FOUNDATIONS OF POLITICAL ANALYSIS
An Introduction to the Theory of Collective Choice

FOUNDATIONS OF POLITICAL ANALYSIS
An Introduction to the Theory of Collective Choice

Robert Abrams

New York
Columbia University Press
1980

Robert Abrams is Associate Professor of Political Science at Brooklyn College, and a member of the Doctoral Faculty at the Graduate Center of the City University of New York

Library of Congress Cataloging in Publication Data

Abrams, Robert.
  Foundations of political analysis.

  Bibliography: p. 347
  Includes index.
  1. Social choice. 2. Political science. I. Title.
JA77.A26   320'.01   79-20850
ISBN 0-231-04480-1

Columbia University Press
New York   Guildford, Surrey

For Natalie, Alexander, Peter, and Jacqueline

Contents

Acknowledgements   xi

Introduction   1

ONE   **Constitutions**   5
  Economic Individualism   7
  The Social Contract   8
  Rationality, Utility, and Costs   9
  The Calculus of Consent   10
  Problems of Consensual Decision-Making   13
  Simple Majority Rule   21
  Rawls's Maximin Principle   26
  Voting Paradoxes   28
    *Condorcet and Borda Methods, 29; The Voter's Paradox, 30;
    Dominated-Winner Paradox, 31; Inverted-Order Paradox,
    32; Winner-Turns-Loser Paradox, 33; Truncated Point-Total
    Paradox, 34; Borda Dominance, 36*
  Strategic Manipulation   36
  Conclusion   38

TWO   **Arrow's General Possibility Theorem**   41
  Social Choice Conditions   42
    *Connectivity and Transitivity, 42; Free Triple, 43; Positive As-
    sociation of Social and Individual Values, 46; Independence of*

*Irrelevant (Infeasible) Alternatives, 47; Citizens' Sovereignty,
52; Nondictatorship, 52; Summary, 52*
Proof of the Impossibility Theorem   53
*The Pareto Principle, 53; Revised Free Triple and Positive
Responsiveness, 54; Decisive Sets, 55*
Clarifying the Proof   60
Conclusion   62

THREE   **Paradox Lost**   65
A Theorem on Two Alternatives   66
Single-Peakedness   66
Value Restrictedness   69
Eliminating Social Transitivity   71
Cardinal Utility and the Independence Condition   76
*Weighing Preferences, 78; Measurement and Scaling, 79;
Lotteries, 81*
Preference Priority   85
The Probability of the Voter's Paradox   88
*The Concept of Probability, 88; The Theoretical Strategy, 89;
More Than Three Individuals and Alternatives, 91; Impartial
and Arbitrary Cultures, 93; Arbitrary Cultures and the Para-
dox Probability, 95; More Than One Dimension, 97*
Summary   100

FOUR   **Logrolling**   103
Logrolling Cycles   104
Stable Outcomes   108
Logrolling and the Voter's Paradox   111
Separability and Additivity   115
Conditions for Vote Trading: Any Number of Individuals and Al-
ternatives   118
Vote Trading and Condorcet Winners   121
Logrolling vs. Vote Trading   124
Proving a Logrolling Theorem   125
Paradox of Vote Trading   129
Summary   136
Conclusion   137

FIVE **Spatial Models** 139
Economic Theories of Politics 139
Spatial Models 140
Rational Voting 145
Downs's Theory of Electoral Politics 146
Parties and Voters, 147; Summary, 156; N Voters, 158; The Effects of Uncertainty, 159; Ideology, Activists, and Political Leadership, 163
Reactions to Downs 165
Equilibrium Points, 171; A Probabilistic Model, 173; Lexicographic Models, 177; Minimax Regret, 182
Conclusion 185

SIX **Game Theory** 189
Prisoner's Dilemma 191
Chicken 193
Levels of Analysis 196
Games in Extensive Form, 196; Games in Normal Form, 198; Games in Characteristic-Function Form, 210
The Rationality of Coalition Formation 213
Essential and Inessential Games, 213; Rationality Conditions, 215; The Core, 217; Solution Concepts, 219; Imputations, 219; Domination, 220; The Shapley Value, 222; The Bargaining Set, 225
Conclusion 229

SEVEN **Coalition Theory** 235
Minimum Winning Coalitions 235
Maximum Positive Gainers 241
Bargaining Cycles 244
Symmetry 245
Competitive Bribery and Indeterminate Outcomes 249
Summary 251
Empirical Tests of the Theory 252
Problems, 252; Findings, 256; Oversized Coalitions, 260; Legislative Evidence, 261; Evidence from the U.S. Supreme Court, 263; General Findings, 265; Summary: Empirical Tests, 265

Minimizing Policy Distance   266
Weighing Competing Criteria   270
The Case of Israel   277

EIGHT   **Collective Goods**   281
The Logic of Collective Action   283
Supply and Costs, 283; Individual Benefits, 285; Marginal Utility and Marginal Costs, 285; Privileged Groups, 288; Large Groups, 291; Intermediate Groups, 292; Carrots and Sticks, 297
Income Effects and Congestion Effects   298
Political Entrepreneurs   304
Collective Action as a Prisoner's Dilemma Game   306
Noncooperation Without Prisoner's Dilemma   315
Altruism   319
Assumptions of the Model, 320; Varieties of Altruism, 321
Conclusion   325

Conclusion   329
Collective Outcomes   331
Decision Rules   332
Individual Choosers   337
Individual Actions   338
Individual Preferences Among Outcomes   339
Results   340

References   347

Index of Names   353

Subject Index   355

Acknowledgements

I AM VERY GRATEFUL to Nicholas Miller and Russell Hardin for their extensive comments on large portions of this book. I have learned a great deal from them and have been spared the embarrassment of transferring my errors from draft to print. I would also like to thank Brian Barry for reading and commenting on the manuscript. Of any errors which remain, I would say—as William Faulkner said of his Yoknapatawpha County—that I am the "sole owner and proprietor."

As a traditionally trained political scientist specializing in Soviet politics, it was my good fortune, about ten years ago, to hear Bill Mitchell discuss the virtues of the "new economic approach" to political science. For several years thereafter I flirted with this field, reading desultorily in the various classics, wondering how they related to Kremlinology. In a short time I was hooked. It was evident to me that collective choice theory—as I now refer to this field—was important, and that its practitioners were scholars of the first order. Since then I have received a remarkable post-doctoral education from my colleagues in the Public Choice Society—an extraordinary collection of political scientists, economists, sociologists, psychologists, philosophers, lawyers, and mathematicians. Interested readers of this book will find at the annual meetings of the Society a rare combination of scholarship, good humor, and camaraderie. I would particularly like to thank Mancur Olson and Charles Plott, past presidents of the Society, for their many personal kindnesses to me.

For the past several years I have used drafts of this book in seminars at

Brooklyn College. My students there have been superb, and I am grateful to them for their serious interest in the subject.

I am especially grateful to my wife, Natalie. In numerous discussions she helped to clarify and make precise ideas which would otherwise have remained hopelessly muddled.

Finally, I wish to thank my former colleague Dennis Palumbo for his encouragement at an early stage of this project; my current colleague Jim Levine for his moral support; Bernard Gronert, my editor at Columbia University Press, for guiding the book through to completion; and Leslie Bialler for his very thorough editing of the manuscript.

FOUNDATIONS OF POLITICAL ANALYSIS
An Introduction to the Theory of Collective Choice

Introduction

I

In recent years a new field has been developing in political science. The names used to describe this field vary: "the theory of collective choice," "rational choice models," "formal political theory," "mathematical political theory," and so on. Substantively, the topics are those of traditional political theory and political science, such as voting, political parties, constitutions, the just society, power, bargaining, and coalition formation. Methodologically, however, there are important differences. The theory developed is primarily deductive (and, in this sense, bears some resemblance to the methodology of traditional political theory), but it draws its analytical tools from formal logic and probability theory, as well as economics. For this reason, it has been beyond the ken of most political scientists, even those trained in the methods of the behavioral approach.

This book is intended as an introduction to the field. It presents theoretical results which I have found interesting, impressive, and worthy of further study. My personal view is that the material presented here represents the beginning of a theoretical development which will emerge as the preeminent approach to political analysis in the next several decades.

II

For the average political scientist, the material presented here will seem complex and technical. For the specialist in collective-choice theory, however, it will seem relatively elementary. My hope is that political scientists without background in this field will find an exciting new way of analyzing traditional questions. More importantly, I hope that the theoretical results contained here will be perceived as a genuine contribution to knowledge in political science. Needless to say, that is my personal view.

For the specialist in collective-choice theory, there might be two points of interest aside from simply the juxtaposition of the most important elements of the field. First, I mention at several points in the book certain ethical questions. For example, Rawls's theory of justice and Strasnick's theory of preference priority are described briefly. While these points are not developed here, I do think that they represent a very important new development—the application of collective-choice questions to problems in ethics. Second, I argue in the conclusion that the material presented here forms the parts of a relatively unified theory. If so, the disparate political processes these theories attempt to explain are also related. Such a demonstration would be a significant step forward in social-scientific explanation.

III

The formal theory of collective choice has a distinguished pedigree. Its origins go back at least to the eighteenth-century mathematicians Jean-Charles Borda and the Marquis de Condorcet, who were fascinated by problems of voting methods. Each developed a method of voting which bears his name and which will be discussed in chapter 1. The Reverend C. L. Dodgson, otherwise known as Lewis Carroll, found it more interesting to study the logical problems of voting on faculty committees at Oxford than to worry about the lackluster substance of the debates. He carried on Borda and Condorcet's work, especially the question of "cyclical majorities."

Other famous mathematicians of the eighteenth and nineteenth centuries, such as Laplace and Galton, also studied the theory of social choice, but there was a substantial hiatus between this work and the renewal of interest in the subject which was marked by the appearance of several articles by Duncan Black in 1948, later collected in his *Theory of Committees and Elections* (1958). Since the publication of Nobel Prize winner Kenneth Arrow's *Social Choice and Individual Values* in 1951, the theory of collective choice has grown dramatically, involving practitioners of a wide spectrum of academic disciplines—economists, political scientists, sociologists, mathematicians, physicists, philosophers, and lawyers. A set of "classics" has also developed in addition to those already mentioned, including Anthony Downs, *An Economic Theory of Democracy* (1957); William Riker, *The Theory of Political Coalitions* (1962); James Buchanan and Gordon Tullock, *The Calculus of Consent* (1962); and Mancur Olson, *Logic of Collective Action* (1965). A related development has been the evolution of game theory from its creation by John von Neumann and Oskar Morgenstern in their *Theory of Games and Economic Behavior* (1944).

In 1966 a new publication appeared, *Papers in Non-market Decision-making*. Edited by Gordon Tullock at the Virginia Polytechnic Institute and State University, it was devoted to topics in the theory of collective choice. Subsequently, the Public Choice Society emerged and with it the journal *Public Choice,* successor to the *Papers.* . . . Today there are over 1200 members of the Public Choice Society, which holds annual meetings at which papers are given in a wide range of areas. These papers have appeared not only in *Public Choice,* but in other professional journals such as the *American Political Science Review,* the *American Journal of Political Science, World Politics,* the *Journal of Politics, Behavioral Science, Journal of Mathematical Sociology, Economic Quarterly, Econometrica,* and the *Journal of Economic Theory.*

Nevertheless, despite the enormous growth of interest in the field across a wide range of disciplines, and despite the fact that courses in the theory of collective choice are taught at universities throughout the United States, Canada, and Europe (there is now a European Public Choice Society), there is no satisfactory introduction to the subject. Riker and Ordeshook's *An Introduction to Positive Political Theory* (1973), which is excellent in so many respects, is simply too difficult to serve as a genuine introduction. More recently, Frohlich and Oppenheimer (1978) have produced a shorter and less difficult text, *Modern Political Economy,* which includes many of the topics covered below. The approach, however, is very different.

While the choice of subject matter here is clearly designed with political scientists in mind, the experience of the field so far suggests that many of the same topics are being dealt with by economists and sociologists as well. It should also be pointed out that there are a number of good introductory books in the more specialized areas of game theory. These include Rapoport's *Two-Person Game Theory: The Essential Ideas* (1966), and his

N-Person Game Theory: Concepts and Applications (1970); as well as Steve Brams's excellent *Game Theory and Politics* (1975).

IV

In the organization of this book I have tried to stress several themes:

A. The work in the theory of collective choice has been cumulative. That is, problems which emerged in the work of the earliest theorists still dominate the field, even though refinements have been made and new problems introduced.

B. Many of the theoretical results are counterintuitive. In the social sciences, unlike the natural sciences, a frequent test of the validity of results has been whether they seem reasonable, or whether they conform to our intuition or common sense. This is in stark contrast to the attitude of natural scientists for whom the intuitive acceptability of results is irrelevant.

C. The disparate results of the theory of collective choice can be related, and the same empirical situation can be analyzed from different perspectives. For example, chapter 4, *Logrolling,* shows the relationship between voting and vote trading, and between vote trading or logrolling and party politics. Similarly, legislative politics can be seen either as a vote-trading or game theoretical situation.

D. The theory has great empirical range. That is, certain theoretical results can be applied to a great many different empirical situations. For example, the analysis of the so-called Prisoner's Dilemma in game theory could be applied to international confrontations, labor-management negotiations, relations between the President and Congress, and so on.

V

Technical details have not been relegated to a separate chapter but have been woven into the discussion of theoretical issues. I have assumed virtually no knowledge on the part of the reader regarding definitions of terms or meaning of symbols. I have also tried to show every step in each analysis. Two simple proofs of theorems are included in chapters 2 and 4.

CHAPTER ONE

Constitutions

A CONSTITUTION IS primarily a set of rules for making collective decisions. These rules may be *prescriptive* (they indicate who will make decisions); they may be *proscriptive* (they indicate who may not make decisions or what kinds of decisions may not be made); or, they may be *numerical decision rules* (they indicate how many individuals must support a policy if it is to be implemented, or a candidate if he or she is to be elected). The American Constitution provides examples. Among the prescriptive rules are the provisions that the President shall be commander-in-chief of the armed forces, that Congress shall declare war, and that the "judicial power of the United States, shall be vested in one Supreme Court. . . ." Most of the proscriptive rules are contained in the Bill of Rights which, for example, denies Congress the power to make laws "respecting an establishment of religion or prohibiting the free exercise thereof. . . ." The numerical decision rules are limited to simple majority and two-thirds or three-quarters majority. Thus, "the Congress, whenever two-thirds of both Houses shall deem it necessary, shall propose Amendments to this Constitution . . ." (Article V).

Of course, any constitution also creates the particular institutions of government and makes some substantive policy as well. Thus, the U.S. Constitution creates our tripartite national government, and declares that "all Debts contracted and Engagements entered into, before the Adoption of this Constitution, shall be as valid against the United States under this Constitution, as under the Confederation" (Article XI).

The central concern of our Constitution, however, is the distribution of power within the system. Thus, the system of checks and balances at the federal level, the separation of powers, and the entire federal system itself—in which powers are shared between state and federal governments—all indicate how the founding fathers felt power should be divided. Moreover, while there were many disputes about how these powers should be apportioned, there was virtually unanimous agreement that power should not be concentrated in the hands of a monarch, or even a few individuals. The American revolution, after all, was the second great reaction against monarchical rule, and was a major development in the struggle against aristocratic rule in general.

This point is important. Historically, democracy is a relatively new system. At the time of the American Revolution, it was so poorly developed, even conceptually, that the Bill of Rights was an afterthought, and suffrage was not given to women, slaves, or white males without property. More importantly, strong arguments have been made recently that current democratic systems are not very "democratic." Power is said to be concentrated in the "military-industrial complex" or the "power elite" or the "ruling families." Our system of legislation is said to be a sham, a cover for the "exploitation of the proletariat" by the "bourgeoisie." Moreover, the advent of sophisticated technology is said to limit the power of individuals, and to provide government with the tools for total control. Such an argument is given added weight by the tendency in recent years toward massive expansion of governmental activity. Finally, widespread corruption and abuse of power in high places—Watergate, "Koreagate," "Floodgate," to name a few recent examples—also seem to suggest that democracy, in any meaningful sense of the word, cannot work.

Given the historical rarity of democracy, then, and the evidence that it sputters at best when tried, it seems rather unusual that there has been a recent resurgence of interest in democratic theory, and in such normative questions as "distributive justice," or "fairness," in political systems. This is not to suggest that the theoretical results have been heartening to democrats—they have not—but that these traditional questions are being taken seriously despite the evident historical problems.

In this chapter, we shall focus on the normative and empirical questions relating to "majority rule." We shall examine some of the literature which asks, what kinds of collective-decision rules *would* rational individuals support? and what kinds of collective-decision rules *should* such individuals support? The thrust of our discussion will be a demonstration that there are serious logical problems with either simple majority rule or the unanimity rule, as well as with more complicated voting procedures. In subsequent chapters we shall show that such difficulties are a general problem for *all* decision rules.

ECONOMIC INDIVIDUALISM

It is interesting that the renewed interest in democratic theory has come primarily from economists who have been concerned with the problem of creating a nonmarket method of allocating resources. In capitalist systems, goods and services are allocated through the market mechanism. The price of goods and services is the device by which supply and demand are equalized. If supply is high relative to demand, for example, the price is lowered in order to stimulate increased demand. Conversely, if demand is high relative to supply, the price increases as a means of reducing some of the demand pressure. It is not clear, however, whether such a system is "good" for a society. Adam Smith argued that through the multitude of individual transactions in the market society will benefit. An "invisible hand," he said, would assure that the social product would be beneficial. Karl Marx, however, was concerned about the "anarchy" of the marketplace, in which the undirected system of individual agreements would lead not to social welfare, but to a system of exploitation.

In recent years, scholars in the field of welfare economics have attempted to determine whether a system of allocation could be devised which had the advantages of the market system, but not its disadvantages. In particular, they wanted to retain the feature of individual preferences. Thus, a "visible hand," in the form of a public planner, would allocate goods and services, based on these preferences.

It is not our intention here to introduce the vast field of welfare economics, but simply to point out that the problem of aggregating individual preferences into public policy for economic goods and services is *struc-*

turally the same as the more general problem of democratic choice—viz, aggregating individual preferences into public policy for any issue. In this sense, then, the problem in welfare economics of devising a so-called social-welfare function, is a special case of the political problem of determining the "people's will."

It is important to stress here that the nonsocialist tradition in economics accepted the normative rule that the goods and services which *ought* to be produced in a society are those which the people want. Even the "visible hand" of the economic planner is not supposed to substitute the planner's preferences for those of the people.

Such a position is open to obvious criticism: suppose that people want things which are not good for them physically (e.g., cigarettes), "morally" (e.g., gambling), or economically (e.g., choosing to purchase an expensive car rather than using the money to improve salable personal skills). Should they be allowed to spend their resources in those ways? There is a clear paternalism implied here. Someone apparently knows what is good for others, and what is good for society. Those who defend "economic individualism"—as we shall call the nonpaternalist position—argue that economic paternalism violates individual liberties. An individual ought to have the right to do what is injurious to himself so long as it does not harm others.

This debate has its counterpart in political theory, where "enlightened monarchies" of one form or another—philosopher king, medieval monarch, independent representative, or city planner—are proposed as an alternative to rule by the *vox populi*. Again, our point here is not to discuss this complex problem, but simply to point out that *for good or ill, the theories discussed in this book assume political and economic individualism.*

THE SOCIAL CONTRACT

In this chapter, we shall be primarily concerned with the question of choosing decision rules. This is the stage of constitution-making analogous to the creation of a social contract which transforms the state of nature, of traditional political theory into a society and a polity. It is the stage when the rules of the game are established. One important assumption we shall make here, and one not necessarily accepted in general by those who have written on this question, is that *anyone who does not like the rules of the game may choose not to play*. If we are really discussing constitutions, it does not seem reasonable to suggest that some individuals may not approve of the rules, and yet must join the society. There are obvious limitations in the real political world to opting out once we see how the rules actually operate; but, presumably, if we are really at the stage of social and and political creation, we must allow the option of not participating. Otherwise, a set of rules is simply being imposed against the will of certain individuals. Once the rules have been adopted, we may expect that policies will be implemented which some oppose, but such policies will be legitimate in the sense that they were produced by a system to which everyone consented. In other words, we shall assume that *the rules of the game require unanimous consent, even though such rules themselves need not be that of unanimity*. Thus, a group of individuals may unanimously agree to a system of majority rule, or even a dictatorship. In traditional political theory, any system produced by unanimous agreement is said to be *legitimate*.

In the case of the American Constitution, the states of the Confederacy indicated by their actions in the 1850s and 1860s that they did not accept the rules of the game. The interesting question posed by the American Civil War is whether a group may secede at any time from a polity to which it has formerly consented. And, whether such a right to secede makes the initial consent meaningless, or whether, in fact, it assures its legitimacy. Clearly, not all members of the original thirteen colonies approved of the Constitution, but it can be argued that their failure to stay out of the Union at the time of its formation implied consent.

Our two-pronged question then is, what decision rules *will* rational individuals support? and what decision rules *ought* to be supported? We shall also ask whether any one set of decision rules could be both empirically predictable and normatively justifiable. That is, is there a set of decision rules which rational individuals will choose, and which will satisfy certain ethical criteria?

RATIONALITY, UTILITY, AND COSTS

A "rational" individual, in the following discussion, is simply *one who has a consistent set of preferences over a set of alternatives*. In other words, suppose there are three alternatives, *x, y,* and *z,* and that our individual prefers x to y, and y to z. We say that this individual is consistent if he or she prefers x to z as well. Such preferences are said to be *transitive*. If z were preferred to x in the example above, the preferences would be *intransitive*, or *inconsistent*. There is a considerable debate about whether intransitive preferences are irrational in any meaningful sense of the term, but for our purposes, "transitivity" and "rationality" will by synonymous.

Sometimes, such preferences are simply taken as given. Sometimes, however, we try to explain such preferences by referring to the *utility* of the alternatives. That is, an alternative which will bring us greater utility will be ranked above, or preferred to, an alternative which provides us less utility.

There are two problems with such a formulation, which we shall simply mention here. First, does the fact that it is an individual who receives utility mean that all action must be narrowly self-centered, or can we receive utility from doing for others? That is, are we assuming self-interested individuals, or is altruism possible? Second, can utility be expressed numerically, or are we limited to saying, simply, that some alternative gives us "more" or "less" utility than another, without being able to specify a numerical difference? This is the distinction between *cardinal* and *ordinal* utility which we shall discuss in more detail below.

The economic notion of "costs" and "benefits," then can be expressed in terms of utility. A "cost" is a *loss* of utility while a "benefit" is a *gain* in utility. Moreover, a "rational" individual is one who wants to minimize his or her costs, and maximize benefits; or put another way, a rational individual wants to maximize the difference between benefits and costs.

THE CALCULUS OF CONSENT

From this relatively simple set of assumptions, Gordon Tullock and James Buchanan develop their arguments for the normative primacy of the unanimity rule in constitutions, and the empirical grounds for expecting simple or special majority rule. Their book, *The Calculus of Consent* (1962) is one of the classics in the collective-choice field. It is an important work because it was one of the first to systematically apply certain economic concepts to the analysis of political constitutions.

Economists distinguish between costs which we voluntarily impose on ourselves, and costs which are involuntarily imposed on us by the actions of

others. The latter are referred to as negative *externalities*.[1] The classic example of an external cost is the factory chimney whose smoke pollutes the
surrounding area. The residents of the area are forced to accept the loss of
utility which accompanies the added dirt and the added health hazard of the
chemical pollutants. Contrast this situation with that of the individual ciga-
rette smoker, who willingly accepts the cost of his or her habit, both in
terms of money and the loss of health, in return for the putative pleasure of
smoking. As indicated above, any costs which such an individual willingly
accepts in return for a particular benefit should not concern others. (We shall
not discuss here the problem of a "free" act.) On the other hand, negative
externalities are essentially a violation of individual rights and are therefore
legitimate social issues. In fact, the Western liberal tradition rests on the notion that the main function of government is to prevent what economists call
negative externalities, and what political theorists and philosophers would
call a denial of rights, or harm.

Tullock and Buchanan argue that each individual is in the best position
to determine when he or she is suffering a loss of utility from the actions of
others. For that reason, they claim that the unanimity rule is best suited to
protect individuals against negative externalities. Thus, if a particular policy
is costly to me, I can simply veto it. And, since every individual has a veto
power with the unanimity rule, only those policies which do not produce external costs will be implemented. Moreover, they argue that there is a direct
relation between the decision rule and the potential loss of utility. Thus,
simple majority rule is the least effective in preventing externalities; a two-
thirds rule is more effective, and, of course, the unanimity rule guarantees
no external costs.

In the graph form of which economists are so fond, this argument can
be summarized in (fig. 1.1). Here, the least inclusive decision rule is "1."
This rule says that a policy will be implemented if any one individual in the
group wants it. At the other extreme is the unanimity rule, *N*—the total
number of individuals in the group. The curve slopes down toward the right
to indicate that external costs decline as the decision rule approaches unanimity.

It should be noted that this argument assumes a certain amount of disagreement at all times. For, if the group were relatively homogeneous—if,

1. Externalities can also be positive. My neighbor's garden can be both aesthetically pleasing
to me and a source of higher property values.

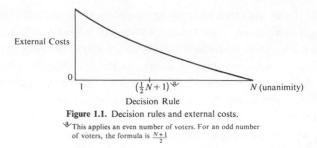

Figure 1.1. Decision rules and external costs.

This applies an even number of voters. For an odd number
of voters, the formula is $\frac{N+1}{2}$

that is, there were relatively little disagreement—the decision rule would be irrelevant. The group would reach the same decision whether the decision rule were simple majority or unanimity. Similarly, if the group were divided into a number of relatively homogeneous subgroups, a change in the decision rule would not necessarily change the external costs. Suppose, for example, that there were 100 group members divided into four relatively homogeneous subgroups of 25 each. Under such circumstances, any decision rule from simple majority to just below three-quarters [i.e., k (decision rule) = 74] would allow any *two* groups to veto policy. Any decision rule from just above three-quarters ($k = 76$) to unanimity would allow any *one* group to veto new policies. Thus, the potential external costs in such a situation would not vary between majority rule and $k = 74$, or between $k = 76$ and unanimity.

Nevertheless, since most real political situations involve considerable conflict and the absence of such strict group (party) cohesion, the Tullock and Buchanan formulation does not appear particularly objectionable on these grounds.

Tullock and Buchanan recognize, however, that it is a time-consuming and difficult process to achieve unanimity where there are important disagreements. Time and effort are necessary to persuade those who oppose a policy to support it, and such support frequently must be purchased by concessions, promises of future support, or other policies. Such time, effort, or concessions are clearly costs. They consume resources and result in a loss of utility, even though the benefits of the policy are presumed to outweigh the costs.

Such costs, however, can be *reduced* by making the decision rule *less* inclusive. Thus, it is less costly to put together a simply majority than a three-quarters majority. Clearly, the most costly project is to get unanimous agreement, where the incentives for blackmail and extortion by single individuals are considerable. Tullock and Buchanan refer to such costs as *decision costs*. In terms of reducing *external costs,* then, an individual should opt for a unanimity rule. In terms of reducing *decision costs,* however, he or she should support a rule of $k = 1/n$. In graphic terms, this latter point is expressed as in fig 1.2.

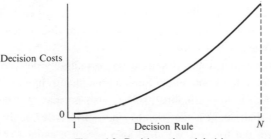

Figure 1.2. Decision rule and decision cost.

The choice of a decision rule, then, represents a trade-off between external costs and decision costs. Thus, while individuals, would prefer a unanimity rule as the best means of protecting against external costs, they will accept less than unanimity rules in order to avoid decision costs. The exact decision rule, presumably, would depend on the relative importance of the potential external costs and the potential decision costs for the individual. In any case, the important point is that *the existence of decision costs makes it rational to consider decision rules other than the unanimity rule.* Nevertheless, Tullock and Buchanan are also saying that, *as an ideal, the unanimity rule is desirable, and that in a world without decision costs, it should be the choice of rational individuals.*

PROBLEMS OF CONSENSUAL DECISION-MAKING

The argument above is not new. It is the traditional suggestion that consensual decision-making (or, the unanimity rule, as we called it) would be the most desirable constitutional rule, but that it is simply too difficult to achieve in practice. Douglas Rae (1975), however, has argued that consensual decision-making may not even be a normative ideal.

Rae begins by pointing out that the Tullock-Buchanan model makes an analogy between the economic marketplace and the polity. That is, in the market, an exchange between the buyer and seller takes place only when both agree to the exchange. Thus, the market exchange is an example of a situation involving consensual decision-making. Either the buyer or the seller can block the exchange simply by refusing to participate. Moreover, it is assumed that the buyer and the seller *both* gain from the exchange. Otherwise, the exchange would not take place. Such an outcome, in which all parties increase their utility, is said to be *Pareto optimal*. This is a very important concept in current economic theory, and one which will reappear frequently throughout this book.

The market model, then, is said to be normatively desirable, because it produces Pareto optimal outcomes. Such a conclusion, however, rests on the assumption that Pareto optimality itself is also normatively desirable. Subsequently, we shall suggest that Pareto optimaltiy is seriously flawed as an ethical standard, but for now we shall also accept it as desirable.

One of the important arguments against the market analogy in the political process is that it fails to take into account that the status quo may be very undesirable for one or more of the participants. In the marketplace, the absence of exchange simply leaves the potential buyer and seller with their original resources. Neither gains, and neither loses. Thus, either party in a potential exchange may *impose the status quo by refusing to trade*. In the political situation, the activity analogous to a market exchange is the policy decision. Thus, a unanimity or consensus rule in political decision-making means that a new policy will be implemented only if everyone agrees to it. Without such agreement, the status quo prevails. The unanimity rule, then, is highly conservative. It gives a decided advantage to those who are already prosperous, and it virtually eliminates the possibility of income redistribution. In general, it favors those who prefer the status quo to those who oppose it.

From such a perspective, it is clear that the status quo should itself be considered an alternative, and not simply the outcome which will prevail when all other alternatives are rejected. Thus, the status quo should also be subject to the unanimous consent rule. In such a case, anyone could veto the status quo. The obvious problem with such a "revised market analogy" (Rae), is that it allows for the possibility that *neither* the status quo, *nor* any alternative to the status quo will receive unanimous consent! This is clearly a situation of anarchy.

Another problem with consensual decision-making involves Rae's notion of "efficiency." A policy change is said to be "efficient" or "efficiency dominant" if it increases the utility of everyone involved or at least does not *reduce* anyone's utility. A policy change is "inefficient," or "counterefficient" if it results in a utility *loss* for everyone. A policy change is "efficiency undecidable" if some individuals gain while some lose utility.

This last condition requires some explanation. In the literature, a distinction is made between *ordinal* and *cardinal* utility. Ordinal utility refers to *nonnumerical* utility. Thus, I can say that *A* gives me *more* utility than *B*, but I cannot specify that utility in terms of a quantity, nor can I specify *how much* greater is the utility of *A* than *B*. In other words, I can rank order alternatives in terms of greater or lesser utility, but I cannot quantify that utility. *Cardinal utility*, on the other hand, is the numerical specification of utility in which I can indicate not only the numerical utility of a single alternative, but also the numerical *difference* in utility between two alternatives.

There has been a great debate in the literature on whether cardinal utility is a meaningful concept, and whether it is possible to compare the utilities of different individuals. In the next chapter, we shall discuss this problem in more detail. For present purposes, our point is, simply, that if cardinal utility and the interpersonal comparison of utility are meaningful concepts, then we can compute things like total utility (for a group), and average utility. Suppose, for example, that a group of three individuals implemented a policy which gave each three utiles (whatever that may mean). Then, the total utility for the group would be nine utiles, and the average would be three utiles. Suppose further that another policy would give two of the individuals three utiles, but would result in a net *loss* of two utiles for the third individual. Here, the total utility would be four utiles $(3 + 3 - 2 = 4)$.

Given the notion of cardinal utility, then, we can always determine whether there is an aggregate gain or loss, or whether there is neither a gain nor a loss. (*Question:* Can you construct a situation in which there is neither an aggregate gain, nor an aggregate loss?) For those who do not find cardinal utility a meaningful concept, however, it is still possible to determine the efficiency of policy changes in terms of ordinal utility. Rae does this by distinguishing first between what he calls *preference sets, rejection sets,* and *indifference sets.* A preference set is that set of alternatives which would result in positive utility (or, at least, not negative utility). A *rejection set* is that set of alternatives which would result in a utility loss. An *indifference set* is that set of alternatives which would bring neither a gain nor a loss of utility. Now, if one rejects the notion of cardinal utility, the only way in which we could determine whether a proposal would result in utility gains or losses, or neither, is to find out whether an individual would support or oppose a particular alternative in a voting situation, or whether he or she would abstain. Presumably, a vote *for* an alternative implies a potential utility gain for the individual, while a vote *against* an alternative implies a potential utility loss. Abstention, of course, implies neither potential gain nor loss.

Rae illustrates these concepts as in fig. 1.3.

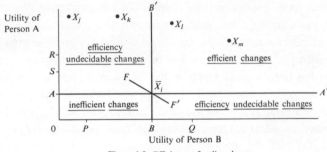

Figure 1.3. Efficiency of policy changes.

In this illustration, we have a two-person society—individuals A and B. We also have a status quo represented by point $\bar{X}_i$ (read, "X bar sub i"), and a number of alternatives to the status quo, X_j ("X sub j"), X_k, X_l, and X_m. Now, notice that the major horizontal and vertical lines (ordinate and abcissa) represent different levels of utility for individuals A and B. Thus, point P represents less utility for individual B than point Q, while point R represents a greater level of utility for A than point S. In other words, as we move from left to right or, west to east in the space above, individual B's utility increases; and, as we move from the bottom of the diagram toward the top (or, from south to north) individual A's utility increases. For example, if alternative X_j is chosen over the status quo, $\bar{X}_i$, A's utility increases, while B's utility decreases. Suppose, then, that alternative X_m is chosen over X_j; Whose utility will increase, and whose utility will decrease? Clearly, B would gain utility while A would lose.

It is evident, however, that neither A nor B will vote for a policy change which reduces his or her utility. Thus, individual A would vote only for those alternatives which lie in the area to the north of line A–A', (e.g., X_j, X_k, X_1, X_m), while individual B would vote only for those alternatives which lie east of line B–B' (e.g., X_1, X_m). Such alternatives would be in the *preference sets* of A and B, respectively. The *rejection set* for A would be all those alternatives south of A–A', while the rejection set for B would be all those alternatives west of B–B'. The *indifference sets* for A and B would be all of the points on the lines A–A' and B–B' respectively.

In terms of our previous discussion, then, all of the *efficient* changes from the status quo are those alternatives in the area bounded by B'–$\bar{X}_i$–A'— the upper right-hand sector. These changes are efficient in the sense that both A and B benefit. The *inefficient changes would be those alternatives in the area bounded by A–$\bar{X}_i$–B*—the lower left-hand sector. A movement from $\bar{X}_i$ to any point in that space would result in lower utility for *both* A and B. The areas designated as "efficiency undecidable" involve alternatives which one individual supports and one opposes. Recall that we are considering here only ordinal utility. Thus, we know that A gains from a move to X_j and that B loses, but we do not know how much. For this reason, we cannot determine whether there has been an aggregate gain or loss of utility, and for that reason we say that such moves are "efficiency undecidable"; we cannot decide whether or not they are efficient as we have defined the term.

Clearly, a decision rule which chooses efficient outcomes is better than a decision rule which chooses either inefficient outcomes or efficiency undecidable outcomes. Moreover, it is evident that the unanimity rule will always choose efficient outcomes. This is because any individual can veto any proposed change which does not increase his or her utility. After all, the status quo is superior to any alternative which reduces my utility. Therefore, given a unanimity rule, every individual can impose the status quo and protect against a utility loss.

At the same time, the unanimity rule cannot assure that *all* efficient outcomes will be chosen. For example, suppose A and B choose alternative X_l over the status quo $\bar{X}_i$. Then, X_1 becomes the new status quo. But, with X_l the new status quo, the alternative X_m, which was an efficient outcome when $\bar{X}_i$ was the status quo, is no longer efficient when X_l becomes the new status quo. Thus, *unanimous consent does assure that only efficient outcomes will occur, but it does not assure that all efficient outcomes will occur.*

In this imperfect world, the fact that a decision rule will not produce all outcomes which are efficient does not seem to be a major indictment. A more serious problem with the unanimity rule, however, is that *it either requires the elimination of the private sector, or it allows situations in which private activity severely limits, or at the extreme, may eliminate, efficient outcomes altogether.*

To see this, consider a diagram based on Rae (p. 1290) (fig. 1.4). This figure is the "efficiency" sector of the previous diagram. That is, X_1 is the status quo, and all alternatives within the boundaries of the figure are efficient changes from the status quo. The curved line which begins at the upper left and descends toward the lower right is the set of points we call the "efficiency maxima." These points represent the highest level of utility possible in that direction. This is not a complicated notion; it simply means that there are limits to the utility levels which we can obtain. Such a set of points is also referred to as a "frontier."

The set of points X_2, X_3, etc., represent successive changes in the status quo. The D_1, D_2, etc. simply refer to the successive decisions by which each new status quo was reached. Each successive stage represents an efficiency improvement over the previous stage. Thus, X_2 is an efficiency improvement over X_1, X_3 over X_2 etc. The outcome X_5 is an *efficiency maximum.*

Such a scenario is clearly desirable. By a succession of steps, each of which is Pareto optimal—i.e., a change in which everyone benefits—a position of maximum feasible benefit is reached.[2] Rae, however, indicates a very interesting and important problem with this picture. Basically, he suggests that *activity in the private sector could change the status quo in ways which were not efficient, and in ways which could eliminate the possibility of efficient changes.* In other words, while unanimous consent can assure that all collective decisions are efficient, it cannot assure that all noncollective decisions are efficient.

In order to see this point more clearly, let us consider an example which economists have grown fond of, and which Rae also uses. Suppose government regulations do not forbid factories from burning their waste near residential areas. This, then, is the status quo. Suppose, further, that factory owner B begins to burn his waste in such a way that the air in the residential

2. Such a maximum may be limited, for example, by technological problems. Thus, in medicine there may be a maximum cure rate for a particular disease because of limited knowledge or technological capacity. Thus, prior to the development of surgical microscopes and mini-instrumentation, vascular grafting in brain surgery was not possible. See Jack M. Fein, "Microvascular Surgery for Stroke" (1978).

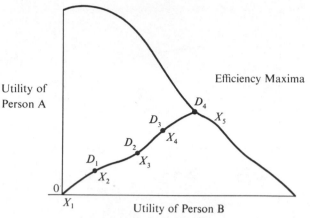

Figure 1.4. Efficient policy changes.

area becomes heavily polluted. Clearly, this is a private (as opposed to a collective) act. Moreover, it is, collectively, "efficiency undecidable." It benefits the factory owner, but hurts the nearby residents. Now, the question is, what should be done? *The problem is that if unanimous consent is the collective decision rule, the factory owner can block any collective move to make him or her either refrain from burning waste or clean up the smokestacks.* Surely, this does not seem fair. The factory owner ought not to be able to impose external costs on nearby residents without providing some kind of compensation. Yet, with the unanimity rule in effect, no such compensation would be approved since the factory owner would always object. For political or personal reasons the factory owner might offer some kind of compensation voluntarily, but social institutions probably cannot count on such generosity where important issues arise.

A way out of this dilemma which would preserve the unanimity rule and prevent such externalities would be simply to require such decisions as waste disposal to be subject to unanimous consent. In that case, the residents would obviously oppose pollution-causing waste disposal, or would require, at least, some limitations and compensation. But this suggestion implies the destruction of the private sector; all decisions would have to be reached collectively. Let us illustrate the problem above diagrammatically (fig. 1.5).

Here, X_1 is the original status quo. Note that all changes in the area bounded by $A–X_1–C$ are efficient. Then, the factory owner starts burning waste and the new status quo is X_2. The southward slope indicates that the

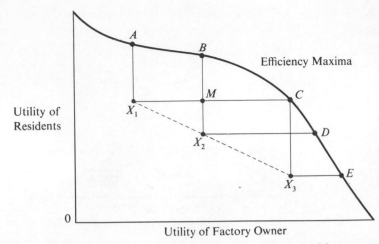

Figure 1.5. Conflict between utility of residents and of factory owner.

residents have lost utility, while the eastward movement indicates that the factory owner has gained utility. From the new status quo the possible efficient changes for the factory owner are in the area bounded by $B–X_2–D$, while the efficient changes for the residents are limited to $B–M–C$. (*Question:* Why is the area of efficient changes for the residents limited to that bounded by $B–M–C$?) It is not difficult to see that if the utility loss for the residents continued to decline, while the utility gain for the factory owner increased—for example, to point X_3, there would be no possible efficient changes available for the residents. This is so because at point X_3, the only alternatives which bring added utility to the factory owner are those in the area bounded by $C–X_3–E$. The residents, of course, would like to return to the original status quo, but, given a unanimity rule, the factory owner can always block such a move. Moreover, the factory owner would always have an incentive to block a return to the previous status quo, since any alternative to the left of line $C–X_3$ would result in a utility loss for him or her.

There is one way out of this dilemma. If the activities in the private sector never produce external costs, or utility losses for others, then the situation described above will never arise. Presumably, however, if everyone can go about his business without adversely affecting others, there would be no need for politics. After all, the state is created, according to social contractarians, to prevent just such intrusions by individuals on the rights, liberty, and property of others. *Unanimous consent, then, succeeds as a decision rule primarily in those situation where it is not needed!*

SIMPLE MAJORITY RULE

In the discussion above, we assumed that our goal was to prevent or limit the imposition of external costs on individuals. It was then shown that unanimous consent cannot ensure the achievement of that goal. It is evident, however, that the prevention of external costs is only one of many possible goals which are normatively desirable. In this section, we shall consider two additional goals, and indicate the decision rules, as well as the very limited conditions needed to achieve them. In particular, we shall show that Rae's (1969) "political individualism" ("having one's way") is best achieved by simple majority rule (and *not* the unanimity rule), but only under three conditions: (1) no one has knowledge of the future, (2) individual choices are independent of each other, and (3) all individuals are equally likely to support or oppose a proposed policy. The first condition, ignorance of the future, is also the critical condition for John Rawls's *maximin principle,* which states that only those policies should be implemented which benefit the members of society who are least advantaged.

Let us consider Rae's "political individualism" first. In a political situation, each individual would like the group to support those policies which he or she supports, and oppose the policies which he or she opposes. Notice that Rae is presenting this notion as a *normative* principle, that is, one which *ought* to be implemented on ethical grounds. We should simply point out, however, that neither Rae's political individualism, nor Tullock and Buchanan's "economic individualism"—in which the normative principle is to prevent the imposition of external costs—is unequivocally desirable. We have seen in the pollution example above, for instance, that the prohibition on imposing external costs through collective action created an unfair situation in which the polluter imposed external costs on others through private action. And, in general, it is not clear that we should always refrain from imposing external costs on others, particularly when there is a more important goal to be achieved. The ending of racial or sexual discrimination, allowing or limiting abortion, preventing pollution, or conserving energy all involved the imposition of external costs. The important point, however, is that the *failure* to impose such costs results in the imposition of other costs. Thus, in most important political situations, we are weighting competing costs, or, as philosophers would say, weighing competing *rights* or *claims*. A blanket prohibition on the collective imposition of external costs, or the denial of certain rights or claims, then, does not achieve its aim of protecting *all* individuals. Rather, it protects only those already advantaged by the status quo. It is, then, a very conservative principle.

Rae's *political individualism* is also weak as a normative principle because it does not evaluate the substance of the policies which the individual supports or opposes. It simply says that it is desirable for an individual to have his or her way as often as possible. The result may be a series of horrendous or illogical policies, which would nevertheless satisfy the principle.

With these problems in mind, let us show briefly how simple majority rule is the single decision rule which satisfies political individualism most often when there is an odd number of individuals in the group. When there is an even number of individuals in the group, simple majority rule and $k = n/2$, i.e., one half of the group can be decisive, share the distinction as the decision rules which most often assure that individuals will have their way.

When an issue comes up for a vote, yea or nay, there are four possible outcomes:

A. The proposal which the individual supports is rejected.
B. The proposal which the individual opposes is passed.
C. The proposal which the individual supports is passed.
D. The proposal which the individual opposes is rejected.

In this case, "the individual" is the generic individual. That is, it can be anybody. Each individual will go through the same calculation; and, since we shall assume that everyone behaves in the same way, the decision rule which any one individual would like is the decision rule which the group would support.

It is evident that our individual wants to limit the occurrences of A and B. Assume, now, that every individual is as likely to vote for any proposal as against, and that voting is independent. That is, no one's vote influences that of any other. In symbols,

$$P_i(X) = P_i(-X) = \tfrac{1}{2}$$

That is, the probability that individual i will vote for proposal X equals the probability that individual i will vote against proposal X, and these probabilities equal ½, since an individual must vote.

Rae then introduces the notion of a *response combination*. A response combination is simply the support and/or opposition to a proposal. Thus, if there are three individuals, a response combination consists of a listing of how each individual voted. Suppose, for example, that individuals h and i supported proposal M, while j opposed it. The response combination would be *HIj*, where the capital letters indicate support, while the lower case letter indicates opposition. It is easily verified that for a group of n members, there are $2^n - 1$ response combinations. To illustrate this, consider the case of three individuals. The possible response combinations include those shown in (fig. 1.6).

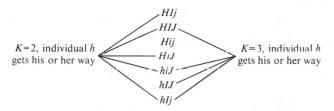

Figure 1.6. Possible response combinations for three individuals who vote for or against a policy proposal.

With three individuals, there are $2^3 - 1 = 7$ response combinations. Notice the absence of *hij*, which would indicate unanimous opposition. This is because it is assumed that a proposal will be placed on the agenda only if at least one person supports it.

Rae then introduces the notion of a *support set,* or the set of individuals who support a proposal. Thus the support set for *HIj* is *HI*. (*Question:* What is the support set for *HIJ* or *Hij?*)

Now, the question is, what proportion of these response sets correspond to outcome A or B for any individual? That is, in what proportion of these sets of outcomes does the individual *not* get his or her way? (We could ask the question the other way: in which response sets *does* the individual get his or her way?). The answer clearly depends on the decision rule. To see this, consider individual h. With three individuals, the only majority rules are simple majority (two out of three) or unanimity (three out of three). Assume that the unanimity rule is in effect. Then, individual h gets his or her way *four* times—that is, once when everyone supports proposal M, (HIJ), and the three occasions where h opposes M (hIJ, hiJ, hIj). In every other instance, h does not get his or her way. In other words, h does *not* get his or her way $3/7 = .43$ of the time. Now consider a simple majority rule. Here, h gets his or her way five out of seven times (HIj, HIJ, HiJ, hiJ, hIj). In other words, h does *not* get his or her way $2/7 = .29$ of the time.

This simple example illustrates a situation in which simple majority rule satisfies the individual voter more often than the unanimity rule. To be more accurate, there is a greater *probability* that a particular individual will be satisfied with majority rule in effect than with the unanimity rule.

It is still possible, however, that some decision rule other than simple majority or unanimity would increase the probability that an individual will have his or her way. Note that in a group of size n, the decision rule k can equal any number from one to n. Thus, $1 \leq k \leq n$ ("$\leq$" means "less than or equal to"). In the example above, suppose $k = 1$. That is, a proposal will pass if only one person supports it. Then h would get his/her way on four occasions: HIJ, HIj, HiJ, Hij. In every other case, where h opposed M, h would not get his/her way since either i or j or both could assure passage of M.

Table (1.1) shows the probabilities or expected frequencies of outcomes A and B for groups of 3 to 12 members, and decision rules $k = (1,2, \ldots, n)$.

TABLE 1.1 EXPECTED SUMMED FREQUENCIES FOR EVENTS A AND B

k/n	3	4	5	6	7	8	9	10	11	12
1	.43	.47	.48−	.49−	.50−	.50−	.50−	.50−	.50−	.50−
2	.29	.34	.39	.43	.46	.47+	.48+	.49+	.50−	.50−
3	.43	.34	.32	.35	.39	.38	.45	.47	.48	.48+
4		.47	.39	.35	.34	.36	.39	.42	.44	.46
5			.48	.43	.39	.36	.36	.38	.40	.42
6				.49	.46	.38	.39	.38	.38	.39
7					.50−	.47+	.45	.42	.40	.39
8						.50−	.48+	.47	.44	.42
9							.50−	.49+	.48	.46
10								.50−	.50−	.48+
11									.50−	.50−
12										.50−

Source: Taken from Rae, 1969, p. 50. Reprinted by permission of the American Political Science Association.

The italicized figure in each column is the lowest relative frequency. This means that with the corresponding decision rule, the likelihood of an individual *not* having his/her way is least. More positively, it indicates the decision which assures the greatest possibility of success. Notice that in every case simple majority rule is the optimum point. Notice also that where *n* is even, either the simple majority rule *or* the rule $k = n/2$ is optimal. Finally, observe that as *n* increases, i.e., as the groups become larger, majority rule does not provide *as much of* an advantage as it does where the group is smaller.

There is another interesting result. Suppose an individual is more concerned in general about either blocking proposals which he/she opposes, or getting passed proposals which he/she supports. This is known as having a *positional preference,* as opposed to a substantive preference. In the United States Congress of the 1950s, for example, the Southern states were more concerned with blocking civil rights legislation than with implementing legislation of any kind. Conversely, Franklin Roosevelt and Lyndon Johnson, in their respective presidencies, were more concerned with implementing liberal welfare state and civil rights policies than with preventing action.

Our intuition suggests that those who want to block group action are best served by *more inclusive* decision rules—with unanimity the most desirable; while those who would push for action would do better with *less inclusive* decision rules, with $k = 1$ as optimal. And, indeed, Rae's results show that for those who want to minimize the frequency of *A* (rejection of favored proposals), the chances of success *increase* as the decision rule becomes *less inclusive;* while for those who would minimize the frequency of *B* (imposition of opposed policy), a *more inclusive* decision rule is more desirable. Table (1.2) indicates the expected frequencies for outcome B with various decision rules.

The italicized frequencies are those associated with simple majority rule. The expected frequency table for Event A is just the reverse of this. So, for example, the expected frequencies for $n = 3$, $k = 1$, 2, or 3 are .00, .14, and .43 respectively.

The main conclusion here, then, is that *simple majority rule is the best rule to employ if our goal is to maximize the probability that an individual will have his/her way.* If, however, the goal is to maximize the probability either of blocking proposals or of imposing proposals, then *no single rule will suffice.* A more inclusive decision rule is required to maximize the former, while a less inclusive decision rule is required to maximize the latter.

TABLE 1.2 EXPECTED FREQUENCY FOR EVENT B (IMPOSITION OF OPPOSED POLICIES)

k/n	3	4	5	6	7	8	9	10	11	12
1	.43	.47	.48	.49	.50−	.50−	.50−	.50−	.50−	.50−
2	.14	.27	.36	.41	.45	.47	.48	.49	.50−	.50−
3	.00	.07	.16	.25	.33	.35	.43	.46	.47	.48
4		.00	.03	.10	.17	.25	.32	.37	.41	.44
5			.00	.02	.06	.11	.18	.25	.31	.36
6				.00	.01	.03	.07	.13	.19	.25
7					.00	.00+	.02	.05	.09	.14
8						.00	.00+	.01	.03	.06
9							.00	.00+	.01	.02
10								.00	.00	.00+
11									.00	.00+
12										.00

Source: Taken from Rae, 1969, p. 49. Reprinted by permission of the American Political Science Association.

Notice, however, our assumption that *all possible outcomes are equally likely.* This is, generally, an unrealistic assumption. Ordinarily, we have some idea of whether we are more likely to be in a majority or minority in a particular group. In fact, a good deal of the political process consists of ascertaining the vote count. Moreover, we learn relatively quickly over time whether we have political allies and the kinds of issues which concern us. Without such information, no good politician would commit himself to a particular decision rule. And yet, in the model above, simple majority rule is shown to be most desirable only in a situation of political ignorance. Once a political picture emerges, no single decision rule is likely to be acceptable to everyone. For this reason, Rae concludes: "I suspect that one must look away from formal institutional choices and toward the standard civic virtues if individual values are to be optimized in factional strife." (1969, p. 55)

RAWLS'S MAXIMIN PRINCIPLE

In the quote above, Rae was suggesting that we cannot look to simple decision rules to assure the implementation of certain values. Indeed, we have seen that both unanimous consent and simple majority rules have serious disadvantages. The only alternative to employing numerical decision rules, is either to permit dictatorship, or to find substantive policy rules or principles which express our values. The problems with dictatorship are too obvious to need comment. The question of finding suitable policy principles is more subtle.

In one sense, the search for policy principles is analogous to the constitutional question of finding the optimal decision rule. We must still ask ourselves what is the best method for choosing among competing policy principles. If this takes us back to the question of unanimous consent versus simple majority, obviously we have not progressed.

John Rawls (1971), however, has made an interesting suggestion which, if not impregnable to serious criticism, at least provides a mechanism for avoiding certain of the problems discussed above. As the title of his very famous book, *A Theory of Justice* suggests, Rawls is concerned with the notion of a "just society." Clearly, such a notion is a normative principle as is Rae's "political individualism" or Tullock and Buchanan's "economic individualism." Unlike any of these authors, however, Rawls presents a fully developed justification for his "just society."

Traditional political philosophers have presented arguments for many different types of political systems. When proposing normative suggestions—what societies or polities "ought" to be like—they usually appeal either to reason or intuition for their justification. Rawls tries to avoid either—though some claim he was not successful—by arguing that a just society is one which would be created by individuals if they had no idea how they would fare in such a society. In other words, by means of a procedural mechanism, Rawls provides a justification for the just society. At the constitutional stage of such a society, individuals would choose the policy principles which would govern them, and they would do so behind a "veil of ignorance." Such a veil would assure that they were choosing only fair principles and not those which would merely benefit themselves. Presumably, such principles would allow for elections on some issues, and would utilize majority rule occasionally, but no policy decision could violate the basic principles enunciated at the constitutional stage.

One of the principles which such a group would support, says Raws, is the so-called *maximin rule*. This says that any policy must work to the advantage of the least advantaged members of the society. Thus, Rawls's just society would be striving constantly to equalize the assets and opportunities of its members. Presumably, such a principle would be supported by all members of the society at the constitutional stage, in view of the possibility that any one of them might be among the least advantaged at a later stage. Of course, in time, those who actually become more advantaged may object to the maximin principle, but their objections would be unjust, since they are simply arguing for their own privilege. Moreover, at the constitutional stage, they supported the maximin rule.

This is, of course, only the briefest of summaries of a very complex position. Nevertheless, it gives a hint of the interesting and important arguments in Rawls's book. For present purposes, it also provides an alternative to the search for simple numerical decision rules to govern policymaking. At the same time, it should be noted that Rawls himself may be accused of imposing his own values rather than eliciting group values through an impartial procedure. For, how does Rawls know what principle will be chosen behind the veil of ignorance? Suppose the group is composed of risk-takers who are willing to take a chance on being disadvantaged in return for the opportunity to achieve extraordinary success, perhaps at the expense of others? Rawls's individuals are clearly conservative and risk-averse. The characteristics of constitution-making individuals, however, would appear to be an empirical question, and not one amenable to intuitive understanding. Moreover, if groups of individuals do differ, they should produce different "just societies." Such a conclusion, of course, leads back to ethical relativism.

VOTING PARADOXES

In the preceding sections we have attempted to show that decision rules such as simply majority or unanimity lead to results which may be normatively undesirable. In other words, we may not be able to achieve certain normative goals through the use of these decision rules. The Rawlsian approach eliminates some of these problems but, as we have indicated briefly, it presents other difficulties. In this concluding section, we want to show that there are decision rules other than those which consider only the first preferences of individual voters, but that these rules have problems of their own: sometimes they cannot indicate a group preference; even when they do, there may be a preferable alternative; and, finally, different voting methods can produce different results.

CONDORCET AND BORDA METHODS

Consider the following preference orders for three individuals and three alternatives:

Alternatives

	A	$x > y > z$
Individuals:	B	$y > z > x$
	C	$z > y > x$

Here the symbol $>$ means "preferred to." In other words, for individual A, x is preferred to y, and y is preferred to z. Now, suppose that this group of individuals was trying to choose one among these alternatives using simple majority rule. The alternatives, by the way, could be policies, candidates for elective office, candidates for a job in a political-science department, and so forth. Obviously, there is no majority winner if we consider only first choices.

The eighteenth-century mathematician, the Marquis de Condorcet, however, suggested another method for choosing among alternatives. He argued that the winner ought to be that alternative which would receive a simple majority over every other alternative in a pairwise, or binary, comparison. For instance, in the example above, individuals B and C prefer y to x, and individuals A and B prefer y to z. In other words, alternative y is preferred by a majority to every other alternative and is the Condorcet winner. Thus, the Condorcet criterion takes account of preferences other than the first preference, and can avoid the kind of stalemate found in the example above. As we shall see, however, the Condorcet criterion has its own problems.

Another voting method which also takes account of preferences beyond the first preference is the so-called Borda method, after the eighteenth-century mathematician Jean Charles Borda. This is a method which should be familiar. Suppose, in the example above, an alterantive was assigned two points for each first-place vote, one point for each second-place vote, and no points for third-place votes. Then, we add these points together. The Borda winner is the alternative which receives the highest point total. (Of course, we could reverse the procedure and assign no points for first place votes, one point for second place votes and two points for third place votes. Then, the inner would be that alternative which received the least number of points.)

Using the Borda method, our example above would be written:

		Alternatives	
		2 1 0	*Rank Points*
	A	$x>y>z$	$y=4$
Individuals:	B	$y>z>x$	$z=3$
	C	$z>y>x$	$x=2$

Thus, alternative x would have one first-place vote and two third-place votes, for a point total of two. Alternative y would have four points, and z would have three points. The Borda winner, then, would be y.

In the remainder of this section we shall illustrate some interesting problems—or "paradoxes" as they have been called—which arise when we apply either of these methods. Our point will be to show that the voting methods which have been devised to go beyond the consideration of first preferences alone also have serious problems.

THE VOTER'S PARADOX

Perhaps the most famous of the problems with the Condorcet method is the so-called "voter's paradox," or the problem of "cyclical majorities." This important problem will be discussed extensively in subsequent chapters. Therefore, we shall simply describe it here.

Consider the following set of individual preference orders:

		Alternatives
	A	$x>y>z$
Individuals:	B	$y>z>x$
	C	$z>x>y$

Using the Condorcet method, we see that A and C prefer x to y, A and B prefer y to z, but B and C prefer z to x. In other words, the group prefers x to y, y to z, and z to x. Such an outcome is said to be *intransitive*. Ordinarily, we expect that if one alternative is preferred to a second alternative, which is preferred to a third alternative, then the first alternative also should be preferred to the third alternative. Such a set of preferences is said to be *transitive*. To see the problem more clearly, ask yourself which alternative in the example above should be the winner. If you select x, we can point out that a majority prefers z to x. If you suggest z, we point out that a majority prefers y to z. And, if you suggest y, we note that x is preferred to y by a majority. In other words, when the set of group preferences in intransitive, there cannot be a majority, or Condorcet, winner. Or we might say, the group does not seem to have a preference among the alternatives, but neither is it indifferent among them! This odd situation is the voter's paradox.

Would it help to use the Borda method? No. The alternatives would each receive an equal number of points. (You can check this for yourself.)

DOMINATED-WINNER PARADOX

In an important article, Fishburn (1974) pointed out several other paradoxes or problems related to the Condorcet and Borda methods. He described one as the "dominated-winner paradox." In this unusual situation, there is an alternative which everyone prefers to the simple majority winner! In more technical language, the winner is "Pareto-dominated" by another alternative.

Such a situation arises in a sequential-elimination, simple-majority voting procedure. This is simply a situation in which the alternatives are compared two at a time, with the simple majority loser being eliminated. The procedure continues until only one alternative is left. That alternative is the winner.

There are two interesting problems which arise in connection with this voting method. First, consider the voter's-paradox example above. Suppose that x and y had been compared first. Since a majority preferred x to y, y would be eliminated in a sequential-elimination process. Then x and z would be compared, and x would be eliminated since a majority prefers z to x. Alternative z, then, would be the winner by this method even though a majority prefers y to z. Moreover, notice that the order of voting is critical. Any alternative which is considered last is the winner! In other words, where there is a voter's paradox, manipulation of the voting agenda can produce a winner. In a subsequent chapter, I refer to such manipulation as the "chairman's gambit," since, if A, B, or C are chairman of this three-person committee, they can assure their desired outcome by appropriate planning of the sequential voting process.

The second problem is the dominated-winner paradox. Consider the following example:

Alternatives

	A	$x>y>z>a$
Individuals:	B	$a>x>y>z$
	C	$z>a>x>y$

Note that by one sequential simple-majority procedure the winner is *y:*

$$a \text{ vs. } x \rightarrow a \ (x \text{ eliminated})$$
$$a \text{ vs. } z \rightarrow z \ (a \text{ eliminated})$$
$$z \text{ vs. } y \rightarrow y \ (z \text{ eliminated})$$

Yet, everyone prefers *x* to *y!* Notice that if *x* and *y* were compared originally, *y* would have been eliminated. Again this points up the importance of the agenda.

Without describing Fishburn's important work in detail we shall say, simply, that he has shown that while such situations are relatively rare in general, they are much more likely to occur given certain preference profiles (sets of individual preference orders).

INVERTED-ORDER PARADOX

This problem arises in Borda-type procedures. As the description suggests, this is a situation in which the group preference order is *reversed* when the original winner is removed. Such a problem could arise, for example, in an election where the winner dies or withdraws for health or legal reasons just before the vote count. To illustrate this, consider the following example:

		Alternatives	
	3 2 1 0	*Rank Points*
A	$x > y > z > a$	$x = 15$
B	$a > x > y > z$	$a = 10$
C	$z > a > x > y$	$z = 9$
Individuals: D	$x > y > z > a$	$y = 8$
E	$a > x > y > z$	
F	$z > a > x > y$	
G	$x > y > z > a$	

Here, *x* is the Borda winner with 15 points. Now delete *x:*

Alternatives

		2	1	0	*Rank Points*
	A	$y > z > a$			$y = 8$
	B	$a > y > z$			$z = 7$
	C	$z > a > y$			$a = 6$
Individuals:	D	$y > z > a$			
	E	$a > y > z$			
	F	$z > a > y$			
	G	$y > z > a$			

The surprising outcome is that when x, the original winner, is deleted, y, originally the alternative with the fewest points, becomes the winner! In fact, the social-preference order among the alternatives with x deleted is exactly the reverse of the social-preference order among those same alternatives when x is included. Computer results indicate that the likelihood of such an outcome is relatively small, but that the likelihood increases as the number of voters increases.

WINNER-TURNS-LOSER PARADOX

The obverse of the Inverted-Order Paradox can also occur. That is, the original winner can become a loser when a loser is removed. Moreover, the likelihood of this occurring increases as the number of voters increases when the number of alternatives remains fixed. The very important political implication of this paradox is that it suggests a strategy for the politically weak to undermine the politically strong. Thus, the decision of a *weak* candidate to *withdraw* from an electoral contest can be used as a threat against a stronger candidate under the appropriate circumstances! Consider the following example:

Alternatives

	3	2	1	0	*Rank Points*
63 voters	$x > a > z > y$				$a = 372$
62 voters	$a > z > y > x$				$x = 370$
61 voters	$z > y > x > a$				$z = 370$
60 voters	$y > x > a > z$				$y = 364$

Individuals:

Notice that we now have 246 voters rather than the three, four, or seven in the examples above. In this case, 63 voters have the preference order $x>a>z>y$; 62 voters prefer $a>z>y>x$, and so on. Notice also that every set of voters ranks every alternative differently, and that each preference order, from top to bottom, is obtained by taking the first preference of the previous order and placing it last. This is referred to as a "forward cycle." The point totals indicate that alternative a would be the winner. Now, eliminate y, the alternative with the lowest point total. The new set of preference orders is:

Alternatives

		2	1	0	*Rank Points*
	63 voters	x	$>a$	$>z$	$x=307$
Individuals:	62 voters	a	$>z$	$>x$	$a=247$
	61 voters	z	$>x$	$>a$	$z=184$
	60 voters	x	$>a$	$>z$	

Here a is no longer the winner! A similar result occurs if we eliminate z:

Alternatives

		2	1	0	*Rank Points*
	63 voters	x	$>a$	$>y$	$y=306$
Individuals:	62 voters	a	$>y$	$>x$	$x=247$
	61 voters	y	$>x$	$>a$	$a=187$
	60 voters	y	$>x$	$>a$	

(*Question:* Would a also become a loser if x were eliminated? Can you devise a five-voter preference profile which gives similar results?)

TRUNCATED POINT-TOTAL PARADOX

You may have wondered whether the choice of particular numbers for the rank points makes a difference. Sometimes it does not. Consider the following example:

Alternatives

3	2	1	*Rank Points I*
2	1	0	*Rank Points II*

		I	II
	A	$x>y>z$ $\quad y=7$	$y=4$
Individuals:	B	$y>z>x$ $\quad z=6$	$z=3$
	C	$z>y>x$ $\quad x=5$	$x=2$

Here the result is the same whether the rank point system is I or II; that is, y is the winner. On the other hand, consider the following example:

Alternatives

1	0	0	0	*Rank Points I*
2	1	0	0	*Rank Points II*
3	2	1	0	*Rank Points III*

		I $\quad x=3$
	A $\quad x>y>z>a$	$y=2$
	B $\quad x>y>z>a$	$z=2$
	C $\quad x>y>z>a$	$a=0$
Individuals:	D $\quad y>z>x>a$	II $\quad y=7$
	E $\quad y>z>a>x$	$x=6$
	F $\quad z>a>x>y$	$z=6$
	G $\quad z>a>x>y$	$a=2$
		III $\quad z=13$
		$x=12$
		$y=12$
		$a=5$

Here there are three different sets of rank points. Notice that two of them do not assign any points to either a third or fourth place vote, and one of them, set I, assigns points only to first place votes. Set I, then, is the usual system for most American elections to political office. Set III is the traditional Borda method.

The unusual result, of course, is that the use of each set of rank points produces a different winner! Alternative x wins when set I is used, y wins when set II is used, and z wins when set III is used.

Borda Dominance

Fishburn's final paradox, which he calls "Condorcet's other paradox," involves a situation in which there is again conflict between the Condorcet and Borda methods. This time, a Condorcet winner is defeated by another alternative when the Borda method is used, and this occurs *for every set of rank points*. Consider the following example:

Alternatives

		2	1	0	*Rank Points*
	A	$x>y>z$			
	B	$x>y>z$		Condorcet:	$x>y$
	C	$x>y>z$			$x>z$
Individuals:	D	$y>z>x$		Borda:	$y=9$
	E	$y>z>x$			$x=8$
	F	$y>x>z$			$z=4$
	G	$z>x>y$			

It is not difficult to show that this occurs when the rank points are 3, 2, and 1 respectively. This will be left to the reader. Fishburn proves that this particular result holds for all sets of rank points. This is called "Borda dominance," because in such a situation the Borda method always produces a winner which beats the Condorcet winner. Fishburn also provides computer data which indicates that the discrepancies between the Borda and Condorcet methods increase as the number of voters increases.

STRATEGIC MANIPULATION

The problems described above are inherent in the particular voting systems which we have considered. They assume that all voters report their honest preferences, or that all voters are "sincere." In this final section, we shall mention briefly, and illustrate the important problems which arise when individuals try to affect the outcome of an election by misrepresenting their preferences. Such voting, which is not sincere, is referred to as "sophisticated." It should be stressed that there are no value judgments implied in the choice of these labels.

Consider the following case:

Alternatives

		3	2	1	0	*Rank Points*
	A	$x > y > z > w$				$x = 7$
Individuals:	B	$w > x > y > z$				$w = 6$
	C	$w > x > y > z$				$y = 4$
						$z = 1$

In this situation, x is the Borda winner. Now, on its face, this does not seem to be the fair outcome. Rather, we would expect that w—the Condorcet winner as well as the simple majority winner—should be the winner. By misreporting their preferences, however, either B or C can change the outcome. Suppose, for example, that C reported his or her individual preference order as $w > y > z > x$. Then the outcome would be:

Alternatives

		3	2	1	0	*Rank Points*
	A	$x > y > z > w$				$w = 6$
Individuals:	B	$w > x > y > z$				$x = 5$
	C	$w > y > z > x$				$y = 5$
						$z = 2$

Now, w is the winner. Individuals B and C can do even better by reporting one of their individual preference orders as $w > z > y > x$. Then the outcome is:

Alternatives

		3	2	1	0	*Rank Points*
	A	$x > y > z > w$				$w = 6$
Individuals:	B	$w > x > y > z$				$x = 5$
	C	$w > z > y > x$				$y = 4$
						$z = 3$

In this case, the collective preference order is $w > x > y > z$ which, of course, is the "sincere" individual preference order for both B and C.

This particular outcome does not seem to be objectionable. Nevertheless, the problem of altering the outcome by misreporting preferences could also be used to prevent the victory of an alternative which appeared to be the fair or proper outcome and which would be chosen if individuals reported their true preferences. Consider the following example:

Alternatives

	3	2	1	0	*Rank Points*
A	$x > y > z > w$				$y = 6$
Individuals: B	$w > x > y > z$				$x = 5$
C	$y > z > w > x$				$w = 4$
					$z = 3$

Here, y is the Borda winner. (*Question:* Which alternative is the Condorcet winner?) Note, however, that individual A is in a position to change the outcome by reporting the preference order $x > z > w > y$. Then, alternatives x and w have the highest point totals:

Alternatives

	3	2	1	0	*Rank Points*
A	$x > z > w > y$				$x = 5$
Individuals: B	$w > x > y > z$				$w = 5$
C	$y > z > w > x$				$y = 4$
					$z = 4$

The possibility of strategic or sophisticated voting obviously complicates the voting process enormously and presents the possibility that an alternative which should be the winner by some reasonable standard of fairness is prevented from winning.

In the literature on collective-choice problems, there has been a interest in devising voting systems which are immune from the effects of strategic voting. Such systems have been described as *strategy-proof*. The very interesting theoretical result of this work, however, is that "all strategy-proof systems are defective as ways to make a social choice depend on individual preferences" (Gibbard, 1976, p. 4. See also, Gibbard, 1973, and Satterthwaite, 1975). This means that we cannot devise a system which protects against the adverse effects of strategic voting without creating other problems of equal severity. For example, a dictatorship is clearly a strategy-proof system, but it is unacceptable as a democratic decision-making process. (*Question:* Why is a dictatorship strategy proof?)

CONCLUSION

The original question of this chapter was, what decision rules *will* rational individuals support, and what decision rules *ought* they to support? We also asked whether there could be any set of decision rules which was both empirically predictable—i.e., likely to occur—and normatively justifiable. Our analysis indicates that there are serious theoretical problems with either simple majority rule or the rule of unanimous consent. It also indicated that more complex decision rules, such as the Condorcet and Borda rules, cannot escape serious difficulties. We concluded by showing that even if the decision systems are not flawed, misreporting of preferences by voters, or strategic voting, could prevent the system from operating as intended.

These are rather negative and disheartening results. They show the limitations of certain formal decision procedures. In the next chapter, moreover, it will be shown that such problems apply to all decision procedures.

Such results can be interpreted in at least two ways. First, we could say that we have merely pointed out problems, but have not been able to provide solutions. A "solution" in this case would be a perfect decision rule. One obvious answer to this criticism is that what we have shown is that a "solution" may not be possible!

Another obvious but cynical response is to point out that life is not perfect either! On the other hand, we could say that we are learning a great deal about the particular problems of particular decision rules. Increasingly, we know what we can and cannot expect from certain decision procedures under certain conditions. Surely, this is progress. In any case, for those whose task it is to create the decision rules for new institutions, the problems presented here and in subsequent chapters, and their implication for the political process, must be considered.

CHAPTER TWO

Arrow's General Possibility Theorem

IN THE PREVIOUS CHAPTER, we examined some of the weaknesses of simple majority rule, the unanimity rule, and the Condorcet and Borda methods of vote counting. The question which remained was whether there were any decision procedures which could avoid these problems. In this chapter, we shall present one of the best-known and most important theoretical results in the collective-choice literature—Kenneth Arrow's (1963) "general possibility theorem.[1] This theorem proves that there is no collective decision procedure which can simultaneously satisfy certain weak normative conditions. By implication, there are no decision procedures which are not seriously flawed.

It probably sounds strange to political scientists to hear of a "theorem" which is said to "prove" something in political theory. Our last contact with such terms was most likely in a high-school geometry course where we learned about Euclid, and about such theorems as "the sum of the angles of a triangle equals 180 degrees." In fact, the theorems of collective-choice theory are precisely the same kinds of statements as the theorems of Euclid-

1. This is sometimes called the "general impossibility theorem" for reasons which will soon be evident; but the choice of names is of no substantive significance.

ian geometry. They make general claims about an entire class of things, and they prove these claims by means of deductive logic. That is, using the basic definitions (axioms and postulates) of the theoretical system, it is shown that certain statements in the system are true, and certain statements are false. It is important to note that these are not empirical claims. Euclid did not go out and physically measure the angles of all triangles, or even a sample. Rather, they are statements about a formal theoretical system with very precise characteristics. What is extraordinary is that theorems of formal mathematical systems, such as Euclidian or Riemannian geometry (a geometry which uses different axioms and postulates from those of Euclid), have enabled us to understand, explain, and function more effectively in the real world. Thus, for example, the processes of surveying land or measuring the speed of light depend upon the truths of formal mathematical systems. Similarly, the claim that is being made here is that analyses of formal systems of collective choice can tell us something about actual collective-choice processes.

SOCIAL CHOICE CONDITIONS

Arrow's theoretical strategy in analyzing social decision procedures—or "social welfare functions" as he called them—was first to look for relatively innocuous conditions which virtually all reasonable individuals would agree must be satisfied by any collective-choice procedure. In other words, he did not demand that a decision procedure produce justice, freedom, liberty, happiness, or any other grandiose goal. Rather, he asked, simply, were there any collective choice procedures which could achieve certain minimal goals. These goals were his "natural conditions." His famous theorem says that no collective choice procedure can always satisfy these conditions simultaneously. But, if we cannot achieve these minimal goals, what hope is there of achieving our more important demands? That is the challenge presented by the Arrow result.

CONNECTIVITY AND TRANSITIVITY

Arrow's first condition—it is called an "axiom" in his original work—is that individual and collective preferences be connected. *Connectedness* or *connectivity* means simply that for any two alternatives, one of two basic relationships holds, either preference or indifference; in symbols, *xPy,* or *xIy.* This is merely a requirement that two alternatives be comparable. It eliminates situations in which two alternatives cannot be compared meaningfully.

The second condition or axiom is transitivity. As indicated in the previous chapter, transitivity means that if an individual prefers alternative *x* to alternative *y,* and *y* to *z,* then he/she must prefer alternative *x* to *z.* Transitivity involving only *preferences* (i.e., not allowing for individual *indifference* among alternatives), along with the condition of connectivity described below, results in a so-called *strong ordering.* Transitivity which allows indifference results in a *weak ordering.* For example, if an individual prefers *x* to *y,* but is indifferent between *y* and *z* (i.e., does not prefer one to the other), then, by transitivity he or she prefers *x* to *z;* but the resulting ordering is said to be *weak* because of the indifference relation between *y* and *z.* In symbols:

$x\,P\,y$ means "*x* is preferred to *y.*"
$x\,I\,y$ means "*x* and *y* are preferred equally.*"
$x\,R\,y$ means "either *x* is preferred to *y,*
or *x* and *y* are preferred equally; but *y* is *not* preferred to *x.*"

Sometimes, the standard mathematical symbols for equality and inequality are also used:

$$x\,P\,y \text{ can be expressed } x > y$$
$$x\,I\,y \text{ can be expressed } x = y$$
$$x\,R\,y \text{ can be expressed } x \geq y$$

Arrow's requirement that individual preferences be connected and transitive is referred to as his condition of *individual rationality.* His requirement that group preferences also be connected and transitive is referred to as his condition of *collective rationality.*

FREE TRIPLE

The most obvious task for a collective decision procedure is to produce a social choice, or social preference ordering, from a set of individual preference orderings. Now, one requirement of any decision procedure might be that it yield a social preference for every possible set of individual orderings. This is a tall order. Arrow refers to such a decision procedure as a "universal social welfare function." Consider, for example, majority rule. In our example of the voter's paradox in the previous chapter, the set of individual preferences did not yield a social preference order when majority rule was used. Instead, we found a so-called cyclical majority, an intransitive social ordering. Arrow labels such a set of individual preference orders as "inadmissible" for majority rule. That is, it constitutes a set of individual preference orders which will not produce a social preference order when majority rule is the decision procedure. An "admissible" set of individual preference orders, then, is "a set for which the social welfare function defines a corresponding social ordering" (1963, p. 24). Such a social ordering must be *connected* and *transitive*. In graphic form,

Admissible set of individual preference orderings $\xrightarrow{SWF}$ social ordering

Arrow, however, does not require that all individual preference orderings be admissible. Rather, he limits admissibility to at least one subset of three alternatives within any set of alternatives. In other words, Arrow's decision procedure is only required to produce a social ordering for every set of individual orderings for some set of three alternatives, and not for all the alternatives. That is, individuals must be free to order some set of three alternatives in any way they wish with no restrictions—hence the label "free triple"—but, there may be restrictions on the orderings of the remaining alternatives.

In order to see what is meant by restrictions on individual preference orders, consider the case of three alternatives, x, y, and z. With three alternatives there are six possible preference orderings:

$$x\ y\ z$$
$$x\ z\ y$$
$$y\ z\ x$$
$$y\ x\ z$$
$$z\ x\ y$$
$$z\ y\ x$$

These different orderings of x, y, and z are also referred to as *permutations*.

The "free triple" condition says that any individual may order these three alternatives in any one of these six ways. If there were four alternatives, there would be 24 individual preference orders. The number of possible preference orders is determined by multiplying the number of alternatives by the next lower number, multiplying that product by the next lower number, and so on, until the number one is reached. The product at that point is the number of possible preference orders. Thus, with four alternatives, there are

$$4 \times 3 \times 2 \times 1 = 24$$

possible preference orders. The process is known as finding "n factorial," written "$n!$" Thus, "4!" means "4 factorial" and involves the process above.

Suppose that a national election involves three political parties, each of which takes a different stand on the question of government involvement in the economy. Suppose, further, that party X believes in extensive government intervention—a socialist or at least a welfare state (we shall call this position the "left" since that is generally the term used in the literature on parties); party Z believes in strict laissez-faire (which we shall call the "right," despite the conservative or even reactionary connotation of that term, to which liberals of the nineteenth-century variety object); and party Y wants a judicious combination of state intervention and free enterprise. Suppose also that this is the only issue in the campaign and that all voters perceive it as such. Finally, suppose that for all voters, any voter who prefers either the left or right extreme as a first choice prefers the centrist position as a second choice, while the opposite extreme would be the last choice.[2] Graphically, this could be represented as in fig. 2.1.

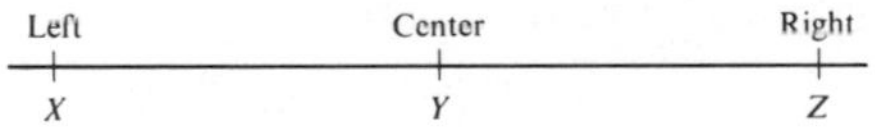

Figure 2.1: Sample alignment of three political parties.

The possible preference orders would then be:

> XYZ   (the leftist position)
> ZYX   (the rightist position)
>
> YXZ⎫   (the centrist positions—note
> YZX⎭   that the centrist position can have
>   either extreme as the second choice)

2. We are excluding from consideration, for purposes of illustration, the situation in which an individual of either extreme would prefer as a second choice the opposite extreme on the grounds that the centrist position accomplishes nothing, while the other extreme might at least provoke a reaction. This, of course, was the position of Lenin and the Bolsheviks in the Russian Revolution.

What has been excluded are the preference orders XZY and ZXY. It is this kind of situation, the exclusion of certain individual preference orders, which Arrow's first condition prohibits when there are only three alternatives. But, as we shall see below, it is just such a restriction that has been proposed as a method of avoiding the voter's paradox.

POSITIVE ASSOCIATION OF SOCIAL AND INDIVIDUAL VALUES (POSITIVE RESPONSIVENESS)

The Positive Association condition says that if an alternative rises or falls in rank in some individual's preference order, and remains unchanged in the preference orders of everyone else, then the relationship among the alternatives in the social ordering must either remain unchanged, or it must change in the direction of the change in the individual's preference order. This condition prohibits an alternative from falling in rank in the social order when it has not fallen in the preference order of any individual. Conversely, it prohibits an alternative from rising in the social preference order when it has not risen in the preference order of any individual. For instance, suppose there are three individuals, three alternatives, and the following *preference profile* (set of individual preference orderings):

I

Alternatives

	A	$x>y>z$
Individuals:	B	$y>x>z$
	C	$z>\underline{x>y}$

Then, suppose that individual C changes his or her mind so that the new preference profile becomes:

II

Alternatives

	A	$x>y>z$
Individuals:	B	$y>x>z$
	C	$z>\underline{y>x}$

What has happened is that alternative y has risen in C's ranking and x has declined. At the same time, the relationship between x and y in A and B's ranking has remained unchanged. The Positive Response condition requires that the social orderings derived from these preference profiles should reflect the change in the relationship between x and y in C's ranking or should remain unchanged. It prohibits a *decline* in y's ranking in the social ordering. Suppose, for instance, that we were using the Condorcet criterion to select a winner—or, more precisely, to establish a social ordering. Then, the ordering in I would be $x > y > z$. In II, the ordering would be $y > x > z$. In other words, alternative y has risen in the social ranking and x has declined, just as it did in C's individual preference order. (*Question:* Can you devise a preference profile in which the social ordering remains unchanged while some alternatives rise or fall in some individual ranking?)

The Positive Response condition is clearly in the spirit of democratic decision making. It requires that the collective choice reflect individual choices in a meaningful way.

INDEPENDENCE OF IRRELEVANT (INFEASIBLE) ALTERNATIVES

The Independence condition is the most controversial of Arrow's conditions. Not only is there a dispute about whether it should be a requirement of decision procedures, there is also substantial disagreement about what the condition means! The wording in the original text of Arrow's book was meant to imply that the preference relation between any two alternatives should not be affected by "irrelevant" alternatives.[3]—i.e., alternatives which were not among the alternatives on the agenda. In other words, an individual's ranking of two alternatives should depend only upon the individual's preferences for the available alternatives.

Stated this way, there does not seem to be anything particularly troublesome about this condition. It seems to be nothing other than common sense. In Arrow's original phrase: "The choice made from any fixed environment S should be independent of the very existence of alternatives outside of S" (1963, p. 26).

Nevertheless, the more formal statement of the condition seemed to suggest something quite different:

If we consider two sets of individual orderings such that, for each individual, his ordering of those particular alternatives in a given environment is the same each time,

3. Recently, Fishburn (1973) and Plott (1976) have suggested that the term "infeasible" captures the spirit of Arrow's meaning better than the term "irrelevant.".

then we require that the choice made by society from that environment be the same when individual values are given by the first set of orderings as they are when given by the second. (1963, pp. 26–27).

More technically:

Let $R_1 . . . R_n$ and $R'_1 . . . R'_n$ be two sets of individual orderings, and let C(S) and C' (S) be the corresponding social choice functions. If, for all individuals i and all x and y in a given environment S, x R_i y if and only if x R'_i y, then C(S) and C' (S) are the same. (1963, p. 27).

The phrase "social choice function" is what we have called a "choice set" or, simply an "outcome" in a collective-choice process. The expression "$R_1 . . . R_n$" refers to a set of orderings, or a "profile" as we have called it. Thus, one "$R_1 . . . R_n$" might be:

Alternatives

	A	$x > y > z$ $= R_1$
Individuals:	B	$y > z > x$ $= R_2$
	C	$z > x > y$ $= R_3$

Stated this way, this Independence condition seems to be a variant of the Positive Responsiveness condition above. That is, positive responsiveness demanded that when an individual preference changed, the social preference should either change in the same way, or remain unchanged. The Independence condition says that if the individual preferences do not change, the social preference also should not change.

Plott (1976) has made a subtle but important change in this statement. He says:

If the feasible set remains fixed and *if* individuals' preferences over the feasible options remain fixed, *then* the social *choice* remains fixed. (1976, p. 32. Italics in the original.)

Here Plott is stressing the *choice set* rather than the social preference ordering. That is, the result of a collective choice procedure is supposed to be a choice. In a presidential election, we choose a single candidate. Sometimes, however, the "choice set" is more than one alternative (as when Congress passes a number of bills, or in proportional representation, or when we choose a committee of several members). In any case, we have a choice set as well as a social ordering of all the alternatives. Thus, in a presidential election, there is an ordering or ranking of all the candidates as well as a winner. While an ordering or ranking is necessary in determining a winner, the two are conceptually different. Plott, then, is focusing on the choice set rather than on the social preference relations.

The question which remains, however, for either version of the Independence condition, is the relationship between these statements about fixed sets of alternatives, fixed individual preference orderings, and fixed choice sets or social preference orderings on the one hand, and the role of "irrelevant" or "infeasible" alternatives on the other.

In Arrow's original version, he used an example to illustrate his point which Plott (1967) later showed to be erroneous. Nevertheless, it gives us an intuitive feeling for Arrow's intended meaning. Consider an election involving candidates x, y, z, w, and three voters, A, B, and C, with the following preference profile:

Candidates

		3	2	1	0	*Rank Points*
	A		$x > y > z > w$			$x = 7$
Voters:	B		$x > y > z > w$			$z = 5$
	C		$z > w > x > y$			$y = 4$
						$w = 2$

If the Borda method is used to determine the outcome, the winner is x, as it would be if we use a simple majority rule and consider only first preferences. The same result holds for the Condorcet method as well. Now, suppose candidate y dies on the eve of the election, or just after the vote tabulation. Then if y were removed from the ballot, the preference profile would be the following:

Candidates

		2	1	0	*Rank Points*
	A		$x > z > w$		$x = 4$
Voters:	B		$x > z > w$		$z = 4$
	C		$z > w > x$		$w = 1$

Here, x and z are tied if we use the Borda method. In other words, even though there was no change in the individual rankings, the outcome changed. Notice, however, that if we had used the Condorcet method, x would have remained the winner. In this case, y is the "irrelevant" or "in-

CITIZENS' SOVEREIGNTY

The Citizens' Sovereignty condition says that the social choice is not to be imposed. "Imposition" means that a particular alternative will be the social choice regardless of the individual preference orders of the members of the group. In formal terms, imposition is expressed as follows:

. . . for some pair of distinct alternatives x and y, $x R y$ for any set of individual orderings $R_1, \ldots, R_n$, where R is the social ordering corresponding to $R_1, \ldots, R_n$. (Arrow, 1963, p. 28)

The expression "$R_1, \ldots, R_n$," as we said above, refers to the preference profile. Each "R_i" is an individual ordering. Notice the expression "$x R y$." This means that x is preferred to y, *or* that x and y are ranked equally; but that y is *not* preferred to x. If such a social choice holds *regardless* of individual preferences, that choice is said to be imposed.

NONDICTATORSHIP

Arrow's final condition is Nondictatorship. This means that no single individual in the group will determine the social choice regardless of the preferences of others. Formally,

A social welfare function is said to be dictatorial if there exists an individual i such that, for all x and y, $x P_i y$ implies $x P y$ regardless of the orderings $R_1, \ldots, R_n$ of all individuals other than i, where P is the social preference relation corresponding to $R_1, \ldots, R_n$. (1963, p. 30)

The term "$x P_i y$" means "individual i prefers x over y." The symbol "R," as we said before, refers to an ordering of the alternatives. Thus, R might be the same as $x > y > z$; and if this is the ordering of individual i, we would refer to that ordering as "R_i," read, "R sub i," and meaning "individual i's ordering."

SUMMARY

These, then, are Arrow's conditions. They are the normative goals which every collective-choice procedure should satisfy, and which reasonable people are expected to accept. They are the weak normative conditions to which we referred initially.

And, indeed, they do not seem objectionable. They first require that we be able to say, simply, whether we have a preference for one alternative over another, or whether we are indifferent between two alternatives (*con-*

nectedness). Then we are required to be able to rank our preferences if more than two are involved; that is, to indicate our first choice, second choice, and so on (*transitivity*). It is also required that there be a group choice, or a social ranking of the alternatives (*collective transitivity or rationality*). Next, Arrow requires that there be no limitation on the way individuals can rank the alternatives for at least some sub-set of three alternatives (*free triple*).

Having established conditions for individual preferences, he then turns to the relation between the set of individual preferences and the social choice (choice set). Here, the first requirement is that any change in individual preferences either should leave the collective choice unaffected, or should result in the same kind of change. The collective choice cannot change in a way which is *different* from individual changes (*positive responsiveness*). Related to this requirement is the demand that when individual preferences do not change, the social preferences also must not change (*independence of irrelevant alternatives*). The two final conditions prevent a social choice from being imposed on the group as a whole (*citizens' sovereignty*) and from being imposed on the group by any particular member of the group (*nondictatorship*).

Certainly such conditions appear to be minimal requirements for a democratic process. They do not demand that the choice mechanism provide love, happiness, justice, prosperity, or any other virtue. The problem is, however, that they are inconsistent goals. That is, as Arrow has shown, they cannot all be satisfied simultaneously by any decision procedure.

PROOF OF THE IMPOSSIBILITY THEOREM

The original proof of Arrow's theorem contained certain flaws which were subsequently revealed by Blau (1957) and others. These problems were not fatal to the theorem, however, and in the second edition of his *Social Choice and Individual Values,* Arrow revised both the proof and the form of the conditions. In this section we shall describe the revised proof and conditions.

THE PARETO PRINCIPLE

In the previous chapter, we introduced the notion of Pareto optimality as a criterion of choice among alternative policies. Arrow incorporated the

Pareto principle into his new set of conditions. Formally, the Pareto principle is expressed as follows:

Pareto Principle: If $x P_i y$ for all i, then $x P y$

In other words, if everyone prefers alternative x to y, then the society or group must also prefer x to y. This is referred to as the *weak* version of the Pareto principle. That is, only strict preference relations are allowed. In the so-called *strong* version, x is the social preference if at least one individual prefers x to y, and if everyone else is indifferent between x and y.

REVISED FREE TRIPLE AND POSITIVE RESPONSIVENESS

Arrow also revised these two conditions, replacing them with the following: I. *Revised Free Triple (Unlimited Domain):* "All logically possible orderings of the alternative social states are admissible" (1963, p. 96).

Here, Arrow is extending the requirement of admissibility from some triple of alternatives to *all* alternatives, or, more precisely, all alternative social states, which are combinations of alternatives rather than single alternatives. This is, of course, a much stronger requirement than the "free triple" condition.

II. *Revised Positive Responsiveness:* "For a given pair of alternatives, x and y, let the individual preferences be given. . . . Suppose that x is then raised in some or all of the individual preferences. Then if x was originally socially preferred to y, it remains socially preferred to y after the change" (1963, pp. 96–97).

(*Question:* How does this differ from the original condition? In what sense is it "stronger"?)

Arrow then shows that the Pareto principle is deducible from II, above, and citizens' sovereignty. The point of showing this relationship is that Arrow's revised proof shows that conditions I (above), independence of irrelevant alternatives, the Pareto principle, and nondictatorship, are inconsistent. And, since the Pareto principle is deducible from II, above, and citizens' sovereignty, the latter are also inconsistent with the unlimited domain, independence, and nondictatorship conditions.

It is important to remember that Arrow's proof shows that no decision procedure can avoid this inconsistency completely. He is not suggesting that decision procedures must always violate these conditions. Majority rule, for example, violates Arrow's conditions when the individual preferences yield a cyclical majority. In many other circumstances, however, there are no problems. In the next chapter, we shall discuss the extensive literature which focuses on this point and inquires into the likelihood of the occurrence of the voter's paradox.

DECISIVE SETS

Arrow's proof begins with a definition of a *decisive set:*

A set of individuals V is decisive for x against y if x is socially chosen when every individual in V prefers x to y and every individual not in V prefers y to x. (1963, p. 98)

Notice that the notion of "decisiveness" is very similar to the notion of "dictatorial" in Arrow's condition of nondictatorship. Notice also the strong requirement that everyone *not* in the decisive set has exactly the opposite preferences from those in the decisive set. This definition closely resembles one of the standard definitions of power in political science: the ability to have one's way despite the resistance of others.[4]

The first part of the proof shows that if an individual is decisive for some pair of alternatives, then he or she is decisive for all pairs of alternatives in the set of alternatives. For example, if there are three alternatives, x, y, and z, there are three pairs of alternatives: xy, xz, and yz. Arrow's point is that an individual decisive for any one of these pairs, is decisive for the other two as well. But this means that the individual is the dictator, since, no matter what the preferences of others, his or her will prevails. Thus, if our individual prefers x to every other alternative, x is the social choice. If he or she prefers y, y prevails, and so on.

Arrow introduces a related notion which we might call "weakly decisive." An individual, I, is weakly decisive if "x is socially preferred to y whenever I prefers x to y, regardless of the orderings of other individuals" (1963, p. 98). Notice that this definition differs from that given above— which we may call "strongly decisive"—in that it allows the preferences of others in the group to be the same as I, different from I, or some combination. Recall that the notion of decisiveness above required that everyone not in the decisive set have the *opposite* preferences from those in the decisive set. In symbols, $x \bar{D} y$ means that I prefers x to y and is weakly decisive;

4. Cf. Dahl (1963).

i.e., x will prevail regardless of the preferences of others. Then, $x \, D \, y$ means that I prefers x to y, everyone else prefers y to x, but that x will prevail. We might also say that "x is weakly decisive over y" ($x \, \bar{D} \, y$), and that "x is decisive over y" ($x \, D \, y$).

Arrow then points out that:

$$x \, \bar{D} \, y \text{ implies } x \, D \, y$$

This means that if an individual is weakly decisive for one alternative over another, he or she is also decisive for those alternatives. (*Question:* Can you explain this?) Arrow then shows that:

$$x \, D \, y \text{ implies } x \, \bar{D} \, z$$

Notice that here he is saying that if an individual is decisive for one alternative over a second alternative, he or she is weakly decisive for the first alternative over a third alternative. In other words, if we can say that x is socially preferred to y whenever I prefers x to y and everyone else prefers y to x, then x is socially preferred to z whenever I prefers x to z, regardless of the preferences of others.

This point is demonstrated by the following example. Suppose that there are three alternatives, x, y, z, and that I is decisive for x and y. Suppose, further, that I prefers x to y to z, and that everyone else prefers y to both x and z, and may order x and z in any way. In symbols:

$$I: x > y > z$$
$$\text{Everyone Else: } y > x \geq z; \text{ or, } y > z > x$$

Since we assume that I prefers x to y and that I is decisive over these two alternatives, the social preference is x over y. In symbols:

$$x \, P \, y$$

Notice that everyone, including individual I, prefers y to z. Thus, by the Pareto condition (if everyone prefers one alternative to another, so does the group),

$$y \, P \, z$$

Now, by the condition of social transitivity, if $x \, P \, y$, and $y \, P \, z$, then:

$$x \, P \, z$$

That is, x is socially preferred to z. But notice that the individuals other than I may prefer z to x. Nevertheless, x will always be socially preferred to z by the argument above. And, since I prefers x to z, and x is socially preferred to z regardless of the preferences of the others, it follows that I is weakly decisive for x against z. Therefore,

$$x \, D \, y \text{ implies } x \, \bar{D} \, z.$$

(*Question:* Suppose everyone else in the group preferred x to y also. How would this affect the argument or proof?)

By similar arguments, Arrow shows that if an individual, I, is decisive for any two alternatives in a set of three alternatives, then that individual is the dictator for those three alternatives:

If $x \, D \, y$, then $u \, \bar{D} \, v$ holds for every ordered pair u, v from the three alternatives x, y, and z (1963, p. 99).

In this sentence, the letters "u" and "v" are variables which can stand for x, y, or z. In other words,

$$u \, \bar{D} \, v = \{x \, \bar{D} \, y, \ y \, \bar{D} \, x, \ x \, \bar{D} \, z, \ z \, \bar{D} \, x, \ y \, \bar{D} \, z, \ z \, \bar{D} \, y\}$$

The brackets indicate a *set,* or a group of things—in this case, pairs of alternatives, one weakly decisive over the other. This also means that $u \, \bar{D} \, v$ can stand for any of the expressions within the brackets.

Arrow then shows that if an individual I is decisive for any pair of alternatives, he or she is a dictator for any *number of alternatives*. That is, if individual I is decisive for any pair of alternatives, not only is he or she the dictator for three alternatives, as shown above, but would be the dictator if that pair were two among ten alternatives, twenty alternatives, and so on.

This is an extremely important result, since it can then be shown that an individual is a dictator simply by showing that he or she is decisive for *some* pair of alternatives. Arrow then uses this point to show that the conditions he has put forward are inconsistent—that is, they lead to a contradiction. He does this in the following way. First, recall that the condition of *nondictatorship* says that no individual can be *decisive*—as we have used the term above—for any pair of alternatives. In other words, the nondictatorship condition forbids $x \, D \, y$. Arrow then shows that the Pareto principle *must* lead to at least one situation in which some individual is decisive for some pair of alternatives, and is, therefore, a dictator—in violation of the condition of nondictatorship. In short, *the Pareto principle and the condition of nondictatorship are contradictory.*

Arrow's demonstration of this point is relatively simple. Recall that the Pareto principle—or, unanimity principle, as we might call it—says that if everyone in the group prefers x to y, then the social or group preference must also be x over y. Now, this means that there must be at least one *decisive set* of individuals in any group, and that is the set of *all* individuals who prefer x to y. In our discussion above, we spoke of a decisive *individual*. This is forbidden by the nondictatorship condition, but the Pareto principle *requires* a decisive *set* of individuals. Notice that such a decisive set is not required in all cases. Obviously, an allowable decisive set exists only when there is unanimity. (*Question:* If the decisive set consists of everyone in the group, who are the "others" who hold opposing preferences as described in our discussion of the decisive individual? In other words, how do we describe the "set" of individuals *not* in the decisive set?)

While the nondictatorship condition forbids individual dictators, and the Pareto condition requires that unanimous groups be decisive, there are no formal restrictions on groups larger than one or smaller than n. Therefore, Arrow says, assume that some group in that range is decisive for the pair x, y. Designate that set V. Then, $1 < V < n$; i.e., the decisive set V contains at least two members, but does not include every member of the group. This means that we are considering groups which contain at least three members. (*Question:* Why could we not be considering groups of *two* members?)

Next, divide V into two groups, V_1 and V_2. Let V_1 contain a single member, V_2 contain the other member(s) of V. In other words, if $V = 2$, $V_1 = 1$, and $V_2 = 1$. (*Question:* If $V = 5$, how many members are there in V_2?) Further, let V_3 contain everyone not in V. Thus, if $n = 3$, $V_3 = 1$, $V = 2$, $V_1 = 1$, and $V_2 = 1$.

Remembering that V is the decisive set for some pair of alternatives, assume that the preference order for V_1 of alternatives x, y, and z is $x > y > z$. Assume further that the preference order for V_2 is $z > x > y$, and that the preference order for V_3 is $y > z > x$. Thus, the preference profile is:

Alternatives

$V_1 \quad x > y > z$

$$\textit{Individuals:} \quad V_2 \quad z>x>y$$
$$V_3 \quad y>z>x$$

There are two important points to notice about this preference profile. First, it is the set of orderings which produces a voter's paradox when the number of individuals in V_1, V_2, and V_3 are equal. Second, the individuals in V_1 and V_2 all prefer x to y, even though they hold opposite preferences over alternatives y and z. This is necessary, of course, since V_1 and V_2 are part of the set V, which is decisive over some pair of alternatives, in this case, x and y. Notice also that everyone in V_3 prefers y to x. This is necessary if everyone in V prefers x to y, and if V is to be called "decisive."

Since V is decisive, and since everyone in V prefers x to y, the social preference is $x\ P\ y$. Now consider the alternatives y and z. Notice that V_1 and V_3 prefer y to z, while V_2 prefers z to y. If the social preference were $z\ P\ y$, then V_2 would be decisive, since everyone else prefers y to z. This would not be a problem unless $V_2 = 1$ (i.e., V_2 contained one member). This could occur, of course, if $V = 2$. Suppose, then, that $V = 2$. This would mean that the social preference could *not* be $z\ P\ y$ since that would make V_2 a decisive individual, which is forbidden by the nondictatorship condition. Remember, we are trying to establish that a contradiction *can* occur, not that it *must always* occur. For that reason, if we find a single case where the contradiction occurs, we have shown that it cannot always be avoided. In this case, our example involves $V = 2$.

Since it cannot be the case that $z\ P\ y$, it must be that $y\ R\ z$, (i.e., the society either prefers y over z, or is indifferent between them). By the condition of social transitivity, however, if $x\ P\ y$ and $y\ R\ z$, then society must prefer x to z. To see this, consider the possibilities separately. If $x\ P\ y$, and $y\ P\ z$, then, clearly, $x\ P\ z$, since only preference relations are involved. If $x\ P\ y$ and $y\ I\ z$ (i.e., society is indifferent between y and z) then it is also true that $x\ P\ z$. To see this, remember that indifference can also be thought of as the mathematical notion of equality, while the preference relation can be thought of as the mathematical notion "greater than." In the above expression, if z is equal to y, then z can be substituted for y in the expression $x\ P\ y$, and we get $x\ P\ z$. In other words, society prefers x to z. But, notice that V_1 (a single individual since $V = 2$), is the only one who prefers x to z. Both V_2 and V_3 prefer z to x. This means that individual V_1 is decisive for alternatives z and x, and, by the previous demonstration is also the dictator. This result, however, which we derived from an initial assumption of the Pareto condition, violates the condition of nondictatorship. It has been shown, therefore, that there is a contradiction between these two conditions.

What we have just done is to prove Arrow's General Possibility Theorem which is expressed as follows:

Conditions 1' (unlimited domain for social preference orderings), 3 (Independence of Irrelevant Alternatives), P (Pareto principle) and 5 (nondictatorship) are inconsistent. (1963, p. 97)

CLARIFYING THE PROOF

Notice that the statement of Arrow's theorem focuses on the inconsistency of his conditions. By the term "inconsistent" he means that their use leads to a contradiction, as illustrated above. That is, one or more of the conditions is violated.

The relationship between the theorem and the proof, however, is not immediately evident. Nor is it immediately clear how the theorem and its proof relates to our previous discussion of decision rules. At least part of the reason for this is the habit of verbal economy which is so characteristic of formal theorists; as well as the assumption that the reader can make the connections which the author has in mind without explicit guidelines. No such assumption is made here.

We note first that there is no mention of a decision rule in either the proof or the theorem. This is not an oversight, but an important element in the generalizability of the theorem. That is, Arrow wants to make a statement about *all* decision rules. In order to do this, he is required to make statements which apply to all decision rules. Such a statement is the Pareto condition or the nondictatorship condition. In fact, all of his conditions must apply to all decision rules. That is the nature of a condition on a decision procedure. *By dealing with the consequences of his conditions, therefore, he is also dealing with the consequences of the decision rules which must satisfy those conditions—i.e., all decision rules.*

The second point to notice is that Arrow uses a particular preference profile—that which we know produces a cyclical majority, or voter's paradox. Now, the immediate question which should arise is whether the Pareto condition and the nondictatorship condition lead to a contradiction if another preference profile is used. Consider the following:

Alternatives

	V_1	$x > y > z$
Individuals:	V_2	$z > x > y$
	V_3	$y > x > z$

The only difference between this profile and the one above is that the preference of V_3 is $y > x > z$, rather than $y > z > x$. In other words, this is not a paradox-producing preference profile. Notice that if V_1, V_2, and V_3 are single individuals, x is the Condorcet winner.

Now, let us run through the Arrow proof using this profile. Here $x \, P \, y$, x is socially preferred to y, since $V \, (V_1 + V_2)$ is decisive for some pair—by assumption—and in this case it must be x, y. (*Question:* Why could V not be decisive for y, z?) Further, z cannot be socially preferred to y since that would make V_2 decisive for z, y contradicting the Nondictatorship condition since V_2 is an individual, by assumption. This means that $y \geq z$ (i.e., either y is socially preferred to z, or the society is indifferent between them). So far, the results are the same as those in the Arrow proof. If $x \, P \, y$ and $y \, P \, z$, then by social transitivity $x \, P \, z$. But, notice that this result does *not* imply that V_1 is decisive—or, the dictator—since V_3 also prefers x to z. Thus, there is no contradiction here. This is also true if $y = z$ (or $y \, I \, z$). *The Arrow result, then, appears to hold only for a particular configuration of preferences and not for all configurations of preferences.* At the same time, because of the demonstration in the first part of the proof that if an individual is decisive for any pair of alternatives he or she is a dictator over any number of alternatives in the same set, the contradiction shown in the second part of the proof applies to any (finite) number of alternatives and any number of individuals. *Thus, the Arrow result holds for all paradox-producing preference profiles, any number of individuals and alternatives, and all decision rules.*

The very important point here also is that the existence of paradox-producing profiles is independent of the decision rule used. The use of majority rule, for example, does not affect the preferences of the individuals in the group, although, as we have shown, it does have a direct bearing on the social preference. Thus, if such a profile is possible, it *may* appear no matter what decision rule is used. In other words, particular decision rules cannot prevent the occurrence of such profiles. In fact, Arrow's condition of *unlimited domain* assures that such profiles are possible. This means, then, that *no decision rule can avoid situations where the contradiction between the Pareto principle and the Nondictatorship condition can occur*. Therefore, no decision procedure can always satisfy Arrow's conditions.

CONCLUSION

The impact of the General Possibility Theorem which follows from these conditions derives from the fact that these conditions appear eminently reasonable. Some, in fact, probably strike us as so obvious that they do not need stating. Moreover, they can be said to be quite weak in the sense that they do not seem to be very demanding conditions. They do not require that the decision procedure produce a "just" society, or a society of full equality and human happiness, or any other utopian ideal. Rather, they seem to be minimum requirements, at best, for a social welfare function. Yet, Arrow shows that there is no social-welfare function which can satisfy all of these conditions. If such weak requirements cannot be met, what possible hope could there be to satisfy more stringent conditions?

It is important to stress that Arrow's General Possibility Theorem is a *logical* conclusion, and not the result of empirical observation or testing of decision procedures. It will undoubtedly appear that his conclusion is counterintuitive, i.e., there seems to be no commonsense reason why all of his conditions cannot be satisfied simultaneously by some decision procedure. But an analysis of the formal proof, which is now commonly accepted as correct, shows that this counterintuitive result does indeed follow from his conditions.

In fact, however, Arrow's conditions are not nearly so self-evidently acceptable as they appear. Rather, they represent a very particular political philosophy, which has had many critics. We shall mention only some of those criticisms here.

First, political philosophers such as Plato would reject such conditions, arguing that individual preferences are irrelevant in the creation of a just society. Thus, even if it were possible to overcome the logical problems of passing from individual to collective preferences which Arrow demonstrates,

Plato would not accept the outcome. Rather, a just society requires an elite of rational intellectuals led by a "philosopher king." Ordinary people, it is claimed, are simply not capable of making important decisions on public issues. The fear of the tyranny of the majority, in De Tocqueville's terms, has also been a recurring theme in political philosophy. The American Constitution recognizes this problem in the Bill of Rights, which protects individuals from the potential excesses of majority rule. José Ortega y Gasset, a Spanish political philosopher, argued that the political problems of the twentieth century, and especially the rise of fascism, resulted from the "revolt of the masses," in which people of no particular ability (not simply the rich) have taken power. Instead, he called for rule by an elite of those who are skilled, dedicated, and qualified (although he did not define these terms with any great precision).

Even many political philosophers who are democrats, however, put little or no faith in overt expression of preference. Rousseau, for example, argued for a "general will" as the basis of political action, but denied that voting or any such mechanism could always be an adequate expression of that general will. Similarly, Karl Marx was a democrat in the sense that he believed that a just society would emerge through the rule of all the people in a classless society, but such a society would not require the electoral or parliamentary mechanisms of "bourgeois democracy" which were designed to implement class rule and the oppression of the proletariat.

For Arrow, on the other hand, the social good is nothing other than the choices which a society makes according to a certain decision procedure: "I regard social values as meaning nothing more than social choices" (1963, p. 106). There is no metaphysical "general good" which must be reasoned out by select individuals, or which somehow inheres in collective action. In this sense, Arrow is very much in the utilitarian tradition of Bentham and Mill.

But this does not mean that individual preferences are without constraints. Indeed, his conditions are the restraints on individual preferences taken as a whole. The interesting question however is, Why should we accept these conditions? What are the grounds for saying that the values expressed in these conditions are acceptable? In fact, Arrow himself recognizes that his conditions are arbitrary and that suitable revisions might eliminate the paradox problem, and, hence, eliminate the contradiction among his conditions. In the next chapter, we shall discuss some of those suggested revisions. Nevertheless, nowhere does Arrow indicate what he believes should be a suitable basis for accepting or rejecting constraints on a social welfare function. Moreover, those who propose alternatives appear to suggest that their recommendations should be acceptable *because* they eliminate the paradox problem! Clearly, this is not a satisfactory answer to our question concerning the justification of his conditions.

Another way of viewing this problem is to note that Arrow conceives of the alternatives in the environment S as "social states"—that is, bundles of policy alternatives—and the social welfare function as a "constitution." But this means that the choice of a constitution itself is *not* an alternative to be chosen by a social welfare function and subject to its constraints. In other words, the choice of a constitution appears to be arbitrary—i.e., whatever decision procedure satisfies certain arbitrary conditions. It would seem reasonable, however, to assume that the choice of a constitution should be one of the most important decisions which a society can make, and, therefore, should also be derived by some kind of collective-choice process.

CHAPTER THREE

Paradox Lost

IN THE PREVIOUS CHAPTER, we saw that the proof of Arrow's impossibility theorem depended upon the existence of preference profiles which yield a cyclical majority or voter's paradox. The elimination of such profiles, then, would eliminate the contradiction among Arrow's conditions. For that reason, a great deal of work in the collective-choice literature has been devoted to establishing conditions which assure that such profiles will not exist. In the first part of this chapter we shall examine two of these, *single-peakedness* and *value restrictedness*. These conditions represent an alteration of Arrow's "free triple" and unlimited domain conditions.

Another change in Arrow's conditions which would eliminate the possibility of a cyclical majority is Fishburn's (1970) suggestion that *social transitivity* not be required. We shall discuss this below.

Perhaps the most controversial suggested change is the elimination of the *Independence of Irrelevant Alternatives* condition. This would clear the way for the use of cardinal utility and, perhaps, interpersonal comparison of utility. Such a move would not eliminate the possibility of the paradox, but it would greatly reduce its probability.

Some theorists, however, argue that even though paradox-producing profiles may be unavoidable in actual collective-choice situations, they are relatively rare and, for that reason, are not particularly important. By implication, Arrow's contradiction remains, but its importance is denigrated. In the second part of this chapter, then, we shall examine the work on the *probability of the paradox.*

A THEOREM ON TWO ALTERNATIVES

Before discussing single-peakedness, we should note that all of the analysis in these first chapters applies to situations of three or more alternatives. For, if there are only two alternatives, Arrow provides the following theorem:

If the total number of alternatives is two, the method of majority decision is a social welfare function which satisfies conditions 2–5 and yields a social ordering of the two alternatives for every set of individual orderings. (1963, p. 48)

The "conditions 2–5" are all of the conditions which we discussed above except for that of the "Free Triple." (*Question:* Why is the "Free Triple" condition not included here?) Arrow suggests that this theorem "is, in a sense, the logical foundation of the Anglo-American two-party system." In other words, if we limit the number of alternatives to two, the voter's paradox and Arrow's contradiction can never arise.

SINGLE-PEAKEDNESS

This condition was first suggested by Duncan Black (1958). We have given an example of single-peakedness in the previous chapter in our discussion of the election of parties from the left, center, and right of a political spectrum. *Single-peakedness is, essentially, a limitation on the allowable preference orders. It says that some alternative cannot be the last choice of any individual.* Recall that in our example x was the leftist position, y the centrist, and z the rightist. We argued, then, that the preference orders xzy, and zxy were ruled out as individual preference orders so long as everyone agreed that the one issue in the campaign was degree of government intervention, that the particular parties did indeed stand for those positions, and that an extremist of the right or left could not take the opposite extreme as a second choice. In this case, then, y cannot be the last choice of any individual.

The term "single-peakedness" is derived from the figure which would be obtained if we diagramed this situation. Thus, the possible preference orders, *xyz, zyx, yzx,* and *yxz* might be presented in two-dimensional form as shown in fig. 3.1, where the height of the dot above the letter on the line in-

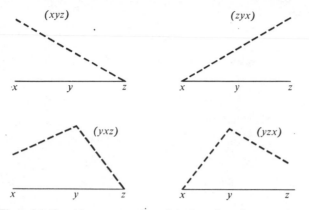

Figure 3.1. Graphic representation of single-peak preference orders.

dicates the ranking. Thus, a first choice is listed higher than a second, and a second choice higher than a third. For each of the above preference orderings, there is a single peak, hence the term single-peakedness.

The individual preference orders *xzy* or *zxy* would appear with two peaks, as shown in (3.2). But, the geometical representation is less impor-

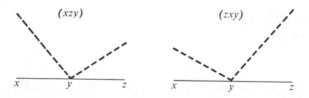

Figure 3.2. Graphic representation of two-peaked preference orders.

tant than the notion that certain alternatives cannot be the last choice. This restriction on the position of certain alternatives then rules out certain preference orders in violation of Arrow's first condition.

It is relatively simple to demonstrate that the restriction of single-peakedness rules out the possibility of the voter's paradox for the case of three alternatives. For three alternatives there are six possible preference orders as indicated above:

xyz
xzy
yzx
yxz
zxy
zyx

The voter's paradox occurs when no two individuals out of three have the same ranking for any alternative. Thus, the following preference profile for three individuals and three alternatives produces the paradox, or as we have called it, a cyclical majority.

$$Alternatives$$

A $x>y>z$

Individuals: B $y>z>x$

C $z>x>y$

Note that each alternative appears in a different rank for each individual. There is one other preference profile which produces the paradox:

$$Alternatives$$

A $x>z>y$

Individuals: B $y>x>z$

C $z>y>x$

Again, each alternative is in a different rank for each individual, but this time an entirely different set of preference orders has been used. Between these two sets of preference orders, however, all six possible preference orders have been used. The important point is that *no other set of three preference orders produces a voter's paradox.*[1] Note also that the preference orders with *y* as the third choice are in *different* sets of paradox-producing preference profiles. This means that if both of these preference orders are eliminated as possibilities, as is the case in single-peakedness, the preference profiles which produce the paradox are also eliminated. But then, there are no paradox-producing preference profiles, and so, the paradox is eliminated! Notice that this result obtains *no matter which alternative is ruled out as the last choice of some individual.* In our example, if either *x* or *z* were

1. You can demonstrate this rather easily for yourself by a simple trial and error method. Simply list all of the other combinations of three of these preference orders and, using majority rule, see if you get a winner.

eliminated as a possible last choice, then again one preference order from *each* of the paradox-producing preference profiles would be eliminated and the paradox could not occur. (*Question:* Does the number of individuals involved affect this result? Explain.)

VALUE RESTRICTEDNESS

It turns out that the paradox is also eliminated if *any alternative cannot be the first, second, or third choice for any individual and for any three alternatives*. This has been called *value-restrictedness*, (Sen, 1966) and is an obvious extension of single-peakedness. Again, a glance at our paradox examples above shows that this is the case for three alternatives.[2] Suppose, for instance, that *x* were eliminated as a possible first choice. Then the preference orders *xyz* and *xzy* are also eliminated, as is the possibility of the paradox. (*Question:* Show that value-restrictedness eliminates the paradox when *any* alternative is eliminated as the first, second, or third choice for any individual when there are three alternatives. Again, is the number of individuals relevant?)

Both single-peakedness and value-restrictedness are violations of Arrow's condition of unlimited domain and his "Free Triple" condition, in the sense that they restrict the possible preference orders. In the case of single-peakedness, we can say either that the individuals agree that some alternative shall not be the last choice, or that *all of the individuals use the same criterion in making their choices*. In other words, the agreement on what *criterion* to use in making choices is equivalent to agreeing that some alternative will not be a last choice. To see this more clearly, let us return to our example of the political parties. There the *alternatives* were parties, but the *criterion* used to order the parties was *ideological position*. By this criterion it would have been contradictory for any individual whose first choice was a party of the left or right extreme to have the opposite extreme as a second choice. That is because the positions left, center, and right are already ordered in terms of the extent of government intervention in the economy. And, once the individuals accept the criterion of government intervention as the basis for their choices, they also implicitly accept that ordering. *This is*

2. The formal proof for any number of alternatives can be found in Sen (1966).

not the same thing as saying that all individuals have the same preference orderings, but simply that the second and third choices are constrained by the nature of the first choice. Thus, the choice of x (left) as first choice limits the second and third choices to y and z respectively.

Suppose, however, that not all individuals used the same criterion. Let individual A judge the parties x, y, and z according to the attractiveness (to A) of the parties' candidates, while individuals B and C use the criterion of ideological position. Suppose also that attractiveness involved willingness to take bold, risky steps, and that everyone agreed that the candidate of party x was the boldest, party z's candidate was next, and party y's candidate was the least bold. The boldness of candidate's criterion then, would order the parties as follows:

$$x \qquad\qquad z \qquad\qquad y$$
More Bold   Less Bold

The preference ordering for any individual who uses this criterion would depend upon one's notion of attractiveness. If boldness were considered attractive, then x would be the first choice, z the second, and y last. But, recall that the absence of the preference ordering xzy had eliminated the paradox. By using a second criterion of choice the possibility of the paradox is reintroduced. The implication of this analysis is that the elimination of the paradox requires some kind of agreement—we might use the term *consensus*. We shall discuss below how the extent of agreement affects the probability of the occurrence of the paradox.

Both single-peakedness and value-restrictedness eliminate the possibility of the paradox by altering Arrow's condition of unlimited domain. They show, in other words, a *sufficient condition* for the elimination of the paradox. In one sense, this is important knowledge if we want to know how to structure a choice situation so that cyclical majorities could be avoided. In another sense, however, both Black and Sen simply avoid the Arrow problem; they do not solve it. They say, in essence, let us assume that a certain amount of agreement exists! But, the traditional problem of political philosophy has been how to deal with situations in which such agreement does *not* exist. These problems cannot be postulated away.

ELIMINATING SOCIAL TRANSITIVITY

Another important alteration in Arrow's conditions has been suggested by Fishburn (1970), who argues that *social transitivity is not necessarily a desirable condition to place on a social welfare function*. He shows, by example, that certain choice outcomes which appear completely acceptable violate Arrow's condition of social transitivity as well as a later condition called *extension*. The *extension condition* is related to the Condorcet criterion. It says that the choice set from environment S shall consist of those alternatives in S that *tie or beat* every other alternative. The extension condition is necessary, says Fishburn, because "transitivity by itself says absolutely nothing about social choice from environments (sets of implementable alternatives) that contain more than two social alternatives. Arrow leaves this task up to E (extension) which prescribes (in a possibly limited way) choices from larger environments on the basis of choices from two-alternative environments" (p. 120).

When the conditions of transitivity and extension are combined (we shall call this TE), they produce a result which says that "if two environments both contain x and y, and if x but not y is the choice set from the first environment, then y shall not be in the choice set from the second environment." (p. 123) Formally this is written:

$$\text{If } x, \ y \in S \wedge S' \text{ and } (x \in F \ (S,D),$$
$$y \notin F \ (S,D), \text{ then } Y \notin F \ (S',D)$$

Where the Greek letter "ϵ" means "are elements in" (or, "is an element in"); S and S' are two environments, or sets of alternatives; the symbol $\wedge$ means "the intersection of" (i.e., the intersection of sets); D is the set of individual weak orderings in S; "$\notin$" means "is not an element of" ("are not elements of"); and $F(S,D)$ means the "choice set for the environment S given the individual weak ordering D." The formal statement then says that if the alternatives x and y ("x, y" is read "x and y") are in the environments S and S', and if x is in the choice set for the environment S given the individual weak orderings D (D is equivalent to "$R_1, \ldots ,R_n$" which was introduced in the previous chapter) and if y is *not* in the choice set for the environment S given the individual orderings D, then y is also *not* in the choice set for environment S' given the individual orderings D. Arrow (1959) shows that this condition (TE) holds *if and only if* both transitivity and extension hold separately. In other words, transitivity and extension *are neces-sary and sufficient conditions* for *TE*. This means that *TE* not only *can* hold if *T* and *E* hold, but that these are the *only* conditions which result in *TE*.

With this explanation we can now turn to one of Fishburn's examples. Suppose there is a three-way electoral contest between candidates *x*, *y*, and *z*, and that there are 21 voters, who rank the candidates in the following way (we are assuming that the voters have been asked to *rank* the candidates and not simply to indicate a first choice):

Candidates

		x	*y*	*z*
	1–10	1	3	2
Voters:	11–20	2	1	3
	21	2 (tie)	2 (tie)	1

In other words, candidate *x* receives ten first-place votes from voters 1–10, ten second-place votes from voters 11–20, and one second place vote from voter 21 who is indifferent between *x* and *y*. Candidate *y* also receives ten first place votes (voters 11–20), but only one second-place vote (voter 21); and ten third-place votes. Candidate *z* receives only one first-place vote, ten second-place votes and ten third-place votes. Another way of represent-ing these preference orders is as follows:

Preference Orders

	(10)	$x > z > y$
Number of Voters for Each Preference Order:	(10)	$y > x > z$
	(1)	$z > (xy)$
		(tie vote)

That is, ten voters have the preference ordering *xzy*, ten have *yxz*, and one has *z*(*xy*). Which candidate, then, should win the election? It would certainly appear that *x* should be the winner even though that candidate does not have a majority of the first place votes, since he or she has eleven second-place votes as well as the ten first-place votes. Candidate *y*, who has ten first place votes, has only one second-place vote, while candidate *z*, who has ten second-place votes, has only one first-place vote. Moreover, *x* is also the winner by the *extension* condition since he or she beats *z* and ties *y*, and since he or she is the *only* alternative here which beats or ties every other alternative in a pairwise comparison. By the Condorcet criterion, x is equal to y (since ten voters prefer x to y, ten prefer y to x, and one voter is indifferent between x and y), x is preferred to z, and z is preferred to y. In other words, there is no candidate who receives a majority of the vote in a pairwise comparison with each of the other candidates; and so, there is no Condorcet winner.

Consider now whether transitivity holds. We have the following binary (pairwise) outcomes:

$$x > z$$
$$z > y$$
$$y = x$$

This means that:

$$xRz$$
$$zRy$$
$$yRx$$

In other words, we do appear to have at least a *weak* ordering here— i.e., one which allows indifference. Yet there is a contradiction. If $y = x$, then y and x can be substituted for each other. This means that if $x > z$ and if $x = y$, then $y > z$. But, this contradicts the preference relation $z > y$. Thus, transitivity does not hold in this case,[3] even though x is the winner by several reasonable arguments.

Now consider the following preference orders with the same 21 voters and candidates x and y as in the first example; but this time, instead of candidate z, substitute candidate w.

Candidates

		x	y	w
	1–10	1	2	3
Voters:	11–20	3	1	2
	21	2	2	1
			(tie)	

The preference orders are:

---

3. I am indebted to Nicholas Miller for pointing this out to me.

Preference Orders

	(10)	$x > y > w$
Number of Voters for	(10)	$y > w > x$
Each Preference Order:	(1)	$w > (xy)$

Notice that since the voters are the same and the two candidates x and y are also the same, the preference relationship between x and y does not change. Thus, the same ten voters prefer x to y, and the same ten voters prefer y to x, while the one voter is still indifferent between them. This time, however, candidate w is third in the order of the first ten voters, moving y to second place; and is second in the ordering of the other bloc of ten voters, moving x to third place. Now it would appear that y should be the winner, since y has ten first-place votes and eleven second-place votes while x has ten first place votes but only one second place vote. Moreover, y is also the winner by the extension condition. Again, however, there is no Condorcet winner, since x is tied with y in a pairwise comparison, and x is defeated by w. Transitivity is also violated. The binary preferences are $y > w$, $w > x$, and $y = x$. Since $y = x$, however, it should be that $x > w$ (since $y > w$); but, $w > x$.

In both of these examples, then, transitivity is violated even though it would appear that x is the reasonable winner in the first example and y in the second. More importantly, if x and y are judged the respective winners, the condition *TE* is violated since there are two alternatives, x and y, which are in two different environments— $S = \{x, y, z\}$; $S' = \{x, y, w\}$—and x is in the choice set of the first environment while y is not, *and* y is in the choice set of the second environment. By *TE*, y cannot be in the choice set of the second environment.

Fishburn also shows that a reasonable *unanimity principle* can lead to a violation of the social transitivity condition as well as *TE*. Recall that in the previous chapter the Pareto principle was defined as follows: if xP_iy for all i, then xPy. That is, if everyone prefers x to y, x must be the social preference in a contest between x and y. *The unanimity principle* is somewhat different. It says that if xR_iy for all i, and if xP_iy for some i, then xPy. That is, if no one prefers y to x (which is another way of saying that if everyone either prefers x to y or is indifferent between x and y) and if at least one individual prefers x to y, then x should be the social preference in a contest between x and y. He then gives the following example. Suppose that there are three alternatives, x, y, and z, and three individuals, A, B, and C. The three individuals order the alternatives as follows:

A: prefers x to y and is otherwise indifferent
B: prefers z to x and is otherwise indifferent
C: prefers y to z and is otherwise indifferent

in symbols:

A: xPy, xIz, yIz
B: zPx, zIy, xIy
C: yPz, yIx, zIx

Then, if the unanimity principle holds, x is the social choice when x and y are compared, since A prefers x to y, and B and C are indifferent. Similarly, z is the social choice when x and z are compared, since B prefers z to x and A and C are indifferent. Finally, y is preferred to z when y and z are compared, since C prefers y to z and A and B are indifferent. But this means that:

$$xPy,\ yPz,\ zPx$$

or, an intransitive social ordering. In other words, the acceptance of the unanimity principle, which appears so reasonable, can result in situations where social transitivity is violated.

Fishburn provides one more example of a situation in which a slightly different unanimity criterion violates TE. The criterion is

U': If S contains an alternative x such that no individual prefers any other alternative in S to x, and if x is the only alternative in S that has this property, then x is the one element in the social choice set.

To show how this condition can lead to a violation of TE, suppose that $S = \{x, y, z, w\}$ and that there are two individuals, A and B with these preference orders:

A: $wPxPz$, wIy, xIy, and zIy
B: $zPyPw$, zIx, yIx, wIx

Then if U' holds, the choice set for $S = \{x, y, z\}$ is x, and the choice set for $S' = \{x, y, w\}$ is y which contradicts TE as we discussed it above. (*Question:* can you explain how this occurs?)

Fishburn's point is not that transitivity should never be a condition for social choice, but that there are situations in which it should not be required. He also questions whether it is desirable to determine social choices for sets of more than two alternatives from choices made in two-alternative subsets as the Condorcet criterion prescribes. The weakening of the transitivity requirement where it appears inappropriate would be an important step in overcoming, rather than avoiding, Arrow's Possibility Theorem.

CARDINAL UTILITY AND THE INDEPENDENCE CONDITION

In our discussion of Arrow's Independence of Irrelevant (Infeasible) Alternatives condition, we pointed out that collective-choice procedures involving cardinal utility would be excluded. Consider, however, the effect of cardinal utility on the existence of preference profiles which yield cyclical majorities. Our basic paradox-producing profile is:

Alternatives

$$
\begin{array}{ll}
\text{A} & x(10) > y(9) > z(8) \\
\textit{Individuals:} \quad \text{B} & y(10) > z(6) > x(2) \\
\text{C} & z(\,7\,) > x(6) > y(5)
\end{array}
$$

The numbers in parentheses are cardinal utilities. Notice that if we consider only the preference order, and if we use majority rule, there is no winner. But, let us consider the total utility which the group obtains when particular alternatives are declared the winner. Alternative x brings a total of 18 utiles (simply add the utiles next to each x); y results in an aggregate of 24 utiles; while z produces 21 utiles. In other words, y should be the first preference of the group, z the second, and x the last choice if we allow these cardinal utilities, and if we use a *sum of utilities* method of choice. Notice that this method is sensitive to interpersonal differences in intensity. The social ordering $y > z > x$ is the ordering of individual B who feels relatively greater concern about the outcome than either A or C. Individuals A and C, for example, see little difference in utility between the outcomes, while B gets much greater utility if y wins than if x wins. Individual B, then, can be said to be more intensely concerned about the outcome than either A or C, and our decision procedure seemed to take that into account. This procedure also satisfies Fishburn's desire that a decision mechanism compare all of the alternatives simultaneously, rather than two at a time.

There is another interesting point to note about this example. Recall our discussion of Rawls's *maximin principle,* in the first chapter, which would lead a society to select that alternative which maximizes the utility of its least advantaged member. In this example, we do not know who started out as the least advantaged, but we can tell who would be the least advantaged individual given certain outcomes. Thus, if x is selected, individual B receives 2 utiles, which is less than that of anyone else. If y is selected, individual C receives the least, 5 utiles; and if z is selected, individual B receives 6 utiles, again less than anyone else. In other words, if we applied Rawls's maximin principle here, the social choice should be z, since that alternative produces the greatest utility for the individual who receives less utility than anyone else.

This brief discussion of Rawls also implies that the maximin principle requires both cardinal utility and interpersonal comparisons of utility. For that reason, it would appear to be ruled out by Arrow's Independence condition. Strasnick (1976), however, argues that this is not the case, as we shall see below.

The importance of cardinal utility, then, is that it could transform a preference profile which produces a cyclical majority into one which produces a clear winner. But this is not always the case. Consider the following example:

Alternatives

	A	$x(10) > y(6) > z(3)$
Individuals:	B	$z(10) > x(6) > y(3)$
	C	$y(10) > z(6) > x(3)$

Here there is a cyclical majority if we consider only ordinal preferences, and a tie in terms of aggregate utility. That is, each alternative produces a total of 19 utiles. Moreover, even using a maximin principle, there is no way of choosing a winner. Thus, the use of cardinal utility here does not overcome the voter's paradox. Nevertheless, the use of cardinal utility would avoid cyclical majorities in all other situations in which the utility distribution were not so symmetrical. For that reason, the acceptance of cardinal utility could severely weaken the impact of Arrow's theorem. At the same time, we should point out that Sen (1970) and Schwartz (1970,

1972) have obtained impossibility results similar to Arrow's, using cardinal utilities! In other words, even if cardinal utility is acceptable, it may not overcome the Arrow problem.

WEIGHING PREFERENCES

It may seem to the reader that every time we make a statement, we produce another statement which negates the first. This is not an illusion. It is, in fact, the way in which this field, and every other scientific field, does develop. Therefore, we shall not apologize for this, but simply point out the theoretical conflicts and hope that political scientists will not be averse to living with such uncertainties. The only consolation is that we are learning!

With that brief aside, let us return to the problem of cardinal utility. Before proceeding, however, there is one more caveat. The literature on utility theory is massive. What we shall be doing here is presenting the briefest introduction to this very complex problem, but we will try to bring out the most basic issues.

Presumably, cardinal utility is involved when we can say not simply that we prefer one alternative to another, but that we prefer that alternative by a specifiable amount. Now, in ordinary discourse, we frequently use words which imply such amounts: "I like him much more than I like her." "I feel very strongly about the issue of civil rights." "She is a much better tennis player than he is." "They are much more concerned about pollution than about military security." Perhaps it is because we use such expressions that we frequently assume that there are no conceptual difficulties with the notion of "intensity of preference." A closer look, however, reveals many problems.

Intensity of preference involves the notion of "degree." For that reason, the expression of intensity requires the use of numbers. We want to indicate not just that we prefer something, but by how much we prefer it. We have referred to such numbers as "utiles," but this simply leads to another question: What is a "utile"? Suppose we try using money as an indicator of utility. Then, the amount that I am willing to spend on an item is a cardinal indicator of my preference. Further, the difference between what I am willing to spend on one item rather than another can be taken as a measure of the intensity of my preference for one item over the other.

Within a certain limited range, money is not a bad cardinal indicator of preference. So long as we are comparing purchasable items within our income bracket, money is probably satisfactory. On the other hand, we frequently are asked to rank alternatives which are not purchasable in the ordinary sense. It makes little sense to say that our preference for one presidential candidate over another can be expressed by the amount of money we are willing to spend on that candidate. At least, this is so for most voters; campaign contributors are a different story! We might say that the intensity of our preference for one candidate is measurable in the time or effort which we are willing to invest in the campaign. One of the problems with such an approach, however, is the difficulty of quantifying such effort. Is it the amount of time involved or the calories which we burn in the process? Moreover, how could we use that measure for invalids, the aged, or those whose work does not permit them to participate in the campaign?

Another problem with using money as a cardinal indicator of preference is that it does not allow meaningful comparisons between individuals. The reason for this is that the amount of money I am willing to spend on an item is heavily influenced by my income and not simply by my preference. Thus, a hundred dollars to a wealthy banker is simply not the same thing as a hundred dollars to an unemployed carpenter.

Moreover, how can we express our preference for items which we cannot afford? If we are asked to choose between federal spending on waste disposal and federal spending on military hardware, we are not being asked how much we are willing to spend on each, since, by ourselves, we can afford neither. The question might be, how much of our tax dollar are we willing to spend on each? Such an estimate might be meaningful, except that we are rarely given precise figures. The question usually involves, simply, whether we want to spend "more" on one or the other. The idea of indicating how each of us would allocate the federal budget might be a relatively good indicator of preference intensity, except that we would be susceptible to "quality" arguments. That is, we might agree on what it is that we want without being able to agree that a particular amount of spending will achieve it. My willingness to spend less on national security does not necessarily indicate that I want less national security. It may mean that I believe there are more efficient ways of achieving that goal.

MEASUREMENT AND SCALING

This measurement problem is not unique to utility theory. Consider the question of temperature. The Fahrenheit scale is a set of arbitrary units at a

specified distance from each other. When mercury in a tube expands or contracts, we say that there has been a temperature change. Moreover, the extent of that change is determined by the number of units past which the mercury moves. Our point is that such measurement is completely arbitrary.
Indeed, temperature can be measured with equal ease—and in fact with
more logic—by the Celsius scale. The notion of "temperature," then, is a
theoretical creation.

Consider also the fact that the zero point on a Fahrenheit scale does not
indicate the "beginning" of temperature in any sense. In fact, temperature
is also measured in "minus" degrees. There is an "absolute zero," however, which is the point at which all molecular motion ceases. The analogous zero point on a scale which measures length is, of course, zero—i.e.,
no length or extension.

An interesting point here is that we do speak of one length or distance
as being twice as long as another. Thus, the distance from New York City to
southern Vermont (about 200 miles) is twice the distance from New York
City to Philadelphia (about 100 miles). Yet, we do not speak of a 100-
degree summer day as being twice as hot as a 50-degree day. This illustrates
a basic difference between two types of scales, the so-called *interval scale*
and the *ratio scale*. A Fahrenheit thermometer is an example of an interval
scale. It does not have a "natural zero" point, and the ordinary operations
of mathematics cannot be employed. On the other hand, it is meaningful to
make statements about degrees of difference. Thus, we say: "It was 20
degrees cooler on Saturday night than on Friday afternoon." Measurement
of length or distance is an example of a ratio scale. There is a natural zero,
and all of the operations of mathematics are applicable.

Cardinal utilities are usually thought of as units on an interval scale.
Thus, we can say that an individual prefers one alternative over another by
10 utiles, but not that one alternative brings twice the utility of another. In
other words, we cannot employ the ordinary operations of mathematics. The
use of a particular scale also does not say anything about the problem of interpersonal comparisons of utility. (We should also note here that the simple
ranking of preferences is an example of an *ordinal* scale.)

The use of a particular scale also affects the units which may be used,
and the so-called transformations which may occur. For example, suppose
we have three alternatives with the following utilities for a particular individual:

$$x = 10$$
$$y = 5$$
$$z = 3$$

Now, suppose that instead of the numbers 10, 5, and 3, we used the numbers 20, 15, and 13, respectively. The relative distances between the members of both sets of numbers are the same: 5 units between x and y, 2 units between y and z, and 7 units between x and z. Such a change from the first set of units to the second is a *transformation*. It was achieved simply by adding ten units to each of the original units. The important point is that, in terms of utilities, the two sets of numbers are equivalent. That is, whether we say that the utilities for x, y, and z are 10, 5, and 3, respectively, or 20, 15, and 13, respectively, we will be saying the same thing. Moreover, *any* set of utility numbers which maintain the same distance between these units is equivalent. A set of numbers which is *not* equivalent, however, is the following: $x = 20$, $y = 10$, $z = 6$. Here we have obtained a new set of utility numbers by multiplying everything by 2. Thus, we maintain the *ratio* between the numbers, but not the numerical difference. For an interval scale, such a move is not allowed.

LOTTERIES

With this discussion of measurement and scaling as a background, let us consider one ingenious suggestion for generating a set of cardinal-utility indicators. This approach utilizes the "lottery" notion, and is generally credited to John von Neumann and Oskar Morgenstern, the inventors of game theory.

In a lottery, we are usually asked to purchase a ticket. Then, there is a drawing, and the individual who holds the same ticket or number is the winner of a certain prize. Obviously, this is gambling. That is, we are risking our money. What we mean when we say that we are "risking" our money is that we are uncertain whether we shall receive anything in return for it. In most lotteries we either receive nothing, or an amount substantially greater than the amount we risked. Moreover, it is usually the case that in a public lottery many people are involved. This means that any particular individual's chance of winning is relatively small. For example, if there are one thousand purchasers of lottery tickets, and if there will be only one winner, then, the probability that any particular individual will win is 1/1000. In other words, in most lotteries, the prize is relatively large, but the chances of winning are relatively low, and the risk is also low. It is this combination of low risk and potentially high return which must counterbalance the relatively low probability of winning.

Compare the purchase of life insurance. Here, a so-called whole life policy guarantees a payoff whether an individual lives or dies. It is a "sure thing" purchase. In other words, there is no risk of losing any money, and there is a guarantee that one will get back more than one invests. Because of this assured gain, however, the initial cost or investment is much higher than in the lottery situation, and the potential gain is much less relative to the investment—unless, that is, an individual dies soon after the policy is purchased. For the insurance company, however, such risks are acceptable, since their data indicate that most people live for many years after buying insurance. Moreover, this risk is lessened further by the rate structure, which provides less expensive insurance for younger people. In fact, given the large population with which insurance companies deal, they face virtually no risk at all. Their business is virtually guaranteed by statistics.

Our decision, then, to gamble or to buy insurance is an expression of our attitude toward risk. It is this attitude which provides the basis for the von Neumann-Morgenstern indicator of cardinal utility. To see how this works, consider an individual who prefers one alternative to another. We want to know how much he prefers the first to the second, and we attempt to determine that in the following way. If we offer the individual a simple choice between the two, he or she will obviously choose the more-favored alternative. This is equivalent to a guarantee that whichever alternative is chosen, that alternative will be implemented. Suppose, however, that there is some uncertainty involved. That is, if I choose one alternative it will certainly be implemented, but if I choose another, it may or may not be implemented. For example, suppose I enter the hospital with a brain tumor. The doctors tell me that if I do not have surgery, I will soon become paralyzed. On the other hand, the surgery is risky. At best I could achieve a full recovery, but, at worst, it could be fatal. My choice, then, is

$$x, \text{ a full recovery}$$
$$\text{or}$$
$$y, \text{ paralysis}$$

In this case, there is no question that I prefer x to y. But, while y is relatively certain, x is problematic. Clearly my decision depends partly upon the probability of x. If the probability of x is 1, or a certainty, I prefer x to y. As the probability of x declines, however, the risk of death increases, and y becomes a more preferable alternative. My decision also depends upon my own attitude toward risk. If I am a gambler, I will be more likely to risk the operation. If I am not a gambler, I may prefer to take the certain paralysis.[4]

Consider now several possible probabilities for x:

$$\left.\begin{array}{l} x = 1.00 \\ x = .90 \\ x = .60 \\ x = .50 \\ x = .30 \\ x = .25 \\ x = .10 \end{array}\right\} \; y = 1.00$$

The numbers from .90 to .10 mean that there is some possibility that the operation will be fatal. (For this example, we are ignoring the possibility that the operation will leave the situation unchanged). In other words, we must choose between a certain paralysis, or a .90 chance of full recovery, .60 chance of recovery, .50 chance of recovery, and so on.

Obviously, in a real-life situation, the medical people make an estimate of the chances of full recovery, and the patient chooses either to risk the operation or not. We can use such a situation, however, to determine the *extent* to which an individual prefers one alternative over another—in this case, full recovery over paralysis.

Suppose that the doctor says, initially, that the chances of full recovery are .90, and the patient chooses to risk surgery. Before surgery, however, a complication is discovered which reduces the chances of full recovery to .70.[5] At that point, the patient changes his or her mind, and decides against surgery. In other words, when the probability fell to .70, the individual preferred y to x. *The point at which the individual would no longer choose that alternative which is more preferred when both alternatives can be implemented with certainty can be taken as a measure of the intensity of preference.* That is, if I still prefer x to y when the probability falls to .20,

---

4. There are, of course, many considerations which would go into such a difficult situation, and not simply our inclination toward gambling. An individual's life situation, for example, or his or her attitude toward a life as an invalid would obviously be important. For present purposes, however, we will not examine such questions.

5. In real situations, of course, such precision and round numbers never exist.

the intensity of my preference is greater than if I prefer x to y only if the probability stays above .50. Intuitively, this can be understood as saying that if I have a very strong preference for one alternative over another, then, I should be willing to take a chance on achieving it even when the odds against it are great. Conversely, a low level of preference intensity means that I hold to a preference only so long as it is relatively likely that it is achievable.

The major advantage of this indicator of cardinal utility is that it allows interpersonal comparisons. If two individuals are faced with the choice above, their relative intensity of preference can be determined by the point at which each chooses the alternative which is less preferred in a situation of certainty. Another advantage is that the utility units are confined to the range between zero and one.

There are, however, important problems. It seems unlikely that in any real situation we can indicate probabilities with any precision. Ordinarily, we speak of probability ranges: "The chances of rain today are between 20 and 40 percent." More importantly, it has been argued that the lottery notion does not measure the intensity of our preferences for alternatives, but rather the "tastes of individuals for gambling" (Arrow, 1963, p. 10).

Harsanyi (1977), however, has argued that this is a misinterpretation of von Neumann-Morgenstern utility functions: "In other words, even though a person's vNM (von Neumann-Morgenstern) utility function is always estimated in terms of his behavior under risk and uncertainty, the real purpose of this estimation procedure is to obtain cardinal-utility measures for the relative personal importance he assigns to various economic (and noneconomic) alternatives" (p. 643).

Perhaps the most important limitation is that this notion applies only to situations of uncertainty.[6] Where the outcomes are certain, the lottery notion cannot play a role for obvious reasons.

At this point, then, there is considerable dispute about whether the elimination of Arrow's Independence condition, and the application of cardinal utility would overcome the voter's paradox and eliminate the basic contradiction among Arrow's other conditions. There is also considerable debate about whether a meaningful indicator of cardinal utility can be found.

6. In the literature, a distinction is made between risk and uncertainty. The former refers to situations in which the probabilities are known, the latter to situations in which the probabilities are unknown.

PREFERENCE PRIORITY

Recently, Strasnick (1976) has proposed a very interesting way of avoiding Arrow's problem. Essentially his method consists of providing an *ethical foundation* for a decisive or dictatorial individual! That is, he suggests that there may be nothing wrong with dictatorships of a particular kind. In fact, it turns out, Strasnick argues, that Rawls's maximin principle can provide just such an ethical justification. While we cannot deal with the full complexity of his argument here, we shall try to show, by example, what he means.

Consider the following two-person, three-alternative profile:

$$Alternatives$$

$$Individuals: \quad \begin{matrix} A & x>y>z \\ B & y>z>x \end{matrix}$$

Note that these individual preference orders are the first two of a paradox-producing profile. (*Question:* What would be the third individual preference order?) Now consider the social preference for this profile. Since A prefers x to y, and B prefers y to x, society should be indifferent between these two alternatives. Thus, xIy. Both A and B, however, prefer y to z. Therefore, by the Pareto or unanimity rule, yPz. The society prefers y to z. But, if xIy, and yPz, then, by transitivity xPz. The point here, however, is that individual A prefers x to z, while individual B prefers z to x. Yet, the social preference is xPz. In Arrow's terminology, then, A is decisive for alternatives x and y, and, hence, the dictator.

One response to this outcome is to say that it is undesirable. Strasnick, however, tries to show that it is justifiable. He does this by first considering intrapersonal comparisons of utility, and then interpersonal comparisons of utility. Interestingly, he does this using only ordinal utility.

Each individual has preferences for the binary comparisons x vs. y, x vs. z, and y vs. z. For A, these are $x>y$, $x>z$, and $y>z$. For B, they are $y>x$, $z>x$, and $y>z$. Now, the question is, if each individual had a choice of winning on only one binary contest, which one would he choose to win? Since A's first choice is x, A would want to win on either x vs. y, or x vs. z. Individual B would want to win on y vs. x or y vs. z, since y is B's first choice. Thus, we can begin to establish an intrapersonal preference priority.

We can say that for A, winning in contests x vs. y and x vs. z is more important, or has priority over winning on y vs. z. In symbols we might say,

$$xP_Ay > yP_Az$$
$$xP_Az > yP_Az$$
$$\text{and}$$
$$yP_Bx > zP_Bx$$
$$yP_Bz > zP_Bx$$

The symbols "P_A" and "P_B" mean "A's preference for" and "B's preference for," respectively. The first line then reads, "A's preference for x over y is more important (to A) than A's preference for y over z." Similarly, the third line says, "B's preference for y over x is more important (to B) than B's preference for z over x."

What can we say about the relationship between xP_Ay, and xP_Az; or yP_Bx, and yP_Bz? One plausible argument is that A should prefer winning on x vs. z rather than x vs. y, since he or she has more to lose if z wins than if y wins since z is A's third choice. By the same reasoning, B would rather win in the binary contest y vs. x, than in the contest y vs. z. In other words, we have the following *preference priorities:*

$$A: xPz > xPy > yPz$$
$$B: yPx > yPz > zPx$$

Thus, A cares more about the outcome xPz than B does. Recall, now, our outcomes above. First, xIy. Notice, that the binary contest x vs. y is the most important to B, and the second most important to A. The outcome xIy does not give B his or her first choice, but neither does it impose his or her last choice. Both are satisfied, of course, with the outcome yPz. The outcome xPz, then, can be justified on the grounds that it gives A what he or she wants most, and is the outcome with which B is least concerned.

Such statements clearly involve interpersonal comparisons of utility. Another way of expressing this is the following. For the alternatives x and y, x is A's first choice, while y is B's first choice. Strasnick thus assumes that, in terms of utility, x would provide A with the same utility as y would provide B. In other words, whichever first choice wins, the utility is the same. In symbols

$$x_A = y_B$$

Similarly, it is assumed that the utility of losing is the same for each. Thus,

$$y_A = x_B$$

This says that A's utility when y is the outcome is the same as B's utility when x is the outcome. The statement above says that A's utility when x is the outcome is equivalent to B's utility when y is the outcome. Notice that while we have made an interpersonal comparison of utility, we have not specified a numerical or cardinal utility.

Given these comparisons, we can make the following symbolic statement:

$$x_A = y_B > z_B > x_B = y_A > z_A$$

This says that in terms of utility, x is most desirable for A, y is most desirable for B, and they are equal. Further, both x and y have a higher utility for A and B respectively than z has for B, and z has a higher utility for B than x has for B. This last statement is simply a reiteration of the fact that B's preference order is $y > z > x$. Finally, the utility of x for B is equal to the utility of y for A, as we noted above, and the utility of y for A is greater than the utility of z for A. Again, this is simply a restatement of A's preference order.

The important point to notice here is that A receives the highest utility from x, and the lowest utility from z. Moreover, while B receives an equally high utility from y, the utility which B receives from x, his or her lowest preference, is *greater than* the utility which A receives from z, his or her lowest preference. By having the society choose x over z, then, less damage is done than if society chooses z over x. In this sense, the social choice xPz, which resulted from a combination of the Pareto principle and transitivity, can be seen as ethically justifiable on utilitarian grounds. Moreover, it is also apparent that this justification is equivalent to Rawls's maximin principle, since we are choosing that alternative (x) which maximizes the utility of the worst-off individual.

This point may be clearer if we introduce utility numbers, although the importance of Strasnick's work is that he makes interpersonal comparisons of utility *without* cardinal utility.

Alternatives

Individuals:
A $x(10) > y(8) > z(7)$
B $y(10) > z(9) > x(8)$

These numbers satisfy all of the equalities and inequalities above, as you can easily verify. Now, our point is that if society chooses z over x, B receives 9 utiles while A receives 7 utiles. If, on the other hand, society chooses x over z, then A receives 10 utiles and B receives 8 utiles. Thus, by choosing x, society assures that the worst-off individual (B) is better off than the worst-off individual (A) if z were chosen. Moreover, x would also be the preferred choice by the sum of utilities criterion, since the aggregate utility would be 18 utiles if x were chosen and only 16 if z were chosen.

Strasnick then generalizes this result with the following theorem:

Given the conditions on the SPF (social preference function) and those on the notion of preference priority, the only acceptable social choice procedure is that which prefers in each choice situation the alternative favored by the individual who would be left worst off if his preference were not satisfied. (1976, p. 262)

We have not discussed these "conditions," and for our purposes here it is not necessary. What we do want to understand is that just as Arrow was looking for a decision procedure to satisfy certain reasonable conditions of social choice, Strasnick was looking for a principle of preference priority which satisfied certain conditions, and which could overcome the problem of Arrow's dictator. Strasnick's theorem purports to have found such a principle, and for that reason it is extremely important and interesting.[7]

THE PROBABILITY OF THE VOTER'S PARADOX

A second type of response to Arrow's theorem is to suggest that while a preference profile which yields a cyclical majority *may* occur, the important question is the likelihood of its occurrence. The thrust of this argument is that no choice procedure is perfect, and that society can live with a certain risk of stalemate or the need to impose a social decision. A good deal of attention, then, has been devoted to the question of the probability of the voter's paradox.

THE CONCEPT OF PROBABILITY

Before discussing this work, we shall begin with a brief exposition of the notion of probability. There have been two approaches to the concept of probability. One, the *subjectivist*, suggests that a probability statement is a statement about our belief in something based on some kind of evidence.

---

7. It is not, however, undisputed. See Wolff (1976) and Goldman (1976).

Thus, I may say that it is likely to rain in view of the fact that there are dark clouds gathering. The *objectivist* view suggests that a probability statement is a statement about events in the world around us. Thus, a statement about the probability of rain is actually a statement about a set of events and not about our subjective belief. The objectivist position is further divided into the *logical* and *relative-frequency* notions. The relative-frequency notion suggests that a probability statement is a statement about a future event based on past events. Thus, if we say that there is a high probability that it will rain, we mean that in similar circumstances in the past it has usually rained. The *logical* notion of probability does not take into account either past events or our subjective feelings. Rather, it is a statement about the *possibility* that a particular event will occur based on all related events which could possibly occur. Thus, to say that the probability of throwing a 4 when a die is cast is 1/6 is equivalent to saying that when the die is cast, there are six possible outcomes, only one of which is a 4. The logical notion of probability, then, is a statement about the number of times a particular event could occur given a set of related events. The probability is expressed in numerical terms as a ratio:

$$\frac{\text{The number of times a particular event could occur}}{\text{The total number of related events}}$$

In virtually all of the collective-choice literature, the logical notion of probability is the predominant one.

THE THEORETICAL STRATEGY

The study of the probability of the voter's paradox does not focus on the experience of actual voting situations for several reasons. First, in most elections, voters are only asked to indicate their first choice and not their preference order for all of the alternatives. Without the individual preference orders, it is not possible to determine whether a paradox exists. Second, it is not difficult to conceal a paradox, even if it does exist, by the manipulation of voting procedures, even when preference orders are known. For example, suppose the following paradox situation existed:

Alternatives

	A	$x > y > z$
Individuals:	B	$y > z > x$
	C	$z > x > y$

Suppose, further, that individual C was the chairman, and that he ruled that, beginning with x and y, each alternative would be compared to every other alternative, and that the loser would be eliminated. Thus, x would defeat y and y would be eliminated; then z would defeat x and be declared winner! In this way, the chairman's first choice becomes the collective choice, even though a paradox existed. Finally, many decisions made by administrative fiat might also have resulted in a paradox if the affected individuals had been permitted to choose among the available alternatives. For these reasons, the empirical study of the occurrence of the paradox is unlikely to produce accurate results, although some attempts have been made (see Riker, 1958; and Bowen, 1972).

Instead, the common method has been to estimate the *logical probability* of the paradox. This means that the total number of possible outcomes in a voting situation are compared to the number of possible paradox outcomes in the following way. Assume, again, that there are three individuals and three alternatives. Now, each individual is free to order the three alternatives in any way. Recall that there are six different preference orderings associated with three alternatives. But, there are three individuals who can choose any one of these six preference orders. This means that there are 216 possible preference profiles when there are three individuals and three alternatives. The formula for computing the number of possible preference profiles in m^n, which is read, "*m* to the *n*th power," where m stands for the number of possible preference orders and n the number of individuals. Thus, with three individuals and three alternatives there are $6^3 = 216$ possible preference profiles. (*Question:* Suppose there are three individuals and *four* alternatives. How many possible preference profiles are there?)

The problem then is to determine how many of these 216 preference profiles produce a paradox. Recall that there are two basic preference profiles which produce the paradox:

Alternatives

		I	II
	A	$x>y>z$	$x>z>y$
Individuals:	B	$y>z>x$	$y>x>z$
	C	$z>x>y$	$z>y>x$

So that there are at least two preference profiles which result in a paradox. But note that any individual can have any preference order. Thus, the following two preferences profiles also yield a paradox:

Alternatives

	Ia	IIa
A	$y > z > x$	$y > x > z$
Individuals: B	$x > y > z$	$x > z > y$
C	$z > x > y$	$z > y > x$

We have simply switched preference orders between individuals A and B in each case. The paradox result has not been altered. This raises the number of paradox-producing preference profiles to 4. Altogether there are 12 such preference profiles. To see this more clearly substitute R_1 for each preference order. Thus $xyz = R_1$, $yzx = R_3$, $zxy = R_5$, $xzy = R_2$, $yxz = R_4$, and $zyx = R_6$. The possible paradox-producing preference profiles are:

Orderings

	1	2	3	4	5	6
A	R_1	R_3	R_5	R_5	R_3	R_1
B	R_3	R_1	R_3	R_1	R_5	R_5
C	R_5	R_5	R_1	R_3	R_1	R_3

Individuals:

	7	8	9	10	11	12
A	R_2	R_2	R_4	R_4	R_6	R_6
B	R_4	R_6	R_2	R_6	R_2	R_4
C	R_6	R_4	R_6	$R_?$	R_4	$R_?$

MORE THAN THREE INDIVIDUALS AND ALTERNATIVES

In other words, only 12 of the 216 possible preference profiles produce a paradox; that is the paradox probability is $12/216 = .056$. If all possible preference orders are equally likely to occur, then the paradox will occur less than 6 percent of the time. In general this has been interpreted as a rather low percentage. But the important question is, how does this percentage change as the number of individuals, or alternatives increases? This question proved rather difficult to answer, since the number of possible preference profiles increases at an extraordinarily rapid rate. For instance, with three individuals and only four alternatives, the number of possible preference profiles jumps to $24^3 = 13,824$! At relatively low levels of alternatives or individuals, then, the number of possible preference profiles is enormous.

Where the number of individuals or alternatives approaches that of most actual political situations, the number of possible preference profiles is so great that even computers are hard-pressed to handle the problem.

This difficulty was handled in two ways, which need only be mentioned here and not described in detail. The first was to select, at random, only certain preference profiles for a relatively few combinations of individuals and alternatives at relatively low levels. In other words, rather than trying to observe all possible preference profiles, a random sample was selected as representative of the whole. The proportion of paradox-producing preference profiles in the sample, then, served as an estimate of the proportion in the whole. Another method was to devise a mathematical formula to estimate the paradox probability for any number of individuals and alternatives. By these methods, it was concluded that *as the number of alternatives approaches infinity, the paradox probability approaches one or certainty. In other words, as the number of alternatives increases the paradox probability also increases, reaching a limit of one.* That is, the proportion of paradox-producing preference profiles becomes an increasing proportion of the total number of possible preference profiles as the number of alternatives increases. Put another way, the paradox probability is a *function* of the number of alternatives. This can be graphed roughly as shown in fig. 3.3.

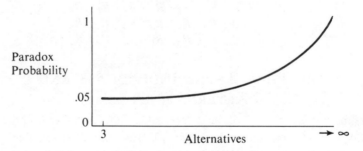

Figure 3.3. Paradox probability as a function of number of alternatives.

Interestingly, however, the paradox probability is *not* affected very much by the number of individuals. In fact, as the number of alternatives remains at three, and as the number of *individuals increases,* the paradox probability rises from .056 to a limit of about .09. In other words, no matter how many individuals are involved in the choice process, the paradox probability never rises above 10 percent, so long as there are only three alternatives.

These would appear to be contradictory conclusions, one suggesting that the paradox probability increases to a very high level and that, therefore, the paradox is, empirically, a likely occurrence; the other suggesting that the paradox is a rather unlikely occurrence and therefore less important so long as there are only three alternatives. This is less of a contradiction than it appears, however, since the paradox probability rises *very* slowly toward a limit of 1.0 as the number of alternatives increases. As one writer concluded: "It would seem that this limit is attained too slowly to be of real concern to behavioral scientists" (May, 1971, p. 146). In other words, given the numbers of individuals and alternatives with which political scientists are generally concerned, the paradox probability is relatively low. For example, suppose there were three candidates in an American presidential election, and 70 million voters. The results of the work on the logical probability of the paradox tell us that if the voters were to rank their preferences, the paradox would arise less than 10 percent of the time *if all six preference orderings of the candidates were equally likely* (the term *equiprobable* is used in the literature).

IMPARTIAL AND ARBITRARY CULTURES

Suppose, however, that not all preference orders were equally likely. Suppose that some alternatives were a priori more likely to be chosen as first preference than others. Would this alter the paradox probability? To some extent, of course, single-peakedness or value-restrictedness represent a priori limitations on the probability of certain preference orders. Thus, in our discussion above, the preference orders which were eliminated as possibilities when all voters used the same criterion had a probability of .00 and, as a result, the paradox probability was also .00. In that case, not all preference orders were equally likely.

In real political situations, the likelihood is that some alternatives do have a better chance of being selected than others because of the nature of the group which is making the choices. Mass transit bonds are clearly more likely to receive support in urban areas than in suburban areas; and federal funds for the interstate highways are the more probable first choice in suburban and rural areas in the United States. It would seem more realistic, then, not to assume that all possible preference orders are a priori equally probable.

In the literature on this question, a situation in which all preference orders are equiprobable is called an *impartial culture*.[8] Conversely, a situation in which some alternatives and, hence, some preference orders are, a priori, more likely than others has been called either a *partial culture* or an *arbitrary culture*. When expressing these concepts in symbols, a so-called *probability vector* is·used. This is nothing other than a listing of the probabilities for each individual preference ordering. For example, where there are three alternatives there are six possible preference orders as indicated above. If these preference orders are equiprobable, then each has a probability of $1/6$ (or, approximately, .16), and the probability vector looks like this:

$$(1/6, \ 1/6, \ 1/6, \ 1/6, \ 1/6, \ 1/6)$$

where each of the fractions stands for one preference order.

Since they are all equally probable, the order is of no consequence. (*Question:* If there were four alternatives, how many possibilities would there be in the probability vector, and how would you express the impartial culture?) Suppose, however, that some preference orders are eliminated, as in the case of single-peakedness. Then it is very important to make it clear which probabilities refer to which preference orders. Thus, a probability vector for single-peakedness is frequently written:

$$(1/4, \ 0, \ 1/4, \ 1/4, \ 0, \ 1/4) = (xyz, \ xzy, \ yzx, \ yxz, \ zxy, \ zyx)$$

In other words, the preference orders xzy and zxy are eliminated as possibilities and, hence, have a zero probability of being chosen. The fact that the rest of the preference orders are equally likely is simply an arbitrary assumption. They could vary in any way. In general, the probability vector for arbitrary cultures can be written as follows:

$$P = (P_1, \ \ldots \ , P_r), \ p_i \geqq 0 \text{ for all } i, \ \sum_{i=1}^{r} = 1, \text{ and not all } p_i = p_j$$

where "p" stands for the probability of any individual preference order; where "$\sum_{i=1}^{r} p_i = 1$" is read "the sum of all the probabilities of all of the individual preference orders from one to r;" and where p_i and p_j are the probabilities for two different individual preference orders.

The probability vector can also be used to express a situation in which there is neither an impartial culture nor single-peakedness. For example,

8. Given the ordinary meaning of the term *culture* as a particular set of values, this is perhaps a strange name for a situation in which no value is dominant. But that is a minor point.

suppose alternative x is slightly more likely to be the first choice than either y or z (the reason is not important at this point). This could be expressed as follows:

$$({}^6/_{30}, {}^6/_{30}, {}^4/_{30}, {}^5/_{30}, {}^5/_{30}, {}^4/_{30})$$

Notice that this probability vector differs only slightly from the impartial case. The first two probabilities are higher than the others, since they represent xyz and xzy, preference orders which are more likely to occur in view of our assumption above that x is slightly favored. Similarly, the third and sixth probabilities are lowest since they represent yzx and zyx; and the fourth and fifth probabilities are in the middle, since they represent yxz and zxy.

Arbitrary Cultures and the Paradox Probability

Now we turn to the question of the relationship between these arbitrary cultures and the probability of the paradox. It turns out that we cannot generalize about arbitrary cultures the way we can generalize about the impartial culture. That is *the probability of the voter's paradox in arbitrary cultures depends not only on the number of individuals and alternatives, but also on the form of the probability vector, i.e. which preference orders have which probabilities.* In our example of single-peakedness, the paradox probability was zero, a drop from the paradox probability of .056 in the impartial culture. Similarly, in the example above in which x is slightly preferred, the probability that x will win exceeds 50 percent once the number of individuals is greater than eleven. In the impartial culture with three alternatives, the probability that *some* alternative will win is about 94 percent, but the probability that a *particular* alternative will win is only about 31 percent (three alternatives with an equal chance of winning in a situation in which it is 94 percent certain that there will be a winner). Again, the paradox probability is lower in the arbitrary culture than in the impartial culture.

On the other hand, some arbitrary cultures result in paradox probabilities which are *higher* than that of the impartial case with the same number of individuals and alternatives. To see this more clearly, let us consider the case of three individuals and three alternatives and the following arbitrary cultures:

Probability Vector	Paradox Probability
$(0, \, ^1/_5, \, ^1/_5, \, ^1/_5, \, ^1/_5, \, ^1/_5 \,) =$	.048
$(0, \, ^1/_4, \, 0, \, ^1/_4, \, ^1/_4, \, ^1/_4 \,) =$	.09
$(0, \, ^1/_3, \, 0, \, ^1/_3, \, 0, \, ^1/_3 \,) =$	.22

The paradox probabilities are computed in the following way. In the first probability vector, one preference order, *xyz*, has been eliminated (we shall not consider now why preference orders are eliminated, but simply make these assumptions for purposes of illustration). This leaves five preference orders which, we assume, are equiprobable (for ease of presentation). With five possible preference orders there are $5^3 = 125$ possible preference profiles. Of these, only 6 result in a paradox. This is because the six paradox results associated with the preference profile *xyz, yzx,* and *zxy* are no longer possible, since *xyz* has been eliminated as a possible preference order. (Note that such an elimination violates Arrow's condition of unlimited domain.) The paradox probability then, for this arbitrary culture is $6/125 = .048$. A similar analysis applies to the second arbitrary culture above, where there are $4^3 = 64$ possible preference orders and again 6 which result in a paradox. This is because the two preference orders which are eliminated, *xyz* and *yzx,* are from the same basic preference profile which produces six of the paradox results. In other words, once any one of the preference orders from either of the paradox-producing preference profiles is eliminated, all of the paradox results associated with that preference profile are eliminated, and the elimination of any other preference order from that profile does not reduce the number of paradox results any further. Thus, once *xyz* is eliminated, it does not change the number of paradox-producing preference profiles to eliminate *yzx* and/or *zxy*. The result would have been the same if we had eliminated preference orders from the other basic paradox-producing preference profile *xzy, yxz, zyx*. It is for this reason that the paradox probability *increases* as *more* preference orders are eliminated in the figure above from $^5/_{125} = .048$, to $^6/_{64} = .09$, to $^6/_{27} = .22$. (*Question:* Can you explain how the final .22 probability is derived?) In other words, given the same number of individuals and alternatives, the paradox probability varies according to the form of the particular arbitrary culture. Notice also that with only three individuals and three alternatives the paradox probability can be as high as .22, rather than the relatively low .056 of the impartial culture. Moreover, as the number of individuals increases with the arbitrary culture $(0, \, ^1/_3, \, 0, \, ^1/_3, \, 0, \, ^1/_3)$, the paradox probability rises very rapidly, so that with only nine individuals, the paradox probability is a very high .57. This means that more than half of the possible preference profiles result in a paradox.

More Than One Dimension

From these examples, it is clear that the probability of the paradox can indeed be high enough to be of significance in the political process; and, more important, the higher paradox probabilities occur in situations which are more realistic than the impartial culture. Another interesting conclusion of this analysis is that restrictions on Arrow's condition of unlimited domain do not necessarily eliminate the problem of the paradox. As in this example, certain kinds of restrictions actually aggravate the problem!

Part of the difficulty with this analysis, however, is that it is not clear what these restrictions mean. For example, what would be the reasoning behind the elimination of xyz, yzx, and zxy in the probability vector (0, ⅓, 0, ⅓, 0, ⅓)? Such a situation obviously could occur, but under what conditions? In the case of single-peakedness, on the other hand, the probability vector (¼, 0, ¼, ¼, 0, ¼) is a direct result of the assumption that all individuals use the same criterion in ordering their preferences. Moreover, varying the single-peakedness assumption has led to the conclusion that with only partial agreement on criteria, the paradox probability is relatively low, as opposed to our conclusion above. Niemi (1969) shows that for three alternatives, any number of individuals, and only partial agreement on the criteria, the paradox probability never rises above .25; and that as the number of individuals, alternatives, and degree of agreement increases, the paradox falls rapidly. A relatively simple model can be used to explain the basis for this conclusion.

To agree on a particular criterion is, as we have shown above, equivalent to limiting an individual's choice of preference orderings. With three alternatives, only four of six preference orderings are admissible if a single criterion is used. But, the criterion can vary and with it the particular alternatives which are admissible. In our example above, the positions "left," "center," and "right" were designated xyz, and the preference orders xzy and zxy were eliminated. We could also have designated these positions zxy, in which case xyz and yxz would have been eliminated; or, we could have designated them zxy, in which case zyx and yzx would have been eliminated. These changes in the labeling would have been tantamount to using different criteria. Notice that for three alternatives, there are only three different ways to order the preference scale. Thus, no matter what criteria are used, or how many different criteria are used by different people, one of these three orderings must be used:

	I	II	III
Scale Ordering	$xyz(zyx)$	$xzy(yzx)$	$zxy(yxz)$
Admissible Preference Orderings:	$\left.\begin{array}{l} xyz \\ yxz \end{array}\right\} 1$	$\left.\begin{array}{l} xzy \\ zxy \end{array}\right\} 3$	$\left.\begin{array}{l} zxy \\ xzy \end{array}\right\} 3$
	$\left.\begin{array}{l} zyx \\ yzx \end{array}\right\} 2$	$\left.\begin{array}{l} yzx \\ zyx \end{array}\right\} 2$	$\left.\begin{array}{l} yxz \\ xyz \end{array}\right\} 1$
Eliminated Preference Orderings:	xzy	xyz	zyx
	zxy	yxz	yzx

In other words, even if one hundred people use one hundred different criteria in ranking the same three alternatives, when it comes to actually indicating their preference order it would not appear that one hundred different criteria were being used. In fact, *for all practical purposes, it would appear as if no more than two criteria had been used.* This can be seen by an examination of the illustration above. Notice first that the scale orderings involve two preference orders which are the reverse of each other—e.g., xyz (zyx). This is because the outcome is the same no matter which ordering is used to designate the scale.

Notice also that the sets of preference orders which we have labeled with numbers always appear together, and that they have the same last choice. Now, suppose that there are three individuals each of whom uses a different criterion to rank the alternatives x, y, and z, and that these criteria correspond to the three different scale orderings. This means that one individual will choose a preference order from among the admissible orders in I, the second individual will choose from II, and the third from III. But, even if each individual chooses preference orders from different sets (i.e., 1, 2, or 3), it would appear that two of the three chose preference orders from the same scale ordering. This is because any two scale orderings (I and II, I and III, or II and III) contain all three sets of preference orders, and so all possible preference orders. Thus, *no matter how many individuals are choosing among the same three criteria, and no matter how many criteria of choice are actually being used, for all practical purposes no more than two criteria can be used.*

What is the paradox probability, then, when two different criteria are used? Niemi (1969) suggests that the paradox probability in this case is .25, which he computes as follows. He assumes, first, that all possible preference orders are equally probable. This means that for the two individuals who use the same criterion the a priori probability of the four preference orders associated with that criterion is ¼. For example, if the scale ordering associated with the criterion is xyz, then the probability vector for those preference orders associated with xyz would be:

$$(¼, ¼, ¼, ¼) = (xyz, yxz, yzx, zyx)$$

On the other hand, for the third individual who uses a different criterion associated, say, with the scale-order xzy, the a priori probabilities apply only to the two remaining alternatives (xzy and zxy) in order to differentiate that individual from the other two. The probability vector here, then would be:

$$(½, ½) = (xzy, zxy)$$

Niemi also assumes that each pair of alternatives with the same last choice (which we have labeled 1, 2, 3 above) is chosen by one individual. Thus, for example, a configuration of voters and preference orders for these three individuals, two of whom use the same criterion in ordering the alternatives might be:

$$A = (xyz, yxz)$$
$$B = (yzx, zyx)$$
$$C = (zxy, xzy)$$

There are eight preference profiles associated with such individual preference orders:

		Alternatives			
		1	2	3	4
	A	xyz	xyz	xyz	xyz
Individuals:	B	yzx	yzx	zyx	zyx
	C	zxy	xzy	zxy	xzy
		5	6	7	8
	A	yxz	yxz	yxz	yxz
Individuals:	B	zyx	zyx	yzx	yzx
	C	zxy	xzy	zxy	xzy

Of these profiles, two produce a cyclical majority. (*Question:* Which two?) In other words, the paradox probability is $^2/_8 = .25$. Niemi also calculates the paradox probability for three alternatives and odd numbers of individuals up to 21. He also varies the proportion of individuals who use the same criterion from ⅔ (which, as our example showed is the lowest possible with three alternatives) to 1.00 (all individuals use the same criterion). He finds that "the conditional probability of the paradox is never more than .25," (p. 492) and that for a given number of individuals, the probability of the paradox *decreases* as the proportion of individuals who use the same criterion increases. He also found that the probability of the paradox decreases as the number of individuals is increased for any given proportion of individuals who use the same criterion. His overall conclusion is that "for very large groups of individuals, as much as 70% agreement on an underlying dimension [criterion] is sufficient to make the paradox a rare occurrence" (p. 493). In other words, the paradox can generally be avoided even if the agreement on the criterion of choice is far less than unanimous.

A similar conclusion was reached by Tullock (1967) who argued that with *large numbers of individuals* and choices involving *more than one dimension,* the voter's paradox is so rare an occurrence that it is generally irrelevant. We shall not present a detailed analysis of Tullock's ingenious argument at this point, since it is rather complicated, and because it utilizes *spatial modeling* which we shall discuss in some detail below in the chapter on political parties.

SUMMARY

In this chapter, then, we have shown the following:

1. It is possible to avoid the voter's paradox by restrictions on Arrow's condition of unlimited domain. The two restrictions which we discussed were Black's *single-peakedness* and Sen's *value-restrictedness.* The former requires that some alternative not be the last choice for any three alternatives[9] for any individual; the latter requires that some alternative shall not be first, second, or third choice for any triple of alternatives for any individual.

---

9. Sometimes written in the literature as any "triple" of alternatives. The general expression used is "*n*-tuple" of alternatives where "*n*" refers to any number greater than one.

We have pointed out, however, that such restrictions *avoid* Arrow's problem but do not *solve* it.

2. Arrow's requirement of *social transitivity* may not be a fruitful condition since, as Fishburn has shown, there are situations in which intuitively reasonable results violate that condition. He concludes, therefore, that social transitivity should not always be a requirement in collective-choice processes.

3. The elimination of Arrow's Independence condition and the use of cardinal utilities may also reduce the problem, but it cannot eliminate it. In addition, there are important conceptual problems with the notion of cardinal utility.

4. Ethical theories of preference priority have been developed which purport to show that Arrow's dictator may be morally justifiable. These theories argue for a connection between the Arrow result and Rawls's maximin principle.

5. Even if it is accepted that the voter's paradox is undesirable and unavoidable, it may not be a very likely occurrence. Most of the literature in the field suggests that in most situations of concern to political scientists, the probability of the paradox is relatively low and that, therefore, the paradox should not be of great concern. Abrams (1976), on the other hand, has suggested that there are important and politically realistic situations in which the paradox probability is quite high and that, therefore, the paradox is important. In the next chapter, we shall show that analyses of the process known as logrolling, or vote trading, have led to results which confirm this concern about the prevalence of the paradox.

CHAPTER FOUR

Logrolling

SOME OF THE MOST interesting work in the theory of collective choice relates to the traditional political activity of logrolling or vote trading. Very simply, logrolling occurs, most frequently in legislative bodies, when individual members agree with others to vote in a particular way. The "trade" involves a mutual decision on the part of at least two members to change their vote on a matter which is of less importance to them in order to receive from the other member a promise of support on an issue which is of more importance. In essence, votes are being bartered, and it is for this reason that logrolling has been attacked as being improper. Legislators, it is argued, should determine what they or their constituents believe is the best position on each issue, and then should vote that way. The notion of trading votes smacks of corruption.

In view of this traditional objection to logrolling, it is interesting that a number of current writers have argued that not only is vote trading unobjectionable, but that it may be a way of benefiting everyone.[1] Gordon Tullock and James Buchanan, for example, in their classic study *The Calculus of Consent: Logical Foundations of Constitutional Democracy* (1962) suggest that:

1. An outcome which has the effect of increasing everyone's utility is said to be Pareto optimal.

[the voter's] welfare can be improved if he accepts a decision contrary to his desire in an area where his preferences are weak in exchange for a decision in his favor in an area where his feelings are strong. Bargains among voters can, therefore, be mutually beneficial. (p. 145)

Tullock and Buchanan recognize that there is a problem when some voters or legislators trade and others do not—the nontraders will lose on issues they thought they would win—but they argue that this difficulty could be overcome by some kind of device for compensating the nontraders for their loss. In this way, everyone would gain.

Before examining this claim in detail, it should be noted that some writers have also viewed logrolling as a way of avoiding the voter's paradox and as a means of expressing intensity of preference—problems which we encountered in the first two chapters. The analysis of vote trading in this chapter will show that logrolling does not avoid the voter's paradox—that, in fact, vote trading can lead to irresolvable cycles in exactly the same way as simple voting; and that vote trading can result in a situation where those who trade are worse off than they would have been if they had not traded, but will be worse off yet if they do not trade while others do. This situation Brams and Riker (1973) call the "paradox of vote trading." In other words, whether vote trading is moral or immoral, it does not appear to be a solution to the problem of the voter's paradox, nor does it appear to lead toward increased utility for all. Rather, it appears simply to benefit some at the cost of others. In that sense, traditional objections to logrolling may have merit.

LOGROLLING CYCLES

We shall begin with a simple logrolling model. Assume that there are three voters—(A, B, and C) and two proposals (x and y). To make matters more interesting, suppose that x is a proposal in Congress (ours is a three-person Congress!) to proceed with the building of a new missile launcher, and that y is a proposal for a nationalized system of welfare. Suppose further that (1) each member of our Congress will vote either for or against each proposal; (2) that a proposal which receives a majority of the votes will be enacted; (3) that each proposal will be voted on separately, one after the other; and, (4) that the preferences of the members are as follows:

Proposals

Members:	Missile Launcher (x or $-x$)	Nationalized Welfare (y or $-y$)
A	x	y
B	x	$-y$
C	$-x$	$-y$
Result of majority vote	x	$-y$

where "$-x$" and "$-y$" are read "not x" and "not y" respectively, and mean that the particular member votes against the proposal (i.e. in favor of the status quo). In other words, member A supports both proposals, member B supports the production of a new missile launcher but opposes a nationalized system of welfare, while member C opposes both proposals. In a simple majority vote, the proposal for a new missile launcher would pass, while the proposal for nationalized welfare would fail.

So far, we have not indicated how each member feels about the issues in relation to each other; we have not said whether the members are equally concerned about the two issues, or whether one issue is more important than the other for any member. Suppose that member A is more concerned about a nationalized-welfare system than about a new missile launcher, even though she would like to see both implemented. Suppose that B is relatively indifferent about the issues. That is, his support for the missile-launcher proposal is no stronger than his opposition to the nationalized-welfare proposal. Finally, suppose that C is more concerned about defeating the missile-launcher proposal than the nationalized-welfare system. Given these preferences, we can then deduce the preference order of each individual for all possible outcomes. That is, the outcome in the example above is $(x, -y)$. The missile-launcher proposal is passed and the nationalized-welfare proposal is defeated. But, there are three other possible outcomes:

(x, y)—both proposals are passed

$(-x, -y)$—both proposals are rejected

$(-x, y)$—The missile-launcher proposal is defeated while
the nationalized-welfare proposal passes

In terms of our individuals, A prefers (x, y) to any other possible outcome; B prefers $(x, -y)$ to any other outcome; and C prefers $(-x -y)$ to any other outcome. Given these first choices, it is easy to deduce the last choice of any individual: A—$(-x, -y)$; B—$(-x,y)$; and C—(x,y). (*Question:* Can you explain how we know that these are the least preferred outcomes for each of our members?) In order to determine the second and third choice for each member it is necessary to know the preference of each for x and y. Thus, since A prefers y to x, and since her first choice is (x,y), her second choice must be $(-x,y)$. (*Question:* Can you explain why?) And since her last choice is $(-x, -y)$ her third choice must be $(x, -y)$. By similar reasoning we can determine the preference orders for outcomes of our three members. They are as follows:

Outcomes

	A	(x,y)	$> (-x,y)$	$> (x, -y)$	$> (-x, -y)$	
Members:	B	$(x, -y)$	$> (-x, -y) = (x,y)$	$> (-x,y)$		
	C	$(-x, -y)$	$> (-x,y)$	$> (x, -y)$	$> (x,y)$	

To see this a bit more clearly, let us assume that each set of outcomes is a single alternative, and let us designate these alternatives with single letters. Thus,

Outcomes		Letter Symbol
(x,y)	=	M
$(-x,y)$	=	N
$(x, -y)$	=	O
$(-x, -y)$	=	P

Then the preferences for each member can be written:

Preference Orders for Outcomes

	A	MNOP
Members:	B	OPMN
	C	PNOM

But, if this is the preference structure, there would be no Condorcet winner; or, in other words, we are again confronted with a voter's paradox since:

Preferences for Outcomes	Members
$M > N$	(A, B)
$N > O$	(A, C)
$O > P$	(A, B)
$P > M$	(B, C)

Before discussing the significance of this point, we shall return to the original example of the vote on the missile launcher and the nationalized-welfare proposal. Notice that the original outcome, $(x, -y)$ is B's first choice. He is, therefore, quite satisfied with the outcome. It is also the third choice of both A and C. At this point the question of vote trading or logrolling arises: Can members A and C change their votes in any way which will alter the outcome to produce a result which is either their first or second choice? Since A and C have different first choices, it is obvious that they cannot both achieve their first choices simultaneously. On the other hand, they both have the same second choice, $(-x, y)$. Thus, A could agree to change her vote on the missile launcher (from x to $-x$) and C could agree to change her vote on nationalized welfare (from $-y$ to y). Then, the new vote would be:

		Proposals	
		Missile Launcher $(x$ or $-x)$	*Nationalized Welfare* $(y$ or $-y)$
	A	$-x$	y
Members:	B	x	$-y$
	C	$-x$	y
Result of *Majority Vote*		$-x$	y

In other words, the missile-launcher proposal would be defeated and the nationalized-welfare proposal would be passed. Both A and C would have achieved their second highest preference in outcomes; but the outcome $(-x, y)$ is member B's last choice. For this reason, B has a definite incentive to look around for a trade which will improve his position. The fact that A and B have both failed to achieve their first preferences provides room for just such a trade. Notice that B's second choices (tie) are $(-x, -y)$, and (x, y), which happen to be the first choice of C and A respectively. This means that B is in a position to deal with either A or C. (*Question:* Suppose B preferred (x, y) to $(-x, -y)$; i.e., he was more concerned that the missile-launcher proposal pass than that the nationalized-welfare proposal fail. With whom would he have to deal?) Suppose that B offers A the following trade: B will change his vote on the nationalized-welfare proposal (from $-y$ to y), and A will change her vote on the missile launcher (from $-x$ to her original position, x). Now the outcome would be:

Proposals

		Missile Launcher (x or $-x$)	*Nationalized Welfare* (y or $-y$)
	A	x	y
Members:	B	x	y
	C	$-x$	$-y$
Result of			
Majority Vote		x	y

Note that we assume member C reverts back to her first preference when excluded from the trade. No other voting by C, however, would change the outcome. Now, the outcome is (x,y), A's first choice, B's second choice, and C's last choice. But, the potential trading is not yet finished. Member C has an incentive to trade with B. By changing her vote from $-x$ to x in return for B's change from y to $-y$, C can assure the outcome $(x, -y)$ which is B's first choice and C's third choice. It is also A's third choice, however, and you will recall that this is precisely the outcome of the very first vote without any trading at all! *In other words, through a series of trades which were advantageous to the traders in each case, the result is not different from what it would have been with no trading.* Moreover, since the initial outcome was not stable (i.e., there was an incentive for trading) the same outcome after a series of trades is also not stable. Thus, in this case, we have a never-ending vote-trading cycle which is exactly like the voting cycles, or voter's paradox, of the preceding chapters.

STABLE OUTCOMES

In practical terms, there are several ways to prevent such cycles. One is simply to forbid vote trading. A second is to arbitrarily call a halt to the trading process at some point. This happens in real legislatures, of course, when the time comes for voting. Nevertheless, such an outcome is clearly imposed, in the sense in which Arrow used the term, since a majority prefers one outcome to the actual outcome, no matter what it is. In such a case, the outcome is said to be *dominated* by another potential outcome, and the result is said to be theoretically (i.e., not necessarily practically) *unstable*. *A stable* or *undominated* outcome is one which is preferred by a majority and which is not susceptible to becoming a minority position as a result of trading. Another way of defining stability or domination is to say that an outcome is unstable or dominated so long as there are at least two individuals who could improve their position by altering the outcome through trading. Or, an outcome is stable or undominated if no two individuals can improve their position by altering the outcome through trading. The literature on vote trading is concerned primarily with the question of finding the conditions which produce stable or undominated outcomes.

We can return now to our point above that when the combined outcomes are treated as alternatives, the result is a cyclical majority. The vote trading which we described above was equivalent to altering individual preference orders. Thus, the initial trade between members A and C involved a change in their voting behavior.[2] After their trade, the new preference orders were:

Preference Orders for Outcomes

	A	*NMPO*
Members:	B	*OPMN*
	C	*NPMO*

In this case, N (i.e., the outcome $-x,y$) is the winner, and, if these preference orders were the true or original (or "sincere," a term frequently used in the literature) preference orders, this would be a stable outcome. Since these are "sophisticated" preference orders, however (i.e., designed to obtain a second choice when the first choice is not obtainable), they are susceptible to further changes when better deals are presented. That, of course, is exactly what happens when member B offers A a chance to obtain her real first choice M (x,y) by agreeing to adopt M as first choice. The resulting preference order is:

Preference Orders for Outcomes

	A	*MNOP*
Members:	B	*MNOP*
	C	*PNOM* ·

2. It should be noted that such a change is not in fact a change of *preference*, even though the effect is similar. Again, I thank Nicholas Miller for pointing this out.

Notice that we have restored the sincere preference order of member C on the grounds that this trade is simply an alternative to the first trade, and that C would have no incentive to do anything but vote sincerely if she were left out of the trade. At this point, however, C had an incentive to offer B a trade, which resulted in the preference orders:

Preference Orders for Outcomes

	A	*MNOP*
Members:	B	*OPMN*
	C	*OMPN*

But, since outcome O $(x, -y)$ is the sincere third choice of both A and C, they have an incentive to join forces and make N $(-x,y)$, their mutual second choice, the actual outcome. At that point, however, the situation reverts to that which obtained after the initial trade. In other words, vote trading did not produce a stable result, and, thus, did not avoid the voter's paradox involved in the original set of preference orders for outcomes.

In this case, we have shown a specific example in which a voting situation led to a cycle of vote trading, and in which the preference orders for outcomes involved a voter's paradox. Suppose, however, that certain of the conditions were different. Suppose, in particular, that both A and C felt that the outcome of the nationalized-welfare vote was more important than the outcome of the missile-launcher vote, even though A supported both proposals and C opposed both. Then, the preference for outcomes would be:

Outcomes

Members:	A	(x,y)	$>(-x,y)$ $>(x,-y)>(-x,-y)$
	B	$(x,-y)$	$>(-x,-y)=(x,y)$ $>(-x,y)$
	C	$(-x,-y)$	$>(x,-y)$ $>(-x,y)>(x,y)$

or:

Preference Orders for Outcomes

	A	*MNOP*
Members:	B	*OPMN*
	C	*PONM*

$$O>M, \ O>N, \ O>P$$

In this case, outcome O, $(x, -y)$ is the Condorcet winner, and, moreover, there is no incentive to trade. (*Question:* Can you explain why there is

no incentive to trade?) In other words, the outcome O is stable, or undominated, and there will be no trading. Thus, in this case, there is no voter's paradox and no vote trading.

LOGROLLING AND THE VOTER'S PARADOX

These two examples suggest that there might be a systematic relationship between the voter's paradox and logrolling. And, indeed, there have been
arguments that vote trading and the voter's paradox are logically equivalent,
or that an "efficacious coalition of minorities" *requires* an underlying voter's paradox. A "coalition of minorities" is simply the voting coalition
formed by vote traders who would be in the minority on their most salient
(important) issues if they did not trade. In our example above, C was in the
minority on the original missile-launcher vote and A was in the minority on
the original nationalized-welfare vote. When they traded votes they formed,
in essence, a coalition of minorities. Another way of expressing the logical
equivalence of vote trading and the voter's paradox is to say that the presence of a preference structure which would yield a voter's paradox is a necessary and sufficient condition for vote trading; or, conversely, that the possibility of vote trading is a necessary and sufficient condition for the
presence of a preference structure which yields a voter's paradox.

Expressed in this general form, however, none of these propositions is
true, as Peter Bernholz (1975) has demonstrated with the following two
simple counterexamples. Suppose that our members A, B and C were again
voting on the missile launcher proposal and the nationalized-welfare proposal, but suppose that this time we could indicate *utility payoffs* (recall our
discussion of cardinal utility in chapter 1) for the outcomes. That is, associated with each outcome there would be a number which represented the
utility of that outcome for each member as follows:

	A	Utility	B	Utility	C	Utility
	$(x,y) =$	10	$(-x,-y) =$	10	$(x,-y) =$	10
Outcomes:	$(-x,y) =$	8	$(-x,y) =$	8	$(-x,y) =$	8
	$(x,-y) =$	6	$(x,y) =$	6	$(x,y) =$	6
	$(-x,-y) =$	2	$(x,-y) =$	2	$(-x,-y) =$	2

In other words, the new preference orders for outcomes for our three
members is:

Preference Orders for Outcomes

	A	*MNOP*
Members:	B	*PNMO*
	C	*ONMP*

Notice that this is different from the original set of preference orders, and notice also that N ($-x,y$) is the Condorcet winner. Nevertheless, if each member voted for his sincere first choice, the outcome would be O ($x, -y$) since A and C would vote for the missile-launcher proposal, and B and C would vote against the nationalized-welfare proposal. That outcome would please C whose utility for O is 10; but it would not please A and B whose utilities for O are 6 and 2 respectively. For this reason, A and B would have an incentive to make the following trade: A would change her vote on the missile launcher to $-x$, and B would change his vote on the nationalized-welfare proposal to y. The new outcome, then, would be N ($-x,y$), a stable, undominated outcome. In other words, *here we have a situation in which there is vote trading, but no underlying voter's paradox.*

Before presenting Bernholz's second example, we shall introduce the notion of a *utility matrix*, which Bernholz uses in his first example, and which is used simply to present a set of utility indicators in a clear, concise fashion. Since this device is used extensively in analyses of game theoretical situations (which we shall discuss in subsequent chapters), we shall introduce it briefly here.

A matrix is simply a two-dimensional array of any kind. In this case, since we are discussing utilities, it is an array of utility numbers. A matrix of outcomes shows the possible outcomes:

		Column 1	*Column 2*
	Moves available to all voters	y	$-y$
Row 1	x	(x,y)	$(x,-y)$
Row 2	$-x$	$(-x,y)$	$(-x,-y)$

The horizontal spaces are called *rows,* the vertical spaces are *columns.* The boxes contain the joint outcomes. Thus, the box for Row 1, Column 1 contains the outcome (x,y), since x is the alternative in Row 1, y the alternative in Column 1. A matrix of utility numbers for our three members would be:

Moves available to all voters	y	$-y$
x	10,6,6	6,2,10
$-x$	8,8,8	2,10,2

where the first number on the left in any box represents the utility of member A for that outcome, the second number the utility of B, and the third number the utility of C. Thus, reading the first box, the utility of A for (x,y) is 10, the utility of B is 6, and the utility of C is also 6. The use of such a matrix does not give us any more information, but it is a convenient and more concise method of presentation.

Bernholz's second example is designed to show that there is at least one case in which a voter's paradox situation does not involve an incentive for vote trading. For this, he assumes a situation of three individuals and three alternatives, but he also assumes that the alternatives all belong to one issue. Thus, the alternatives could represent three proposed bridges, only one of which can be built because of budgetary considerations. The group must decide which bridge will be built. But, even if the preference orders of the three individuals result in a cyclical majority, there can be no trading since there is only one issue.

David Koehler (1975) however, has argued that the existence of a voter's paradox *is* a sufficient condition for vote trading, using the three-alternative case. Koehler begins with the standard paradox situation:

Alternatives

	A	$x>y>z$
Individuals:	B	$y>z>x$
	C	$z>x>y$

He then suggests that A and C could trade by exchanging their preference for y,z and x,z respectively. The preference profile after such a trade would be:

Alternatives

	A	$x>\underline{z>y}$
Individuals:	B	$y>\overline{z>x}$
	C	$\underline{x>z}>y$

In other words, A agrees to vote for z against y in return for C's vote of x against z. The letters underscored indicate the preference changes. As a result, says Koehler, x will defeat z which A wants, and z will defeat y, which C wants. Neither of these results would be obtainable without trading. Moreover, x will be the Condorcet winner. But, in the original preferences, C and B preferred z to x. Therefore, there would be an incentive for C to break the agreement with A and trade with B, so that the new profile would be:

Alternatives

	A	$x > y > z$
Individuals:	B	$z > y > x$
	C	$z > y > x$

In this case z will defeat y (and will be the Condorcet winner), which C wants, and y will defeat x, which B wants. But, this trading can be carried on indefinitely. Nevertheless, Koehler argues that this demonstrates that the presence of the preference pattern for a voter's paradox is necessary for vote trading. The Bernholz counterexample is designed to show that Koehler assumes a particular relationship among individual preferences which is not made explicit, and that is, *separability* or *independence*. That is, a preference pattern which produces a voter's paradox will lead to vote trading only if the preferences are separable. In other words, the preferences on any one issue are independent of the preferences on any other issue.

Before discussing this point further, there is one other problem in the Koehler analysis which should be mentioned. If there is a Condorcet winner, the choice set contains a single element. In his example, however, Koehler speaks of both Condorcet winners *and* binary winners. That is, he speaks of y defeating x, for example, as *satisfying* B as well as z defeating y and becoming the Condorcet winner. But, if there is a Condorcet winner, there can be *only* one winner, and it makes no sense to speak of additional binary winners. On the other hand, if there are binary winners, then each member should be satisfied without trading, since each is a majority winner on his first choice in one binary contest, as follows:

Binary Contests

		x vs. *y*	*y* vs. *z*	*x* vs. *z*
	A	*x*	*y*	*x*
Members:	B	*y*	*y*	*z*
	C	*x*	*z*	*z*
Binary Winner:		*x*	*y*	*z*

SEPARABILITY AND ADDITIVITY

To a great extent, the disagreements above are based on the fact that different conditions are being assumed. For example, Koehler makes two assumptions which Bernholz does not make: that voter preference for issues are *separable* and *additive*. We shall discuss briefly these different but related notions.

In our earlier example, we assumed that an individual's highest preference among alternative outcomes uniquely determined the lowest preference. Thus, a voter who supports both the missile-launcher and the nationalized-welfare proposals, would be least satisfied if they were voted down. A first preference for (x,y), then, implies a last choice of $(-x, -y)$. This example illustrates a consequence of the notion of *separability,* but does not define it. Strictly speaking, separability refers to preferences.[3] It says that my preference for a particular outcome on one issue shall be unaffected by my preference on any other issue. Now, in one sense, this is a suspect definition. My position on different policy issues must surely be related and, most probably, based on a set of principles or an ideology. So, to say that issue positions are completely unrelated is somewhat of an exaggeration.

In the logrolling literature, however, separability has a very specific and limited meaning, and is related to the notion of additivity. To see this, recall our example of nationalized welfare and missile launcher. Suppose that a voter prefers passage of both. Then, suppose that he or she cannot have both. What would his or her second choice be? One kind of answer is, "If I cannot have both, I would like at least one, and I would like that one

3. My thanks to Nicholas Miller for pointing this out to me.

which I prefer more than the other.'' By implication, though having both is of greatest value to the voter, having at least one is second best. In other words, there is nothing about the issues which makes them valuable only as a package.

Another answer, however, is, "If I cannot have both, I do not want either." Here there is something about the issues which makes them valuable only as a package deal. For example, suppose that a voter believes that government has been too active, and that it has collected and spent too much taxpayer money. For that reason, he or she opposes spending on either the missile launcher or nationalized welfare. Suppose, however, that our voter feels that if spending cannot be reduced significantly, it ought to be raised precipitously in order to bring about a financial crisis and demonstrate the folly of government spending. In such a case, the voter has as his or her first choice no spending at all, but, as a second choice, spending on both missiles and welfare. In this case, the preferences of the voter are related, i.e., non-separable.

The *additivity* condition is related to separability, but involves cardinal utility. To see this, let us assign cardinal utilities to our voter preferences. Suppose for example, that a voter supports spending on both the missile launcher and nationalized welfare. This must mean that the utility of spending the money is greater than the utility of not spending the money in each instance. In symbols:

$$u_i(x) > u_i(-x)$$
$$u_i(y) > u_i(-y)$$

The symbol "$u_i(x)$" is read, "the utility for individual i of spending on the missile launcher." Similarly, the sum of the utilities for spending must also be greater than the sum of the utilities for not spending. In symbols:

$$u_i(x) + u_i(y) > u_i(-x) + u_i(-y)$$

Now, the question is, what is the relationship between the utilities for not spending anything—$u_i(-x) + u_i(-y)$—and the utility from spending on *one* item, that is, *either* the missile launcher *or* the nationalized welfare? Let us assume that we are considering spending only on the missile launcher—i.e., $(x, -y)$. By the additivity condition, it must be true that

$$u_i(x) + u_i(-y) > u_i(-x) + u_i(-y)$$

That is, the sum of the utilities for spending on the missile launcher and not spending on nationalized welfare must be higher than not spending on either. That is clear from the utilities—$u_i(-y)$ is the same on both sides of the inequality sign, and $u_i(x)$ is greater than $u_i(-x)$ by assumption. Therefore, the sum of the utilities on the left above must be greater than the sum of the utilities on the right.

If this is the case, however, it must also be true that

$$u_i(-x) + u_i(y) > u_i(-x) + u_i(-y)$$

(*Question:* Can you explain this?)

This also means that a voter who has the highest utility for spending on both issues must receive the least utility from no spending at all. In other words, the issue positions which bring the highest utility are ranked first. The lowest-ranked options are those with the opposite position on each— i.e., those which bring the least utility. It is evident, then, that the notions of separability and additivity are closely related. The former applies to ordinal preferences, the latter to cardinal.

In the Bernholz example, the preferences of individual A are additive, but the preferences of B and C violate additivity. Thus, the utilities for B indicate that $(-x, -y)$ is the first preference. By additivity, then (x,y) should bring the least utility, but we see that $(x, -y)$ is the lowest in terms of utility and, therefore, in terms of preference.

The interesting point here is that *separability and additivity constitute restrictions on individual preference orders*. As such, they violate Arrow's condition of unlimited domain, which we discussed before. Nevertheless, separability and additivity appear to be conditions which *assure* vote-trading cycles! Recall that limitations on the unlimited domain condition—such as single-peakedness—assured that there would be no voting cycles. Here, a limitation on preferences assures just the opposite. This is also similar to a point made in the last chapter, where limitations on the form of the probability vectors for preference orders also resulted in a worsening of the paradox problem.

It is also interesting to note that the separability condition is like an independence condition for individual preferences. That is, Arrow's Independence condition, which we discussed before, required that the *social* preferences remain unchanged if the set of individual preferences remain unchanged. The separability condition requires that individual preferences for each part of a complex alternative remain unchanged if the individual preferences among the alternatives remain unchanged. Thus, in the Bernholz example, the utilities for member B indicate that

$$(-x, -y) > (-x, y)$$

This implies that $-y > y$. But, the utilities also indicate that

$$(x, y) > (x, -y)$$

which implies that $y > -y!$ In other words, there is no consistent preference on the nationalized-welfare issue even though the preferences among the joint outcomes (i.e., $P \ N \ M \ O$) do not change. This is precluded by the separability and additivity conditions.

CONDITIONS FOR VOTE TRADING: ANY NUMBER OF INDIVIDUALS AND ALTERNATIVES

Up to this point, we have seen that for three individuals and two dichotomous (two-sided) issues, logrolling and the voter's paradox are logically equivalent only if we assume separability of preferences. We also want to know if this is true for any number of individuals and alternatives, and for decision rules other than simple majority. For this we shall turn to a theorem of Oppenheimer (1975):

If unrestricted vote trading is permitted with regard to a finite number of independent (i.e. separable) m-sided issues with any simple or special majority rule, precisely those preferences which allow for an effective logroll lead to a voting cycle, or cyclic majority. Furthermore, if (in such situations) the individuals' preferences do not support a cycle then such a logrolling coalition is not efficacious. (p. 963)

In this statement, the term "effective" is ambiguous. In Oppenheimer's previous work (1972), he showed that logrolling cycles are based on underlying voting cycles (voter's paradox), and yet there too he spoke of voting cycles as a prerequisite for "efficacious" coalitions of minorities, which, as mentioned above, are simply the traders who would be in the minority on their more preferred alternatives unless they traded votes. Presumably, Oppenheimer intends "efficacious" to mean that votes can be traded to the advantage of the traders on any particular issue, and not that the trading process will lead to a stable outcome.[4]

On the other hand, the term "coalition of minorities" has also been used by Anthony Downs (1957) to refer to a *party platform* designed to secure a party electoral victory by appealing to minority views on two or more issues, but obtaining thereby an overall electoral majority. Although we shall discuss this in more detail in a subsequent chapter on spatial modeling and political parties, we shall describe a victorious or "efficacious" coalition-of-minorities strategy here. Suppose that three voters (or three large blocs of voters) had the same preferences on the missile-launcher and nationalized-welfare proposals as in our first example above. But, we shall make one change. Assume that member B cares more about the outcome of the missile-launcher proposal. Then, suppose there were two political parties, D and R, which were presenting candidates for election to these voters, and which were called upon to take a stand on each issue in order to win votes. If party D supported the missile launcher and opposed nationalized welfare, we would speak of a *majority strategy*. In other words, party D adopts the positions which would receive a majority of the vote on each issue according to the known preferences of the voters. Party R, however, could defeat D by adopting a *minority strategy*, i.e. by supporting the minority, or losing position, on each issue! This occurs for the following reason. Recall our assumption that member A is more concerned about nationalized welfare than about missile launchers, and that C is more con-

4. Miller, in a personal communication, has suggested that what Oppenheimer really meant to say was that conditions which allow for logrolling lead to a cyclical majority, and that *the absence of such conditions implies the absence of a cyclical majority*. In short, Oppenheimer says:

> Logrolling $\xrightarrow{\text{(implies)}}$ Cyclical Majority
> Absence of Cyclical Majority $\xrightarrow{\text{(implies)}}$ the Absence of Logrolling

In symbols,

$$LR \longrightarrow CM$$
$$-CM \longrightarrow -LR$$

Miller's point is that the two parts of this statement are logically equivalent, and that in this form the theorem is redundant. The more appropriate expression would be:

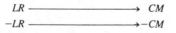

$$LR \longrightarrow CM$$
$$-LR \longrightarrow -CM$$

The conditions for logrolling produce a cyclical majority, and the absence of such conditions imply an absence of a cyclical majority.

cerned about missile launchers than nationalized welfare. Therefore, A will support party R for adopting her position (y) on nationalized welfare, and C will support R for adopting her position ($-x$) on the missile-launcher proposal. Thus, a majority of the voters supports party R, which wins the election. This is what is meant by a successful or efficacious coalition-of-minorities strategy. Oppenheimer then shows that any efficacious coalition of minorities strategy depends upon an underlying voter's paradox. But, it is important to note, as Anthony Downs (1957) pointed out, that a coalition-of-minorities strategy can only be successful if one party must take a position before the other party, and then cannot change its position. If unlimited changes in strategy are allowed, and if the election involves an incumbent party, the opposition party can never win.

This can be shown rather easily. The four possible strategies for R and D are:

Strategies

I	$(x, -y)$	majority strategy
II	(x, y)	majority–minority strategy
III	$(-x, -y)$	minority–majority strategy
IV	$(-x, y)$	minority strategy

Now, if D adopts the majority strategy, R will adopt a minority strategy. But then, D can defeat R by adopting the majority–minority strategy. This occurs for the following reason. Suppose D supports a majority–*minority strategy (x, y)*. Then A will support D because of its support for A's more salient alternative. Voter C, on the other hand, will not support D since the latter does not support either of C's positions. But, B will support D since the latter supports his more salient alternative. Nevertheless, the contest is not over. Party R can defeat D's majority–minority strategy by adopting the majority strategy $(x, -y)$. In this case, A still supports D because of its support for y; but B now switches to R which supports *both* of B's positions (as opposed to D which only supports one), and C also supports R, since it supports its $-y$ position. At this point, however, the majority strategy can be defeated by the minority strategy and a cycle develops. We can summarize these results as follows:

Winning Strategy	Winning Coalition
minority $(-x, y)$ defeats majority $(x, -y)$	(C,A)
majority—minority (x, y) defeats minority $(-x, y)$	(A,B)
majority $(x, -y)$ defeats majority-minority (x, y)	(C,B)

In other words, coalitions of minorities are sure to win only if the procedural rules set certain limits. With unlimited changes in policy positions allowed, cycles of strategies result, even though practically speaking an election requires an arbitrary halt to the process, at which point the last strategy (not necessarily a coalition of minorities) is the winner. Further, as Koehler has pointed out, the coalition of minorities in an electoral contest is different from vote trading in a legislature *since the former requires sincere voting while the latter requires sophisticated voting.* Nevertheless, the two processes are structurally similar if no limitations are imposed, and the analysis of both leads to the conclusion that vote trading and the voter's paradox are related in an important way.

VOTE TRADING AND CONDORCET WINNERS

Even the Oppenheimer theorem on the relation between logrolling and the voter's paradox, however, requires further restrictions before it can be considered valid. Schwartz (1977) has shown by example that *it is possible to have a Condorcet winner in a voting situation, and yet have an incentive to trade. In other words, a defeated minority can block a victorious majority by trading.* This can be shown by the following example. Suppose that there are now five members of our legislature with the following preference orders on our missile-launcher and nationalized-welfare proposals.

Outcomes

	A	$(x,-y)$ $> (x,y)$	$> (-x,-y) > (-x,y)$		
	B	$(x,-y)$ $> (-x,-y) > (x,y)$		$> (-x,y)$	
Members:	C	$(-x,y)$ $> (x,y)$	$> (-x,-y) > (x,-y)$		
	D	$(-x,y)$ $> (-x,-y) > (x,y)$		$> (x,-y)$	
	E	$(-x,-y) > (x,-y)$	$> (-x,y)$ $> (x,y)$		

In terms of our letter equivalents:

Preference for Outcomes

	A	$O\ M\ P\ N$
	B	$O\ P\ M\ N$
Members:	C	$N\ M\ P\ O$
	D	$N\ P\ M\ O$
	E	$P\ O\ N\ M$

Condorcet outcomes: $P > M$, $P > N$, $P > O$.

In other words, $P(-x, -y)$ is the Condorcet winner. (Notice that P is also the Borda winner). But, P ranks only third in the preference orders of A and C, who can block that outcome by trading votes: A votes for y instead of $-y$, and C votes for x instead of $-x$. The new outcome, then, is $M(x,y)$ which is the second choice of both A and C. But, M is the third choice of B and D, and the last choice of E. Members B and D, therefore, have an incentive to change their preferences in order to restore the Condorcet winner P. This can be done by B's change from x to $-x$, and D's change from y to $-y$. This process could go on indefinitely, of course, but Schwartz's point is simply that there is a situation in which there is a Condorcet winner (i.e., no voter's paradox) *and* an incentive to trade. Moreover, if we assume certain practical conditions—for example, suppose it is too costly, for some reason, for B and D to trade—then the minority, A and C can frustrate the wishes of the majority, B, D, and E. In this case, the vote-trading outcome results in a lower aggregate utility than that of the simple voting outcome without any trading.

In Schwartz's analysis, the majority coalition, B, D, and E is referred to as a decisive coalition. The size of a decisive coalition depends upon the decision rule. If the decision rule is simple majority, a decisive coalition is any group which includes more than half of the total number of voters. (*Question:* What is the minimum size of a decisive coalition if the decision rule is a 2/3 majority?) Using this notion, Schwartz shows that "if . . . the outcome chosen in the absence of vote trading . . . is stable, and if cooperation costs do not keep winning coalitions from cooperating, then vote trading cannot block [that outcome] . . ." (pp. 1002–1003). Of course, in the example, if there are no limitations on trade, the decisive majority cannot impose its will either.

The Schwartz example, then, demonstrates a specific case for this generalization. In the coalition-of-minorities situation, however, unlike the Schwartz example, it is a decisive coalition which wants to trade in order to overturn the outcome chosen in the absence of vote trading. Thus, Schwartz shows that the Oppenheimer thesis must be altered to take into account the position of any decisive coalition in a voting situation. He concludes that the *Oppenheimer thesis is correct only when limited to situations of vote trading in which decisive coalitions want to overturn the outcome chosen in the absence of vote trading.*

In reaching this conclusion, Schwartz made two major assumptions:

I: The issues involved are *separable*.
II: There is a collective preference on each issue in the absence of vote trading.

He also assumed a *"collective preference* or *dominance* relation," P, among "feasible outcomes," which he interprets as "the relation of unanimous preference by any one of certain *winning coalitions* of voters" (p. 1000, italics in original). These are the "decisive coalitions" discussed above.

Schwartz also posits a "winning coalition rule" which says: "choose the position voted for by all the members of some winning coalition, if such a position exists; otherwise, choose randomly" (p. 1000). This is essentially a collective decision rule for coalitions which is analogous to majority rule in simple voting situations.

The Schwartz theorem, then, is as follows:

Suppose Assumptions I and II hold, P satisfies (2), and issues are decided according to the winning coalition rule. Then Ω contains no stable outcome if there is a potential vote trade involving issues drawn from among $w_1, \ldots, w_n$ such that the members of some winning coalition all prefer that trade (i.e., the outcome issuing therefrom) to $(m_1, \ldots m_n)$. (p. 1004)

Conversely,

Suppose Assumptions I and II hold, P satisfies (2), and issues are decided according to the winning coalition rule. Then, Ω contains no stable outcome if, and only if, there is a potential vote trade involving issues drawn from among $w_1, \ldots, w_n$ and preferred to $(m_1, \ldots, m_n)$ by all the members of some winning coalition. (p. 1004)

In these statements, (2) refers to the relation of "unanimous preference" mentioned above; Ω is the set of feasible outcomes; and $w_1, \ldots,$ w_n is a set of issues, each a set of feasible alternative positions. In terms of our examples above, w_i might be $\{x, -x\}$, w_j might be $\{y, -y\}$, etc. The term $(m_1, \ldots, m_n)$ refers to the set of positions which would be the collective preference in the absence of vote trading.

Notice that this formulation also implies that if the set of outcomes on each issue is a stable choice set supported by a decisive majority, then vote trading should not ensue. Or, if the choice set is unstable, then the members of some decisive coalition should prefer some vote trade. In the Schwartz example, however, the original outcome is what we might call *Condorcet stable,* i.e., the outcome $P(-x, -y)$ is preferred to every other alternative in a pairwise comparison. Yet, the fact that A and C have an incentive to trade means that the outcome P is not really stable, for with no restrictions on trading there would be a never-ending cycle of changes: first A and C would change their votes, then B and D would change their votes, and then A and C would change their votes, and so on. In each case, two voters who are in a position to alter the outcome through trading would prefer the new alternative to the old outcome and the situation would be unstable. Moreover, the coalition which prefers trading to the original outcome in each case is not a decisive coalition, since at least three voters constitute such a coalition with a total of five members. Thus, if the original outcome is considered unstable, it is not true that unstable outcomes are a necessary and sufficient condition for vote trading involving a decisive coalition. In other words, Schwartz is correct only if the original Condorcet stable outcome is considered stable. If not, his own example is a counterexample to his theorem.

Miller[5] has argued, however, that "stable" in Schwartz's terms means that there is no other alternative which is preferred by a majority to the Condorcet stable outcome. In that sense of the word, of course, Schwartz's example is not a counterexample to his own theorem, since no other alternative is preferred by a majority to P.

LOGROLLING VS. VOTE TRADING

So far, we have used the terms logrolling and vote trading interchangeably. In the literature, however, a distinction has recently been drawn (see, for example, Miller, 1977, and Enelow, 1976) between the two concepts. Miller (1977) describes *logrolling* as follows:

. . . the formation of a coalition including a majority of voters that engages in "decisive" strategic collaboration in order to impose on the voting body a voting decision different from, and preferred to, the individualistic voting decision. (p. 53)

The term "decisive strategic collaboration" means an agreement to change votes in such a way that there is a new result. The term "individualistic voting decision" refers to the result which occurs when all voters vote for the alternative which is highest on their preference scales.

5. Personal communication.

Vote trading, on the other hand, involves

Concerted action among voters who may lack the power to impose a decision on the voting body but who engage in "marginal" strategic collaboration in order to bring about a voting decision different from, and preferred to, the individualistic voting decision. (p. 53)

The critical distinction, then, between logrolling and vote trading is whether the collaborators constitute a majority or a minority. If the coalition is a majority, they are logrolling; if a minority, they are trading votes. *Where there are only three voters, logrolling and vote trading are equivalent,* since there must be at least two collaborators, and since any two voters constitute a majority.

This distinction is not simply a semantic refinement. Rather the theoretical results indicate, as we have tried to illustrate, that *there is a systematic relationship between logrolling and the voter's paradox, but that there is not a systematic relationship between vote trading and the voter's paradox.*

PROVING A LOGROLLING THEOREM

So far, we have only stated various theorems and have used examples either to illustrate the theorem or to disprove it. At this point we shall present a relatively simple general proof of the Oppenheimer theorem in order to illustrate once again a general proof.

An example is a single case or single situation. What we want to know, however, is whether all other possible examples exhibit the same characteristics. A theorem is a statement about all cases of a particular type, and in order to prove a theorem, the proof must be in a general form, as we saw in the case of the Arrow theorem. For example, a situation of simple majority rule could involve any number of individuals. Thus, in a group of three voters, two is a simple majority; in a group of five voters, three is a simple majority, and so on. Our problem is to express that notion in a general form which would include all such instances. This might be done as follows. Let m and n stand for two positions on a dichotomous—two-sided—issue. Further, let m be the majority position, and let n be the minority position. Then, let $N(m)$ mean, "the number of voters who hold the majority position," and let $N(n)$ mean, "the number of voters who hold the minority position." The general notion that a simple majority can involve two or more voters, then, can be expressed as follows:

$$N(m) > N(n)$$

That is, the number of voters who hold the majority position, no matter how many, is always greater than the number of voters who hold the minority position. Notice that this statement includes all possible majorities of $N(m)$ over $N(n)$—a simple majority, two-thirds majority, etc.—and is thus a completely general statement. In other words, no matter what kind of majority rule, and for any number of voters, it must be true that $N(m) > N(n)$.

Now, let us include more than one issue. We shall designate each issue by a subscript number. Thus, our statement for issue 1 would be

$$N(m_1) > N(n_1)$$

For issue 2,

$$N(m_2) > N(n_2)$$

That is, the number of voters who hold the majority position on issue 1 is greater than the number of voters who hold the minority position on issue 1; and the number of voters who hold the majority position on issue 2 is greater than the number of voters who hold the minority position.

To make this illustration more concrete, let issue 1 be our missile-launcher proposal, and issue 2 be our nationalized-welfare proposal. Each individual voter, then, will hold either the majority or minority position on each issue. In our earlier example, $N(m_1)$ represented those voters who supported the missile-launcher proposal, $N(n_1)$ those who opposed it. $N(m_2)$ represented those who opposed nationalized welfare, and $N(n_2)$ those who supported it. It is important to note that we are not specifying any particular position on any issue by our symbols, but rather whatever positions are the majority and minority.

For any voter, then, the choice of issue positions for two dichotomous issues will fall into one of four categories:

$$(m_1 m_2)$$
$$(n_1 m_2)$$
$$(m_1 n_2)$$
$$(n_1 n_2)$$

In other words, a voter can choose a position on each issue which turns out to be a majority position or a minority position, and his or her position on both issues can be expressed in terms of whether it is a majority or minority position. Thus, the symbol (m_1m_2) means the majority position on both issues (whatever it is); (n_1n_2) means the minority position on both issues, and so on.

For example, in the original vote on the missile launcher, x, support for the proposal, was the majority position, while $-y$, opposition to the nationalized-welfare proposal, was the majority position on that issue. Individual A, then, who voted for both proposals, was in the majority on the first issue, but in the minority on the second. This can be expressed (m_1n_2). Moreover, every individual's preferences can be expressed this way—that is, in terms of whether they hold a majority or minority position.

Consider now the number of possible orderings of these joint positions. With no restrictions, there are 24 permutations of the four joint positions— (m_1m_2), (n_1n_2), (m_1n_2), (n_1m_2). Oppenheimer, however, assumes separability. Once again, this means that if, say, (m_1m_2) is the most preferred position, then (n_1n_2), the opposite preference on each issue, must be the lowest preference. This restriction reduces the possible orderings of the joint positions to eight:

1	2	3	4
$\underline{(m_1,m_2)}$	$\underline{(m_1,m_2)}$	(n_1,m_2)	(n_1,m_2)
(m_1,n_2)	(n_1,m_2)	$\underline{(m_1,m_2)}$	(n_1,n_2)
(n_1,m_2)	(m_1,n_2)	(n_1,n_2)	(m_1,m_2)
$\underline{(n_1,n_2)}$	$\underline{(n_1,n_2)}$	(m_1,n_2)	(m_1,n_2)

5	6	7	8
(m_1,n_2)	(m_1,n_2)	(n_1,n_2)	(n_1,n_2)
(n_1,n_2)	$\underline{(m_1,m_2)}$	(n_1,m_2)	(m_1,n_2)
$\underline{(m_1,m_2)}$	(n_1,n_2)	(m_1,n_2)	(n_1,m_2)
(n_1,m_2)	(n_1,m_2)	$\underline{(m_1,m_2)}$	$\underline{(m_1,m_2)}$

This would be equivalent to our listing above of preferences for outcomes such as:

$$(x,y)$$
$$(x,-y)$$
$$(-x,y)$$
$$(-x,-y)$$

Now, by definition, a coalition of minorities is a group which prefers a minority position on each issue. Thus, a coalition of minorities is a group which prefers the minority positions on each issue to the majority position; or, for whom

$$(n_1, n_2) > (m_1, m_2)$$

To see this more clearly, recall our initial example in which the majority outcome, (m_1, m_2) was $(x, -y)$. The minority outcome, (n_1, n_2) was, therefore, $(-x, y)$, and both A and C preferred $(-x, y)$ to $(x, -y)$, or $(n_1, n_2) > (m_1, m_2)$. Thus, a general condition for efficacious coalitions of minorities is that

$$N\,(n_1, n_2) > N\,(m_1, m_2)$$

That is, the number of voters who prefer both minority positions must be greater than the number who prefer both majority positions. Another way of expressing this is to say that the number of voters who hold preference orders 4, 5, 7, and 8 above, must be greater than the number who have the preference orders 1, 2, 3, and 6. This could be written:

$$N(4) + N(5) + N(7) + N(8) > N(1) + N(2) + N(3) + N(6)$$

Oppenheimer refers to this as *Condition I*. A second condition is that the number of people who prefer the majority position on any issue must be greater than the number who support the minority position, by virtue of the definitions of majority and minority. In terms of our symbols, this means that

$$N(m_1) > N(n_1)$$

That is, the number of people in the majority coalition on issue 1 is greater than the number in the minority coalition on issue 1. In our list of eight possible preference orders listed above we see that m_1 is preferred to n_1 in preference orders 1, 2, 5, and 6; and that n_1 is preferred to m_1 in preference orders 3, 4, 7, and 8. To see this more clearly, note that in preference order 1, the first choice is (m_1, m_2). This outcome is preferred to (n_1, m_2) which is the third choice. But this means that m_1 must be preferred to n_1, since both outcomes contain m_2. Conversely, in preference order 3, (n_1, m_2) is preferred to (m_1, m_2) and, therefore, n_1 is preferred to m_1. In general terms *Condition II* is:

$$N(1)+N(2)+N(5)+N(6)>N(3)+N(4)+N(7)+N(8)$$

Do not be confused by the fact that the sign ">" means "greater than" when numbers are involved, and "preferred to" when we are ranking outcomes. Condition II says that the number of individuals who have preference orders 1, 2, 5, and 6 must be greater than those who have preference orders 3, 4, 7, and 8. This condition does not contradict the first condition, since different groupings of preference orders are involved on each side of the inequality sign (we would say "equation" if both sides were equal).

Similarly, *Condition III* says that the number of individuals who prefer m_2 to n_2 must be greater than those who prefer n_2 to m_2. Thus,

$$N(1)+N(2)+N(3)+N(4)>N(5)+N(6)+N(7)+N(8)$$

Now, recall that a minority strategy can defeat a majority strategy where the conditions for vote trading hold. This would mean that

$$N(n_1, n_2)>N(m_1, m_2)$$

And, Condition I tells us that this would be the case. But, Condition II tells us that (m_1, n_2) would be preferred to (n_1, n_2) and that, therefore,

$$N(m_1, n_2)>N(n_1, n_2)$$

Condition III, however, says that (m_1, m_2) would be preferred to (m_1, n_2). Therefore,

$$N(m_1, m_2)>N(m_1, n_2)$$

Yet, we have already seen that (n_1, n_2) is preferred to (m_1, m_2). Thus, a cycle of preferences over outcomes exists. This analysis, then, constitutes a proof that, for any number of individuals and two two-sided issues, if the conditions for vote trading exist there is an underlying voter's paradox. This is, of course, a more general statement than our earlier example, which was limited to the case of three individuals. Oppenheimer also presents a general proof for more than two issues, but we shall omit that here.[6]

PARADOX OF VOTE TRADING

One of the most interesting results in the theory of vote trading is Brams and Riker's paradox of vote trading. Unlike our examples above, Brams and

6. See also Miller (1977) for a direct proof for any number of issues and issue positions.

Riker were concerned not only with the stability of vote trading and the voter's paradox, but also with the question of whether vote trading increased the utility for all voters. In other words, were the individuals better off after logrolling than they were before?

Brams and Riker do not provide a general proof for their claim, but merely provide examples to show that there are situations in which there is an incentive for vote trading, but that if voters do trade, the results are outcomes which provide *lower* utility than would obtain without trading. Yet, if some voters trade while others do not, the nontraders will be even worse off than they would have been had they traded votes. Thus, everyone has an incentive to trade, which forces an outcome which is worse than if no one traded!

To illustrate this point, consider a legislature of three members (or three blocs of members) and six two-sided issues. Suppose also that two issues are considered at each round of voting, and that once a trade is made it cannot be altered. This last condition is a severe restriction on the process, but it tends to accord more with reality since, in most legislatures, once a bill has finally been voted on it cannot be reopened. Brams and Riker argue, however, that this condition is not crucial to their argument.

The first round of voting involves our old friends A, B, and C, and issues x and y. But this time we shall indicate the utility values for each individual of winning or losing on his other preference. That is, if an individual prefers x to $-x$, his or her utility will be higher if x is the majority choice than if $-x$ is the majority choice. In our example we assume that an individual in fact loses utility if his or her preference is defeated. That is, a defeat *costs* the losers a certain amount in terms of utility. The material below, then, indicates both the utility of winning (of being in the majority) and the utility of losing (of being in the minority) for each individual.

		A	
		Proposals	
		$x(-x)$	$y(-y)$
Members:	A	$x\,(1) > -x\,(-2)$	$y\,(1) > -y\,(-2)$
	B	$x\,(1) > -x\,(-1)$	$-y\,(2) > y\,(-2)$
	C	$-x\,(2) > x\,(-2)$	$y\,(1) > -y\,(-1)$
Result of majority vote		x	y

The number in parenthesis after the preferred alternative represents that member's utility if his or her preference becomes the majority preference. The number in parenthesis after the less preferred alternative is the cost to each member of having that alternative become the majority preference. Thus, for example, member A receives a utility of 1 if her preferred alternative (x) is the majority choice, but loses 2 utility units (whatever that may be) if $-x$ is the majority choice. In the initial vote on x, both A and B would be in the winning majority and would receive 1 utility unit, while C would lose 2 utility units. In the initial vote on y, A and C would be in the winning majority, each receiving 1 utility unit, while B would lose 2. The preference orders for outcomes on x and y would be:

Preference Orders for Outcomes

$$
\begin{array}{lll}
\text{A} & (x,y) = 2 > (-x,y) = -1 = (x,-y) = -1 > (-x,-y) = -4 \\
\textit{Members: } \text{B} & (x,-y) = 3 > (-x,-y) = 1 > (x,y) = -1 > (-x,y) = -3 \\
\text{C} & (-x,y) = 3 > (-x,-y) = 1 > (x,y) = -1 > (x,-y) = -3
\end{array}
$$

The positive or negative numbers after the joint outcomes is the sum of the utilities for each member on each outcome. Thus, for A, x and y each yield one unit if they are the winning outcome. At the other end of the preference order, the outcomes $-x$ and $-y$ cost A 2 units each for a total cost of 4 utility units, symbolized by "-4." Notice that the condition of additivity is satisfied in this example—(x,y) is A's first choice, $(-x,-y)$ the last choice—and that the structure of preferences is exactly the same as in our original vote-trading examples above.

The sincere outcome, (x,y), is A's first choice, but is the third choice of B and C who can then trade votes (change their preferences) in order to change the outcome to $(-x,-y)$, their second choice. The columns below list the utility outcomes before and after trading:

		Results without Trading (x,y) Utiles	Results with Trading $(-x,-y)$ (Traders: B and C) Utiles
	A	2	−4
Members:	B	−1	1
	C	−1	1

The trade has resulted in an increase of utility for B and C from -1 to 1; and a decrease in utility for A from 2 to -4.

Now, we shall introduce two more two-sided issues with the following preference structure:

B

Proposals

		$w(-w)$	$z(-z)$
	A	$w(1) > -w(-1)$	$-z(2) > z(-2)$
Members:	B	$-w(2) > w(-2)$	$z(1) > -z(-1)$
	C	$w(1) > -w(-2)$	$z(1) > -z(-2)$

Result of
majority vote w z

Notice that this is exactly the same as the first case except that now C is in the initial majority on both issues and A and B are the potential traders. Here the preference orders for outcomes are:

Preference Orders for Outcomes

$$
\begin{array}{ll}
\text{A} & (w, -z) = 3 > (-w, -z) = 1 > (w, z) = 1 > (-w, z) = -3 \\
\text{Members: B} & (-w, z) = 3 > (-w, -z) = 1 > (w, z) = 1 > (w, -z) = -3 \\
\text{C} & (w, z) = 2 > (-w, z) = -1 = (w, -z) = -1 > (-w, -z) = -4
\end{array}
$$

The traders are A and B, and the utility outcomes are:

		Results without Trading (w, z) Utiles	Results with Trading $(-w, -z)$ (Traders: A and B) Utiles
	A	-1	1
Members:	B	-1	1
	C	2	-4

The results are exactly the same as those above except that it is now C who comes out the big loser.

The final example is also exactly like the first two except that B is the loser after trading.

C

	Proposals	
	$t(-t)$	$v(-v)$

		$t(-t)$	$v(-v)$
	A	$-t(2) > \ t(-2)$	$v(1) > -v(-1)$
Members:	B	$t(1) > -t(-2)$	$v(1) > -v(-2)$
	C	$t(1) > -t(-1)$	$-v(2) > \ v(-2)$

Result of
majority vote t v

Preference Orders for Outcomes

	A	$(-t, v) = 3 > (-t, -v) = \ \ 1 > (t, v) \ = \ \ 1 > (t, -v) \ = -3$	
Members:	B	$(t, v) \ = 2 > (t, -v) \ \ = -1 = (-t, v) = -1 > (-t, -v) = -4$	
	C	$(t, -v) = 3 > (-t, -v) = \ \ 1 > (t, v) \ = -1 > (-t, v) \ = -3$	

		Results without Trading (t, v) Utiles	Results with Trading $(-t, -v)$ (Traders: A and C) Utiles
	A	-1	1
Members:	B	2	-4
	C	-1	1

The result of this trading is that each member receives 1 utile on each issue where he or she is a trader, but loses 4 utiles on the one issue where he or she does not trade. This is a net *loss* of two utiles for each member. Without any trading, each member loses 1 utile on two issues and gains two utiles on one issue for a net outcome of zero. In other words, trading *reduces* the utility for all members who trade. The follow tabulation summarizes this result:

		Utilities without Trading			
		(x, y)	(w, z)	(t, v)	Totals
	A	2	-1	$-1 =$	0
Members:	B	-1	-1	$2 =$	0
	C	-1	2	$-1 =$	0

Utilities with Trading

		(x, y)	(w, z)	(t, v)		*Totals*
	A	-4	1	1	=	-2
Members:	B	1	1	-4	=	-2
	C	1	-4	1	=	-2

Since it is better for everyone not to trade, suppose that one member decides to set an example by refusing a trade where it is available. Assume that member A refuses a trade with B on (w, z), and refuses a trade with C on (t, v). Then there will be only one trade, between B and C on (x, y). Let us now look at the results with only that one trade:

Utilities with Trading on One Issue

		(x, y)	(w, z)	(t, v)		*Totals*
	A	-4	-1	-1	=	-6
Members:	B	1	-1	2	=	2
	C	1	2	-1	=	2
		(trade)	(no trade)	(no trade)		

In this case, the nontrader A loses 6 utiles while B and C each gain 2 utiles. This is obviously the best outcome for B and C, and the worst outcome for A. Moreover, the result is the same no matter who is the nontrader. (Work this out for yourself.) In other words, by trying to induce B and C toward a more rational collective outcome, A has become the "sucker" by advancing the interests of her colleagues at her own expense. The specter of becoming the sucker, moreover, forces each member to trade, and the outcome is worse for all than if no one had traded.

The obvious answer to this dilemma is some kind of common agreement not to trade. The equally apparent difficulty with such a solution, however, is that there is a definite incentive for two of the members to enter such an agreement in order to induce the third member not to trade, but then to renege on their promise and trade on one issue. Presumably, this could only happen once, after which the betrayed sucker would never again agree not to trade. Another solution, however, is for two of the members simply to agree never to trade with the third. This assures the best outcome for the traders, and the nontrader cannot alter that situation alone.

It is on this point that Tullock (1974) has criticized Brams and Riker.

He argues that we must assume that rational traders will only make those trades which are advantageous to them. And, if it is apparent that certain trades are not advantageous in the longer run, even though they are advantageous on a particular issue, then rational traders would avoid them and no paradox would occur. The counterargument to this point is that although rational traders would not make such trades if they were known to be disadvantageous in the long run, the uncertainty of most real political situations would force all voters into any advantageous trades in order to protect against being the sucker. In other words, in most real situations, in which there is uncertainty about the future, it would seem wiser for any member to enter any trade which is immediately advantageous. In a situation of complete information, however, trades which are disadvantageous in the long run would certainly be shunned by rational traders, and on this point Tullock's objection has merit.

Schwartz (1977) has argued that the Brams and Riker results are limited in another sense. He provides an example to show that there are situations in which vote trading can improve the position of every voter, making all better off. His example involves three individuals, and three alternatives which have dollar values to each of the individuals, as follows:

Alternatives (with Dollar Values)

A	$x(500) > z(400) > y(-1000)$
Members: B	$y(500) > x(400) > z(-1000)$
C	$z(500) > y(400) > x(-1000)$

The numbers in the parentheses represent dollar values of each alternative for each member. The alternatives are proposals which can be passed or rejected as above. Thus, if x is passed it is worth $500 to A, and $400 to B; but it would cost C $1000. (Perhaps the issue is a tax or a tax rebate.) The three members are to vote yes or no on each alternative. For example, A would vote for x and z, but against y. Member B would vote for y and x, but against z; and C would vote for z and y, but against x. Without trading the outcome would be (x,y,z) since each alternative would receive two of three votes for passage. But, the outcome (x,y,z) would result in a net loss to each member of $100. This is because each member receives $500 for his first choice and $400 for his second—a total of $900—but loses $1000 when his third choice is passed. Suppose, however, that every alternative had been defeated. Then, no member would receive any money, but neither would any member have lost anything. This outcome is clearly preferred by everyone to the outcome in which everyone loses $100, and can be easily achieved by a general agreement to vote against each of the alternatives.

The difficulty with this example, however, is that the outcome $(-x, -y, -z)$ does not appear to be stable, since any two members could trade votes, exclude the third member, and reap a great benefit at the expense of the sucker. Suppose, for instance, that A and B agreed to vote for x, and against y and z. The outcome would be $(x, -y, -z)$, which would result in a $500 gain for A, a $400 gain for B, and a $1000 loss for C. Or, suppose that B and C voted for y and against x and z. Then the outcome would be $(-x, y, -z)$, which would give B $500 and C $400; but would cost A $1000. *Notice, however, that any result is unstable, since one of the traders receives less than the other and is open to an offer from the original nontrader to increase his original gain of $400 to $500.* At that point, however, the new nontrader is in a position to offer the member who receives $400 a better deal, and so on. In other words, an endless cycle of trades results. Notice also that the underlying preference structure in this case is a paradox-producing profile. With a time limit, the trading will stop and two voters will gain at the expense of the third. Without a time limit, however, a cycle of trades will ensue. In no case does it appear that all voters will be better off trading than not trading. The Schwartz example is also open to Tullock's objection that rational voters do not take less advantageous trades if they can do better.

SUMMARY

In this chapter, we have made the following main points:

1. Given certain conditions the possibility of logrolling, or vote trading, *requires* an underlying preference structure which supports a voter's paradox.

2. Nevertheless, if the conditions exist for logrolling, and if the trading begins, the result will be an endless series of trades unless the process is halted by an arbitrary device, such as a time limit on trading.

3. We have drawn a distinction between logrolling and vote trading. The former involves a decisive majority, the latter a minority which can block sincere outcomes. While there is an equivalence between logrolling

and the voter's paradox, that relationship does not hold for vote trading and the paradox.

4. There are situations in which vote trading or logrolling makes each individual worse off than he or she would have been without trading; but any individual who eschews trading runs the risk of an even greater loss. There is, therefore, an incentive for all voters to act in a way which reduces their utility, i.e., irrationally.

5. For these reasons, logrolling and vote trading are not ways of avoiding the voter's paradox, nor can they guarantee an increased utility for all voters.

CONCLUSION

In conclusion, we shall briefly relate our theoretical analysis to actual political situations. Our first point is that if the conditions for logrolling described above actually exist, then the potential for cycles of trading also exist. But, since votes are taken in real legislatures or committees, we can conclude that the outcome is imposed in those cases which satisfy our theoretical conditions. While it is not news to students of politics that decisions are frequently imposed over the wishes of a majority, it is news that such a situation may be unavoidable even in principle, and even if no one intends it.

Second, vote trading in actual legislatures or committees frequently does not resemble the theoretical vote trading situation described above. That is, there seem to be situations in which vote trading takes place but without full symmetry of rewards. For example, in legislatures, trading frequently takes place among individuals who are not, by themselves, pivotal to the outcome of the voting on a particular issue. One member may agree to switch his or her vote in return for the vote of the other trader on an issue of greater importance to him, but the desired outcome is only assured if others also trade. What happens if two members trade votes but in the actual voting one trader's preferred alternative is defeated while the other trader's preferred alternative is passed? Presumably, the political obligations have been mutually satisfied—after all, each trader kept his word—but in terms of the utility of the outcomes, one trader has gained while the other has not. Moreover, the trader who loses cannot claim any future obligation from the successful trader since the latter fulfilled his part of the bargaining.

In such a case, the losing trader has simply made a bad deal, or an irrational trade if rationality is defined in terms of utility maximization. Obviously, however, the source of the irrationality was a lack of information about the intentions of other voters. Presumably, the losing trader would not have entered into such a trade if he or she could have known the adverse outcome. In this case, we see the importance of information in rational decision making. *The implication of our analysis, however, is that increasing the amount of information available may not lead to more rational outcomes, but rather to social intransitivities.*

There are also instances in which legislators accumulate political obligations by agreeing to vote with other legislators on their pet projects in return for future support. Until those political debts are paid off, however, the legislator who has simply given a vote to a colleague has made an irrational deal.

Empirical studies of legislatures and committees, then, could investigate the extent to which vote trading cycles exist but are suppressed, as well as the extent of irrational vote trading.

CHAPTER FIVE

Spatial Models

IN 1957, Anthony Downs published his *Economic Theory of Democracy*. This work has become a classic in the field and is the starting point for all work involving so-called "spatial models" of political parties. It also develops a theory of rational voting which stands as an alternative to psychological or socioeconomic theories.[1] In this chapter, we shall present the major points in Downs's analysis, the subsequent developments in spatial modeling and the theory of rational voting, and the relationship between this work and the voter's paradox.

ECONOMIC THEORIES OF POLITICS

The notion of an "economic" theory of politics has been widely misunderstood. Since the field of economics deals with the distribution of goods and services, it has been assumed that an economic theory of politics contends that politics involves only material issues. This is incorrect. Economic theories of politics assume that decision makers (voters, candidates) weigh the costs and benefits involved in their choices and then make the decision

1. For an analysis and critique of these theories, see Robert Abrams, *Some Conceptual Problems of Voting Theory* (1973).

which produces the greatest net benefit. This *net* benefit is what we have referred to before as *utility*. In symbolic terms, $B - C = U$, where B means "benefits," C means "costs," and U means "utility."

The "economic" decision maker is one who tries to *maximize utility*. The important point, however, is that this utility does not have to be expressed in terms of money or material goods. For example, one of the costs of voting is simply the time it takes to register and actually vote. Similarly, the benefits of governmental policies can be such intangibles as civil rights and liberties, or the preservation of individual privacy. Economic theories of politics assume, however, that such costs and benefits are calculable and comparable, and that the utility to be maximized is expressible in numerical terms. In other words, *unlike Arrow, these theories accept the notion of cardinal utility*.

SPATIAL MODELS

Each decision maker, then, can calculate the costs and benefits of any outcome. It is important to stress here that these costs and benefits are determined subjectively by the decision maker. There are no objective costs and benefits which determine the utility for any individual. The utility to be maximized is that which the decision maker alone can determine by asking, "What is the utility of this outcome for *me?*" [2]

Thus, any political outcome or issue position is associated with a numerical utility for all individuals involved, and this utility is the difference between the benefits and costs of that outcome for each individual. For example, assume that an election has come to focus on a single important issue, such as the extent of government control of the economy. At the extreme left, the socialists argue that all industry should be nationalized. At the extreme right, the laissez-faire capitalists argue that government should keep its hand out of private business (except, perhaps, for favorable tax policies, subsidies, lucrative contracts, and so on). Each citizen, then, weighs the costs and benefits to himself of every position on that scale, and would like to find and support a candidate who espouses that position which brings the highest utility. Suppose for instance, that a particular citizen supports a position which is just to the left of center. (See fig. 5.1.)

2. In Chapter 8, Collective Goods, we shall discuss "altruistic" decision makers who consider the utility of *others* in their calculations.

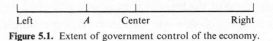

Figure 5.1. Extent of government control of the economy.

This means that any position either to the left or right of position *A* has a lower utility for that citizen. In other words, if a government came to power which implemented policies which could be described as left of center (*A* above) then our citizen would receive the greatest utility. Any policy which is farther left or right, however, would reduce that utility. This could be represented diagrammatically as in fig. 5.2.

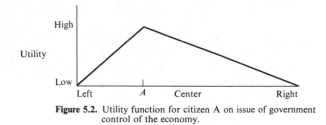

Figure 5.2. Utility function for citizen A on issue of government control of the economy.

Notice that this is the graph of single-peaked preferences which we discussed in chapter 2. And, it means that our citizen has a weak ordering (indifference allowed) over all of the alternative policies available.[3] (*Question:* Why is this a *weak* ordering rather than a *strong* ordering?) Similarly, a citizen whose highest utility is to the right of center might have the graph shown in fig. 5.3.

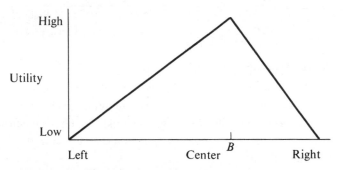

Figure 5.3. Utility function for citizen B on issue of government control of the economy.

3. We shall defer for the moment the question of whether there are any difficulties in assigning a "left" or "right" position to any bundle of policies.

The actual slope of the lines in both graphs above would be determined by the utility calculations of each individual. If, for example, our first citizen were strongly committed to his left of center position, then the lines would drop sharply down as one moved away from that position. If the commitment were weak, on the other hand (i.e., if the utility associated with positions either farther left or farther right was not much lower than that at the most preferred position) then the lines would slope gradually. This can be illustrated by the graphs in fig. 5.4.

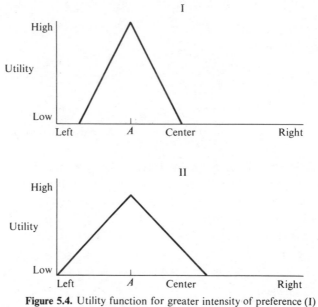

Figure 5.4. Utility function for greater intensity of preference (I) and lesser intensity (II).

Notice that the utility for the most preferred position in I, i.e., A is higher than that of A in fig. 5.4-II. In addition, the lines slope much more sharply in fig. 5.4-I than II. This means that any citizen whose utility function (the term we use to describe these figures) looks like I has a much stronger preference for his or her most preferred position than the citizen whose utility function looks like II.

Each citizen, then, has a most preferred position in a *policy space*. In the example above, the policy space was a single issue or dimension. But, there could be any number of issues or dimensions. For example, suppose there were two issues involved in an election, such as the extent of government intervention in the economy and the war in Vietnam. Suppose further that the Vietnam issue involved positions from "hawk" to "dove," i.e., from those who wanted the United States to increase its military activity to those who wanted the United States to get out of Vietnam altogether. Then, suppose that our citizen who preferred a somewhat left of center position in the example above (A) was also a strong dove on the war, while the citizen who preferred a slightly right of center position on the economy (B) was a "hawk" on the war. Such a set of preferences might be graphed as in fig. 5.5.

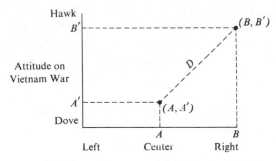

Figure 5.5. A two-dimensional policy space.

The letters in parentheses, (A, A') and (B, B'), refer to the point at the intersection of the dotted lines which originate at points A and A', B and B' respectively on each axis.[4] The letter "D" on the line connecting points (A, A') and (B, B') is the *distance* between the two positions.[5] In a one-dimensional model, this distance could be shown as in fig. 5.6.

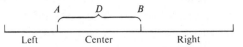

Figure 5.6. Distance between most preferred issue positions of citizen A and B in one-dimensional policy space.

4. An "axis" is a line on a two-dimensional plane. A "two-dimensional plane" is a flat surface, such as this page, which has length (one dimension), and width (another dimension) but not depth. The term "three dimensional," which we use in ordinary speech, includes length (height), width, and depth.

5. Notice that in this example the positions on each issue are assumed to be of equal weight in determining the combined position. We shall discuss below alternatives to this assumption.

In both the one- and two-dimensional models, it is assumed that it is meaningful to speak of such distances in numerical terms. Notice, however, that these numerical distances are *not* the same thing as the numerical utilities discussed above. Each position has a utility value for each individual, but the same position can have different utility values for different citizens. For example, the position A has a higher utility value for the citizen whose first preference is position A than for the citizen whose first preference is B, and conversely, position B has a higher utility for the citizen whose first preference is position B than for the citizen whose first preference is position A.

The term "spatial model" then, refers to those analyses which use graphic representations such as those above, and which posit spatial (from the word "space") distances between issue positions. Thus, in spatial models we can refer to one issue position as being "farther away from" a second issue position than from a third, as for example, in fig. 5.7. Here D is the distance from issue position A to B, D' is the distance from A to C, and D'' (read, "D double prime") is the distance from C to B (or B to C, the direction is not important.) Without specifying numerical distances, it is evident that the distance D is greater than either D' or D''. Thus, A can be said to be farther from B than from C. We also know that the distances, D' and D'' together equal D, or

$$D' + D'' = D$$

and, using simple algebra,

$$D' = D - D'', \text{ or}$$
$$D'' = D - D'$$

Moreover, we can also specify simple relations between D' and D''. That is, D' is either greater than, less than, or equal to D''. If $D' > D''$ (D' greater than D'') then issue position C is farther from A than from B. Thus, without actually assigning numerical distances to positions in a policy space, we can say a great deal about their relationship. And in fact a great deal of the theory of political parties based on spatial models has been developed without specifying such numerical values. In principle, however, they are specifiable, and any empirical work must face the problem of assigning numbers to issue positions.

Notice that there is a similarity between this discussion of spatial mod-

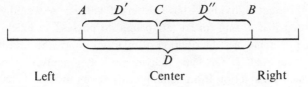

Figure 5.7. Distance between issue positions in a one-dimensional policy space.

els and our ordinary notions of someone being "closer to" or "farther from" the position of another. In labor-management negotiations, for example, it is common to speak of the two sides as being "far apart." To some extent, spatial modeling is an attempt to give more precise meanings to such terms and to clarify analyses of political situations where issue positions are relevant.

RATIONAL VOTING

"Economic" theories of politics, then, posit individuals who consider costs and benefits in making decisions, and who make those decisions which bring them the greatest possible utility. Although there is general agreement that such utility need not be financial or material, there is less agreement about whether utility maximization rules out unselfish or altruistic behavior. The economist Adam Smith claimed that our food is provided not because of the good will of the farmer and baker, but because of their selfish desire for personal gain. In other words, social goods are, paradoxically, the product of individual actions designed for individual benefit. For many economists, the desirable social end of plentiful production served as a justification for individual behavior which neglected such virtues as altruism. Would the same hold true in politics? Could we look forward to social goods such as justice in a system of self-centered citizens?

The implication of this question for a theory of rational voting was straightforward. If utility maximization meant only the benefits (material or otherwise) which accrued to an individual—whether or not they accrued to others—then those decisions which could be described as altruistic or idealistic would be considered irrational. Thus, it would be irrational for a wealthy individual to vote for a candidate who advocated higher taxes on the rich. The difficulty with such a judgment, however, is that it neglects the fact that different individuals have different values. A wealthy individual may feel that it is wrong for so few people to possess so much wealth and that justice demands a redistribution of material goods. Should that be considered "irrational"? Or, an individual may receive some kind of psychological satisfaction from helping others even though there is no material benefit involved—and perhaps there is even a material loss. Should such satisfaction be considered any less of a utility than, say, additional financial income?

The difficulty with extending the boundaries of the term *utility* is that there does not seem to be a natural limit. If anything which an individual does brings some benefit to him in some form, then there is no such thing as irrational behavior. Even apparently detrimental behavior can be explained by psychoanalysts as the satisfaction of a subconscious desire for certain kinds of gain.

The dilemma, then, for a theory of rational voting is that a narrow definition of utility excludes certain kinds of benefits which we feel are important in many decisions; while a limitless definition makes all behavior rational, thereby stripping the notion of its significance. One way out of this dilemma, of course, is to drop the notion of rationality altogether on the grounds that it is simply a label with normative connotations which does not add to our understanding of human behavior.

DOWNS'S THEORY OF ELECTORAL POLITICS

With these problems in mind, we shall turn to Anthony Downs's analysis of electoral politics. Downs begins by postulating a political system composed of voters and political parties. Voters, in his system, are rational, as described above, in the sense that they seek to maximize their utility. But Downs makes an important stricture. His voters are rational only to the extent that their decision to vote or abstain, and their particular party preference, are determined solely by the benefits they expect to receive from the policies which would be implemented if their party were elected. No other benefit or utility is to be considered. Thus, for example, it would be irrational for an individual to vote or abstain, or to vote for a particular party, simply to please a spouse. Here a clarification must be made. From the perspective of conjugal harmony, voting to please one's spouse certainly could be rational. For this reason, Downs distinguishes *political rationality* from rationality in general. The advantage of this distinction is that it avoids some of the problems mentioned above. By limiting the definition of rationality for purposes of analyzing a particular system (the political system) he obviates the need to define the concept for all activities.

Political parties in Downs's system are groups of individuals— *teams,* he calls them—who all share the same values and goals, and who seek election to office solely to obtain the perquisites of office for themselves, i.e., money, power, status, and so on. In other words, Downsian parties do not seek office in order to implement a particular policy. They will advocate any policy which attracts votes. The only restriction in Downs's system is that parties cannot "pass" each other in a one dimensional situation. That is, if party R takes a position to the "left" of party D on a single dimension then the two parties can move *toward* or *away* from each other, but cannot pass each other and reverse their position.

These two characteristics or parties in Downs's system—their *unity* and *desire for self-gain*—are certainly applicable to some parties in the real political world at some times; but as the only attributes they appear unrealistic. What Downs does is to ask what a political system would be like which contained such parties and politically rational voters. Surprisingly, the political systems which Downs shows to be based on these supposedly unrealistic assumptions are very much like those with which we are familiar in Western democracies. This result implies that a *rational* (suitably defined) *model* may be an appropriate explanatory device for electoral systems. On the other hand, one of the implications of Downs's analysis, which we shall describe in more detail below, is that *it is generally not rational for individuals to vote in national presidential elections.* This conclusion from the theory, however, does not seem to be supported by the empirical fact that a majority of the American electorate does vote in presidential elections. For if the theory suggests that voting is irrational, but if most individuals do vote, then either most individuals are irrational, the theory is wrong, or the notion of rationality must be redefined.

PARTIES AND VOTERS

In an election, then, voters are trying to determine whether to vote (and, if so, for whom) while parties are trying to determine voter preferences in order to adopt a policy position that will attract a majority of the votes. While there is no indication of how particular issues arise, Downs makes two important initial assumptions about issues and voter preference: (1) both parties and voters have *complete information* about the available issue positions and about voter preferences and party positions; (2) voter preferences are fixed, while party positions can vary within certain limitations. Both of these assumptions are unrealistic—the first obviously more so than the second—and are altered later in Downs's analysis. He begins with a simplified system, however, because it is easier to analyze.

To illustrate this simple model, assume that there are three voters, A, B, and C, and two parties, R and D. Assume further that a single issue, say nationalized welfare, dominates the election campaign, and that the voters are divided as in fig. 5.8.

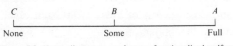

Figure 5.8. Voter alignments on degree of nationalized welfare.

The parties in turn, have initial positions on this issue based on their preferences as voters (the members of the party are, after all, voters even though in this example their votes are not counted). Downs, however, is not really clear about what determines this initial position. He simply posits voter preferences and party positions prior to any electoral maneuvering. Suppose, for example, that party R initially took a position halfway between that of C and B, while party D took a position halfway between A and B. Again, these initial positions are prior to ascertaining voter preferences.

This could be illustrated as in fig. 5.9.

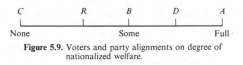

Figure 5.9. Voters and party alignments on degree of
nationalized welfare.

In such a situation, voter C's first choice is closer to the position of R than D, while A's first choice is closer to D than R. Voter B's first choice is equidistant from D and R. Now, recall that the highest utility for any voter is associated with that voter's first choice. Any other position has a lower utility. In our example, we also assume that voter preferences are single-peaked. This means, as we discussed above, that C's second choice must be position B (i.e., voter B's first choice), and C's third choice must be A (i.e., voter A's first choice). Similarly, A's second choice is B, and third choice

C. For B, the second choice could be either C or A, and this will determine the electoral strategy for both parties.

Clearly, voter C would vote for R, and A for D. This is because R is closer to C than D, and D is closer to A than R. In general, then, a voter's decision is based on the difference in utility between his or her own most preferred position and the position which either political party advocates. In symbols, this can be expressed:

$$U(A) - U(D); \text{ or } U(A) - U(R)$$

which is read, "the utility of voter A's most preferred position less the utility of the position advocated by party D or R." Or, more generally,

$$U(V_i) - U(P_j)$$

that is, the utility of voter i's (i.e., any voter's) first preference less the utility of the position of party j (any party) for voter i. If the two positions are the same, then $U(V_i) = U(P_j)$ and there is no difference between voter i's most preferred position and the position advocated by party j. As the party position moves farther from the voter's first choice, the utility (for the voter) declines, and the utility difference grows larger.

This utility calculation involves not only the benefits of a particular policy for the voter, but also the cost of voting. Now ordinarily the cost of voting is quite small, frequently involving only the time, energy, and expenditure of financial resources necessary to gather information about the candidates. For the present, however, we are assuming *complete and costless information*. This means that the voters know the position of all the parties, and the parties know the preferences of all the voters. Therefore, the only costs are those involved in voting.

An individual will vote for a particular party over another, then, if the utility difference between the voter's first preference and the position of one of the parties is smaller than the utility difference between the voter's first preference and the position of the other party. That is, if

$$[U(V_i) - U(P_j)] < [U(V_i) - U(P_k)]$$

Then, voter i will vote for party j rather than party k. In our example:

$$[U(C) - U(R)] < [U(C) - U(D)]; \text{ or, } U(R) - U(D) > 0$$

That is, the difference between the utility for C of C's first choice and party R's position is less than the difference between the utility for C of C's first choice and party D's position; or, the difference in utility for i between R's position and D's position is greater than zero. By implication, of course, R's position brings i greater utility than does D's position.

Suppose, however, that the utilities of the party positions for i are equal. (The difference between the utilities of the parties for a voter is what Downs called the *party differential*.) Under such conditions the rational voter should abstain, and thus save the cost of voting without affecting the benefits of subsequent policies. Downs refers to this situation as *abstention from indifference*. There is another condition which also results in abstention. Suppose the parties advocate different positions, or even the same position, but that the difference between the voter's most preferred position and the position of either party is so great that for all practical purposes the voter does not care who wins. In other words, the voter expects so little benefit from the victory of either party that it does not pay to vote. Presumably, such a situation arises when the cost of voting exceeds the benefits expected, or when

$$C > B$$

in which case there is no net utility.

It should also be noted that the electoral outcomes might actually bring added costs to the voter and not simply minimal amounts of positive utility. In such a case, not voting saves the costs of voting, but, of course, cannot prevent the costs of particular party policies.

Downs refers to abstention under such conditions as *abstention from alienation*. In his earlier discussion, however, he assumes that there are no abstentions—i.e., all eligible voters vote.

Returning to our example, then, each party would initially receive the one vote of the voter whose first preference was closest to its position. The pivotal voter, however, is B. Suppose that B is indifferent between positions A and C, i.e., suppose he feels that if a moderate nationalized-welfare policy cannot be introduced, then it does not matter whether a full policy is introduced or whether there is no nationalized welfare at all. Such a voter would be said to have a *symmetrical utility function* about position B. That is, as one moves away from position B either toward A or C, the utility for voter B declines at the same rate. The graph for this situation would be the same as that of fig. 5.4. above.

What would the parties do in such a situation if they wanted to win the election? Clearly, the only move for *both* parties is to alter their positions so that they are closer to B's first preference, i.e., R moves right, and D moves left, both moving toward the center. By "moving" we mean, simply, enunciating a somewhat different policy. Thus, for example, R may have announced initially that, while it advocates some nationalized welfare, it is inclined toward none at all. A policy "move" might be an announcement that it was leaning toward a moderate amount of nationalized welfare and away from a total rejection of the policy. Where abstention was possible, however, R would have to watch its left flank to see that it did not lose C's vote. As each party moves toward B, however, the other will have an incentive to move even closer to B in order to win B's vote. The situation is obviously one in which both parties are bidding for B's vote. The logical outcome is for *both* parties to adopt B's position since either party which adopts a position different from B's first choice will be defeated. Figure 5.10 shows the movement of R from R to R' and D from D to D'.

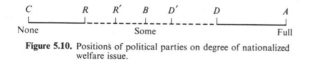

Figure 5.10. Positions of political parties on degree of nationalized welfare issue.

If we think of the positions along this dimension as alternatives, than it is clear that in terms of the electoral contest, position B defeats all other alternatives. Recall from chapter 1 that an alternative which defeats every other alternative is a Condorcet winner, and that if there is a Condorcet winner the situation is described as *stable,* or in *equilibrium;* and that the Condorcet winner is an *undominated outcome. In other words, electoral competition can be viewed as a search by political parties for a stable outcome in the same way that groups of decision makers in earlier chapters were searching for a Condorcet winner, or undominated policy alternative. This suggests an underlying structural similarity between electoral politics and policymaking.*

In electoral politics, a party position is also referred to as a *strategy* and, for this reason, the goal of political parties can be described as a search for a *winning strategy.* This is, of course, very similar to the way in which we ordinarily describe the activity of political parties.

What are the consequences, however, for a situation with an equilibrium strategy in a model of complete information? Here we see the importance of abstention. Suppose B, in our example, knows that both parties will adopt his position. In such a situation the party differential is zero and B should be indifferent. If abstention were allowed, B would abstain, but if the parties knew that B would abstain (there is complete information in our model) then they would have no incentive to move toward *B;* but, if B knew that the parties were not moving toward him, he would not abstain, and then the parties would have to move toward him . . . and so on. In other words, the possibility of abstention serves to *destabilize* a situation which has an equilibrium position without abstention, even in a situation of perfect information.

It could be argued that R and D should converge toward *B* whether B abstains or not. That is, *B* is an equilibrium position. This is true only if both A and C will vote with certainty when D and R are at *B*. That result, of course, would be a tie. The position *B,* then, would be an equilibrium but only if tie votes are stable. A more important counterargument is that, with abstention, either A or C might abstain if D or R moves toward *B*. In fact, as D and R move away from *A* and *C,* the probability of abstention increases. For that reason, if B abstains, D and R would want to move back toward *A* and *C* to prevent abstention by A and C. Presumably, however, since there is complete information, both D and R know whether or not they can move to *B*.

Without abstention, however, both parties would move toward *B*. Under such conditions, would a winner emerge? Presumably, some kind of technical device would have to be used to allow one party to choose the equilibrium position. For example, the rules (written or unwritten) might be that one party adopts a position first, and then the second party must choose a different position.

Downs does imply one such device in his assumption that the parties cannot pass each other along the single dimension. That is, if party R starts out to the left of D, it cannot end up on the right of D. Similarly, D cannot move to the left of R. Thus if D or R were given the first opportunity to take a position, either one could assure victory by moving beyond *B*. For example, R could move to the right of *B* and prevent D from adopting *B* (which would place it to the left of R); or if D moved first, it could adopt a position to the left of *B* thereby preventing R from taking position *B*.

Such devices, however, are artificial and do not solve the theoretical dilemma of cyclical strategies described above. This is similar to the situation in which a voter's paradox exists, but a winning alternative is imposed by a device such as the chairman's gambit or a time limit on the deliberations. In our example above, B would have no way of choosing between R and D if they converged to his position other than through some random device (flipping a coin) or the addition of information which would, in fact, differentiate the parties in terms of utility for B. The latter alternative, however, would violate our initial assumption that the election involved a single, one-dimensional issue, as well as our assumption that, in terms of utility to B, R and D were initially equivalent.

In the example above, we assumed that B was indifferent between A and C as a second choice. Suppose, however, that B preferred either A to C, or C to A; that is, either A had a higher utility for B than C, or C had a higher utility than A. This could be graphed as in fig. 5.11.

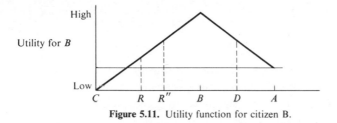

Figure 5.11. Utility function for citizen B.

In this case, A has a higher utility for B than C, and so B would initially prefer D to R. This would force R to move toward B, past position R'' which would have the same utility as D. At that point, however, D would begin to move toward B and we would be back to the same situation as above. In other words, it does not matter whether B's utility function is symmetrical. The outcome will still be theoretically unstable. It should be pointed out that if the set of alternatives is continuous, and if the utility function is continuous, then all the orderings of the set of alternatives must be weak, since an individual will be indifferent between any pair of alternatives which are equidistant from his or her first preference. A *continuous* set of alternatives is one in which there is an alternative at every point along a numerical scale. Moreover, since there are an infinite number of such points, the number of alternatives is infinite. A continuous utility function, then, is one which assigns a certain level of utility for every alternative in that infinite set.

A finite set of alternatives is said to be *discontinuous* or *discrete,* as is the utility function which characterizes that set. It is convenient to visualize a continuous function as a solid line, and a discrete function as a set of points with gaps between them.

Suppose, however, that we allow abstention based on alienation and construct an ordering of the alternatives for A or C in such a way that R or D are constrained in their movement toward B as we suggested above. This could come about by postulating that either A or C feel so strongly about their first preference that the utility of B for them is virtually zero, or at least less than the cost of voting. In such a case we would say that A or C are *extremists*. A graph of such an extremist position might be as in fig. 5.12.

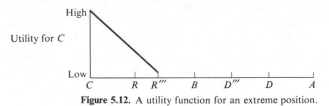

Figure 5.12. A utility function for an extreme position.

Here the utility for C falls to virtually zero at point R''' ("R triple prime") and party R cannot move beyond that point without causing C to abstain. Party D, then, can move to some point toward B beyond D''' (which is exactly the same distance from B as R''') and win the election.

This conclusion supports our ordinary political notion that extremist support for political parties is brittle (or elastic, as the economists say) in the sense that it will not tolerate deviation from a fixed position. *But notice that this result is based on rational or economic assumptions. In other words, by assuming that voters are politically rational, and that political parties are homogenous teams of office seekers who adopt policy positions simply to win elections, we deduce the well-known political conclusion that extremist parties do not compromise their political position. In this case, however, such inflexibility is shown to be a requirement of political survival rather than the product of an alleged extremist mentality.*

Let us review the elements of our electoral model and the results so far. There are three rational voters, two political parties, and an election involving one, unidimensional (single dimension) issue. There is complete information, abstention (or no abstention), and *utility functions* with different characteristics. By "utility function" we mean the relationship between a particular issue position along our single dimension, and the utility of that position for any particular voter. A utility function, then, is a *set of points* which indicate the level of utility to be associated with particular issue positions. Recall that in chapter 1, a social welfare function was a decision rule which designated a subset (choice set) from among a set of alternatives. *A utility function is a rule that relates a set of issue positions to a set of utility values.* One such rule, or characteristic, is *symmetry*. Let us assume an individual's utility function is symmetric. If so, all issue positions at the same distance from the most preferred position in each direction are equal in terms of utility. The term "each direction" applies to unidimensional models such as we have been discussing. In an *n*-dimensional model we would simply speak of "any direction." For example, in a two-dimensional model, an indifference curve[6] (that is, a set of points which have equal utility for a particular voter) generated by a symmetrical utility function would be a circle about a point (the most preferred position). Any movement away from that point in any direction would result in a lower utility, and any two points which were equidistant from that point would have the same utility for the individual. Moreover, any set of points which were equidistant from the most preferred position would be of equal utility for an individual. This is shown graphically in fig. 5.13.

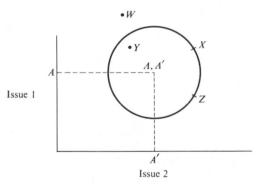

Figure 5.13. An indifference curve for two dimensions.

Point (A,A') is individual A's most preferred position in this two-dimensional space. The points on the circle around (A,A') are all equidistant from (A,A'), and are therefore of equal utility for A. This set of points, then,

6. "Indifference" here does not mean that the individual does not care; but, rather, cares equally about the alternatives.

which constitutes the circle around (A,A') is one of individual A's indifference curves. (*Question:* Is point Y higher or lower in utility for A than points X and Z? Is point W higher or lower in utility than Y?) Any point on the circle is preferred by A to any point *outside* the circle; but any point *inside* the circle is preferred by A to any point on or outside the circle.

An asymmetrical utility function would be one in which equal distances in opposite directions from a most preferred position are not necessarily associated with the same level of utility. Figures 5.2 and 5.3 are examples of an asymmetric utility function for one dimension. (*Question:* What would be the shape of one possible indifference curve for a two-dimensional asymmetric utility function?)

In our one-dimensional model, the symmetric utility function is, simply, two lines sloping down toward the axis from a most preferred point at the same angle, as in fig. 5.14.

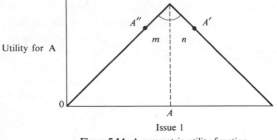

Figure 5.14. A symmetric utility function.

Here, angle m equals angle n, and point A' has the same utility as point A''.

SUMMARY

There are, then, six basic variables in our model so far (a "variable" is an element which can assume different values or change in some way):

1. Number of voters
2. Number of political parties
3. Information (complete or incomplete)
4. Number of issues
5. Abstention (or no abstention; also, type of abstention)
6. Utility functions (symmetrical or asymmetrical; single-peaked, etc.)

Basically, we are concerned with the relationship between these variables and the existence of a dominant position, or equilibrium. So far, our model has consisted of three individuals, two parties, a single one-dimensional issue, and complete information. We have varied the abstention variable, and the characteristics of the utility functions. Our results are as follows:

1. When abstention is not allowed, and when all utility functions are symmetric, there is a dominant position or a single equilibrium point. In our example, this point was position B in the center of the scale.

2. Despite the existence of such an equilibrium point, it appears that one of the parties could win the election only if there were some kind of artificial device to prevent some parties from adopting the equilibrium point simultaneously. The problem here is that an equilibrium point is the same thing as a dominant or winning strategy; but if there can be only one winner in that election then this strategy must be unavailable to all but one candidate or party. With perfect information and symmetrical utility functions, this can only be done through some kind of arbitrary rule which, in essence, imposes a winner.

3. When abstention is allowed, with symmetrical utility functions, a cycle of strategies will result, in which both parties first converge toward the center, but then diverge when the individual in the center abstains from indifference, and then converge again toward the center when the individual in the center is forced by that divergence of the parties not to abstain as his party differential rises above zero. With such assumptions, and without arbitrary devices to stop it, such a cycle cannot be halted.

4. When absentention is allowed, when utility functions can be asymmetric, and when some voters are extremists—i.e., their utility functions fall sharply to zero as one moves any distance away from their most preferred position—the party which does not represent the extremists can win by adopting the dominant strategy and without artificial devices. This is because the party which must count on the votes of the extremists is limited in its capacity to acquire new votes by modifying its position.

Do not forget, the above results apply so far only to situations in which there are three voters, one single-dimensional policy issue, and perfect information. Our next step is to alter these conditions to see whether these results will still hold.

N Voters

Let us increase the number of voters in our model to any large number (thousands, millions, etc.). Then we would want to know the distribution of these voters' first preferences across a particular issue dimension. Such a distribution is referred to in the literature as a *preference density function*. A sample distribution is shown in fig. 5.15.

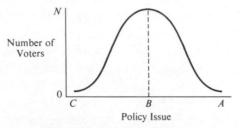

Figure 5.15. Normal distribution of preferences.

This is the so-called "normal curve" or "bell-shaped" curve which is familiar in statistics. It illustrates a situation in which most voters have as their first preference a position just to the left or right of B. Figure 5.15 is also meant to illustrate a symmetrical distribution (or preference density function) in the sense that half the voters are situated to the left of B, half are situated to the right, and every position which is equidistant from B is associated with the same number of voters.[7]

This distribution is also *unimodal* in the sense that it has a single "mode." In statistics, a mode is the most frequent value of a set of numbers. Preference density functions can also be *bimodal* as in fig. 5.16.

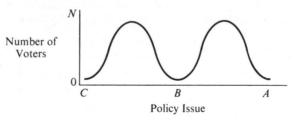

Figure 5.16. Bimodal distribution of preferences.

7. Recall that in a symmetric individual utility function, every issue position which was equidistant from the individual's most preferred position was associated with the same level of utility.

In this case, the greatest number of voters is concentrated at the extremes rather than in the center. A society characterized by such a distribution of voters may be said to be *polarized*.

Finally, a preference density function can be *multimodal* as in fig. 5.17.

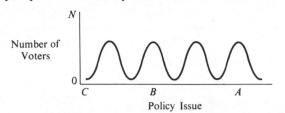

Figure 5.17. Multimodal distribution of preferences.

In analyzing these different voter distributions, Downs suggests that parties facing a unimodal distribution would tend to converge toward the center. This, of course, is said to be characteristic of the American party system where the Republican and Democratic parties appear desperate to beat each other to the middle ground in any Presidential election.

The bimodal distribution, on the other hand, should produce a situation in which two parties take positions at the extremes, and do not converge toward the center. Finally, a multimodal distribution would be the basis of a multiparty system. That is, with voters clustered at several positions along a single dimension, two parties would not be sufficient to keep many voters from abstaining. Additional parties would develop in order to satisfy voters at the several modes.

Notice that in our analysis of situations with a large number of voters, we have introduced a seventh variable, and that is the *shape of the preference density function*. The interesting result here has been that *both the type of party system (i.e., two-party or multiparty) and the strategies of parties in a two-party system (i.e., whether to converge or diverge) are heavily dependent upon the distribution of preferences*. In Downs's words, "it is clear that the numerical distribution of voters along the political scale determines to a great extent what kind of democracy will develop" (p. 121).

THE EFFECTS OF UNCERTAINTY

So far, in our model we have assumed complete information—voters knew for certain the positions of the parties, and the parties knew the preferences and utility functions of the voters. This is, of course, an unrealistic assumption, and one which we shall now alter.

If voters are uncertain about parties, (a) they do not know for certain the position of the parties on particular issues; (b) they do not know for certain whether parties would in fact implement policies they espouse during an election campaign; and (c) they do not know for certain whether the policies they do favor will in fact benefit them as they expect.

If parties are uncertain about voters, they do not know for certain the preference density or utility functions of the electorate. Uncertainty for parties also means that they do not know the electoral strategy of their opponents.

The initial effect of uncertainty on voters is that they cannot calculate their policy distance from the parties, or the party differential, with certainty. This means that they must obtain information in order to reduce the uncertainty. But, gathering information can be costly in time, effort, and financial resources. Moreover, even with additional information, the voter is still uncertain not only about the policy distances and party differential, but also about whether the level of uncertainty has been reduced. For example, suppose a voter spends the time, effort, and money needed to gather information about parties R and D, and concludes, tentatively, that party R is closer to his position than party D. Nevertheless, the voter must also make a judgment about the quality of the acquired information. If the information is wrong, his conclusion about R and D is also likely to be wrong. The voter is then forced to spend more resources checking the reliability of his information. But this process is never-ending. By definition, there is no point at which the voter becomes certain of his information. Therefore, the voter is in the position of a scientist who must constantly gather information, make inferences, check and recheck his conclusions, develop theories, and test his results against the theory.

Now, the question is, Should a rational voter become a "political" scientist? Would the potential payoff justify such an effort? Let us put this question aside and ask a logically prior question. Suppose a voter somehow knew with 99 percent accuracy (whatever that may mean) that party R was closer to her position than party D, and that this conclusion followed an expensive process of investigation. Now, one question is whether the utility for the voter which would come from a victory for R would be greater than the cost of information gathering. If the benefit does not exceed the cost, it would be irrational for the voter to make the effort. But, more importantly, especially in a two-party sysem, *Would it matter whether an individual voted?* Suppose our political scientist voter becomes fully informed and her candidate loses? Then she will have expended considerable resources but will have received no benefit at all—although if her calculations are faulty, the voter may think that her best candidate has lost, when quite the opposite may have occurred. The rational voter, then, must not only decide whether or not to expend resources to become informed, but also whether, even if well-informed, her vote would have an effect on the outcome of the election. If the vote did not affect the outcome, it would be irrational to vote. Let us look for a moment at the choices and outcomes facing a voter. A voter has only three choices when two parties are involved: to vote for one of the parties or to abstain. There are several outcomes of the election:

1. R wins (and would have won without V's vote).
2. R wins (but would have lost without V's vote).
3. D wins (and would have won without V's vote).
4. D wins (but would have lost without V's vote).
5. Tie (V votes).
6. Tie (V abstains).

In the case of (1) and (3), V's vote does not affect the outcome. In (2), (4), (5), and (6), V is crucial to the outcome—the outcome changes if V either changes his vote, or changes his decision to vote or abstain. In those cases V is called the *pivot*, since he is pivotal to the outcome.

While there are more instances in which V can be pivotal, the important question is whether such instances are more or less probable than those in which V's vote is irrelevant to the outcome. Given a large electorate (and 70 million voters cast ballots in American presidential elections), it seems safe to say that the possibility of a tie is virtually zero. It seems equally safe to assume that no one voter will be pivotal to the outcome, since this would imply that there are an odd number of voters and that one party wins by only one vote. If the probability of a tie is virtually zero, the probability of both an odd number of voters and a victory by one vote must also be very close to zero. If this reasoning is correct it would appear to follow that *it is irrational for a voter either to expend resources in becoming informed, or to vote, on the grounds that what she receives, or does not receive, as benefits is unrelated to her vote.* In symbolic terms this can be shown as follows:

$$B(P) - C = U$$

where P is the probability of any one voter's affecting the outcome, or being pivotal to the outcome. Since P is a very small fraction (near zero), the costs will outweight the benefits unless the cost of voting (C) is very small. But, since we are now dealing with a world of uncertainty, C also includes the cost of acquiring information and, therefore, must be fairly substantial. For that reason, costs will be greater than the benefits and the rational voter should abstain.

This result has bothered everyone, including Downs himself, for two reasons. First, if it is irrational to vote, then the relatively large turnout in American presidential elections cannot be explained except by saying that a great many voters are irrational. To most writers in the field, this has not been a very satisfactory explanation. Second, the rational voter should also reason that other rational voters will come to the conclusion that it is irrational to vote and, if all voters are rational, no one will vote. In such a situation, our rational voter would be the only voter if he voted, and would decide the election himself. But, if all other voters were rational they would be reasoning in the same way and they too would vote in an attempt to be the sole and deciding vote. At that point it would become rational to abstain, but then, . . . etc. In other words, the decision to vote could be seen as the attempt by rational voters to outwit other rational voters and become the sole vote, while abstentions could be explained as the rational conclusion by some rational voters that many other rational voters will choose to vote, and that the probability of affecting such an election will be infinitesimal. This explanation views *all* voting as rational, saying simply that those rational voters who vote are gambling on being the sole vote,[8] while those who abstain view the probability of being the sole vote as very small.

A more common way of explaining the relatively large American presidential turnout, without simply consigning it to the realm of the irrational, has been to posit some kind of *psychic benefit* or satisfaction which voters receive simply from participating in the democratic process. In this sense, voting is a social act in which voters affirm their allegiance to the community or to their party. By this reasoning, even if there is no direct policy benefit from the election of a particular candidate (or, even if the opposing candidate wins) the psychic benefit outweighs the cost of voting (and, pre-

---

8. See our discussion below of the "minimax regret" decision rule for individual voters.

sumably, the cost of becoming informed). By including such personal satisfaction as part of the utility calculation, voting on a large scale can be viewed as having a rational foundation. Of course, as Downs defines political rationality, psychic satisfaction cannot count as a benefit, since it is not a direct result of governmental policy.

Another type of explanation which has been suggested, is that voters reason as follows: "Suppose everyone thinks like I do, and no one votes. What will happen to the political system?" In other words, while the Downsian rational voter decides to abstain, he hopes (and assumes) that most other voters will vote. But, if they are also rational, why should they vote? Because of this reasoning, the rational voter adopts a kind of Kantian ethical principle and votes on the grounds that he would want everyone to vote in order to preserve the system. Of course, it must be assumed that the preservation of the system is beneficial. Voting itself, then, is an indication that the existence of a particular political system does bring benefits, even if they are not the direct governmental benefits of the Downsian rational voter.

IDEOLOGY, ACTIVISTS, AND POLITICAL LEADERSHIP

One of the most interesting results of uncertainty in Downs's model is that it leads to the development of ideologies. *An ideology is a general view of what the world should be like and the kind of governmental policies which should be implemented in order to bring about such a world.* For example, socialist ideologies call for relative equality in the distribution of goods and services in a society, and a system in which the important economic decisions are made by the government, which is controlled by the people through democratic decision-making processes. The traditional capitalist ideology urges limited government involvement in the economy, and a system of individual enterprise and freedom in which the success or failure of an individual is determined by his own efforts. Both ideologies, of course, argue that their approach is better—more fair, more productive, more humane, and so on.

In Downs's model, the development of such ideologies is a direct result of uncertainty. That is, since it is irrational for a voter in an uncertain world to become fully informed, he must either forgo any serious attempt to gather information, or find some kind of substitute. One kind of substitute is ideology. An ideology provides a general image or world view and, presumably, the party which espouses a particular ideology will implement policies designed to realize that world view. The voter's task, then, is reduced to comparing his ideology with that of the political parties in deciding how to vote.

Uncertainty also produces voters of different levels of information, and different levels of commitment to the political parties. Downs distinguishes among these and argues that political activists are those with higher levels of information and commitment. Their function is to persuade voters who are less informed and less committed. Interestingly, this theoretical conclusion finds support in the empirical studies of the American electorate, which show that voters who are more informed also tend to be more strongly committed to a particular political party.

Downs's model suggests that political leadership itself is a function of uncertainty. Leadership here is defined as the "ability to influence voters to adopt certain views as expressing their own will" (p. 87). Leaders are those "with influence over voters—usually not full control of their votes, but at least some impact on their views about the best policies for parties to espouse" (*Ibid.*). *In this sense, political leadership can only exist in an uncertain world.*

One of the obvious dangers of uncertainty is irresponsibility in goverment—if voters do not know what government is doing, certain groups will be given favors, and others will be discriminated against. Downs suggests that while this is true to an extent, there are nevertheless inherent limitations on governmental irresponsibility or, even, corruption. First, the existence of party competition limits government discrimination. Presumably, the party out of power will ferret out corruption and mismanagement, and publicize it during the election campaign, as well as during the period between elections. Second, governments can practice favoritism within limits, but certain kinds of policies have effects which are felt so directly by the voters that they cannot be hidden. Thus, for example, government can, with relative impunity, favor certain companies when giving out lucrative contracts, but cannot very well hide major changes in rates of taxation, social-security benefits, military-conscription policies, or subsidies to farmers.

Uncertainty, then, has two effects which seem to pull in opposite directions. On the one hand, it allows governments to treat citizens differently, i.e., to favor certain groups. On the other hand, it requires governments to try to be consistent and fair at least in general, as part of a need to convince relatively uninformed citizens that the party represents their ideology.

The picture of the political system we are sketching is remarkably like the American political system: voters with little political information; general party orientations or ideologies; political leaders and activists trying to convince voters that they represent their interest; "patriotic" voting; and the coexistence of political favoritism with some degree of consistency, honesty, and responsibility on the part of the government. The point to stress, however, is that this system was deduced from an assumption of rationality on the part of voters and parties. *In other words, it appears as if the American voter and the American political parties are rational utility maximizers whose decisions are based on a cost-benefit analysis and on estimates of the behavior of the other members of the political system.* The thrust of Downs's point is that few people have ever argued that a *rational* political system would look like ours! Instead, we are more accustomed to stress the *irrationality* of our system, and to urge rational policies and political activities. Downs shows that the present system *is* the product of rational behavior, given a certain definition of the term *rational.* Our natural resistance to such a conclusion is probably based on our feeling that the American political system cannot possibly be rational in any meaningful sense of the term, and that rational governmental policy would have to be superior to the present policies. Downs's analysis, however, shows that the notion of rationality implied by such a conclusion would have to be one which meant imposing the views of an omniscient policymaker who somehow knew what was best for all of us. Presumably, if such an individual or group of individuals existed, it would be "rational"—even from Downs's perspective—to let that individual or group make all of our decisions. The analysis of the voter's paradox in previous chapters, however, suggests that such policies could not emerge from the aggregation of individual preferences, but would represent a severe form of paternalism.

REACTIONS TO DOWNS

One of the major criticisms of Downs was his use of a single dimension in analyzing party strategies. Researchers at the University of Michigan's Survey Research Center pointed out that their extensive studies showed no such single ideological dimension in American electoral politics, nor any common frame of reference for parties and electorate. As Stokes (1963) put it:

"We may, in fact, have as many perceived spaces as there are perceiving actors" (p. 375). As a result, a number of subsequent studies (Davis, Hinich, Ordeshook, et al.) has assumed that there could be many dimensions in the policy space. The thrust of this work has been mainly to determine party strategies for "*n* dimensions" (any number of dimensions) and to determine whether equilibria exist. It has not been concerned with the broader issues of political leadership, ideologies, and so on. One of the important concerns of this work, then, has been to determine the characteristics of multidimensional models as opposed to undimensional models.

One of the major results of this work is to confirm Downs's argument that parties will converge toward the center where the preference density function is unimodal:

Davis and Hinich demonstrate the dominance of the mean when all eligible citizens vote. Our analysis proves that the mean continues to dominate the strategic considerations of the candidates when abstentions from alienation are permitted. (Hinich and Ordeshook, 1969, p. 90)

The mean, of course, is the center of a symmetric, unimodal preference density function. On the other hand, this work also shows that there are other important considerations in determining party strategy in addition to the number of issues. For example, one of the best known articles in this literature, Hinich and Ordershook's (1970) "Plurality Maximization vs. Vote Maximization," points out that the goal of candidates is not always to *maximize votes* but may be to *maximize plurality*. To "maximize votes" means, simply, to focus on obtaining as many votes as possible without regard to the votes of competing candidates. To "maximize plurality" means to try to maximize the difference in the vote between oneself and the nearest competitor. In a two-party system, maximizing votes and maximizing plurality are equivalent since, by trying to obtain as many votes as possible, a candidate is also putting the maximum distance between himself and the other candidate. In a multicandidate election, however, such as an American presidential primary, or a French Assembly election, the goal may be to beat one's nearest rival by as great a margin as possible in order to establish oneself as the most popular of the candidates. In terms of party strategy, a vote-maximizing candidate, in either a two-party or multiparty contest, would try to take the position closest to the first preference of as many voters as possible. A plurality-maximizing candidate would focus more on a particular segment of the electorate, and would be less concerned with the preferences of all voters. Such a situation is common in American presidential primaries, where candidates tend to be more concerned with beating particular rivals. Thus, a moderate Republican would be most concerned about the challenge of a conservative Republican in the primary, while in a general election such a candidate would be more concerned about the broad spectrum of the American electorate.

In any case, Hinich and Ordeshook assume that the goals of candidates in these two situations will be different, and that the difference in goals leads to different conclusions about the behavior of the candidates. Thus

. . . we conclude that although plurality maximizing candidates converge, vote maximizing candidates do *not* converge under some identical conditions. We also demonstrate that, for suitable conditions, if candidates mazimize votes, the strategies the candidates prefer are sensitive to uniform variations in the cost of voting; if candidates maximize plurality, however, such variations in cost do not affect preferred strategies. (*Ibid.*, p. 773)

They demonstrate further that candidates might not only differ in terms of whether they seek to maximize votes or plurality, but also in terms of whether they have "mixed motives," i.e., whether they might also be trying to elicit financial support by adopting certain positions. Under such conditions, "two competing candidates who maximize plurality might diverge from the mean of a symmetric, unimodal preference density" (*Ibid.*).

In other words, while the number of issues does not affect Downs's conclusion that candidates converge toward the center of a symmetric, unimodal preference density function, both the number of parties (candidates) and the motives of the parties (candidates) may produce a situation in which rational parties (candidates) move away from the center. Similarly, Davis, Hinich, and Ordeshook (1970, p. 442) conclude that rational candidates generally converge even when preference density functions are bimodal:

Downs offers the intuitively satisfying but mathematically unproved proposition that whenever preferences are distributed bimodally, the forces of abstention prohibit rational candidates from converging. Our analysis demonstrates, however, that this proposition generally is false. . . .

This conclusion is related to still another variable, and that is the *sensitivity of turnout to variations in strategy:*

Candidates diverge when preferences are bimodally distributed and when alienation causes abstentions only if the sensitivity of turnout to variations in strategy is sufficiently great. Bimodal distributions and abstentions caused by alienation, then, are not sufficient conditions for nonconvergence (*Ibid.*, p. 443)

The authors admit that "sufficiently great" is imprecise, and, in fact, suggest that

The incentives for convergence or divergence are sensitive to so many parameters of $f(x)$ and of turnout that generalization appears impossible. (*Ibid.*, p. 443)

This rather startling conclusion is qualified somewhat:

We can generalize only by stating that, as the sensitivity of turnout increases, the incentive for nonconvergence increases if $f(x)$ (the preference density function) is bimodal. (*Ibid.*)

The notion of sensitivity of turnout is related to the so-called *loss function*. A loss function is the *relationship between a citizen's most preferred position and all other possible positions*. In our one-dimensional example above, we pointed out that the utility of any position other than the most preferred for any individual was less than the utility of that most preferred position. In figures 5.11 and 5.12 we illustrated two different utility curves for positions other than the most preferred. At that time we said simply that the utility for any individual declined as the distance from his most preferred position increased.[9] We did note, however, that the decline could be sharp if the intensity of the first preference was high, or it could be gradual if the intensity of the first preference was low. The slope of the loss function, however, is not necessarily related to the intensity of the first preference. It is conceivable that an individual could have a relatively high utility for his first preference and relatively high preferences for his or her other alternatives, in which case the slope of the loss function would not be steep. This happy situation, however, is probably unusual. *The set of declining utilities is the individual's loss function.* The *sensitivity* of the loss function is said to be *greater* if the slope is sharper, i.e., if the utility falls at a *more rapid rate* as one moves away from the individual's most preferred position. And, if abstention is allowed, an individual will abstain if the utility which could accrue from the policies of any (either) of the candidates is so low that it is outweighed by the cost of voting, information gathering, and so on. The

9. Davis, Hinich, and Ordeshook (1970), p. 432, define the loss function more specifically as the *square* of the distance between the individual's position and that of the candidates.

sensitivity of turnout, then, in any election, is the loss functions of all voters. If the sensitivity of turnout to variations in candidate strategy is high, this means that the candidates cannot make significant changes in their positions without causing many voters to abstain. Under such conditions, candidates would not converge to the center of a bimodal distribution of preferences. On the other hand, if the sensitivity of turnout to variations in strategy is *low,* candidates can change their positions rather significantly without losing votes and so will converge even when preferences are distributed bimodally. This is an important qualification of Down's conclusion about candidate strategies in the presence of bimodal preference distributions.

Sensitivity of turnout also has an interesting affect on candidate behavior if the preference density function is unimodal:

If both candidates maximize votes, if citizens abstain because of alienation, and if $f(x)$ is the multivariate (i.e., more than one issue) normal density, then an equilibrium exists; and if the sensitivity of turnout to variations in strategy is sufficiently *low* [note!] the candidates do not converge. (Hinich and Ordeshook, p. 781)

Recall that vote maximization occurs when candidates focus on the total vote, and that the multivariate normal density is unimodal. This result says that *sensitivity of turnout to variation in candidate strategy does not always have the same effect.* Above, we saw that a *low* sensitivity of turnout allowed candidates to *converge* to the center of a bimodal distribution of preferences. Now we see that *vote maximizing* candidates do *not* converge when the preference density function is unimodal if the sensitivity of turnout is *low* where there is more than one issue.

The thrust of this work, then, has been to demonstrate that the electoral situation is more complicated than Downs has suggested, and that the conclusions about party or candidate behavior depend upon the assumptions about the goals of the candidates (e.g., vote maximization or plurality maximization), the shape of individual utility functions (loss functions), and the distribution of first preferences in a population (preference density function). The problem is that there are virtually no limitations on the possible combinations of these variables in all of their forms, or, indeed, in the inclusion of additional variables. For that reason, a variety of simplifying assumptions has generally been made which are as "unrealistic" as Downs's one-dimensional assumption, but which make a model easier to analyze. Davis, Hinich, and Ordeshook (1970), for example, make the following assumptions:

1. All voters have a *preferred position for every dimension*. In other words, no citizen is so unconcerned about an issue that he has no preference on that issue.
2. All voters use the *same indices to measure any given policy*. This means that different voters will not use different criteria in judging the same issue.
3. All voters make *identical estimates of the candidates' positions*. This is a very controversial assumption which says that there will be no misperception about the policy stands of the candidates, despite the well-known attempts of most elected politicians to cloud many of their positions, and despite the well-known empirical finding that most voters are ill-informed, and that levels of information vary considerably among voters.
4. Candidates are assumed to have *perfect spatial mobility*. That is, they can take any possible position on an issue regardless of previous commitments or the stand of any opponent. This means that a McGovern-type candidate could take a hawkish stand on the Vietnam War, and a Barry Goldwater could advocate socialized medicine.
5. All voters assign the *same relative weight to any dimension*. This means that no issue is any more important to one individual than another. "The model does not allow some citizens to be concerned while others do not care whether or not schools are integrated" (p. 434). Further, they assume that there is some average level of concern for each issue, and that this concern is not related to preference. That is, an individual who supports integration of public schools is not assumed to have a greater or lesser concern for that issue than one who opposes integration.

There are also simplifications regarding utility functions. For example, it is sometimes assumed that *all utility functions or loss functions have the same shape for all individuals*. This does not mean that all individuals have the same first preference, but that the utility of all alternatives at the same distance from the first preference is the same for all individuals. Such a situation can be described by saying that, for all individuals, the utility loss associated with any position is equal to the *square of the distance* between that position and an individual's first choice. This means that if an alternative is, say, twice the distance from the most preferred position (optimum), the utility loss associated with that alternative would be four times that of the first preference. Obviously, this is only one of a great many relations which could exist between the utility loss of an alternative and its distance from the first choice. For example, the utility loss could also be the cube of the distance, or it could be directly proportional to the distance, in which case the utility loss would be one unit for every unit of distance from the first preference.

Regardless of the specific formulation, however, any relationship between utility values and the distance from the first preference in which the utility declines as a function of the distance is said to be *concave*. The reason for this terminology is that a graph of such a relationship for a single dimension is concave, with a single peak, such as the normal distribution mentioned above.

EQUILIBRIUM POINTS

One of the questions asked in spatial modeling is, as described above, whether electoral candidates will converge or diverge along any issue dimensions. Another question, however, which relates to our discussion in earlier chapters of the voter's paradox, is whether there is a *single* dominant position—that is, a position guaranteed to attract the most votes and win the election. Such a position would be an *equilibrium point,* or a stable, undominated outcome. Earlier in this chapter, we noted that there could be such a point, and that a situation could arise in which one of the candidates was prevented from adopting that position because of limitations on spatial mobility (the candidates could not "pass" one another on a single dimension) or because abstentions owing to alienation would reduce their vote as they altered their position. Subsequently, the assumption of perfect spatial mobility eliminated that problem, but it still left the problem of whether every situation had a "pure" equilibrium—that is, a dominant outcome for any candidate.

In certain situations there is always a pure equilibrium. For example, for symmetric, *unidimensional* unimodal distributions of preferences, the pure equilibrium is the *mean.* On the other hand, Davis, Hinich, and Ordeshook (1970) conclude that *dominant strategies generally do not exist in a multidimensional world* (p.438). This is equivalent to suggesting that *the voter's paradox is also an important element in the electoral process where parties or candidates are the alternatives*. In order to see this more clearly, consider the simple situation depicted in fig. 5.18, where there are three voters, two issues, and three candidates.

Here V_1, V_2, and V_3 are voters, while the half-circles drawn near each voter are the indifference curves which we mentioned above. That is, every

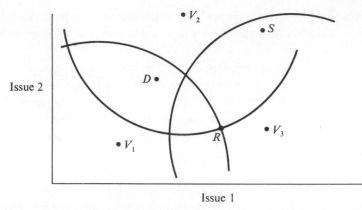

Figure 5.18. Voter's paradox with three voters, two issues, and three candidates.

point on the curves is the same distance from the voter and, therefore, has the same utility for him or her. Any point closer to the voter, i.e., within the half circle, has a higher utility for that voter. Thus, position R is on the intersection of the indifference curves of V_1 and V_2, while position D is on the inside of the half-circles for voters V_1 and V_2. Therefore, V_1 and V_2 will prefer D to R. Position S, on the other hand, is closer to V_2 and V_3 than is D. Therefore, V_2 and V_3 prefer S to D. But, V_3 and V_1 prefer R to S. (Note that R is on an indifference curve which is closer to V_3 than is S, and is also on an indifference curve closer to V_1.) Summarizing, then,

$$V_1 \text{ and } V_2 \text{ prefer } D \text{ to } R$$
$$V_2 \text{ and } V_3 \text{ prefer } S \text{ to } D$$
$$V_3 \text{ and } V_1 \text{ prefer } R \text{ to } S$$

In other words, the collective preference relation (using majority rule) is $D>R>S>D$, and we have a cyclical majority. No matter which of the three positions were to be adopted by either of two candidates, a majority of the voters would prefer another position. Now, in a real election, parties would have to adopt a position, and at some arbitrary point the voting would take place. Then the parties could no longer maneuver. At that point a winner would emerge even though that "winning position" was not the majority choice. To see this more clearly, suppose that just before the election, one party had adopted position S to counter and defeat position D, which the other party had taken to counter the first party's original position R. Then, the first party would be elected even though a majority preferred R to S. The existence of such a time limit assumes that in practice a party will be elected even if a cyclical majority over the alternatives exists. Since we have discussed this problem above, we shall not raise it again at this point.

A PROBABILISTIC MODEL

In the spatial models we have discussed so far, there have been several possible outcomes, depending on the assumptions employed. Some situations have had a so-called *unique or pure equilibrium point*. This is a position which assures the greatest possible vote for any party which adopts that position. If such an equilibrium exists, both (or all) parties converge toward that point. Theoretically, a voting situation in which every party adopts the same unique equilibrium position should produce a tie or a victory for one party based on some tie-breaking device. That is, voters would be indifferent among the parties, and would either abstain or use some random device to choose among them.

Another kind of equilibrium involves a situation where different parties adopt different positions. One party wins, the other(s) lose(s), but the losing party(ies) can do no better, given the preference density function of the electorate, individual utility functions, and so on.

A third kind of situation we have discussed is one in which there is no equilibrium. That is, no matter which position a party chooses, there is another position which defeats that position. As in the voter's paradox case, such a situation is inherently unstable.

All of these situations in the spatial model literature assume a certain relationship between the utility which any voter associates with a particular position, and the decision to vote for a particular candidate. More specifically, if the utility which voter A associates with the position taken by candidate D is greater than the utility which voter A associates with the position taken by candidate R, then A votes for D for certain if he or she votes—i.e., if he or she does not abstain. There is no chance that A will vote for R under the circumstances just described. In other words, if an individual votes, he or she votes for the candidate "nearest" to him or her with a probability of 1.

Some interesting work by Hinich, Ledyard, and Ordeshook (1973), however, has suggested a probabilistic model whose basic assumption is that *any voter has a probability* p, *greater than zero, of voting for a candidate whose issue position would provide that voter with less utility than that of another candidate.* This unusual assumption, together with theorems on the existence of unique equilibria, attempt to provide an explanation for the victory of any one candidate when there is a unique equilibrium point toward which both (all) candidates should converge.

Before describing the assumptions and theorems of this model, we should consider more closely the basic notion of probabilistic voting. It would seem irrational for a voter to vote for a less preferred candidate. The explanation which Hinich, Ledyard, and Ordeshook offer is that the candidate may be less preferred on the basis of a particular issue position—or set of issue positions—but more preferred on some nonissue position such as personality:

In lieu of relegating such acts to the realm of the irrational, however, observe that it is difficult, and perhaps, impractical to represent many of the criteria citizens use to evaluate candidates—such as the candidates' personalities—in spatial terms. Instead of attempting to conceptualize and to measure such criteria so that we can represent them as spatial dimensions, [our] assumption(s) . . . allow us to leave considerations like the candidates' personalities as variables that are exogenous to spatial analysis. Thus, while the citizen prefers ψ to θ [positions of candidates 2 and 1, respectively] for the identified spatial dimensions, he may vote for candidate one because of the positive weight he assigns to the candidate's personality. We require only that personality act as a random variable so that the citizen votes for candidate one probabilistically. (p. 165)

One of the conceptual difficulties with this analysis is that it brings variables such as personality into a theory which assumes that issue positions determine behavior. Some theorists consider such a move legitimate, but I have argued elsewhere (Abrams, 1973) that it is inconsistent.

There is another problem. Hinich, Ledyard, and Ordeshook assume that the probability of individual A's voting for candidate 1 increases as the utility of 1's position increases for him. This sounds reasonable, but if exogenous variables such as personality can intervene in a voter's decision in an unpredictable way, then it seems that there are no grounds for making such a strong assumption. Suppose, for example, that during the course of an election candidate 1 shifts her issue position in such a way that it comes closer to those of voter A. By that move, the utility for A of candidate 1's issue positions has increased. By the assumption of this model, the probability of A's voting for 1 has also increased. But, suppose that while the candidate is shifting her position, voter A learns more about her personality which causes him to develop a severe dislike for her. In that case, the probability that A will vote for candidate 1 has probably declined while the utility associated with 1's issue position has increased!

Nevertheless, Hinich, Ledyard, and Ordeshook make the following assumptions:

1. Individual utility functions are continuous and concave, i.e., "the utility which a citizen associates with a candidate decreases at a constant or an increasing rate as that candidate moves his strategy, θ, away from the citizen's most-preferred position, x" (p. 163). A concave function is shown in fig. 5.19.

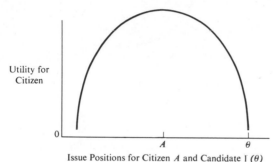

Issue Positions for Citizen A and Candidate 1 (θ)
Figure 5.19. A concave utility function.

A continuous function is one in which there are values for every point along the curve.

2. The probability of voting for a candidate increases as the utility associated with that candidate's issue position increases.

3. The probability of voting for one candidate decreases or remains constant as the utility associated with the issue position of the *other* candidate increases.

4. The probability of voting for a candidate decreases at a constant or increasing rate as the candidate moves his strategy position away from the citizen's most preferred position; and increases at a constant or increasing rate as the candidate moves his strategy position toward the citizen's most preferred position. Technically, "p_1 is concave in $U(\theta/x)$, and convex in $U(\psi/x)$, and p_2 is concave in $U(\psi/x)$ and convex in U(θ/x)." (p. 165.) Here, p_1 and p_2 are the probabilities of voting for candidates 1 or 2 respectively; $U(\theta/x)$ is the utility which a voter associates with candidate 1's issue posi-

tion θ—the Greek letter "theta"—given that the voter prefers position x; $U(\psi/x)$ is the utility a voter associates with candidate 2's issue position ψ—the Greek letter "psi"—given that the voter prefers x. A convex probability function is illustrated in fig. 5.20.

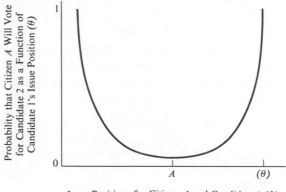

Issue Positions for Citizen A and Candidate 1 (θ)

Figure 5.20. A convex probability function.

These assumptions establish a more rigorous relation between a citizen's probability of voting for a particular candidate, and the issue position of that candidate. With these relatively simple assumptions, moreover, Hinich, Ledyard, and Ordeshook show that whether candidates are vote-maximizing or plurality-maximizing, there is a unique, "pure-strategy" equilibrium.[10] In other words, in a multidimensional issue space, there is a single alternative which defeats all other alternatives in a majority vote. Thus, candidates should converge to the same position. Nevertheless, since the voting choice itself is probabilistic, we can expect that one candidate will receive a plurality even if both candidates adopt the same position. In other words, even if there is a single best position which both candidates adopt, there should be a winner.

What is particularly interesting about this result is that it does not require some of the unrealistic assumptions of earlier spatial models which we discussed above. For example, there is no restriction on the shape of the voters' preference density function. That is, it can be unimodal, biomodal, or multimodal; and it can be symmetric or asymmetric. Also, where pre-

10. We shall discuss the notion of a "pure strategy" in the next chapter.

vious models required that individual utility functions be symmetric, the Hinich, Ledyard, and Ordeshook formulation requires only that they be concave. (*Question:* Must a symmetric utility function be concave?) There is also no assumption that citizens all weight the issues in the same way, nor that they all use the same calculus of voting. For example, two citizens can have the same issue preference and yet not necessarily vote for the same candidate; nor need both necessarily vote. At this point, of course, we must question whether we are still dealing with spatial models! Finally, the absence of these assumptions also implies that candidates who adopt the same issue position are not identical.

We should make one final point about the Hinich, Ledyard, and Ordeshook analysis. Perhaps the most important aspect of this article is that it relates the theory of games to spatial modeling. In particular, the electoral contest is viewed as a *two-person, zero-sum game* in which the payoff is a vote plurality. Since we have not yet discussed game theory, however, we shall not develop this point further.

This work is particularly important for another reason. The empirical work on voting behavior in the American electorate has found very little evidence to support the notion that previous spatial assumptions are realistic.[11] Thus, the Hinich, Ledyard, and Ordeshook approach, which provides new assumptions about voting behavior and dispenses with many of the old assumptions may provide a firmer foundation for the explanation of electoral behavior.

LEXICOGRAPHIC MODELS

Working with multidimensional models involving a number of variables is extremely complicated. Some writers in the field (e.g. Taylor, 1970, Taylor and Rae, 1971) have suggested a way to simplify the problem and make it more manageable. Essentially they have proposed an alternative assumption about the way individuals arrive at policy positions in a multidimensional world. This assumption is the basis for the so-called *lexicographic model*.

Davis, Hinich, and Ordershook assume that voters take a position on every issue and that the position of any voter (or candidate) is some kind of composite or summation of his position on each issue. It is not at all clear,

11. See, for example, the summary by Page (1977).

however, that such a summation process is meaningful. Suppose, for example, that there are two issues, the question of nationalized welfare, and the question of spending funds on a new missile launcher. Suppose further that three individuals, A, *B* and C took the following positions on these two issues: A favored a fully nationalized welfare system, B favored a partially nationalized welfare system, and C opposed any nationalization of welfare; A opposed spending any funds on a new missile launcher, B wanted a great expenditure, and C favored a moderate expenditure of funds. This might be expressed as follows:

Nationalized Welfare

None	*Partial*	*Complete*
C	B	A

Missile Launcher (Expenditures)

None	*Moderate*	*High*
A	C	B

Now suppose we wanted to determine how "close" A, B, and C were to each other on these two issues, or, at least, whether A was closer to C or B. Clearly, A is closer to B than C on the nationalized welfare issue, but A is closer to C on the question of missile launcher expenditures. Does this mean that A, B and C are *equidistant* from each other? Or is there some sense in which A is closer to B on the first issue than A is to C on the second, and so, overall, is closer to B? If the distances on both scales were measured in the same units, there would indeed be a way to measure closeness and to speak meaningfully about it. For example, if the scale were expressed in dollar expenditures, and if one end of each scale were zero and the other end, say, $2 billion, then we could compare A, B, and C in terms of their desired levels of expenditure. In doing so, however, we would be subtly reducing a two-dimensional space to a single dimension—i.e., budget expenditures. In most cases, however, real political issues cannot be reduced to simple measures which allow comparison between issues. This is particularly true when the elements which compose the multidimensional space include not only issues but also "style, partisan identification, and the like" (Davis, Hinich, and Ordeshook, 1970, p. 429).

In order to overcome this problem, Rae and Taylor (1971) and Taylor

(1970) began with the assumption that voters first order the relevant dimensions according to their importance to them. The result is a hierarchy of *dimensions* ordered according to *salience*. This means that one individual may rank the question of nationalized welfare as his greatest concern, another may rank foreign policy consideration highest, and a third may consider the question of defense spending as most important. In choosing among the candidates, then, a voter's task is reduced to determining where the candidates stand on his most salient issue alone. Only if there is no difference between the candidates on that issue does the voter involve another issue, comparing the candidates on the issue which is next most important to him. This process continues until the voter selects one of the candidates. One advantage of the lexicographic model is that there is no need to find a way of combining positions on a number of issues. Each individual has a utility function for each dimension, and there is no overall utility function for the *n* dimensions in a multidimensional space. A second advantage is that there is no need to specify a relation between the utility of the alternatives and their distance from the voter's first preference. Since the voter in a lexicographic model uses only one dimension at a time in judging the candidates, it is only necessary to determine which of the candidates is closest to him.

Using the lexicographic assumption, Rae and Taylor also try to determine whether equilibria exist. Their results are interesting. They show that a unique equilibrium point does exist when a group of voters has an odd number of members, when there are *n* dimensions, and when *all voters have the same salience ordering of the dimensions*—i.e. when all voters rank the dimensions in the same way. Note that this does not mean that all voters have the same preferences on each dimension, but simply that they agree on which dimensions, or issues, are more important than others. On the other hand, *when all voters do not rank the dimensions in the same way there is generally no equilibrium point*. There is, however, an *equilibrium set* of points for the situation in which there are *two dimensions*, majority rule, any number of individuals, and any distribution of first preferences, even if the individuals have different salience rankings of the two dimensions. An "equilibrium set" of points is a set of alternatives or issue positions which is preferred by a majority of the group to any other alternative; but, the majority is indifferent among the alternatives in the equilibrium set. In other words, for the majority of voters, every alternative in the equilibrium set is as desirable as any other alternative in that set; but any alternative in the equilibrium set is more desirable than any alternative outside the set.

Without presenting Rae and Taylor's analysis in its full complexity, we shall simply illustrate here the graphic presentation which they use in proving their theorems on equilibria. For the two dimensional case, suppose that there are five voters whose first preferences on each of the issues are distributed as in fig. 5.21.

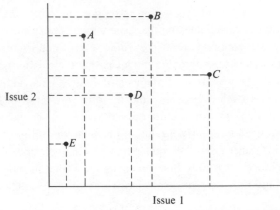

Figure 5.21. Distribution of the preferences of 5 voters
on 2 issues.

Now, draw two lines, one perpendicular to the issue 2 axis, one perpendicular to the issue 1 axis; and in such a way that there is not a majority of the voters on either side of the line. Since there are five voters, this means that the lines must be drawn with two voters on either side. Such lines are called median lines because they pass through the median position among the voters. Median lines for fig. 5.21 would appear as in fig. 5.22.

Notice that median line m passes through D, and line n passes through C, with A and E on one side of m, B and C on the other; and with A and B on one side of n, E and D on the other.

Now, suppose that all voters felt that issue 1 was more important than issue 2. Then they would judge all of the alternative positions along dimension 1. It is clear from the graph that position D, the median, is the equilibrium point for issue 1 since it is the point which is preferred by a majority to any other (recall our discussion of single dimension elections earlier). Suppose, on the other hand, that issue 2 were considered more important than

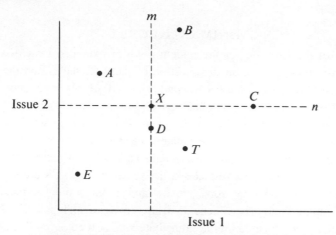

Figure 5.22. Median lines for positions of the 5 voters
in figure 5.21.

issue 1. Then, by the same reasoning, position *C*, the median of issue 2,
would be the equilibrium point. Position *X*, then, the intersection of the median lines, is the unique equilibrium point for this group of voters *no matter
which issue is more important than the other in the voter's salience hierarchy*. To see this more clearly, take any point not at *X*, say *T*. Along dimension 1, *X* is preferred to *T* by voters A, E, and D, because *X* is closer to their
first preference (or "optima," the term which Rae and Taylor use). Along
dimension 2, *X* is preferred to *T* by voters A, B, and C for the same reason.
It can be shown that *X* is preferred to any other point in this two-dimensional
space and is, therefore, the unique equilibrium point.

Rae and Taylor thus demonstrate that with a lexicographic model, and
with certain restrictive assumptions, equilibria do exist. Davis, Hinich, and
Ordeshook had also shown that equilibria exist under restrictive assumptions
when preferences over *n* dimensions are summed, i.e., when a single utility
function describes a voter's position or the distribution of first preferences.
Both approaches, however, show that *in a multidimensional world equilibria
generally do not exist*. This means, essentially, that unless certain restrictions are either imposed or occur spontaneously, e.g., on the shape of individual utility functions, loss functions, preference density functions, lexicographic orderings, and so on, the choice of alternatives or candidates will
be imposed in much the same way as described in chapter 1. Such results
provide further evidence for the importance of the voter's paradox.

MINIMAX REGRET

Most of the work on spatial modeling which extended Downs's work focused, as we have seen, on the question of party strategies and the existence of equilibria under a variety of conditions. All of this work, moreover, accepted Downs's notion of rational voters as *utility maximizers,* i.e., individuals trying to determine the possible benefits which they would receive from the policies of a particular candidate if elected, and the probability that their preferred candidate would be elected. This decision resembled an *investment decision* in the marketplace in the sense that voters were spending current capital (time, energy, some money, and so on) in order to receive an uncertain future return (i.e., benefits from governmental policy). Those, such as Riker, who focused on the immediate and assured psychological satisfaction derived from the voting act were treating voting as a *consumption decision,* i.e., voters were acting like consumers in the marketplace, in the sense that they received an immediate return from the expenditure of their resources.

Recently, Ferejohn and Fiorina (1974) have suggested a way to avoid the problems created by Riker's postulating of a psychic satisfaction as the basis for voting, and Downs's rational utility maximizer. The difficulty with the Riker formulation is that it is not particularly discriminating—it simply accounts for all those voters whose vote appears irrational by cost-benefit analysis. Downs's analysis, as we saw, led to the conclusion that most voting in large elections was irrational.

Ferejohn and Fiorina assume that voters first determine the possible outcomes of the election—e.g., their preferred candidate wins without their vote, their preferred candidate wins with their vote, and so on. Then, they determine the difference in terms of benefits to them between what they could have obtained had they known the true "state of nature" before the vote, and the actual benefits (or costs) from any particular choice. In other words, any possible decision—voting for either candidate or abstaining—is associated with a certain benefit or cost. For example, it I vote for my preferred candidate and he wins, I receive the benefit of his policies—but, since it cost me something to become informed and to vote, I subtract that cost from the benefits in order to determine my *net* benefit. Suppose, though, that I had not bothered to become informed and vote, and my preferred candidate won. I would then be better off, since I would receive the same benefits without having to subtract costs. Now, if I had known beforehand that my preferred candidate would win without my vote, I could have saved the cost of voting. In other words, the difference between what I receive by voting or not voting for my preferred candidate, given that my preferred candidate wins, is the cost of voting.

Suppose, however, that the other candidate wins, and that I had voted for my preferred candidate. In that case, I would not receive any benefits from the outcome of the election, and I would still incur the costs of voting. If I had known that the other candidate would win, I could have saved myself the cost of voting, and simply not received any benefits. In the first instance I have a net loss (the cost of voting) in the second instance I have neither gain nor loss. The difference between the two outcomes, again, is the cost of voting.

As a third case, suppose that I abstain and my preferred candidate loses by one vote. Now I receive nothing, and I have saved the cost of voting; but if I had known the outcome I would have voted, brought my candidate to a tie and received ½ of the benefits (less the cost of voting).[12] In this case, the difference between voting and not voting is the benefits (less the cost of voting) which I would get from a tie.

To see all this more clearly, let us assign the benefits from victory a number 1, the benefits of a tie ½, the costs of voting $-c$, and the absence of benefits (victory of the opposition) 0. Figure 5.23, then, summarizes our discussion above.

Outcomes

		1	2	3
	V_R	$1-c$	$-c$	$\frac{1}{2}-c$
Acts	A	1	0	0
Difference Between Voting and Abstaining		c	c	$\frac{1}{2}-c$

Figure 5.23. Utility matrix.

12. For purposes of analysis, Ferejohn and Fiorina assume that in a tie, all voters receive half of what they would have gotten if their candidate had won.

Here outcome 1 is the victory of my preferred candidate R, who would have won without my vote; outcome 2 is the victory of the other candidate (say, D) who also would have won without my vote; and outcome 3 is a victory for D if I abstain, but a tie if I vote for R. The numbers and/or letter in the boxes indicate the utility for me of my particular act combined with a particular outcome. *The difference between what I would have done if I had known the outcome in advance, and what I would have done without such knowledge, is known as the regret which I associate with the decision I take in ignorance. The minimax regret decision rule says that I should make that decision which minimizes the maximum regret associated with various possible outcomes.* In Fig. 5.23, for instance, the regrets associated with voting for my preferred candidate R are $c,c,$ and 0. Therefore, c is the maximum regret associated with voting for my preferred candidate. The regrets for abstaining are computed in the following way. If I planned to abstain, I would receive a payoff of 1 in benefits if my preferred party R won the election. If I knew that in advance, I would still abstain and still receive a payoff of 1. In other words, there is no difference between what I would do if I had prescience, and what I intended to do in this case—if I intended to abstain. The regret associated with abstaining, where outcome 1 is the actual outcome, is zero. Similarly, the regret associated with abstaining when outcomes 2 and 3 obtain are zero and $\frac{1}{2} - c$. (*Question:* Can you explain why?) The matrix in fig. 5.24 summarizes these regrets.

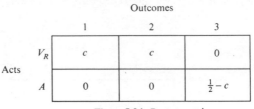

Figure 5.24. Regret matrix.

The minimax regret criterion says that I should vote for R rather than abstain if the maximum regret associated with that act is less than the maximum regret associated with abstention. It is clear from this regret matrix that my decision depends upon the magnitude of c, i.e., the cost of voting. If c is ½ then the maximum regret for voting for R is ½, while the maximum regret for abstaining is 0. Under such conditions, abstention is the appropriate minimax regret decision. If voting costs are *less than* ¼ then the maximum regret associated with voting for R is *less than* $\frac{1}{4}$, while the maximum regret associated with abstaining is *greater than* $\frac{1}{4}$ (if $c > \frac{1}{4}$, then $(\frac{1}{2} - c) < c$; if $c < \frac{1}{4}$, then $(\frac{1}{2} - c) > c$). Under such circumstances, the minimax regret decision should be to vote for R. The thrust of this analysis is that *as the cost of voting declines, voting for one's preferred candidate rather than abstaining becomes the more rational decision, using the minimax regret criterion.*

Ferejohn and Fiorina also consider the option of voting for one's less preferred candidate, but conclude that this is never rational by minimax regret criteria. (*Question:* Using the example above, can you show why this is so?) This result contrasts with Downs's conclusion that the probability of affecting the election is so small that even minimal voting costs make voting irrational (in fact, however, Downs also recognizes that the maintenance of a political system can provide a goal and rationale for voting, even when the direct benefits from a particular government are minimal or nonexistent); and with Riker's conclusion that because of psychic satisfactions, even higher costs of voting should not deter the rational individual from voting.

One important criticism of this analysis, however, is that the possible outcomes are viewed as equally likely. That is, in the example above, outcomes 1, 2, and 3 are obviously weighed as if they are equally likely occurrences, when it seems fairly clear that outcomes 1 and 2 are very probable, while the probability of outcome 3 is negligible. But, if that is the case, then the maximum regret associated with abstaining from a one-vote plurality election should scarcely be considered, and the minimax regret decision should coincide with the utility maximization decision—i.e., the voter should abstain. Ferejohn and Fiorina, however, argue that utility maximization is not the only criterion of rationality, and that other concepts, such as minimax regret, should be considered.

CONCLUSION

In this chapter, we have considered collective-choice situations in which the alternatives were either political parties and their candidates, or issue positions in a one-dimensional or multidimensional policy space. Where the alternatives are political parties and their candidates, the choosers are voters in an election. Where the alternatives are issue positions in a policy space, the

choosers are the political parties. Recall that in previous chapters the alternatives and choosers were either left unspecified (chapters 2 and 3) or were
policies and legislators, respectively, in a legislative or committee setting
(chapter 4). In other words, we have defined a problem—the voter's
paradox—at a general level and, subsequently, we are considering specific
instances of collective-choice situations in order to see whether the paradox
is really a general phenomenon.

In previous chapters, we have considered situations in which choosers
always select their first preference among the alternatives (sincere voting),
and in which choosers select an alternative other than that first preference
(sophisticated voting), as in the logrolling or vote-trading situation. In this
chapter, voters sometimes select their first preference, and sometimes abstain, but never select an alternative which is not their first choice. Parties,
on the other hand, always select their first preference among alternatives in a
policy space, since party preference is *defined by* the preference distribution
of the voters. In other words, in the Downsian analysis on which we focus
in this chapter, parties take positions *only* to win elections. Therefore, they
have no preference ordering among policy alternatives separate from the
preference ordering given by the distribution of voter preferences.

The initial discussion of Downs's work focused on voter preference.
Downs assumes that voters are *rational utility maximizers*. This means that
they vote for the party whose policies are most likely to bring them the
greatest benefit. This also means that there is no other reason for preferring
one party to another. Thus, "rationality" in Downs's system is limited to
political rationality. Voters abstain if the costs of voting outweigh the benefits, or if the parties are so similar that it does not matter which party is elected.

In a world of complete information—i.e., one in which the voters know
for certain the policy positions of the parties and the level of benefits which
will flow to them from the implementation of these policies—voters can determine with certainty whether to vote or to abstain, and, if they vote, for
whom. The real political world, however, is uncertain. Voters do not know
for certain the policy positions of the parties, nor do they know for certain
how particular policies would affect them, even if they were implemented.
This situation creates a need for information. But, information is costly in
time, effort, and financial resources. Therefore, voters in an uncertain world

must consider the cost of reducing that uncertainty in calculating the utility to them of any party's election.

The costs of reducing uncertainty have several consequences for the political system. First, the voter looks for inexpensive shortcuts. This leads to the development of *ideologies,* which are general political orientations or world outlooks designed to summarize party positions and to suggest future policy. Second, *political activists* appear, whose function is to explain party policy to the voters. Finally, political uncertainty gives rise to *political leadership,* whose function is to persuade voters that the policies of their parties are in the voters' interests. In a world of certain information, ideologies, activists, and leaders are not required.

Even with all of this help, however, rational voters in Downs's system generally should not vote, since the likelihood of their affecting the outcome of an election involving millions of voters is virtually nil. That is, even if voters were quite certain that one party rather than another would be better for them, it is also quite certain that no single vote is of any practical significance in an election with many voters. The apparent implication of this conclusion is that the large number of voters who cast ballots in an American political election are irrational. Downs himself, however, suggests that there may be some benefit to voters in simply maintaining the American system and, for that reason, voting may be rational. After all, if no one voted there would be no political system. It might also be suggested that rational voters would gamble on being the sole and deciding voter in an election where other rational voters abstain. Such an explanation of American voter turnout, however, sounds strained. Riker has suggested that individuals may vote primarily for the psychic rewards which come from participating in a community activity. Ferejohn and Fiorina suggest that voters may be *minimax regret* decision makers whose voting is based upon the admittedly slim but potentially critical possibility of being the deciding factor in an election. Despite the variety of attempts to present voting in a large election as a rational act, however, no analysis has proven fully convincing, and we are left with the distinct possibility that such voting is essentially irrational.

The other side of Downs's analysis is the theory of party competition, where parties or candidates are the choosers, while the alternatives are positions in a policy space. This analysis is known as *spatial modeling.* Here there are two major questions: Under what conditions will parties tend to converge toward or diverge from a similar position? And, is there an optimum or best position, such that either (any) rational party should want to adopt that position to win the election? The latter question is analogous to attempts in previous chapters to determine whether stable outcomes, or equilibria, exist.

The results of Downs's work, as well as subsequent developments by Riker, Davis, Ordeshook, Hinich, Ledyard, and others, indicate that the convergence or divergence of political parties depends upon several factors, the most important of which are the distribution of voter preferences over the policy space, the goals of the parties, and the nature of individual preference. In other words, it is not necessarily the case, as Downs has suggested, that the distribution of voter preferences is the factor which determines whether parties will converge or diverge.

The major problem with much of this analysis, however, is that certain unrealistic assumptions have to be made. Most importantly, it is assumed that all voters have identical utility functions. This does not mean that all voters have the same preferences, but that, given their first preference, the differences in utility between those first preferences and any other alternative at the same distance from that alternative are identical.

An important exception is the Hinich, Ledyard, and Ordeshook work on probabilistic voting. Here, the only assumptions necessary are those which relate the probability of voting to the change in distance between the positions of the parties and the voters.

A major conclusion of much of the spatial modeling work is that in a multidimensional world unique equilibria generally do not exist. Even the simplifying assumptions of Taylor and Rae's lexicographic model yield the same results. Such conclusions tend to provide further evidence for the importance and prevalence of the voter's paradox. Again, an important exception is the probabilistic model in which unique equilibria do exist even if the party goals are different.

CHAPTER SIX

Game Theory

IN THE PREVIOUS chapters, we have analyzed situations in which individuals have been called upon to choose among a given set of alternatives, and in which they would like to choose that alternative which ranks highest in their preference ordering. Occasionally, however, the situation demands that individuals choose alternatives which are *not* their first preference. This has happened in the vote-trading situation, where individuals agree to vote for an alternative which is not their first choice on an issue which is less important to them, in return for a similar action by another individual on an issue which is more important to them. It also happens where political parties are looking for winning strategies in an electoral campaign. In each case, the decision to choose an alternative other than the first preference depended upon the circumstances of the voting or collective-choice situation. *Game theory is essentially the study of collective-choice situations in which individual decisions depend not only upon individual preferences, but upon the preferences of the other individuals involved, and upon the outcomes which result from different sets of individual choices.* In graphic terms we might portray that relationship as follows:

Individual preferences
Preferences of others ⎫ *Individual Decision*
Outcomes of various sets of choices ⎭

In other words, in deciding how to choose, an individual must make estimates of the preferences of others as well as the possible outcomes. But the situation is really more complicated, since each individual must also estimate the *intentions* of others, given these variables. That is, it is not sufficient simply to know the preference orders of others. It is also necessary to know how others *perceive* the situation, and especially how they perceive the intentions of other individuals. This is, of course, a situation of infinite regress: I estimate another individual's perception of my intentions, and my intentions are based upon my perception of his intentions, which are based upon his perception of my intentions, and so on. Moreover, all of this presumes that we do in fact know the real (or "sincere") preferences of others. The absence of such information can complicate the problem enormously.

The use of the term "game" does not imply that the theory is concerned with frivolous activities or activities which are simply for fun. Rather, it implies that there are certain structural characteristics of leisure-time games which are isomorphic with certain serious political, economic, or social activity.

All games, for example, involve players, rules, moves or strategies, and outcomes. Moreover, most leisure games—e.g., chess, tennis, poker—involve winners and losers. In the theory, such games are referred to as *zero sum games*. This term derives from the fact that when utilities are assigned to the various possible outcomes, the magnititude of the positive payoff to the winner is equal to that of the loser's loss of utility. The sum of these utilities, therefore, is zero. In poker, for example, the dollar amount the winner receives is exactly the amount the loser gives up. It is literally the loser's money. In tennis, one player's loss is another player's victory. Such situations involve pure conflict.

Some social situations also involve pure conflict. When two people are competing for the same job, or when two political parties are competing for the same office, there can be only one winner. Nevertheless, there are also many social situations in which both (all) individuals can benefit. When a group of neighbors gets together to clean up a local park, everyone "wins."

Although these situations are different from such games as chess in important ways, there are certain structural similarities. For that reason, game theory also considers such "cooperative"[1] games.

1. In game theory, the terms "cooperative" and "noncooperative" have a particular meaning. In a "cooperative" game the players communicate and bargain with each other, while in a

PRISONER'S DILEMMA

To make matters more interesting, it is frequently the case that individuals are faced with the choice of conflict *or* cooperation with others. One of the most intriguing examples of the problems inherent in such situations is the so-called prisoner's dilemma, one of the most famous games in the game theory literature.

The name "prisoner's dilemma" developed because of the example used to illustrate this situation. Suppose you are one of two accomplices in crime who have been apprehended and put in separate cells. The district attorney comes to each of you and makes the following offer: If you confess to the crime and become a state's witness while your accomplice remains silent, you will be released without punishment, while your accomplice will receive a 10-year sentence. If *both* of you remain silent, however, the district attorney does not have enough evidence to convict you of a crime which carries any more than a one-year sentence. On the other hand, if you both confess, conviction would result in a five-year jail sentence for each of you.

Let us summarize the situation by means of a matrix of possible outcomes (fig. 6.1). The numbers in the lower left-hand corner of each box represent the "payoffs" to prisoner Haldeman in various situations, while the numbers in the upper right-hand corner represent the payoffs to prisoner Nixon. The letters in parentheses (e.g., *cc, cs,* etc.) represent the joint outcome when both prisoners confess, one prisoner confesses, and so on.

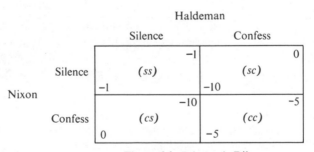

Figure 6.1. Prisoner's Dilemma.

"noncooperative" game there is no bargaining or communication. The object of communication, of course, is to coordinate strategies in order to improve the outcome for all players where possible. In the text above, however, we are distinguishing games of "conflict" and "cooperation" where these terms refer only to the structure of the payoffs. Of course, in games of pure conflict there can be no bargaining even if there is communication.

The "dilemma" in this situation is the following: each prisoner would like to go free; however, given the choices, the freedom of either prisoner can only be achieved through the sacrifice of the other. Now, that is simply a moral dilemma. There is also a practical dilemma. If both prisoners reason in the same way, and if both are willing to sacrifice the other for their freedom, then both prisoners will confess. Moreover, the "confess" strategy is what is called in game theory a *dominant* strategy. This means that *no matter what the other player does, each is better off confessing.* To see this, notice that if Nixon confesses, Haldeman gets only five years in jail, rather than ten, by confessing. Similarly, if Nixon remains silent, Haldeman goes free if he confesses. The same analysis applies to Nixon. Therefore, they should both confess.

A glance at the payoff matrix, however, reveals that the situation where both confess (*cc*) results in prison terms of five years each. This outcome is next to the worst possible outcome for both prisoners.

In other words, while each player prefers the outcome which he would receive from choosing the dominant strategy rather than the nondominant strategy for *each* strategy choice of his opponent, it is *not* true that *both* outcomes associated with the dominant strategy are preferred to *both* outcomes associated with the nondominant strategy. Thus, the mutually cooperative outcome which results from each choosing nondominant strategies is preferred to the mutually noncooperative outcome when both choose dominant strategies.

This might lead both prisoners to reason that it would be better to remain silent (the "cooperative" solution) in which case each would receive only one year in jail. But if both prisoners concluded that the other would decide to remain silent, then the way would be open for a double-cross in which one would confess while the other remained silent. Yet, if both prisoners were reasoning in the same way, both would confess with the resulting five-year term. The dilemma is that if one prisoner takes a chance on cooperating by remaining silent, in order to avoid the five-year jail term, the other prisoner has an incentive to confess. In other words, the fear of becoming a "sucker"—i.e., remaining silent while the other confesses—provides an incentive for both prisoners to stay with their dominant "confess" strategy, a result which is undesirable for both.

To see the problem more clearly, let us list the outcomes in order of preference for each prisoner:

	Nixon	Haldeman
	cs	sc
	ss	ss
	cc	cc
	sc	cs

Obviously both prisoners cannot have their first preferences simultaneously. Their mutual second choices, however, are preferable to their mutual third choices. Nevertheless, the fear of becoming the sucker forces both prisoners to opt for the less preferred outcome. In one sense, such a result is irrational, since an outcome which is *mutually* less desired is chosen over an outcome which is mutually more desired. Nevertheless, in terms of individual choice, it is clearly rational. What we have here is a conflict between individual and collective rationality—i.e., what is rational for each individual, is not rational for the group.

This result, moreover, is not dependent upon the fact that the prisoners cannot communicate. For, even if they could communicate, and even if they agreed to cooperate by remaining silent—the only outcome which could come from a direct meeting—each would have to assess the sincerity of the other. In such circumstances, it is unlikely that any other outcome but *cc* would result, since each prisoner still must fear the worst. It is clear from this analysis that a very high degree of trust must exist before the mutually advantageous cooperative solution *ss* could be achieved.

The prisoner's dilemma is essentially a situation in which individuals choose a relatively undesirable strategy in order to assure against an extremely undesirable outcome. Now, it is not clear that all individuals would make such a choice. Obviously, some people would choose the riskier cooperative strategy in order to try to improve the outcome. Nevertheless, *the situation is structured in such a way that cooperation is more risky than disloyalty*. Notice that anyone who chooses the strategy of disloyalty has chosen a *minimax strategy,* as defined in the previous chapter—i.e., a strategy which minimizes the maximum loss which can occur.

CHICKEN

In order to see the importance of the structure of the situation, let us look at another game called "chicken." This game is familiar to anyone who has ever seen a James Dean movie, or who grew up in the 1950s, when chicken was a rather popular game among thrill-seeking teen-age drivers. The example associated with this game is that of two cars heading toward each other at high speeds. The "chicken," a term of opprobrium, is the driver who swerves at the last minute to avoid hitting the other car; and, presumably, the "winner" is the driver who does not lose his nerve and refuses to swerve. The payoff matrix of such a situation might be as in fig. 6.2.

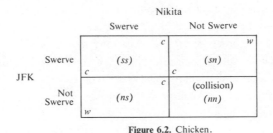

Figure 6.2. Chicken.

Here the *"c"* stands for "chicken," the *"w"* for "winner." In box *ss*, both players are chicken; in *sn*, JFK is the chicken; in *ns* Nikita is the chicken; and in *nn*, neither is chicken, but both are destroyed in the collision. The ranking of alternatives for the players here is:

JFK	*Nikita*
ns	*sn*
ss	*ss*
sn	*ns*
nn	*nn*

Again, both players cannot obtain their first preference simultaneously. On the other hand, unlike the prisoner's dilemma game, both players have a mutual worst alternative which they would like to avoid—i.e., a collision. The "cooperative" strategy is *ss*—both players swerve to avoid a collision.

Now, how would players in the chicken game reason? Nikita might say, "If I were JFK, I would not want to collide; therefore, I will swerve at the last minute. On the other hand, if I were JFK, I might also reason that Nikita would not want to collide either, and will swerve; therefore, it is unnecessary for me to swerve." Again, there are good reasons for assuming that one's opponent will take either course of action. Remember, however, that the collision outcome is a devastating negative one, on a par with, say, nuclear warfare as opposed to conventional warfare. In other words, *this situation is structured in such a way that cooperation is the less risky strategy* (unless, of course, death is preferable to dishonor), and a minimax strategist would swerve rather than not swerve. Notice that in the chicken game there is no dominant individual strategy as there is in the prisoner's dilemma. Thus, if Nikita swerves, JFK should not swerve; but if Nikita does not swerve, JFK should swerve.

One of the interesting implications of this analysis of the prisoner's dilemma and chicken games is that *if the players use a minimax-loss decision rule, and if cooperation is the desired outcome, then the worst possible penalty for noncooperation must be higher than the worst possible penalty for cooperation.* This was the case in the chicken game but not in prisoner's dilemma. In international affairs this result has an interesting implication for the debate over whether the existence of nuclear weapons is a stabilizing or a destabilizing device—i.e., whether the existence of nuclear weapons makes war more or less likely. Some have argued that the proliferation of nuclear weapons increases the probability of warfare by putting an equalizing device in the hands of weaker nations. Behind this reasoning is the assumption that the proliferation of nuclear weapons, and the dispersal of control over these weapons, makes it increasingly likely that some "madman" will ultimately start a nuclear conflagration. There is no doubt that such a scenario is possible. Morevoer, as our analysis above indicates, it is not necessary to postulate a madman in order to increase the probability of nuclear warfare; it is simply necessary to assume that decision makers are not minimax-loss strategists—i.e., they are not risk-averse. Nevertheless, there is ample evidence to indicate that a strong sense of self-preservation is a dominant motive behind the actions of most political leaders. After all, if they had been bent on suicide, even glorious suicide, why bother with the drudgery of politics? It would seem that political assassination rather than political leadership would be the more likely route to personal Armageddon. But, *if most political leaders are minimax-loss strategists, then the existence of nuclear weapons should deter war by creating the alternative of total destruction.* By this reasoning, the existence of destructive but *limited* weaponry is more of a threat to international peace than the existence of nuclear weapons.

Our discussion above is intended to illustrate that one of the goals of game theory is to elucidate the underlying structure of certain collective choice situations, and to show the structural similarity between apparently disparate situations. Thus, it is suggested that international affairs has certain properties in common with a dangerous teen-agers' game called chicken, and that situations which militate against cooperation may resemble the prisoner's dilemma. Presumably, such insights might help us to alter situations which are undesirable, or, at least, to understand them.

LEVELS OF ANALYSIS

GAMES IN EXTENSIVE FORM

We have suggested above that any "game" must involve players and rules; and that the rules indicate the available moves, the possible outcomes, and the potential payoffs to each player. Now games can be analyzed at three levels. First, the individual moves and countermoves could be analyzed. In the game of chess, this would amount to analyzing the possible responses to any particular move, the possible responses to that response, and so forth. In order to do this, it would be necessary to set up what is called in game theory a *game tree*. A game tree is simply a drawing of the possible moves and countermoves available to each player. Suppose, for example, that a game involved only two moves, say L and R. The first player would choose L or R and then the second player would respond by choosing L or R. Suppose further that the game terminated after three moves, and that different payoffs were associated with the different sets of moves. For example, if each player chose move L at each turn, the sets of moves would be (L, L, L). If the first player always chose L and the second $R,$ the outcome would be (L, R, L). There are, in all, eight such outcomes which we will show by setting up the game tree for this simple game (see fig. 6.3):

The payoff to the first player is indicated by the first number in the parentheses under "payoffs," the payoff to the second player is indicated by the second number. In other words, if the outcome is (L,R,L) the first player receives a payoff of 2, the second player 1. Now a *strategy* is a *set of moves*. For example, player one's strategy might be (L,L), (L,R), and so on. That is, he might make move L at first, and L again after player two has moved. Player two, in this game, has only two moves L or R.

In terms of strategies, (L,L) or (R,R), and so on, for player 1 are called *noncontingent* strategies. That is, they simply express the strategy choices

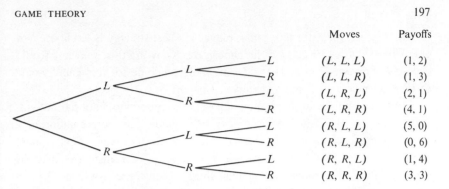

Figure 6.3. A game in extensive form.

which a player has available without making reference to the possible moves of the other player. A *contingent* strategy, on the other hand, relates the strategy choices of one player to the strategy choices of the other. Thus, the sets of moves listed in fig. 6.3 are player 1's contingent strategies. For example, the first two strategies show the alternative responses to player 2's choice of *L* or *R*, once player 1 has chosen *L*. Similarly, player 2's contingent strategies are $(L,L, . . .)$, $(L,R, . . .)$, $(R,L, . . .)$, and $(R,R, . . .)$. That is, player 2 can choose *L* or *R* contingent upon player 1's choice of *L* or *R*.

The idea behind this game, of course, is to achieve the highest possible payoff. Note that this game is not zero-sum, since the sum of possible payoffs to both players is never zero. In a zero-sum game, a payoff might be, (-1, 1), or (-4, 4), etc. Looking at the payoffs, we see that player 1 would like the outcome (R,L,L) best while player 2 would like (R,L,R). In each case, one player receives his or her highest payoff, the other his or her lowest. Each player can prevent either outcome which is detrimental. Player 2, for example, can prevent (R,L,L) simply by choosing *R no matter what player 1 does*. Player 1 can prevent (R,L,R) simply by making his first and second choice different, or by choosing *L* both times.

Suppose player 1 chooses *R* first. If player 2 chooses *L* next, player 1 would certainly choose *L*. Suppose, however, that player 2 chose *R* after player 1's choice of *R*. Then player 1 would also choose *R* as his second choice. Similarly, if player 1 chooses *L* first, and player 2 responds with *L*, then it would not matter to player 1 whether he chose *L* or *R*, since the payoffs associated with $(L,L,L,)$ and (L,L,R) are the same for him. If player 1 chose *L* first and player 2 chose *R*, then, player 1 would choose *R*.

In general, then, for this game, player 2's best strategy is to choose R if player one chooses R, and L if he chooses L. Knowing this, player 1 would choose R first and R last. Thus, the probable outcome for this game would be (R,R,R) where each player receives a payoff of 3.

In this example, we have seen that what is important is not the individual moves, but the strategies. Moreover, the game tree representation of a simple game such as this is manageable, but for an even slightly more complicated game it becomes unwieldy. Suppose, for instance, that the game involved four moves rather than three. Then there would be $2^4 = 16$ possible outcomes. Imagine, then, the problem of characterizing a game such as chess by means of a game tree, where there are an extraordinary number of moves. For these reasons—the greater importance of strategies, and the difficulty of presenting complex games—games in *extensive form* (the technical term for the diagraming of a game in a game tree) have not played an important role in game theory.

GAMES IN NORMAL FORM

At the first level, then, is the analysis of a game in extensive form by means of a game tree. For each game, moreover, there is a unique representation, since different games have different rules or moves. At the second level are games in *normal form*. The so-called normal form is simply the representation of games in terms of the strategies available to each player and the payoffs associated with certain outcomes. In our discussion above of the prisoner's dilemma and chicken games, we used the normal form.

In the literature on game theory, the generalized representation of games in normal form is as shown in fig. 6.4. This formidable looking array of letters and numbers is really not complicated or difficult to understand. It simply lists the possible combinations of strategies for two players. The entry T_1S_1, for example, means that player A has chosen strategy T_1 and that player B has chosen strategy S_1. In our chicken example above (fig. 6.2) this might correspond to the ss combination. The T_i and S_i simply stand for strategies somewhere between the first two strategies and strategy T_n or S_n which are the last available strategies.

The advantage of the normal form is that it allows us to summarize a great deal of information, and to compare different games. Games with many possible moves and very different rules can be seen to be structurally similar to each other by comparing them in normal form. Thus, any two-per-

Strategies S (Player B)

	S_1	S_2 $\cdots$ S_i $\cdots$ S_n
T_1	$T_1\ S_1$	$T_1\ S_2 \cdots T_1\ S_i \cdots T_1\ S_n$
T_2	$T_2\ S_1$	$T_2\ S_2 \cdots T_2\ S_i \cdots T_2\ S_n$
$\vdots$	$\vdots$	$\vdots$
T_i	$T_i\ S_1$	$T_i\ S_2 \cdots T_i\ S_i \cdots T_i\ S_n$
$\vdots$	$\vdots$	
T_n	$T_n\ S_1$	$T_n\ S_2 \cdots T_n\ S_i \cdots T_n\ S_n$

Strategies T (Player A)

Figure 6.4. General representation of games in normal form.

son, non-zero-sum game with two strategies, and with payoffs similar to that of the prisoner's dilemma, *is* a prisoner's-dilemma game. Moreover, once a game is recognized as a certain type, the analysis which applies to the one applies to the other as well.

There is another important reason for focusing on games in normal form. In any game of skill, a good player does not simply respond to a particular move by an opponent, but rather tries to develop a set of moves, or a strategy, which will be effective no matter what the opponent does. Such a goal is generally unattainable, but good players are always seeking approximations. In chess, for example, particular kinds of offensive strategies—e.g., the Queen's gambit—or defensive strategies—e.g., the Sicilian defense—are constantly being developed. The idea is that a particular *set* of moves will be capable of dominating other sets of moves. Much of the work in chess theory is an attempt to see how powerful particular strategies are—i.e., how many competing strategies they can overcome. No major chess player ever thinks in terms of simple moves, but rather in terms of such overall strategies.

The same is true in physical sports. A tennis player, for example, does not simply wait to see what his opponent will do, but determines in advance what kind of game he will play, for example, whether he will aggressively rush the net, or play a base-line game; whether he will try to win points by maneuvering his opponent, or simply return every shot until his opponent makes a mistake. Similarly, athletic teams develop "game plans," which are nothing other than strategies or sets of moves. The idea is that a particular strategy will produce the best overall outcome, even though any particular move in the strategy may be unsuccessful. Thus, a football team does not give up a game plan which calls primarily for passing even though one pass is intercepted. On the other hand, a strategy which shows itself to be unsuccessful must be altered. Nevertheless, planning for most important activities takes place at the *strategic level*. In fact, any set of moves which is not coordinated and guided by some ultimate goal we describe as ad hoc, or improvised. Foreign policy, for example—which, as we have seen, can be viewed as a kind of game—can either be improvised or planned. An improvised foreign policy deals with each situation as it arises, without reference to an overall goal and a strategy designed to reach that goal. The absence of such strategies in foreign policy can have dire consequences.[2]

Two-Person Zero-Sum Games

Pure Strategies

The simplest type of game in normal form is one which involves two players and two strategies, as in our prisoner's dilemma game above. Given that simple type, however, there are many variations involving many possible combinations of payoffs. In fact, the variety of payoffs is limitless. Game theorists, however, have classified games in normal form according to the configuration of payoffs. One of the most famous types, and the one which was subjected to the earliest and most exhaustive analysis by Von Neumann and Morgenstern, the creators of game theory, in their *Theory of Games and Economic Behavior* (1944), is the *two-person zero-sum game* illustrated in figure 6.5. In the literature, the zero-sum-game ma-

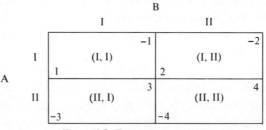

Figure 6.5. Two person, zero-sum game.

2. Of course, an inappropriate or ignorant strategy can also be disastrous, as our involvement in Vietnam indicated.

trix is usually simplified (see fig. 6.6) to show only the payoffs for the row player, in this case A. The payoffs to the column player, or B in this case, are simply the opposite.

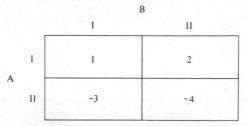

Figure 6.6. Zero-sum game showing only row payoffs.

Here the payoffs for each outcome involve a *positive* payoff for one player, and a *negative* payoff *of the same magnitude* to the other player. Clearly, as we mentioned above, this is a game of pure conflict in which one player wins only what another player loses. In this particular configuration of payoffs, player A would clearly choose strategy I, since no matter which strategy B chooses A will be better off than if he had chosen strategy II. In turn, B, would choose strategy I since this would limit her loss to −1. Of course, B would have preferred strategy II with its opportunity of obtaining a payoff of 4, but A's obvious strategy makes that choice more costly. In this case, *A's choice is best for him no matter what B does*. Such a strategy, as we discussed in the analysis of the prisoner's dilemma game above, is called a dominating strategy. Here, player A has a dominating strategy, while B does not.

The outcome (I,I) in fig. 6.6 is stable or in equilibrium in the sense that neither player can improve his or her position by choosing a different strategy, so long as the opposing player is also free to choose a different strategy. This notion of stability or equilibrium is the same as that used in previous chapters.

This particular outcome is also known as a *pure strategy* equilibrium. This means that the players both chose a single strategy. In a non-iterative game—i.e., a game played only once—it is obvious that every strategy choice must be a pure strategy. Where games are played more than once, however, a player may choose either to use a pure strategy, or to choose more than one strategy, alternating from game to game on the basis of some preconceived pattern, or at random. The latter is referred to as a *mixed strategy*. We shall discuss mixed strategies in more detail below.

It is important to note that an equilibrium point is not necessarily a "good" thing for each player. (In fact, in a zero sum game it must be bad for at least one player.) It simply represents the best that each can do in the circumstances of the particular game. In the equilibrium of fig. 6.6, for example, B's payoff is "−1," and this is only good in relation to her possible loss of 2 in (I,II).

Saddle Points

It is clear that if both players have dominating strategies, each will choose that strategy and there will be a stable outcome. Suppose, however, that neither player has a dominating strategy. Will there then be a stable outcome? Consider fig. 6.7. Here there are three strategies for each player and

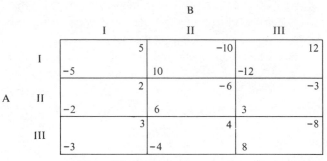

Figure 6.7. A game with no dominant strategies.

nine outcomes. While there are no dominant strategies, player A can guarantee himself a minimum of −2 by selecting strategy II. (*Question:* Can you explain why there are no dominant strategies here?) If he selects strategies I or III he runs the risk of losing −3 or −5 should player B choose strategy I. At the same time, player B can guarantee herself a payoff of at least 2 by choosing strategy I. (*Question:* Can you explain why player B can guarantee herself a positive payoff and yet there is no dominating strategy for player B?)

In this situation, then player A will choose strategy II, and player B will choose strategy I. This outcome (II, I), moreover, is stable or in equilibrium, since neither player can improve his or her position given the choice of the opponent. If B chose strategies II or III, for example, while A chose II, she would lose −6 or −3. Thus, even if B knew that A's choice was II, B would still choose I. Similarly, even if A knew that B's choice was I, he would still choose II.

The outcome $(-2,2)$ is referred to as the *saddle point* of this game. It is also known as the *minimax* solution. The term minimax refers to the *minimum of the column maxima, and the max*imum of the row minima. To see this more clearly, consider fig. 6.8.

		B I	II	III	Row Minima
	I	−5	10	−12	−12
A	II	−2	6	3	−2
	III	−3	−4	8	−4
	Maxima Column	−2	10	8	

Figure 6.8. Computation of Minimax solution.

The payoff -2 is simultaneously the maximum payoff among the row minima, and the minimum payoff of the column maxima. The imagery of a saddle to describe this point is simply an attempt to give pictorial representation to what is essentially a mathematical notion.

A game can also have more than one saddle point, as in fig. 6.9. Here A can guarantee a minimum payoff of 1 by choosing either strategy I or III. But if A chooses I or III, then B must choose strategy II or V in order to minimize her loss. (Remember, these numbers are the payoffs for A, and a *negative* payoff for A is a *positive* payoff for B.) If B chose any other strategy while A chose I or III, she would lose more than if she had chosen II or V. The *four* saddle points in this game, then, are: (I, II), (I, V), (III, II), (III, V).

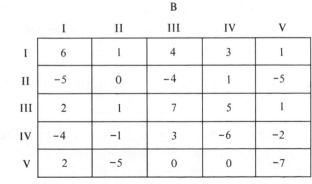

		B I	II	III	IV	V
	I	6	1	4	3	1
	II	−5	0	−4	1	−5
A	III	2	1	7	5	1
	IV	−4	−1	3	−6	−2
	V	2	−5	0	0	−7

Figure 6.9. A game with more than one saddle point.

Notice that these four saddle points have equal payoffs. This must be the case. If either player could achieve a higher payoff, then he or she would move to that point. When one speaks of "the" saddle point of a game, then, it means one outcome which may result from more than one set of strategies.

Mixed Strategies

Consider the game in fig. 6.10.

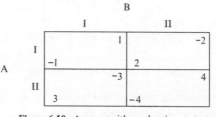

Figure 6.10. A game with no dominant strategies
and no pure strategy equilibrium.

Here, as in fig. 6.7, neither player has a dominant strategy. Suppose, however, that player A attempted to minimize his losses by choosing strategy I. In that case, player B can do best by also choosing strategy I with the joint outcome (I,I). But, if B chooses I, player A can improve his position by choosing strategy II; then B should choose II also, but then, etc. This is a never-ending process, unlike fig. 6.7 in which a point is reached from which neither player has an incentive to move.

Suppose, however, that this game were played many times rather than only once, and that each player tried to obtain his or her maximum payoff. This means that A would try to obtain a payoff of 3 by choosing strategy II, and B would try to obtain 4 also by choosing strategy II. Now, when B uses strategy II, A would like to use strategy I and obtain a payoff of 2 (I,II); and when A uses strategy I, B would like to use strategy I and obtain a payoff of 1 (I,I). But neither player knows when the other is going to use a particular strategy. Is there, in this situation, a way of choosing strategies which assure a desired payoff in the long run no matter what the other player does? The answer is yes.

Suppose each player simply flipped a coin at each play of the game and used strategy I if the coin came up heads, strategy II if tails. In a long series of plays each strategy would be used an equal number of times and the probability of any of the four outcomes would be equal. In other words, one quarter of the time the outcome would be (I,I), one quarter (I, II), one quarter (II,I) and one quarter (II,II). This means that both players would have a total payoff of zero—for A: $(-1+2+3-4)$; for B: $(1-2-3+4)$. Now the question is, can either player do better than this? Since the game is zero-sum, it is obvious that both cannot improve their payoffs simultaneously.

A glance at the payoffs indicates that if player A used only strategy I while B continued to flip a coin, A's total payoff would be $+1$ $(-1+2)$. If A had used only strategy II, however, while B flipped a coin, he would receive a payoff of -1 $(3-4)$. Thus, it is better for A to use strategy I more than strategy II. But he cannot use it exclusively since B would stop flipping her coin and use only strategy I. Similarly, B would like to use II more than I since it results in a total payoff of $+2$ $(4-2)$. The problem, then, for both is to use the better strategy more often but, at the same time, maintain the element of uncertainty. This can be done by the use of some random device such as drawing a number from a hat. A "random device" is one which assures that there will be no pattern to the selection process. The flip of a coin is such a random device. The proportion of times each strategy will be used overall, however, is determined in the following way. If the frequency of occurrence of one strategy is x, then the frequency of the other strategy is $1-x$. For example, if A decided to use strategy I 60 times out of 100 plays (i.e., 60 percent of the time), then he would use strategy II 40 times (i.e., 40 percent of the time). Thus, if $x = .60$, $1-x = 1 - .60 = .40$. Similarly, if player B decides to use strategy II 70 percent of the time, she would use strategy I 30 percent of the time. The joint probabilities, then for the four possible outcomes would be as follows:

$$
\begin{aligned}
(I,I) \ \ &= (.60) \times (.30) = \ \ .18 \\
(I,II) \ &= (.60) \times (.70) = \ \ .42 \\
(II,I) \ &= (.40) \times (.30) = \ \ .12 \\
(II,II) &= (.40) \times (.70) = \underline{\ \ .28} \\
& \hspace{4.5cm} 1.00
\end{aligned}
$$

In other words, the outcome (I, I) would occur 18 percent of the time, outcome (I,II) 42 percent of the time, outcome (II,I) 12 percent of the time, and outcome (II,II) 28 percent of the time. Notice that the joint probabilities add up to 1.00. This is another way of saying that it is certain that one of these four outcomes will be the outcome of the game each time it is played. This also means that each player would receive the following payoffs:

A	B
.18 $(-1) = -$ .18	.18 $(\ 1) =$ .18
.42 $(\ 2) =$ .84	.42 $(-2) = -$ .84
.12 $(\ 3) =$ .36	.12 $(-3) = -$ .36
.28 $(-4) = \underline{-1.12}$	.28 $(\ 4) = \underline{\ 1.12}$
$-$ .10	.10

But is this the best that either player can do? To determine this, let us first generalize the calculations we did above. If the probabilities for player A's strategies are designated x and $1-x$, let us call the probabilities of B's strategies y and $1-y$. Then, let us refer to A's strategy I as x, and strategy II as $1-x$; B's strategy I as y, and strategy II as $1-y$. What we did in our calculations was to first multiply the probabilities of each strategy, and then multiply the resulting probability by the value of each outcome for each player. In other words, player A's total payoff can be expressed as follows:

$$-1(x)(1-y) + 2(x)\ (y) + 3(1-x)(1-y) - 4(1-x)\ (y)$$
$$\ \ (.60)\ (.30) \quad\quad (.60)\ (.70) \quad\quad (.40)\ (.30) \quad\quad (.40)\ (.70)$$

For B, the payoff can be expressed in the same numbers and letters but with opposite signs:

$$1(x)(1-y) - 2(x)(y) - 3(1-x)(1-y) - 4(1-x)(y)$$

Using simple algebra this becomes (for A):

$$y(10x - 7) - 4x + 3$$

Now, recall that x is the proportion of times player A uses his more preferred strategy I. If he sets $x = .70$, then $10(.70) - 7 = 0$, and

$$-4(.70) + 3 = .20$$

In other words, no matter how many times B uses strategy I or II, A can assure himself a payoff of .20 by randomly selecting his strategies I and II from a device which is programmed to produce strategy I seven times out of ten. For instance, A might put 70 white balls and 30 red balls in a large bowl, draw out one of the balls, replace it in the bowl, draw a second time, replace that, and so on. When a white ball is drawn, A plays strategy I; when a red ball is drawn, strategy II.

Now, since this is a zero-sum game, B's payoff will be $-.20$. (*Question:* Can you show how B would compute y and the total payoff from the equation above?) The important point about this result is that *either player can assure a particular outcome in the long run no matter what the other player does.* In this case, A can assure himself a minimum gain of .20, while B can assure herself a maximum loss of .20. In other words, *the outcome (.20, $-.20$) is a minimax solution or a saddle point for this series of games with this particular set of outcomes and when both players use mixed strategies.*

When we combine this result with that demonstrated in our discussion of pure strategies, we arrive at a famous conclusion in game theory: *All two-person zero-sum games have an equilibrium point. In other words, for every two-person zero-sum game there is a "best" strategy (pure or mixed) for each player.*

N-Person Games

In game theory, any situation involving more than two players is referred to as an *n-person game.* As we noted in previous sections, games involving many moves or strategies are extremely complex. When we consider the addition of an unlimited number of players, the possible complexities become overwhelming. For that reason, game theorists have tried to simplify the analysis, and in so doing have produced a body of work on *coalitions* which could be of great significance in the social sciences.

Recall that in our discussion of the prisoner's dilemma, the possibility of coordinating strategies was considered, but was rejected as a means of achieving a cooperative solution, because it was necessary for each player to protect himself against being the sucker. Interestingly, this result holds also for the prisoner's dilemma game involving three players. In this game, there are also just two strategies which we shall call I and II.

The payoffs for particular outcomes are as follows (see fig. 6.11):

1. If all three choose strategy I, then each receives a payoff of 1.
2. If two players choose I and the third chooses II, each player who chooses I gets 0, while the lone player gets 4.
3. If two choose II, and one player chooses I, each of the two who chose II gets 3, while the third player gets a payoff of -4.
4. If all three choose II, each receives a payoff of -1.

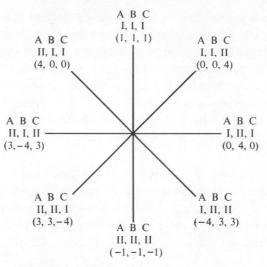

Figure 6.11. A 3-person Prisoner's Dilemma game.

Notice that this is neither a zero-sum game nor what is called a constant sum game—i.e., the sum of the payoffs is not the same for each outcome as it is in the zero-sum game. For example, when all three players choose strategy I (I,I,I), the total payoff is 3. On the other hand, when all of the players choose strategy II, the total payoff is −3. Notice also that the largest payoff goes to the individual who does *not* join the coalition (I,I). In (II,I,I), (I,II,I), and (I,I,II), the single player who chooses strategy II receives a payoff of 4, while the two players who chose strategy I receive a payoff of zero.

What, then, is the "rational" choice for each player? The "cooperative" solution is the grand coalition (I,I,I) in which each player gets a payoff of 1. Any greater payoff to either one or two other players requires that one or two players receive less than 1. What all players want to avoid is the outcome in which they are the single individual who has chosen strategy I. The obvious way to avoid this possibility is to choose II. The choice of II is also the way of achieving the highest possible payoff, as we saw above. Thus, the choice of strategy II is the dominant strategy for all three players, in which case the outcome is (II,II,II), and the result is a payoff of −1 to each individual. In other words, as in the two-person prisoner's dilemma, there is an incentive—the existence of a dominant strategy—not to participate in a cooperative solution which brings a higher payoff than the "safe" noncooperative outcome. The problem cannot be overcome, moreover, by a gradual formation of the cooperative grand coalition, since no player would have an incentive to join the coalition (I,I) once it had formed. By staying out of the coalition (I,I) the "noncooperative" player assures himself the highest payoff.

This three-person prisoner's dilemma game illustrates a difficulty in coalition formation. It is a situation in which each individual has an incentive *not* to join with others in a "cooperative" solution which is better for everyone than the noncooperative solution which occurs. Let us illustrate another impediment to coalition formation. Suppose three players could split $100 among themselves in any way, and that any two players could split the $100 between them—leaving the third player with nothing—simply by agreeing on a disbursement of the money. For instance, if two players agreed to split the money evenly between them, they would each get $50. But, the third player is allowed to offer either of the other two players a better deal as a way of inducing someone to join with him in a new coalition. Moreover, the game does not end until a particular disbursement is agreed upon which cannot be altered by another offer, i.e., the point at which no player who shares the payoff has an incentive to try to gain a larger share. Naturally, a settlement which involved any two players would always leave the third disgruntled.

One cooperative solution in such a game might be to divide the money evenly among the three players. Such a result, however, could always be upset by any two players who thought they could get more. For example, suppose players A and B agree to split the money evenly. In such a situation player C could come along and offer either A or B $51, while C would get $49. Player A or B would be better off with $51 than with $50, and C would be much better off with $49 than with nothing. Therefore, a new coalition would form between C and A or B. At that point, however, the odd man out would have an incentive to offer C a 50-50 deal. This improves C's position as well as that of the third player, but it puts us right back where we started. Let us summarize the results:

		A	B	C
First coalition	$(\overline{ABC})$:	(33⅓,	33⅓,	33⅓)
Second coalition	$(\overline{AB})$:	(50,	50,	0)
Third coalition	$(\overline{AC})$:	(51,	0,	49)
Fourth coalition	$(\overline{BC})$:	(0,	50,	50)

The bar over the letters is the conventional sign in the literature for a coalition. The coalition of all the players is referred to as the *grand coalition* or the *coalition of the whole*. The listing of the payoffs in the parentheses is referred to as the set of *disbursements,* or the *payoff vector*. This is different from the *probability vectors* which we discussed in chapter 2. In symbols, the set of disbursements is described in general terms as:

$$\vec{X} = (X_1, X_2, \ldots, X_n)$$

where $\vec{X}$ is the symbol for the payoff vector, and where $X_1, X_2, \ldots$ are the payoffs to players 1, 2, etc. In our example above, the letters A, B, and C are equivalent to the numbers 1, 2, etc. It is better, however, to use numbers in the general form to indicate that there is no limit on the number of players.

The point of our example above is to illustrate another impediment to coalition formation. This time, any coalition of two players which forms will be broken up by an offer from the third player, and this process will proceed without end very much like the cyclical majority of the voter's paradox which we discussed in chapter 1. Here, the coalition $\overline{AC}$ is preferred to the coalition $\overline{AB}$ by both A and C; but the coalition $\overline{BC}$ is preferred to $\overline{AC}$ by both B and C. The coalition $\overline{BC}$, however, could be defeated by the coalition $\overline{AB}$: (49, 51, 0), and so on. Thus:

$$\overline{AB} > \overline{BC} > \overline{AC} > \overline{AB}$$

In the three-person prisoner's dilemma, then, no coalitions formed because of the fear of being the sucker, while in the game above no stable coalition forms because there is always a preferable deal. It might be argued, however, as it was in the case of the voter's paradox, that such situations are unusual, and that, for the most part, stable coalitions will form. Yet, one of the most interesting and important results of game theory is that *stable coalitions form only under the most restrictive conditions*. In order to demonstrate this we shall focus on the third level of analysis in game theory, i.e., games in *characteristic-function form*.

GAMES IN CHARACTERISTIC-FUNCTION FORM

Recall that the presentation of games in *extensive form* listed all of the possible *moves* in a game by means of a game tree, as well as the possible *strategies* and *payoffs*. The *normal form* presented games only in terms of *strategies* and *payoffs*. Games in *characteristic-function form* deal only with *payoffs*. The most important result of this change in focus is that games which are very different in terms of their basic moves and strategies can be compared in terms of the distribution of their payoffs. In other words, no matter how different in terms of moves and strategies, games whose various payoff configurations are similar present similar problems for coalition formation. It becomes increasingly evident, therefore, that the goal of game theory is not to tell us how to play particular games with more skill, but how to make rational choices among competing strategies given different payoff configurations in *any* game. It is also evident that games of *cooperation* are as prevalent and important as games of *conflict,* and that the task is to find cooperative solutions, or to indicate the problems involved in finding such solutions.

The graphic representation of a game in characteristic-function form is simply a listing of certain payoffs to various coalitions. For example, the characteristic function of the three-person prisoner's dilemma game can be described as follows:

$$v(\phi) = 0$$
$$v(\overline{A}) = v(\overline{B}) = v(\overline{C}) = -1$$
$$v(\overline{BC}) = v(\overline{AC}) = v(\overline{AB}) = 0$$
$$v(\overline{ABC}) = 3$$

The letter v can be read, "the value of" or "the payoff to." The letters in the parentheses with the bar on the top are, of course, the particular coalitions. You will notice that even single players are designated by a bar. This is essentially a coalition of one. This notion is used to indicate that there are other coalitions of more than one player. The Greek letter ϕ (phi) refers to the "null set," or the absence of coalitions. The term "function" in the phrase "characteristic function" is, as in previous chapters, a *rule*. In this case, it is a *rule which specifies the value of the game to each subset of the* n *players*. Thus, the characteristic function of the three-person prisoner's dilemma game above states that the value of the game to the null set is zero. The value of the game to each player alone is -1. This means that any player *acting alone* can assure himself or herself a payoff of no less than -1. In this case, the payoff -1 is also referred to as the *security level* for every player in this game.

A similar explanation applies to any two-player coalition. If two players decide to use strategy II, the third player can have an adverse affect on them by also choosing strategy II. As a result, each player receives a payoff of -1. If the third player had chosen strategy I, however, each of the first two players would have gotten payoffs of 3, while the third player would receive -4! It is for this reason that the third player would not choose strategy I, but rather strategy II. Knowing this, any two-player coalition which forms must do so on the basis of choosing strategy I.

This assures the coalition of at least a zero payoff, regardless of the third player's strategy, and creates the possibility of a payoff of 2. The important point is, then, that the actions of the third player cannot drive any two-player coalition below the zero payoff if it chooses strategy I. In the same way, the security level of the three-player coalition must be three—which means a payoff of 1 to each player—since the only alternative is -3, in which case each player receives -1. Since each player could assure himself or herself a payoff of -1 by playing alone, however, there would be no incentive to join the grand coalition unless it offers a payoff greater than -1.

Value

In this discussion, the term "value" is used in a way which may be misleading. In ordinary speech we would say that the "value" of something is what it is worth to us. We also imply that value or worth can change. As the term "value" is used in our discussion of characteristic functions, it also means worth, but in a more restricted way. That is, the value of a game to an individual could be viewed as the payoff which an individual *actually* receives in the play of the game. Or, it might mean the *possible* payoffs which he or she might receive. As the term is used here, however, it means only *one* of the possible payoffs, and, more particularly, the lowest payoff or minimum payoff an individual can assure himself or herself. This applies also to the "value" of any coalition of more than one player. Thus, the "value" of a game to an individual is the *lowest* possible payoff an individual can count on, no matter what the other players do. The value of a game does not change, then, nor is it necessarily the payoff a player receives. Rather, it is the *least* a player can expect from a particular game. Admittedly, this is an odd and, perhaps, pessimistic use of the term "value," but it is the meaning game theorists use. Since it can cause confusion, we suggest that you be sure to understand the term before proceeding with the rest of the analysis.

THE RATIONALITY OF COALITION FORMATION

In the study of politics, we want to know why some coalitions form rather than others, and why some coalitions are more stable than others. We assume, further, that there are good reasons for the formation, cohesion, or instability of coalitions. We may not know the exact reasons, but we generally believe that those who form coalitions do so because they achieve something which they would not have achieved otherwise. In other words, we assume that there is some rationality in coalition formation.

ESSENTIAL AND INESSENTIAL GAMES

Game theorists have also been interested in this question of rationality in coalition formation and have tried to specify the characteristics of such rationality. This work bears an interesting resemblance to Arrow's attempt to find noncontradictory conditions for democratic choice, which we discussed in chapter 1. Recall that Arrow proposed several apparently innocuous conditions for democratic choice and then showed that there was no decision rule which could always satisfy them simultaneously. Similarly, game theorists have demonstrated that even mild requirements for rationality in coalition formation cannot be satisfied in whole classes of situations. In the following sections we shall illustrate this point.

Suppose that there were a game in which no player could receive a greater payoff in *any* coalition than he or she could receive by remaining alone. It would seem reasonable, then, to assume that no coalitions would form. Game theorists call all such games *inessential*. No particular value judgment should be read into this term—it is simply a label. *Essential games,* then, are those in which the payoffs to individuals in at least one coalition are greater than the payoffs to individuals alone. In symbolic terms this is written:

$$v(S \cup T) > v(S) + v(T), \text{ if } S \cap T = \phi, \text{ for some } S \text{ and } T$$

The v here means what it meant above—that is, the security level of an individual or a coalition. The symbol $\cup$ means the "union of (sets)." The symbol ∩ means the "interaction of (sets)." The expression $S \cap T = \phi$ is simply another way of saying that the two coalitions S and T are different, or that no member of set S is a member of set T. Note that S and T can be *any* subsets of the n players.

Technically, this condition of essential games is called strict *superadditivity*. This means, basically, that the whole is greater than the sum of its parts. In this case, the whole is the security level of the coalition, $S \cap T$, which is greater than the sum of the security levels of the individual members of the coalition. This notion is to be contrasted with that of *additivity*, in which the whole equals the sum of its parts. The intuitive idea in coalition theory is that individuals will join coalitions only if they can do better than they can alone.

In order to illustrate the notion of an essential game, let us consider the three-person prisoner's dilemma game above. In that game there are four possible coalitions: $(\overline{AB})$, $(\overline{AC})$, $(\overline{BC})$, $(\overline{ABC})$. Let us consider the coalition $(\overline{AB})$, in which $(\overline{AB})$ would be equivalent to $S \cup T$ in the equation above, and where A could be S, and B could be T. Substituting, then we see that

$$v(\overline{AB}) > v(\overline{A}) + v(\overline{B})$$

since

$$0 > -1 - 1 = -2$$

Further, this applies to every coalition in this game. For this reason, *the three-person prisoner's dilemma game is an example of an essential game.* In general, all *inessential games* are constant sum, though the converse does not necessarily hold. That is, there are constant-sum games which are essential. As an example of an *inessential* game, consider the following:

$$v(\overline{A}) = v(\overline{B}) = v(\overline{C}) = 2$$
$$v(\overline{AB}) = v(\overline{AC}) = v(\overline{BC}) = 1$$
$$v(\overline{ABC}) = 0$$

If we assume that these are the only payoffs, then it is clear that no coalitions will form, since each player is better off alone than in any coalition. In symbols,

$$v(\overline{AB}) < v(\overline{A}) + v(\overline{B})$$
$$v(\overline{AC}) < v(\overline{A}) + v(\overline{C})$$
$$v(\overline{BC}) < v(\overline{B}) + v(\overline{C})$$
$$1 < 2 + 2$$

The point about the distinction between essential and inessential games, then, is that we expect coalitions to form in the former, but not in the latter. In other words, in essential games at least some individuals are better off in some coalition than they are by themselves.

RATIONALITY CONDITIONS

The assumptions which we have been making so far in regard to the *value* of a game for individuals or coalitions can be generalized as follows. First, we have assumed what we may call *individual rationality*. This means, simply, that *an individual will not join a coalition unless his or her payoff in that coalition is greater than his or her security level*—i.e., that payoff which an individual can guarantee by his or her own actions regardless of the actions of others. In symbols:

$$I$$
$$x_i \geq v(\bar{i})$$

where x_i stands for individual i's payoff in a particular payoff configuration. This says that an individual will either receive a payoff *higher* than his or her security level or will receive an amount *equal to* it. A rational player will not accept *less than* his security level.

The second condition, which we may call *collective rationality* or the *group Pareto condition*,[3] says that, for all coalitions, the *sum of the payoffs to the members of a coalition must be greater than or equal to the value of that coalition*. The notion of the "value" of a coalition is the same as that of the security level for an individual. Thus, the value or security level of a coalition is the *minimum* payoff the members of a coalition can obtain *regardless* of the actions of those *not* in the coalition. And, just as a rational player will not accept a payoff below his or her security level, so a rational group in coalition will not accept a payoff below its security level.

On the other hand, it may be possible for clever players to obtain more than their security level. Thus, both rationality conditions—individual and collective—allow for the possibility that an individual will obtain a payoff higher than the security level. Such an outcome could occur, for example, where one player bribes another.[4] Thus, it may be advantageous for B to bribe A *not* to join C in a coalition. The only source of B's bribe, however,

3. Russell Hardin suggested this term.
4. In game theory, the term "side payment" is used where we would say "bribe."

is her own payoff in the game. Thus, B may agree to give A some of his payoff in return for A's promise not to join C. We must assume further than this arrangement will benefit both A and B. In any case, the point is that A will receive not only his security level, but also B's bribe. In such a case A's total payoff (X_A) will be greater than A's security level—$v(\overline{A})$. The same analysis applies to coalitions of two or more players. In symbols, the condition of collective rationality can be expressed as follows:

$$\text{II}$$
$$v(S) \leq \sum_{i \in S} x_i \text{ for all } S$$

Finally, what of the *grand coalition,* or the *coalition of the whole?* The first point is that the value of the grand coalition cannot be greater than the payoff available in any game. If for example $100 is to be divided among three individuals, the sum of the payoffs to the three cannot exceed $100. Moreover, in this game, a grand coalition is an agreement among all three individuals on how to divide the $100. If two of the three can get together and exclude the third, a coalition of two has formed. Whether this can happen, of course, depends upon the rules of the game—and these are limitless.

In any case, it would also seem reasonable that rational players in a grand coalition will not accept *less than* the total payoff available. In our example above it would be strange indeed for the group to share $90 and not bother with the additional $10. Thus, we may conclude that if the grand coalition forms, the sum of the payoffs to the individual members will equal the value of the grand coalition. In symbols,

$$\text{III}$$
$$v(N) = \sum_{i=1}^{n} x_i$$

Remember, the grand coalition will form only if the individual members of the coalition cannot do better by themselves or in coalition with a subset of the members of the group. Thus, the value of the grand coalition must be greater than the sum of the security levels of the individual members of the groups. In symbols,

$$v(\overline{N}) > v(\overline{1}) + v(\overline{2}) + \ldots + v(\overline{n})$$

THE CORE

These three conditions, then—(I, II, III)—can be considered criteria for rational coalition formation. That is, it seems reasonable to expect that only those coalitions would form which do not violate any of these conditions. Game theorists call any such set of disbursements (payoffs to individual members of a coalition) the *core* of the game. The core, then, is essentially a rational outcome of a game—the set of disbursements which rational players would accept in a game of perfect information. One of the striking conclusions of game theory is that *all constant-sum n-person games have empty cores!* In other words, there is no disbursement or set of disbursements in any n-person constant-sum game which does not violate at least one of the above conditions. This theoretical result is especially surprising in view of the fact that the conditions for a rational outcome are apparently so weak. As in the case of Arrow's conditions, we made no stricture which seemed particularly difficult to surmount. Yet, as innocuous as those conditions are, they preclude a rational outcome in an entire class of games—n-person constant-sum. Recall that a constant-sum game is one in which the total payoffs are always the same no matter how they are distributed.

In order to illustrate the notion of an "empty core," consider again the game in which three players are to divide \$100. The characteristic function of such a game is:

$$v(\overline{A}) = v(\overline{B}) = v(\overline{C}) = 0$$
$$v(\overline{AB}) = v(\overline{AC}) = v(\overline{BC}) = 100$$
$$v(\overline{ABC}) = 100$$

This says that an individual alone cannot guarantee himself or herself anything, while coalitions of two or three can obtain the full \$100.

Notice that every outcome listed above in our analysis of this game is Pareto optimal in the sense that no change is possible which does not reduce the payoff to at least one player. On the other hand, for every disbursement of payoffs, and every coalition structure, there is another coalition structure and set of disbursements which two of the three players prefer. Thus, we would not expect any stable coalition to form, nor would we expect the game to end without some kind of arbitrary decision. For example, once everyone realizes that no two-person coalitions are stable, they might agree to the even division of the grand coalition. On the other hand, two of the players might also realize that if they resist all bribes and hold firm in their two-member coalition, they will do better than in the grand coalition.

Either of these possibilities, however, violates the condition of collective rationality. To see this, consider first the grand coalition. The payoff to each member is $33.33. But, the *value* of every two-person coalition is $100.00. This means that the actual payoff to any *two* members of the grand coalition ($66.66) is less than the sum of their payoffs in a two-member coalition ($100.00) involving those two. Thus, for example, we have,

$$
\begin{array}{cccc}
 & A & B & C \\
(\overline{ABC}): & (33\frac{1}{3}, & 33\frac{1}{3}, & 33\frac{1}{3})
\end{array}
$$

But,

$$
v(\overline{AB}) > X_A + X_B
$$
$$
100 > 33\frac{1}{3} + 33\frac{1}{3}
$$

Similarly, consider any two-person coalition:

$$
\begin{array}{cccc}
(\overline{AB}, \overline{C}): & A & B & C \\
 & (50, & 50, & 0)
\end{array}
$$

Then,

$$
v(\overline{AB}) = X_A + X_B; \quad 100 = 50 + 50
$$
$$
v(\overline{AC}) > X_A + X_C; \quad 100 > 50 + 0
$$
$$
v(\overline{BC}) > X_B + X_C; \quad 100 > 50 + 0
$$

In this three-person constant-sum game, therefore, there is no core.

Interestingly, however, the three-person prisoner's dilemma game *does* have a core. One of the outcomes in the core is $(1,1,1)$. This, however, is not the only outcome. In fact, every disbursement in which all three members receive more than zero is in the core. To see this, recall that the security level of any individual in the three-person prisoner's dilemma is -1, which can be achieved by choosing the defection strategy. Also, the security level for any two-member coalition is zero. This can be achieved by two players choosing the cooperative strategy. For the outcome in which everyone receives 1, then, all players receive more than their security level, the sum of the payoffs to individuals in every two-person coalition is less than this payoff in the grand coalition, and finally, the sum of the payoffs to the individuals in the grand coalition is equal to the value of the grand coalition. The oddity, of course, is that despite the existence of a core, an outcome which is *not* in the core, $(-1,-1,-1)$ is the rational outcome in the three-person prisoner's dilemma. This raises rather starkly the conflict between individual and collective rationality.

SOLUTION CONCEPTS

The core is what is known as a *solution concept*. In game theory a solution concept is simply a set of *conditions* on possible *outcomes* of a game. In contrast, recall that the Arrow conditions applied to *decision procedures* rather than outcomes. In the conclusion we shall discuss the relationship between the Arrow conditions and solution concepts.

A solution concept, then, sets out the criteria for a collective choice, just as majority rule sets out a criterion for collective choice. In the case of the core, the collective outcome must satisfy the conditions of individual and collective rationality. In the case of majority rule, any outcome is acceptable which receives the support of a majority.

In subsequent sections, we shall consider several other solution concepts which impose different conditions. We shall be interested in the nature of these conditions and the outcomes which they yield.

IMPUTATIONS

One of the problems with the core as a solution concept is that, for an important class of games, it does not exist. This is analogous to the problem with the Arrow conditions which cannot be satisfied in a certain class of situations—i.e., those with paradox-producing preference profiles. Moreover, even when the core does exist, it does not necessarily indicate a unique outcome. This, of course, is analogous to the tie vote where majority rule is used.

The question, then, is whether it is possible to alter the conditions of the core in such a way that we do not seriously violate the spirit of these conditions, and yet produce outcomes for all games. We would also like to produce just one outcome as the collective choice. In the case of the Arrow problem, we saw that the alteration of the Transitivity condition, the condition of Unlimited Domain, and the Independence of Irrelevant Alternatives condition have all been suggested as ways of avoiding that undesirable result.

Of the core conditions, however, which should be altered or eliminated? It has generally been argued that the condition of individual rationality is essential for any solution concept. Without this restriction, individuals could accept less than their security level. The spirit of the notion of rationality would certainly be violated were this to occur. A similar argument has been made for the condition of collective rationality involving the grand coalition. There seems to be no good reason for expecting that individuals in a grand coalition might rationally accept less than the total payoff available.

This has left the condition of collective rationality involving coalitions smaller than the grand coalition. This, of course, is our condition II above. It has been argued that this condition could be eliminated with the least damage to the rationality notion. That is, it could be considered rational for an individual to accept a smaller payoff than he or she might obtain in a particular coalition as long as the payoff was greater than the security level. Thus, in the example above, where $100 was to be divided, the outcome (33⅓, 33⅓, 33⅓) violates the collective rationality notion—II above—but not individual rationality—I above—nor the grand coalition condition—III above. The set of disbursements which satisfy conditions I and III is referred to as the *imputation* of a game. Clearly, the set of imputations is going to be at least as big as the core set, and will generally be bigger. In our example of the $100 game, for instance, all four disbursements—those associated with the grand coalition as well as the two-person coalitions—are imputations! Such a result is clearly of little help to us in our attempt to find a single "best" outcome.

The problem with the core concept, then, is that it is too strong a requirement and cannot be satisfied in a great many cases. The difficulty with the imputation notion, however, is that it is too weak a requirement and does not discriminate sufficiently among the possible outcomes.

What we are looking for, then, is a solution concept which provides a *minimum number of possible satisfactory outcomes*—i.e., outcomes which satisfy the conditions of the solution concept—*for all games*. Ideally, we would like to find a solution concept which indicates a unique outcome for every game.

DOMINATION

We might ask whether any of the myriad outcomes in the imputation could be considered preferable to any other. Toward this end game theorists

use the notion of *domination*. One outcome or disbursement is said to dominate another *for a particular subset of players in coalition* if the payoff to
each of the members of the coalition in one of the outcomes is greater than
the payoff in the other. For example, consider two of the possible disbursements in the $100 game above:

$$
\begin{array}{cccc}
 & A & B & C \\
\vec{X}_1: & (50, & 50, & 0) \\
\vec{X}_2: & (0, & 60, & 40)
\end{array}
$$

In this case, players B and C prefer $\vec{X}_2$ to $\vec{X}_1$ since both receive a
higher payoff in   than in $\vec{X}_1$. Thus, $\vec{X}_2$ is said to *dominate* $\vec{X}_1$ via individuals A and B.

Ideally, then, we would like to be able to rank order all of the possible
imputations by means of the domination notion. Then, the best outcome
would be that imputation which was dominant. The problem here, however,
is that some imputations may be dominant for some players, while other imputations are dominant for others. In a sense, what we are doing is asking
how the players would "vote" in an "election" involving imputations. Unfortunately, it turns out that the domination notion also involves cyclical
majorities. To see this, add a third disbursement to the two above:

$$
\begin{array}{cccc}
 & A & B & C \\
\vec{X}_1: & (50, & 50, & 0) \\
\vec{X}_2: & (0, & 60, & 40) \\
\vec{X}_3: & (40, & 0, & 60)
\end{array}
$$

Here, players B and C prefer $\vec{X}_2$ to $\vec{X}_1$. Players A and C prefer $\vec{X}_3$ to $\vec{X}_2$,
and players A and B prefer $\vec{X}_1$ to $\vec{X}_3$. In other words, we have a cyclical majority among imputations:

$$\vec{X}_2 > \vec{X}_1 > \vec{X}_3 > \vec{X}_2$$

and no imputation is dominant for all players. Thus, the notion of domination cannot necessarily be used to narrow down the range of choices produced by the imputation notion, since it cannot avoid the problem of intransitivities.

THE SHAPLEY VALUE

Some interesting solution concepts have been developed for non–constant-sum games which appear more satisfying than the imputation notion. A non–constant-sum game is simply one in which the sums of the payoffs in various outcomes are not always the same. Consider the following characteristic function of such a game:

$$v(\overline{A}) = 1; \ v(\overline{B}) = 2; \ v(\overline{C}) = 0$$
$$v(\overline{AB}) = 4; \ v(\overline{AC}) = 5; \ v(\overline{BC}) = 4$$
$$v(\overline{ABC}) = 12$$

This says that player A in a coalition by himself can get a payoff of 1, player B can get 2, and C could get nothing alone. Coalition $\overline{AB}$ can get a payoff of 4, $\overline{AC}$ can get 5, and $\overline{BC}$ can get 4. The grand coalition can get a payoff of 12. While we have specified the payoffs to various coalitions, we have not indicated how the payoffs would be divided among the members of the coalition. Let us examine this situation and see if we can determine *which* coalition ought to form and why.

Suppose the grand coalition formed and the payoff was divided equally. Then, each player would receive 4. But, should all three players accept that outcome? The answer to this question depends upon the available alternatives. Notice, first, that the players do not all fare as well by themselves. Player B does best with 2, A next with 1, and C receives no payoff at all in a coalition of one. It would seem, then, that C should be more anxious than A or B to join a coalition, and that B should be the least anxious. For this reason, B would have to be induced to join a coalition with either A or C. But, how much could she expect to receive as an inducement? Consider coalition $\overline{AB}$. Without B, A can get only one unit; with B, the coalition gets four. Therefore, B can be said to have brought 3 units to the coalition, and this should be the limit of her expectations. On the other hand, while A may be more anxious than B to form a coalition, it is certainly in B's interest to encourage the formation of the coalition $\overline{AB}$. Therefore, it would seem that B might also solicit A to form a coalition. In that case, A would expect an inducement. Since B can get 2 units by herself, A can be said to bring 2 units to the coalition, and this is the limit of A's expectation.

This reasoning forms the basis of a solution concept known as the *Shapley value* after its creator, L. S. Shapley (1953). It *indicates the payoff each player can expect to receive in the grand coalition,* and depends upon two factors: (1) the configuration of the characteristic function; and (2) the order in which the grand coalition is formed. That is, Shapley assumes that the grand coalition will be formed in stages, first by the formation of a two-player coalition and then the grand coalition. He also assumes that *all two-player coalitions are equally likely to form, and that it is equally likely that any one player will solicit any other player to form a coalition.* That is, in our example, it is as likely that A will solicit B as it is that B will solicit A. This particular assumption does not appear realistic, but it leads to an interesting result.

Returning to our example, then, we shall demonstrate how the Shapley value is calculated. If it is equally likely that the grand coalition will be formed in any order, then the probability of the grand coalition's forming by A soliciting B and then C joining $\overline{AB}$ is $\frac{1}{6}$ since there are five other possible orders:

$$(B,C,A), (C,B,A), (C,A,B), (A,B,C), (A,C,B)$$

Remember, these represent the *order* in which the grand coalition is formed. Shapley then points out that in two orderings out of six, each player is the first to solicit another. For example, B solicits C in (B,C,A) and B solicits A in (B,A,C). Remember, too, that the limit of any player's payoff expectation in the two-player coalition is the difference between the total value of the coalition and the amount which the first player (the "solicitor") would receive alone. Let us list the expectation of the solicited player in each ordering:

Order of Coalition Formation		Maximum Expected Payoff
(B,A)	:	$4\ (V(\overline{AB})) - 2\ (V(\overline{B})) = 2$
(B,C)	:	$4\ (V(\overline{BC})) - 2\ (V(\overline{B})) = 2$
(C,B)	:	$4\ (V(\overline{BC})) - 0\ (V(\overline{C})) = 4$
(C,A)	:	$5\ (V(\overline{AC})) - 0\ (V(\overline{C})) = 5$
(A,B)	:	$4\ (V(\overline{AB})) - 1\ (V(\overline{A})) = 3$
(A,C)	:	$5\ (V(\overline{AC})) - 1\ (V(\overline{A})) = 4$

The second player in the coalition is the one who has been solicited, and the number at the far right is his or her maximum expected payoff. Note that this does not mean that a player should expect such a payoff. Rather, it is the *upper limit* to any player's expectations. Shapley then uses this figure in computing the expected payoff in the grand coalition.

The process of forming the grand coalition is similar to that in which the two-player coalition is formed, except that a single player is solicited by the other two. At that point, the expected payoff to the solicited player is the difference between the total value of the grand coalition, and the value of the two-player coalition which precedes it. Thus, if the coalition $\overline{AB}$ formed, with a value of 4, the expected payoff to C for joining with $\overline{AB}$ would be

$$12\ (V(\overline{ABC})\ ) - 4\ (V(\overline{AB})\ ) = 8$$

The expected payoff for the other players as third (solicited) members of the grand coalition would be computed in the same way:

Order of Coalition Formation	Maximum Expected Value
$(\overline{BA},\ C)$	$: 12\ (V(\overline{ABC})) - 4\ (V(\overline{AB})) = 8$
$(\overline{AB},\ C)$	$: 12\ (V(\overline{ABC})) - 4\ (V(\overline{AB})) = 8$
$(\overline{BC},\ A)$	$: 12\ (V(\overline{ABC})) - 4\ (V(\overline{BC})) = 8$
$(\overline{CB},\ A)$	$: 12\ (V(\overline{ABC})) - 4\ (V(\overline{BC})) = 8$
$(\overline{AC},\ B)$	$: 12\ (V(\overline{ABC})) - 5\ (V(\overline{AC})) = 7$
$(\overline{CA},\ B)$	$: 12\ (V(\overline{ABC})) - 5\ (V(\overline{AC})) = 7$

Notice that every player is in the same position twice: each solicits one other player for a two-player coalition; each is solicited by another player to form a two-player coalition; each is a member of a two-player coalition which solicits a third player; and each is the third player solicited by a two-player coalition. *Remember, each of these situations is assumed to be equally likely for purposes of calculating the Shapley value, or the expected payoff to each member of the grand coalition.*

For any player, then, the probability is $1/6$ that he or she will receive only his or her payoff as a coalition of one when he or she is the initiator of the grand coalition. But, since there are two such situations for each player [e.g. (A,B,C), or (A,C,B) if we are considering player A], there is a $2/6$ or $1/3$ probability of that payoff. Continuing our computation for player A, there is a probability of $1/6$ that he or she will receive a payoff of 2, and a $1/6$ probability that he or she will receive 5 as the solicited member of coalitions $(\overline{BA})$ and $(\overline{CA})$ respectively. Finally, there is a probability of $2/6$ that A will receive a payoff of 8 as the solicited third member of the grand coalition which forms in the orders (B,C,A) and (C,B,A). The total expected payoff for player A, then, is the sum of these expected payoffs, or,

$$\text{Player A: } \tfrac{1}{3}(1) + \tfrac{1}{6}(2) + \tfrac{1}{6}(5) + \tfrac{1}{3}(8) = 4\tfrac{1}{6}$$

For players B and C the total expected payoffs are:

Player B: $\frac{1}{3}(2) + \frac{1}{6}(4) + \frac{1}{6}(3) + \frac{1}{3}(7) = 4\frac{1}{6}$
Player C: $\frac{1}{3}(0) + \frac{1}{6}(2) + \frac{1}{6}(4) + \frac{1}{3}(8) = 3\frac{2}{3}$

These expected payoffs are called the *Shapley value* of the game for these players. Notice that the sum of these values is equal to the total payoff of the grand coalition. In other words, these three players—A, B, and C—will divide the payoff of the grand coalition $4\frac{1}{6}$, $4\frac{1}{6}$, and $3\frac{2}{3}$ respectively. Recall that our original suggestion was simply an even division of the payoff. What the Shapley value does is to divide the payoff according to the characteristic function of the game. This includes not only what each player would have received alone, but the value of two-player coalitions and the grand coalition. The Shapley value uses all of this information in calculating expected payoffs. The Shapley value can also be thought of as the *relative power* of each player in the game, and, as such, has been used as a *power index*. In other words, a player with a higher expected payoff could be said to be more powerful than a player with a lower expected payoff. In this case, the power of an individual comes from his or her position in the game, and not from any personal skill, ability, or characteristic. The Shapley value, then, is an indication of the relative position of each player in the game, and the payoff each can command. It is a *solution concept* in that it prescribes an outcome which is stable as long as the players accept the assumptions which lead to that outcome.

There are two important points to note about the Shapley value. First, it assumes that the grand coalition has formed. Thus, the problem is simply to determine the appropriate distribution of the payoff among the players according to their position in the game. Second, the Shapley value always provides a *unique* outcome. In that respect it is superior to the core or imputation as a solution concept.

THE BARGAINING SET

The Shapley value still leaves us searching for a solution concept which is useful when the grand coalition is generally *not* expected to form. As our final example of such a solution concept, we shall discuss the *bargaining set*.

Suppose that we dropped the condition of group rationality as it applies to all *n*-players together, and simply required that, for any coalition other

than the grand coalition, the value of that coalition is equal to the sum of the
payoffs to the members of the coalition. In symbols,

$$\sum_{i \in B_j} x_i = v(B_j)$$

where "B_j" is any coalition which is not the grand coalition. Any set of coalitions, then, which satisfies this condition, as well as the condition of individual rationality, is said to be an *individually rational payoff configuration*
(IRPC). In symbols, the IRPC is written

$$(\vec{X}, B)$$

where B denotes the set of coalitions $(B_1, B_2, \ldots, B_m)$ which does not
include the grand coalition. The set of such coalitions is generally rather
large. There is, however, a way to reduce the size of the set, though without
indicating a unique result as in the Shapley value.

Suppose that two players, j and k, are members of a coalition. Each
might receive a higher payoff in another coalition. Suppose further that there
is a coalition, C, which includes k but not j, and in which every member of
C receives a higher payoff than in their present coalition. In symbols,

$$\sum_{i \in C} Y_i = v(C)$$

$$Y_i > X_i, \ i \in C$$

where "Y_i" is the payoff to player i (any player) in the new coalition C, and
X_i is the payoff to player i in a coalition *other than* C. In such a case, player
k is said to have an *objection* against player j. In simpler terms, this means
that k has a better option or alternative than to be in a coalition with j. Conversely, j can have a *counterobjection* by being able to find another coalition
which excludes k, and in which all of the members of that new coalition are
better off than they were. Either player has a *justified objection* against the
other if there is no counterobjection. These terms are not meant to imply any
particular judgment about the players. They are simply conventional terms
in the literature.

*The set of all individually rational payoff configurations in which no
player has a justified objection against any other member of the same coalition is referred to as the bargaining set. In symbols, an element of the*

bargaining set is denoted by the disbursements followed by the coalition structure. For example,

$$(0, 50, 50; \overline{A}, \overline{BC})$$

Let us indicate the bargaining set of two simple games. First, consider the game above in which three players divide $100. In the payoff configuration $(0, 50, 50; A, \overline{BC})$, whatever B could offer to A to form a new coalition, C could match. If, for example, B offered A 49, while B received 51, then B could be said to have an *objection* against C since both A and B would be better off in the new coalition than they had been before. On the other hand, this is not a *justified objection* against C since C has a *counterobjection* against B. (*Question:* What is C's counterobjection?) Therefore, this payoff configuration *is* a member of the bargaining set. What about $(60, 40, 0; \overline{AB}, \overline{C})$? Here B has an objection against A since B could offer C the payoff configuration $(0, 55, 45; \overline{A}, \overline{BC})$. Moreover, this is a justified objection since A cannot offer C an equal or better deal. To see this, suppose A offers C 45 as B had done. Then A would have to receive only 55, which is less than A received in the original coalition $\overline{AB}$. This violates the second condition above which says that *each* member of the new coalition must be better off. Therefore, A does not have a counterobjection to B's objection, and the configuration $(60, 40, 0; \overline{AB}, \overline{C})$ is not a member of the bargaining set.

Another way of saying this is that configuration $(60, 40, 0; \overline{AB}, \overline{C})$ is not a stable outcome, since B and C can find a better alternative, while A cannot both improve his position and offer B or C a better deal. The configuration $(0, 50, 50; \overline{A}, \overline{BC})$, on the other hand, *is* considered stable since any move by B or C to form a coalition with A can be countered by an even more advantageous move. Thus, B and C cannot move to a position which is both more advantageous and stable. For that reason, they have an incentive to remain in the original position. Of course, we have not considered how the players formed that particular coalition with those particular payoffs. The bargaining set, however, does not concern itself with that question. It simply asks whether a coalition configuration *once formed* will be stable.

For this particular game, the payoff configurations which are part of the bargaining set are all those in which the payoffs to the members of a coalition are equal. This includes:

$$(0, 0, 0; \overline{A}, \overline{B}, \overline{C})$$
$$(50, 50, 0; \overline{AB}, \overline{C})$$
$$(0, 50, 50; \overline{A}, \overline{BC})$$
$$(50, 0, 50; \overline{AC}, \overline{B})$$
$$(33\tfrac{1}{3}, 33\tfrac{1}{3}, 33\tfrac{1}{3}; \overline{ABC})$$

Notice that the bargaining set here includes the unlikely situation in which no coalition forms.

We can also indicate the bargaining set for a nonconstant-sum game such as the following:

$$V(\overline{A}) = 0; \ V(\overline{B}) = 0; \ V(\overline{C}) = 0.$$
$$V(\overline{AB}) = 50; \ V(\overline{AC}) = 30; \ V(\overline{BC}) = 40.$$
$$V(\overline{ABC}) = 60$$

Let us first consider an equal division of the payoff within each coalition:

$$(25, 25, 0; \overline{AB}, \overline{C})$$
$$(15, 0, 15; \overline{AC}, \overline{B})$$
$$(0, 20, 20; \overline{A}, \overline{BC})$$

Note that these are all individually rational payoff configurations. In the first configuration, neither A nor B has an objection to the other given only those payoffs presented. In any other coalition, A and B would be worse off than they are together. If A joined with C he would receive only 15; if B joined with C she would receive only 20. It would appear, then, that $(25, 25, 0; \overline{AB}, \overline{C})$ is in the bargaining set. But, C would certainly have an incentive to entice B into a new coalition by offering B 26 in the coalition $(\overline{BC})$. This would result in the configuration $(0, 26, 14; \overline{A}, \overline{BC})$. Notice that this is preferable to C than offering 26 to A, since that would result in the configuration $(26, 0, 4; \overline{AC}, \overline{B})$, in which C receives only 4. But then A would have an incentive to offer C 15 in a coalition $\overline{AC}$: $(15, 0, 15; \overline{AC}, \overline{B})$. At that point B could offer A 25 in the original coalition and the process would begin again. It is evident, then, that $(25, 25, 0; \overline{AB}, \overline{C})$ is not part of a stable bargaining set. For this game, the bargaining set would be:

$$(20, 30, 0; \overline{AB}, \overline{C})$$
$$(20, 0, 10; \overline{AC}, \overline{B})$$
$$(0, 30, 10; \overline{A}, \overline{BC})$$

Here, there are no justifiable objections. For every new coalition which any member of any coalition proposes, the original partner can propose a new coalition in which he or she also improves his or her position. Thus, if A proposes to join C, B can offer C the same deal without being worse off herself. Since this is true for every coalition listed here—that is, since every objection meets a counterobjection—these payoff configurations are part of the bargaining set.

The bargaining set is thus an improvement over the imputation notion, but it still does little to narrow down our search for reasonable outcomes. Once again it appears that the attempt to impose reasonable conditions on a collective-choice process leaves us with no outcome at all in many important situations, while a relaxation of these conditions produces a plethora of possible outcomes and no method of choosing among them.

CONCLUSION

In this chapter, the decision makers are *players* in *games* which have *moves, rules, strategies,* and *payoffs.* Strategies are sets of moves. The alternatives vary, depending upon the level of analysis. For games in extensive form, the alternatives are moves. For games in normal form, the alternatives are strategies. And, for games in characteristic-function form (or coalitional form) the alternatives are coalitions.

The basis for choosing a move or strategy or coalition is the payoff associated with each. Players are utility maximizers. They want to obtain the largest possible payoff in any given situation. The payoff configuration is determined by the game itself. Any particular payoff, or outcome, is determined by the joint choices of moves, strategies, or payoffs of the players involved. The goal of game theory is to determine whether there is a "best" move, strategy, or coalition for rational, utility-maximizing players in any game.

Since the variety of possible games is unlimited, and since, therefore, game theorists cannot examine every game individually, the theoretical strategy has been to classify games according to the configuration of the payoffs, and to try to generalize about classes of games. The most famous classification is the *two-person zero-sum* game, in which the total of the payoffs to the players is zero for every outcome. In other words, one player wins exactly what the other player loses. Such games are examples of *pure conflict* situations. They are also a special case of the general classification of games known as *constant-sum*. In constant-sum games, the total payoff remains the same for every outcome. This total may be zero in the case of zero-sum games, or any other number in the case of non-zero sum games. In constant sum games which are not zero sum, both (all) players may receive positive payoffs. Thus, one player's winning (or receiving a positive payoff) does not require another's losing (or receiving negative payoff). In other words, these are games in which there are not necessarily losers. Nonconstant-sum games are those in which the total payoffs to the players may vary for each outcome. Game theorists also distinguish between two-person and *n*-person games, the latter involving more than two players. The focus of game theory is primarily on games in normal form and characteristic-function form, rather than on games in extensive form, since the latter are generally too cumbersome and, in any case, are not easily amenable to generalization.

For games in normal form, game theorists distinguish between *pure* and *mixed* strategies. A pure strategy is simply the choosing of a single strategy. A mixed strategy is the choosing of more than one strategy, each with a particular probability. A pure strategy may be thought of as a mixed strategy in which the probability of some one strategy is 1.00, while the probability of any other strategy is zero. Pure strategies are distinguished according to whether or not they are *dominant*. A dominant pure strategy is one in which every outcome associated with that strategy is at least as good as the equivalent outcome for any alternative strategy against the same pure strategy of the opposing player. The *security level* of every player is the minimum payoff of a dominant pure strategy—the least that any player can guarantee himself or herself, regardless of the actions of other players. The object of rational utility-maximizing players is to maximize their payoffs.

One of the most important results in game theory is that for every two-person zero-sum game of complete information, there is at least one outcome which is *stable* or *in equilibrium*. Depending upon the strategies used by the players, these are referred to as *pure or mixed strategy equilibria*. A stable outcome is one which no rational player has an incentive to alter by choosing another strategy. This stable outcome is the best that each player can achieve, given the particular payoff configuration, and, as such, is the outcome which should result from the strategic choices of rational players.

Notice, however, that this result occurs under very restrictive conditions—two players, complete information, and payoffs which always total zero. This is analogous to the situation described in chapter 1 in which the restriction of single-peaked preferences assured a noncyclical or stable outcome. It is also similar to the situation in the previous chapter in which limitations on the number of dimensions, individual utility functions, and the preference density function (distribution of first preferences) yielded a stable outcome.

On the other hand, notice that the situation of pure conflict in the game-theory situation does produce a stable outcome, while the situation of pure conflict in the voting situations of chapter 1 (e.g. the three-individual, three-alternative case, which resulted in the voter's paradox or cyclical majority) yields an unstable outcome.

The relaxation of restrictions in game theoretical situations tends to produce unstable situations, or situations with peculiar problems. For example, one of the most famous nonconstant-sum games is the two-person *prisoner's dilemma,* where the circumstances of the situation provide an incentive for rational players to choose strategies which produce an outcome which is mutually less desirable than another possible outcome. This result also holds where three players are involved.

Where the restriction on the number of players and configuration of payoffs is relaxed, the situations become rather complex. It is partly for this reason that n-person games are usually analyzed in terms of their payoffs alone, i.e., in characteristic-function form. Another reason is that analyses of games in characteristic-function form allow much greater generalization about classes of games. Thus, games with very different moves and strategies may be quite similar in terms of the configuration of their payoffs. The analysis of n-person games also raises the possibility of *coalition formation,* in which two or more players agree to concert their strategies in order to achieve a particular payoff configuration. That is, if a game has a variety of possible outcomes, a coalition is a group of players which agrees to coordinate its actions in such a way that the outcome which they mutually desire is the outcome of the game. Obviously, an effective coalition must be one that is in a position to determine the outcome, regardless of the actions of the other player(s).

The main question of n-person game theory, then, is which coalitions will form. That is, which payoff configurations will rational, utility-maximizing players agree to? The obvious answer appears to be, "the payoff which will bring the greatest return to all members of the coalition." In fact, however, the search for *stable coalitions*—i.e., coalitions which no member has an incentive to leave, and which cannot benefit from the inclusion of any other member(s)—has shown that such coalitions are rare. The problem, of course, is that rational outcomes require the *mutual* satisfaction of all members of the coalition where alternative coalitions are available. When expressed this way, the difficulty does not seem unusual or counterintuitive.

Stable coalitions in n-person games are also referred to as *solutions* to the games. A rule for determining which coalitions are stable, or whether a game has a solution, is known as a *solution concept*. Most of the work in n-person game theory has been an attempt to devise solution concepts which do not violate our intuitive sense of rationality, and which produce as few candidates as possible for the solution—ideally, just one. This is similar to the quest for a Condorcet winner in a voting situation, and to Arrow's attempt to find a social welfare function which satisfies certain intuitively acceptable conditions. It also resembles the attempt to produce a stable result through vote trading or logrolling.

Initially, we considered three conditions which seemed reasonable for any solution concept:

1. The payoff to the players should be equal to, or greater than, their individual security levels. This is the condition of *individual rationality*.
2. The payoffs to the players should not be less than they can obtain in a coalition. This is the condition of *group rationality*.
3. The sum of the payoffs to all of the players must be equal to the value of the grand coalition. This is the condition of group rationality applied to the grand coalition.

The payoff configurations and coalitions which satisfy these three conditions are called the *core* of a game. The core is thus a solution concept. It says that any coalition(s) and payoff configurations which satisfy these conditions are the coalitions which ought to be formed by rational, utility-maximizing players, and the disbursement of payoffs to which they should agree. One of the most important results in n-person game theory, however, is that *all essential constant-sum* n-*person games have empty cores*. In other words, there are no coalitions and payoff configurations in essential, n-person constant-sum games which satisfy these three conditions. On the other hand, cores do exist in essential, n-person nonconstant-sum games, such as the prisoner's dilemma.

Since these apparently reasonable conditions set too stringent a requirement for rationality, game theorists have weakened them in several ways. First, they have eliminated the second condition. Then, all payoff configurations which satisfy just the first and third condition are referred to as the *imputations* of a game. Unlike the core, imputations always exist, but generally there are too many of them to serve as a satisfactory solution concept.

In order to distinguish among imputations, and perhaps rank-order them, the notion of *domination* has been suggested. One imputation is said to dominate another if some subset of players in a coalition can obtain at least the sum of their payoffs, and if each player receives more in the dominant imputation than in the dominated imputation. While the notion of domination can serve to rank imputations, it cannot avoid the possibility of intransitivities.

One of the more interesting and satisfying solution concepts, the Shapley value, has been suggested for nonconstant-sum games in which the grand coalition is expected to form. An advantage of the Shapley value is that it provides a unique outcome, and it takes into account the characteristic function of the game. In other words, it reflects the relative position of the players. The Shapley value is the expected payoff for each player when the grand coalition is formed in stages. The Shapley value has also been used as an index of the relative power of individuals in a collective-choice situation. In that case, the power of an individual derives from his position in the game, and not from any personal ability or attribute.

Another approach to finding a solution has been to look for a *set* of outcomes in which each particular outcome (coalition and payoff configuration) is stable *if it forms*. In other words, while the solution is not unique, it is stable. One such concept is the *bargaining set,* which does not tell us which particular coalition and payoff configuration should (rationally) form, but does indicate that if any member of a specified *set* of coalitions and payoff configurations forms, it will be stable. The bargaining set is the set of all *individually rational payoff configurations* (IRPC) in which no player has a *justified objection* against any other member of the same coalition. An IRPC is a set of payoffs which satisfies the conditions of individual rationality and a modified condition of group rationality, in which the sum of the payoffs to individual members of any coalition *other than* the grand coalition is equal to the total value of the coalition. A player who has a *justified objection* against another player in the same coalition has an opportunity to join a new coalition from which the other player is excluded, and in which each member receives a higher payoff than in his previous coalition; at the same time, the excluded player cannot find such a new coalition.

The analysis in this chapter has shown that the goal of game theory is not to tell us how to play any particular game better, but to find out whether particular *classes* of games have "best" or "better" outcomes for rational players. The results which we have described are *formal* results, just as the Arrow Impossibility Theorem is a formal result. In other words, game theorists have not studied all, or almost all, two-person zero-sum games, for example, but have found ways of proving statements about all two-person zero-sum games, using logic and mathematics. Since such proofs are difficult, however, we have not included them here.

In applying game theory to real political situations, then, the first step is to ascertain what kind of game that real situation resembles. This is not an easy task and, in fact, would be the main work in applied game theory. Once the political situation is identified as an example of a particular class of games, however, the formal results can provide satisfactory explanations. In the next chapter we shall look more closely at real political coalitions.

CHAPTER SEVEN

Coalition Theory

WE HAVE SEEN in the previous chapter that coalition theory developed from the analysis of n-person games, in which various solution concepts were proposed as a way of determining which coalition(s) would form, or which payoff configuration(s) would prevail. These solution concepts were, essentially, restrictions on the possible outcomes of any game, while characteristic functions were restrictions on possible outcomes for each specific game. In the present chapter, we shall extend that analysis by considering further restrictions on possible outcomes which attempt to make coalition theory more relevant for the analysis of real political situations. In the first section, we shall consider William Riker's notion of *minimum winning coalitions*. The next section will focus on some recent debates about this so-called size principle. The final section will examine alternative criteria for coalition formation, such as Leiserson's notion of ideological diversity and Gamson's size principle.

MINIMUM WINNING COALITIONS

The notion of "winning" may be viewed as a part of the characteristic function of a game and, as such, a restriction on possible outcomes. For example, suppose we are considering a "parliamentary" game in which a winning coalition—i.e., the party which will govern—must obtain more than half of the votes in the parliament. This can be seen as a two-person zero-sum game in which there are no payoffs to anyone until a majority has formed. Notice that the restriction called "winning" reduces any n-person game to a two-person game. To see this more clearly, suppose we have a parliament composed of five parties—Q, R, S, T, U—each of which has twenty members. With a simple majority rule in effect, at least three of the parties will have to join together to form a winning coalition, while the other two parties will be the losing coalition. The "two persons" in this game, then, are the winning coalition (WC) and the losing coalition (LC). How the WC divides its spoils is another story—in fact, an n-person story!

Although the notion of "winning" need not imply a zero-sum game, most of the work on coalition formation has made that assumption. This is similar to the assumption which we encountered in chapter 5, "Spatial Models," where the zero sum referred to the plurality of the winners and losers. That is, the plurality of the winner was a positive number, while the "plurality" of the loser was a negative number of equal magnitude—hence, the zero sum.

The notion of "winning," then, in political contexts is basically a size restriction on the coalition-formation process. In a game involving five players—such as the parliamentary parties referred to above—the rule which requires the governing coalition to be a majority limits the winning coalition to any three, four, or five parties; and the losing coalition to one party, two parties, or no parties. It also implies that no payoff will be forthcoming if no majority coalition is formed. Such a situation is, of course, a stalemate—such was the *immobilisme* of the French Fourth Republic.

While the rule for a winning coalition limits the possible outcomes, it still does not aid very much in empirical prediction, since it allows for the possibility of a great many winners, without telling us which winning coalition will form. William Riker, in his classic work *The Theory of Political Coalitions* (1962) suggests that the coalition which will form is the minimum winning coalition (MWC). *A MWC is defined as a coalition which would not be winning if any one of its members defected.* For example, in the five-party parliament above, any combination of three parties is minimal winning, while any combination of four or five parties is *not* minimal winning. In this case, since all parties have the same number of members, the minimal winning coalitions are all the same size—60 members. But, this is not always the case. Suppose we had a parliament of five parties with the members distributed as follows:

$$Q = 20, \quad R = 15, \quad S = 10, \quad T = 25, \quad U = 30$$

With majority rule, the coalition $\overline{TU}$ would be a minimum winning coalition with 55 members, while $\overline{QSU}$ would also be a minimum winning coalition but with 60 members. That is, if Q or S or U defected from the coalition $\overline{QSU}$, it would no longer be winning; and if T or U left $\overline{TU}$ it would no longer be winning. In other words, a *MWC has no surplus members*.

Riker derives his *size principle* (the term used to describe his prediction of the formation of MWC's) from an analysis of the relationship between various characteristic functions and coalitions of various size. To see how he does this, consider a five-person zero-sum game with the following characteristic function:

$$V(\overline{Q}) = -1; V(\overline{R}) = -1; V(\overline{S}) = -1; V(\overline{T}) = -1; V(\overline{U}) = -1$$

$$V(\overline{QR}) = -2; V(\overline{QS}) = -2; V(\overline{QT}) = -2; V(\overline{QU}) = -2; V(\overline{RS}) = -2;$$
$$V(\overline{RT}) = -2; V(\overline{RU}) = -2; V(\overline{ST}) = -2; V(\overline{SU}) = -2; V(\overline{TU}) = -2;$$

$$V(\overline{QRS}) = 2; V(\overline{QRT}) = 2; V(\overline{QRU}) = 2; V(\overline{QST}) = 2; V(\overline{QSU}) = 2;$$
$$V(\overline{QTU}) = 2; V(\overline{RST}) = 2; V(\overline{RSU}) = 2; V(\overline{RTU}) = 2; V(\overline{STU}) = 2;$$

$$V(\overline{QRST}) = 1; V(\overline{QRSU}) = 1; V(\overline{QSTU}) = 1; V(\overline{QRTU}) = 1; V(\overline{RSTU}) = 1$$
$$V(\overline{QRSTU}) = 0.$$

A less cumbersome way of expressing this characteristic function is as follows:

Size of Coalition	Payoff
0	0
1	−1
2	−2
3	2
4	1
5	0

Or, in other words, any single-member coalition receives a payoff of −1; any two-member coalition receives a payoff of −2; any three-member coalition receives a payoff of +2; any four member coalition receives a payoff of +1; and the grand coalition receives nothing. (*Question:* Why must the grand coalition *always* receive nothing in a zero sum game?) This is an example of what has been called a *simple game* in the game-theory literature. In graph form, this game would be portrayed as in fig. 7.1.

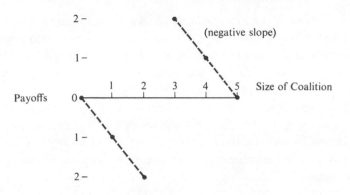

Figure 7.1. A simple game, with negatively sloped characteristic function.

Notice that the positive payoffs to three and four-member coalitions are the opposite of the negative payoffs to the two-member and single-member coalitions respectively. This is, of course, a result of the fact that this is a zero-sum game.

Notice also that the dotted line in fig. 7.1 slopes downward from the upper left toward the lower right. This is referred to as a *negative slope*. A *positive slope* would be one which slopes upward from the lower left to the upper right as in fig. 7.2.

In this case, a coalition of three members receives a payoff of +1, while a coalition of four members receives a payoff of +2. The dotted line which connects these two payoff points is said to have a positive slope.

Notice the significance of these two graphs. Figure 7.1 says that when a coalition *increases* in size from three to four members, the payoff *decreases* from +2 to +1. Figure 7.2 says that when a coalition *increases* in size from three to four members, the payoff *increases* from +1 to +2. In the former case, there is an incentive to form three-member rather than four-member coalitions. In the later case, there *may be* an incentive to form a four-person coalition so long as the slope is sufficiently steep. For example, if the members split the payoffs equally, the three members of the winning coalition in fig. 7.2 would split +1 and receive ⅓ each; the four-member coalition would split +2, in which case each would receive ½. Thus, the slope of

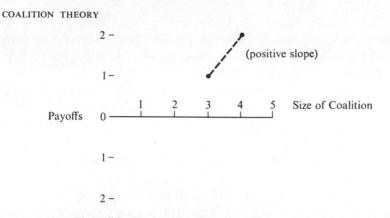

Figure 7.2. Characteristic function with a positive slope.

this particular characteristic function is steep enough to encourage the formation of a four-member coalition. Notice that a four-member coalition is *not* minimum winning since the exclusion of any one member (we assume that no one would want to *defect* in this case) still leaves a winning coalition. A *zero* slope would be one in which the payoff neither increased nor decreased, but remained constant as the number of members increased or decreased. Such a slope would, of course, be simply a straight horizontal line, as in fig. 7.3.

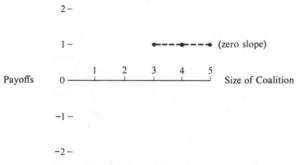

Figure 7.3. Characteristic function with a zero slope.

Figures 7.1–7.3 are representations of *different* characteristic functions. Figure 7.1, for example, is the representation of the simple game illustrated above. The slope of the graph line is said to be the *slope of the characteristic function*. To say that a characteristic function has a negative slope, then, is to say that when the value of the payoffs is plotted in graph form against coalitions of various sizes, the slope of the line connecting those points is negative. A similar interpretation holds for characteristic functions of positive or zero slope.

These distinctions are important for our present discussion because Riker's prediction of MWC's *assumes a nonpositively sloped characteristic function*. In other words, so long as an *increase* in the size of a minimum winning coalition is accompanied by a *decrease* in the payoff, or by no change at all in the payoff, only minimum winning coalitions will occur. This is, of course, intuitively obvious. It means, simply, that a larger number of coalition members would have to share a payoff of the same size or less than a smaller winning coalition. Under such circumstances, each member of the larger winning coalition would receive *less* than each member of the smaller winning coalition. Therefore, the larger coalition would have an incentive to reduce its size by the exclusion of one or more of its players.

It is not necessarily the case, however, that the coalition would always be reduced to minimum winning size. Suppose the characteristic function had a shape as shown in fig. 7.4. Here, n is the total number of members,

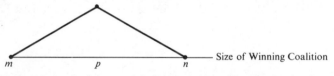

Figure 7.4. Graph of characteristic function with positive and negative slope.

and m is the minimum number needed to win. This graph is, of course, only a portion of the previous graphs. It corresponds to the area on the horizontal axis from 3 to 5 in figs. 7.1–7.3. In any case, the slope of the characteristic function is *positive* from m to p, and then *negative* from p to n. This means that as coalitions increase in size from m to p, the payoffs *increase;* but that as the coalitions increase in size from p to n, the payoffs *decrease*. Under such circumstances, larger than minimum winning coalitions would form. Nevertheless, Riker argues that, empirically, "n-person zero-sum social situations can always be represented by games in which the graph of the characteristic functions in the range of winning coalitions has a negative or zero slope" (p. 46). In other words, in actual situations, we would not expect to encounter coalition games with the characteristic function represented by fig. 7.4.

Now, it is not intuitively clear why this should be so. Surely, we have no trouble with the *idea* of positively sloped characteristic functions in the range of winning coalitions (all coalitions of minimum winning size or larger). Nevertheless, Riker shows that, even theoretically, MWCs will occur even if part of the slope of the characteristic function is positive. His argument is complex and we shall not go into it here in any detail, but it is related to the problem of dividing the payoff among the winners. Riker also supports his theoretical result with an intuitive claim that "there may exist in nature some situations that display these features (i.e. positive slope) but if they do exist, they are so rare and obscure that one who has searched diligently to find them has been unable to do so" (p. 45). (*Question:* Can you think of an actual situation in which an increase in the size of a coalition is accompanied by an increase in the payoff? Consider the case of federal aid to local schools based on a population formula—i.e., an *increase* in the number of children results in greater federal aid. Is this a counterexample to Riker's claim?)

Riker's main conclusion, then, is that "in n-person, zero-sum games, where side-payments are permitted, where players are rational, and where they have perfect information, only minimum winning coalitions occur" (p. 32).

The term "side-payments" means, as we explained in the previous chapter, that one player offers to, or receives from another player, an additional portion of the payoff in order to induce that player, or be induced by that player, to join or leave a particular coalition. The notion of side-payments is structurally similar to that of a "bribe" in ordinary parlance, but without the pejorative connotations.

As we noted above, however, there may be several minimum winning coalitions. For that reason, Riker also analyzes the problem of determining which MWC will form. This is analogous to the search for a "solution," which was described in the previous chapter. Before discussing Riker's solution concepts, however, we must consider several recent arguments which contend that Riker is wrong, and that MWC's *may* occur, but not necessarily.

MAXIMUM POSITIVE GAINERS

Robert L. Butterworth (1971) opened the debate by claiming that Riker's MWC principle should be replaced by what he called a *Maximum Positive Gainers* (MPG) Principle:

In n-person, zero sum games with a non-positively sloped characteristic function, where side-payments are permitted, where players are rational, and where they have perfect information, the largest possible number of positive gainers that can occur is the number of players necessary to comprise a minimum winning coalition. (p. 744)

In other words, a winning coalition could be larger than minimum, but the number of players who receive a positive payoff cannot be greater than the number necessary for a MWC. The winning coalition, then, will be composed of some players who receive *negative* payoffs! This apparently strange notion can be illustrated by an example. Suppose a five-person, zero-sum game has the following characteristic function:

Size of Coalition	Payoff
1	-20
2	-30
3	30
4	20
5	0

It is also assumed that payoffs are dollars and are divided equally among the members of a coalition. This game is presented in tabular form in table 7.1.

TABLE 7.1 A FIVE-PERSON COALITION GAME

Number of Players in Winning Coalition	Individual Payoffs				
	Q	R	S	T	U
5	0	0	0	0	0
4	5	5	5	5	-20
3	10	10	10	-15	-15

For purposes of illustration, we have assigned payoffs to particular players, but any payoff could be assigned to any player without changing the results. It would appear that the three-member coalition in which the winners split the payoff of 30 should form. Butterworth argues, however, that it would not. He begins by assuming that a four-member coalition, say $\overline{QRST}$, has formed. Then he asks, would $\overline{QRS}$ expel T to form a winning three-member coalition? If T were expelled from the coalition, he would lose $15 in the losing coalition $\overline{TU}$. For that reason, T would have an incentive to offer Q, R, and S an *additional* $6 each—i.e., in addition to the $5 they would receive in the original division of the winning payoff—for a *total* winning of $11 each. T, on the other hand, would have the $5 from the original division, but he would have to use that $5 and an additional $13 of his own (there is no indication where this money comes from) in order to provide Q, R. and S with their additional $6 each, as a bribe to let him remain in the coalition $QRST$. In other words, Q, R, and S would receive a net payoff of $11 each, while T would have a net loss of −$13! But, Q, R, and S prefer this outcome to the three-member coalition in which they would receive only $10 each; and T would also prefer this outcome, since he would lose only $13, as a member of the winning coalition $\overline{QRST}$, rather than losing $15 as a member of the losing coalition $\overline{TU}$. Let us summarize these deals in table 7.2.

TABLE 7.2 GAME REPRESENTED IN TABLE 7.1 AFTER DEALS ARE MADE

	Individual Payoffs				
	Q	R	S	T	U
Initially: four members of winning coalition	5	5	5	5	−20
T bribes Q, R, and S	+6	+6	⌐6	−18	0
Net payoffs to four-member winning coalition	11	11	11	−13	−20

Another way of presenting this is to say that the outcome $(\overline{QRST},\ \overline{U};$ 11, 11, 11, −13, −20) *dominates* the outcome $(\overline{QRS},\ \overline{TU};$ 10, 10, 10, −15, −15), since Q, R, S, and T all prefer the former to the latter. But, the coalition $\overline{QRST}$ is a four-member coalition, while $\overline{QRS}$ is a three-member coalition in the game in which the characteristic function is negatively sloped; and yet, the four-member coalition would form rather than the minimum winning coalition, as Riker has predicted. On the basis of this example, Butterworth recommends that Riker's size principle he replaced by his Maximum Positive Gainers principle (MPG). Notice that in the example there are only three "positive gainers" even though the "winning coalition" has four members. Essentially, the fourth member T has accepted a loss in a winning coalition because it is less of a loss than he would have suffered in a losing coalition.

There were a number of objections to .Butterworth's analysis. Riker argued that Butterworth had violated the rules of the game (as expressed in the characteristic function) which he himself had established, since three players, Q, R, and S, shared $33 rather than $30. Butterworth pointed out in response that the coalition which formed was a four-member coalition, not a three-member coalition; and that the net payoff to the coalition was $20 ($33 − $13) as indicated in the rules.

BARGAINING CYCLES

A more important objection to both Riker's original analysis and Butterworth's suggested alteration, however, is that there does not seem to be a good reason for the formation of *any* particular winning coalition. To see this, suppose that the coalition ($\overline{QRS}$; 10, 10, 10) had formed in the first round of bargaining. This would leave a losing coalition of (*TU*; −15, −15). In such a situation, it would seem reasonable for either T or U to offer any *two* of the original three members of the winning coalition a better deal in order to induce them to eject their third colleague and join with T or U. For example, suppose T offers Q and R $11 each in a coalition ($\overline{QRT}$; 11, 11, 8). Such a coalition dominates the original coalition ($\overline{QRS}$; 10, 10, 10). But then, either S or U, who are now part of the losing coalition ($\overline{SU}$; −15, −15), have an incentive to induce T and Q or R to join them in a new coalition, such as ($\overline{QTU}$; 12, 9, 9). Moreover, such a process should continue without end since each member of every two-member losing coalition always has an incentive and an opportunity to induce two members of the winning coalition to form a new winning coalition. In other words, *the three-member winning coalition appears to be inherently unstable.*

Suppose, however, that the players see this situation and try to form four-member winning coalitions as a way of avoiding a stalemate in which no one receives a payoff. At this point, we return to Butterworth's original example, in which four members divide $20 equally. But now, we assume that the one loser will try to induce any three members of the winning coalition to expel the fourth and form a new four-member coalition. For example, suppose the coalition ($\overline{QRST}$; 5, 5, 5, 5) has formed. Then U, who loses $20 as the one loser, has a clear incentive to offer to join, say, Q, R, and S in the coalition ($\overline{QRSU}$; 6, 6, 6, 2). In such a coalition, Q, R, S, and U are all in a better position then before. But now, T has an incentive to bribe his way into a coalition with U and two other members—e.g. ($\overline{QRTU}$;

7, 7, 3, 3). Again, as long as there is a single loser, the situation is unstable, since that loser has both the incentive and the opportunity to make three of the four members of the winning coalition a better offer. (*Question:* Can you show that this is the case?)

SYMMETRY

In our discussion of this five-person game so far, we have assumed that any player could receive any payoff obtainable in the bargaining process. In other words, any payoff was available to any player. Such a situation is said to be *identically symmetric*. A game can also be simply *symmetric*. This means that *the payoff to any coalition is determined only by the size of that coalition, and that all coalitions of the same size receive the same payoff*. An *asymmetric game* would simply be one in which coalitions of the same size could receive *different* payoffs. In our example, all four-member coalitions received $20, all three-member coalitions received $30, all two-member losing coalitions lost $30, and all one-member losing coalitions lost $20. This game is identically symmetric as long as we allow any player to be a member of any coalition and receive any payoff. If, however, certain players received different payoffs in coalitions of equal size and payoff, then the game would be symmetric but not identically symmetric. Thus, for example, in the game above, player Q might receive a payoff of 10 in every three-member coalition in which she participated, while player R might always receive 15 in the three-member coalitions in which he participated. Clearly, then, Q and R are not identical.

The set of identically symmetric games, then, is a subset of the set of symmetric games. Put another way, an identically symmetric game must be a symmetric game, but a symmetric game need not be identically symmetric. The class of symmetric games, then, is larger than the class of identically symmetric games (see fig. 7.5).

Before discussing our five-person game with the restriction of symmetry alone, we should make two more points about the notion of symmetry. First, it is possible to have a situation in which the payoff matrix in normal form is asymmetric while the characteristic function is symmetric. That is, all payoffs to coalitions of the same size are the same, but, not every player can obtain every payoff. Hardin (1976) gives the following example

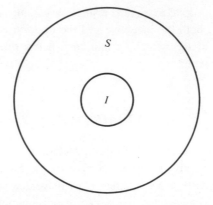

Figure 7.5. The set of identically symmetric games *(I)* as a subset
of the set of all symmetric games *(S)*.

of such a game: three players, A, B, and C, must choose by majority
agreement among three outcomes— (1,1, −2), (2, −2, 0) and (−2, 1, 1).
The first number in each set of parentheses is the payoff to the first player,
the second number is the payoff to the second player, and the third number
is the payoff to the third player.

If A and B agreed on the first outcome, then each would get +1 and C
would get −2. If B and C agreed on the third outcome, then each would get
+1 and A would get −2. If, for some strange reason, A and C agreed on the
second outcome (perhaps C was bribing the first player to join with her
rather than B, in which case C would lose 2) then A would receive +2, C
would get zero, and B would lose 2. In other words, *any two-member coalition receives a payoff of +2, while the complement, any one-member coalition, receives −2.* Moreover, any three-member coalition receives zero.
(Question: Why is this the case?) Thus, the payoffs are equal to different coalitions of equal size, and so this game is symmetric. But, it is not identically symmetric since different players receive particular payoffs in certain
coalitions, and the positions of the three players within any coalition are not
interchangeable.

Our second point is that there exists a notion of *supersymmetry,* which
is an even stronger restriction than symmetry. Recall our discussion in the
previous chapter of security levels. We said that a player's security level
was the highest payoff he or she could guarantee for himself or herself no

matter what the opposing player(s) did. Let us return to our example in table 7.1 above. Assume that the game is asymmetric and that the only outcomes are those listed. In that case the security level of Q, R, and S is zero, while the security level of T is -15, and the security level of U is -20. In other words, while Q, R, and S cannot assure themselves a position in a winning three- or four-member coalition, they can be sure of receiving at least a zero. Similarly, T and U can be assured of -15 and -20 respectively. That is, T does not have to accept less than -15 in any coalition, U does not have to accept anything less than -20, and Q, R, and S do not have to accept less than zero. Obviously, T and U are in relatively poor positions, and Q, R, and S are in relatively good positions, but the point is that there are limits given by the game to the losses that any player has to suffer, and these limits are the security levels of the players. In a symmetric game, the security levels of all players are the same. (*Question:* Can you explain this?)

The important point about security levels is that they determine the players' incentives—especially those in the losing coalition of asymmetric games such as our example above—to bribe their way into a winning coalition. For example, in table 7.1 above, it does not pay U to offer $\overline{QRS}$ a bribe greater than $5 in order to be in the winning coalition. In such a situation, ($\overline{QRS}$; 10, 10, 10) would receive an additional $5 to be split among three players, while U would lose $15 (her original loss) plus the $5 bribe, for a total loss of $20. But, U would have lost no more even if the four-member coalition ($\overline{QRST}$; 5, 5, 5, 5) had formed. Thus, $5 is the *upper limit* of the bribe U would offer Q, R, and S. From T's perspective, a bribe by U to keep the four-member coalition ($\overline{QRST}$; 5, 5, 5, 5) from forming is detrimental. Therefore, he would like to induce $\overline{QRS}$ to form that four-member coalition. Since U has offered $\overline{QRS}$ *less than* $5 (an offer of exactly $5 would not improve U's position) T must offer $\overline{QRS}$ more than $5. In fact, since $\overline{QRS}$ would only receive $5 each as members of the four-member coalition ($\overline{QRST}$; 5, 5, 5, 5), while they would receive more than $10 as members of the four-member coalition ($\overline{QRSU}$), T must offer more than $15 to $\overline{QRS}$. In fact, T can offer $\overline{QRS}$ up to $20, since T would receive $5 as a member of ($\overline{QRST}$) which he could give to $\overline{QRS}$ along with an additional amount under $15 from his own pocket. T, then, would be a net loser of less than $15, his security level. Thus, $\overline{QRS}$ can expect bribes up to a limit of $5 from U, and up to a limit of $15 from T. Now, the payoff to the three-member coalition ($\overline{QRS}$) is $30, and the greatest possible bribe they could receive is \$15. Therefore, by expanding to a four-member coalition, $(\overline{QRS})$ can expect to receive \$45. Thus there is an incentive in this case for a minimum winning coalition to become larger even though the slope of the characteristic function is negative. This, of course, was Butterworth's point. But this analysis also leads us to a more precise specification of the conditions under which a minimum winning coalition would *not* expand. That is, we have seen that a negatively sloped characteristic function by itself is not sufficient. This new condition is *supersymmetry*. *A game is supersymmetric if the payoff to the winning coalition is equal to the negative sum of the security levels of the members of the losing coalition.* In symbols:

$$v(W) = -(\sum_{i \notin W} q_i)$$

Where "W" is the minimum winning coalition, "i" is the symbol for the players who are *not* in the winning coalition, and "q" is the security level for any player i. In our example above:

$$v(W) = 30 \qquad (\overline{QRS};\ 10,\ 10,\ 10)$$
$$\sum q_i = -45\ (T = -15, U = -20)$$

Therefore,

$$v(W) < -(\sum_{i \notin s} q_i)$$
$$\text{or } 30 < 45$$

Thus, our game above is *not* supersymmetric.
Consider the following game:

Player	Q	R	S	T	U
Outcome I	0	0	0	0	0
Outcome II	20	20	20	-30	-30

In this case, $v(W) = 60$, and $-(\sum_{i \notin W} q_i) = 60$. Therefore, the payoff to the MWC is *equal to* the negative of the sum of the security levels of the members of the losing coalition, and this game *is supersymmetric.* If a game is supersymmetric, no member of the losing coalition has an incentive to try to bribe his or her way into the MWC, and so there is no incentive for the MWC to expand. In other words, in order for Riker's size principle to hold, i.e., his contention that only MWC's will form, it is not only necessary that the slope of the characteristic function be negative, but also that the game be supersymmetric. It should be noted, however, that MWC's can also form in asymmetric games so long as the members of the losing coalition receive exactly their security level and no more.[1]

COMPETITIVE BRIBERY AND INDETERMINATE OUTCOMES

We have seen, then, that when a game is supersymmetric, and the characteristic function is negatively sloped, only minimum winning coalitions will form. We have also seen that when a game is identically symmetric endless bargaining cycles will result and the situation will be unstable. The Butterworth example is symmetric only so long as we restrict the possible payoffs to certain players. In such a situation, says Butterworth, larger than minimum winning coalitions will occur as one of the potential losers bribes his or her way into the MWC. Shepsle (1974), however, has pointed out that *competitive bribery* would probably result in the formation of a minimum winning coalition.

That is, if one potential loser in our five-player example above tries to bribe his way into the minimum winning coalition, the other potential loser has an incentive to try to outbid his colleague in bribing his way into the MWC. To see this more clearly, let us return to Butterworth's example:

TABLE 7.3 A FIVE-PERSON COALITION GAME

Number of Players in Winning Coalition	Individual Payoffs				
	Q	R	S	T	U
5	0	0	0	0	0
4	5	5	5	5	-20
3	10	10	10	-15	-15

Suppose that the coalition $\overline{QRS}$ forms, and that T once again tries to bribe his way into $\overline{QRS}$. Then, Shepsle argues, U could either try to outbid T, or try to bribe T back into the losing coalition $\overline{TU}$. Let us see how this

1. See Hardin (1976), pp. 1207–1208.

might work out. Recall that T had offered $\overline{QRS}$ an additional $6 each to let him remain in the coalition $\overline{QRST}$. In order to outbid T, U would have to offer $\overline{QRS}$ more than $6 each. Suppose U offered $\overline{QRS}$ $7 each. Then the payoffs would be as shown in table 7.4.

TABLE 7.4 GAME REPRESENTED IN TABLE 7.3 AFTER DEALS ARE MADE

| | Individual Payoffs | | | | |
	Q	R	S	T	U
Initially: four members of winning coalition	5	5	5	−20	5
U bribes, Q, R, and S	7	7	7	0	−21
Net payoffs to four-member winning coalition	12	12	12	−20	−16

Here, U loses $16 while T loses $20. Is this an improvement for U? In relation to a possible loss of $20 as the single member of a losing coalition, it certainly is. On the other hand, T and U also have the option of losing only $15 each as members of the losing coalition $\overline{TU}$. In relation to that outcome U has not done better by bribing Q, R, and S $7 each to remain in the winning coalition $\overline{QRSU}$. Moreover, T can also protect himself by giving Q, R, and S more than $7. If T offered $8, for example, the total payoff for T would be $-19(5-24)$, which is still preferable to -20. But, it is obvious to both T and U that *competitive bribery makes the situation worse for both of them*.

For that reason, T and U have an incentive *not* to try to bribe their way into a four-member winning coalition, but rather to accept a minimum combined loss of $-\$15$ as members of the losing coalition $\overline{TU}$. (*Question:* Is this situation similar to or different from the prisoner's dilemma? Explain.) In such a case, the MWC would form. On the other hand, Q, R, and S, receive only $10 as members of this MWC, while they receive more than this amount as members of a four-member winning coalition. For this reason, Q, R, and S would have an incentive to try to induce either T or U back into a four-member winning coalition by offering them a better payoff. We have seen above that this is possible. But then, the lone loser would once again have an incentive to try to bribe his or her way into the four-member winning coalition, and the process of competitive bribery would begin all over again. *The point of all this is that in our five-player example, it is not possi-*

ble to predict whether a MWC or a larger than MWC will form. Such a result is said to be *indeterminate.* Moreover, Frohlich (1975) demonstrated that this is true for *any n*-person, essential symmetric game. *In other words, for all essential, symmetric, n-person games except those which are supersymmetric, the minimum winning coalition is an unstable outcome.* This means that Riker's size principle applies only to a narrow class of games, and does not hold in general.

SUMMARY

Let us summarize our points thus far:

1. *N*-person zero-sum games in which coalitions may be expected to form can be classified according to the *symmetry* of their characteristic functions and payoff configurations.

2. The notion of *symmetry* in regard to characteristic functions means that all coalitions of the same size have the same payoff.

3. *Symmetry* in regard to individual payoffs means that all players have the same payoff configuration—i.e., all possible payoffs are available to all of the players. This is also referred to as *identical symmetry.*

4. The notion of *asymmetry* in regard to payoffs simply means that certain players have available to them certain payoffs, while other players have different payoffs, and the groups are not interchangeable. In regard to the characteristic function, asymmetry means that coalitions of the same size do not all have the same payoff.

5. The notion of *supersymmetry* means that the payoff to the winning coalition is equal to the negative sum of the security levels of the members of the losing coalition, and that the characteristic function form of the game is symmetric.

6. For *n*-person zero-sum games involving rational players, perfect information and side-payments, *minimum winning coalitions* will form if the following conditions hold: (*a*) a negatively sloped characteristic function and a supersymmetric payoff configuration; or (*b*) a negatively sloped characteristic function and an asymmetric game in which the members of the losing coalition receive exactly their security levels.

7. *In all other cases, the outcome will be indeterminate.*

In relation to our discussion of previous chapters, it is important to note that *supersymmetry is more of a restriction than is symmetry*. That is, a game which is supersymmetric must also be symmetric; but a game which is symmetric need not be supersymmetric. Supersymmetric games, then, are subsets of symmetric games. Intuitively, a game which is symmetric simply requires that all coalitions of the same size receive the same payoff. If the members of any coalition of a symmetric game are interchangeable, then the game is *identically symmetric*.

For symmetric games, however, the determinate outcome—i.e., the formation of minimum winning coalitions—only occurs in the more restrictive supersymmetric games. Similarly, the MWC is expected to occur only in the subclass of asymmetric games in which the losing players receive exactly their security levels. Moreover, if the restriction of supersymmetry is relaxed, the outcome is indeterminate, which means, essentially, that there is no outcome which dominates every other outcome. Such a situation is, of course, the same as that of cyclical majorities. Once again, then, we see that only by imposing restrictions on choice situations can we assure an outcome and avoid endless cycles.

EMPIRICAL TESTS OF THE THEORY

We have, then, conflicting arguments about the validity of the size principle. Riker claims that it holds generally, except for situations where ideology is a strong factor. We shall discuss this exception below. Hardin and others, on the other hand, claim that it is valid only in very limited situations. Nevertheless, it is possible that even if the size principle applies to very limited *theoretical* situations (supersymmetric games constitute a small portion of all theoretically possible symmetric games) it might be that such situations are *empirically* prevalent. That is, we might just live in a world of supersymmetric games! For this reason, empirical evidence on the size principle is important. In this section we shall first outline the problems of testing the size principle, and then review some of the empirical results which, as we shall see, do not conclusively confirm or refute Riker's prediction of minimum winning coalitions.

PROBLEMS

One advantage of the size principle is that it is easily testable. That is, it makes a rather clear statement about an attribute of coalitions that is both quantifiable and unambiguous. After all, a coalition in any setting—e.g., a parliamentary cabinet, a legislature, the United States Supreme Court—is composed of discrete units—parties, individuals, or groups of any kind. And the numerical composition of such coalitions is seldom in doubt, even though we may not know precisely which individuals, parties, or groups were involved. For example, Congress does not record the particular votes of its members on all bills, but it almost always records the size of the vote for or against.

Compare this advantage of the MWC notion with Butterworth's maximum positive-gainers principle. In order to test MPG, it is necessary to ascertain the nature and division of the payoffs. For most political situations, however, this is virtually impossible. Consider, for example, parliamentary coalitions attempting to form a government. The general "payoff" to the winning coalition is, of course, control over the government and cabinet positions. But, such payoffs are not quantifiable in any meaningful way, and it seems to make little sense to try to determine the number of "positive gainers." Moreover, if the payoff is a plurality vote, as in Hinich, Ledyard, and Ordeshook (1973), there are no "gains" to be distributed.

Despite this singular advantage of the size principle, there are important problems. Recall Riker's conditions for minimum winning coalitions:

1. N-person zero-sum games
2. Rational players
3. Perfect information
4. Side-payments
5. Negatively sloped characteristic functions
6. Control over membership

In real political situations, the *n-person condition* (more than two players) and the *rationality condition* (utility-maximizing players) are not difficult to satisfy. The *zero-sum condition,* however, is more difficult.

Since a zero-sum game is one in which the winner wins what the loser loses, a good model for the zero-sum game is poker, in which the "pot" is composed of money bet by the players. The gains of the winner in such a game, then, are the losses of the defeated players. But are political situations of this type? Consider an election. We certainly speak of "winners" and "losers" in elections, but does the unsuccessful candidate "lose" the election or the office in the same way that a poker player loses money? Presumably we might say that the defeat of an incumbent is *like* a zero-sum game, but does this mean that it is *not* a zero-sum game if the incumbent is not running or if the incumbent wins?

The zero-sum condition presents an even greater problem when we consider such coalition-formation situations as, say, Supreme Court decisions or many legislative committee decisions. In the former, coalitions certainly do form, but can we speak meaningfully of "winning" or "losing" coalitions on the Court? Can the justices in the minority on any decision be said to have lost anything? Perhaps they have lost control over legal or judicial policymaking, but is this analogous in any meaningful way to the poker player's loss of money? In order to apply the size principle to these cases, then, it is necessary to assume that being in the majority on a legislative committee or on a Supreme Court decision *is* akin to winning the pot in poker!

The condition of *perfect information,* however, is rarely satisfied in politics. For that reason, theorists must make further assumptions about the likely effect of uncertainty on the size of coalitions. This is precisely the question we considered in chapter 5, where we discussed Downs's theory of voting.

There are at least two possible effects of uncertainty. The first, which Riker and others (e.g. Koehler, 1972) have suggested, is that uncertainty results in the formation of coalitions which are larger than minimum. The argument here is that the extra members in a congressional coalition act as a kind of insurance against misjudgments or miscalculations on the part of the coalition builders. On the other hand, Rosenthal (1970) has suggested that, "without perfect information, defense of the ego leads to overestimation of resources. In the French case, this proposition seems true: coalitions tend to be too small" (p. 46). Rosenthal was speaking about the problems of the French Fourth Republic (for the years 1951 and 1956) in forming majority governments in parliament, and in forming party majorities in local districts.

There are several difficulties with either of these positions. The Riker-Koehler position assumes that *coalitions have control over their membership*. In the case of cabinet formation in parliamentary governments, this is indeed true. But in legislative coalitions which form to vote on a particular bill, it is generally not possible—nor desirable—to limit the size of the voting coalition. This is also true for judicial "coalitions" in the Supreme Court. Further, if the lack of information results in the formation of coalitions larger than minimum winning, how would we know whether our data confirmed or refuted the size principle? For example, if the decision rule was simple majority, and if we found that winning coalitions averaged about 60 percent of the total membership, would this be confirmation of the size principle? The problem here is that once we admit the notion of coalition "insurance," it is necessary to specify how much insurance a MWC would need in a situation of uncertainty. But, there is no theoretical rationale to distinguish oversized coalitions from minimum winning coalitions with "insurance." Thus, it is virtually impossible to determine whether the size principle has been either confirmed or refuted by the data.

Rosenthal's problem is similar. Does the presence of undersized coalitions—i.e. coalitions smaller than minimum winning—indicate that coalition strength was underestimated in a situation of uncertainty? Does the same explanation hold where no party or parties manage to put together a majority coalition?

The *side-payments* condition also presents difficulties. Presumably, a side-payment, or bribe, must be a commodity whose value is measurable, comparable to other commodities, and capable of being transferred from one individual (or group) to another. Money is, of course, the paradigm of such a commodity. But, assuming that the formation of coalition governments, the passage of bills in Congress, and decision making on the Supreme Court do not involve money payments, what commodities could be used for side-payments? Apart from the corruption which characterizes all governments at some time, the basic side-payment commodity is *votes*. That is, what we called vote trading or logrolling in chapter 4 is equivalent to side-payments in our present discussion. The problem with this condition is that since the process of side-payments is almost universally condemned and almost universally practiced, it is extremely difficult, if not impossible, to determine when trading has taken place. This problem is less difficult where parties are forming a parliamentary government. There the distribution of cabinet positions is clearly visible, even though there may be more trading going on in private, involving other, less legitimate commodities. In any case, it is not necessary to know *what* trades are being made. It is sufficient to know *that* trades are being made.

Riker's final condition, *negatively sloped characteristic functions,* does not present any problems for him, since he assumes that positively sloped characteristic functions simply do not exist in real life. For those less certain, the difficulty of determining the slope of the characteristic function in any situation is enormous. Recall that the characteristic function indicates the payoffs for particular coalitions, or for coalitions of a particular size. In actual situations, this is equivalent to finding out what any coalition is worth to any participant. Here again the data problems are enormous, especially if illegitimate side-payments are involved.

FINDINGS

Despite these difficulties there has been a significant amount of work designed to test the size principle, including not only "natural" situations but also experimental ones. We shall report on some of these briefly.

In Riker's original book (1962) he pointed to several historical events which seemed to confirm the size principle. One was the presidential election of 1824, involving the so-called corrupt bargain between Clay and Adams. In this election, four candidates—Andrew Jackson, Governor of Florida Territory; Henry Clay, Representative from Kentucky; John Quincy Adams, Secretary of State; and William H. Crawford, Secretary of the Treasury—initially split the electoral votes as follows:

Candidate	Electoral Votes
Jackson	99
Adams	84
Crawford	41
Clay	37
Total	261

At that time, a majority winner needed more than 130 electoral votes. With no majority winner, the election went to the House of Representatives where, according to the twelfth amendment of the Constitution, only three candidates could be considered, and where each state had one vote. Jackson had the support of 11 states in the House, Adams 7, Crawford 3, and Clay 3. But, since Clay had fewer electoral votes than Crawford, and since the House could only consider three candidates, Clay's support had to be divided among the other candidates.

The question, then, was where Clay's support should go, and whether the support which the other candidates had won in the election would hold in the House. Riker bases the analysis of this situation on his analysis of zero-sum coalition games. Recall that in a zero-sum game, the value of the grand coalition is always zero, since without any losers, there is nothing for the grand coalition to win. Similarly, the value of any winning coalition other than the grand coalition is simply the obverse of the value of the losing coalition. Now, when applied to political coalitions, the notion of winning a particular value and losing a particular value, as we pointed out above, is not unambiguous. To clarify this notion Riker introduces the concept of *weight*. That is, each coalition member—*proto-coalition,* the term used by Riker to denote any coalition smaller than a winning coalition—comes to the bargaining with a certain weight or, we might say, power. In the previous chapter, for example, computation of the Shapley value required that we indicate the initial weight or value of each coalition member. In this case, the weight of each candidate in the presidential election of 1824 was the number of votes which he could expect in the House. Thus, Jackson with eleven votes had a greater weight than any of the other candidates. So far, the analysis is rather straightforward. But then it is necessary to assign *values* to the proto-coalitions, and to the winning and losing coalitions respectively. Oddly, the value of any proto-coalition—that is, any nonwinning coalition— is the sum of its *weights*. Thus, the value of Jackson in a coalition by himself is 11, while the value of a Crawford-Clay coalition would be 6. These same numbers also relate to winning and losing—a winning coalition must receive a majority of the votes, or 13. *But, the value of a winning coalition is not the sum of the weights of its members, but rather the positive sum of the weights of the losing members.* Thus, a winning coalition of Jackson-Adams (which wins with a total of 18 votes) would have a *value* of only 6—the sum of the weights of the losing Crawford-Clay coalition! This strange situation is the result of the zero-sum condition. For, if the value of the winning coalition were the sum of the weights of *its* members, then the value of the losing coalition could not be the negative of that value as required by the zero-sum condition. Moreover, the value of the grand coalition would not be zero, but rather the sum of the weights of *all* the members.

With this discussion as background, then, we are ready to analyze this election. First, the minimum winning coalitions and their values would be as follows:

Minimum Winning Coalition	Number of Votes	Value of Coalition
Jackson-Adams	18	6
Jackson-Crawford	14	10
Jackson-Clay	14	10
Adams-Crawford-Clay	13	11

Given Riker's reasoning, then, the MWC of Adams-Crawford-Clay has the highest value. But, should it be the one which forms? In our discussion of *solution concepts* in the previous chapter, we pointed out that the coalition which ought to form—that is, "rationally ought to" form—is the coalition which receives the highest payoff as a whole; and whose members receive at least as great a payoff in that coalition as in any other. In the example above, the Adams-Crawford-Clay coalition receives the highest payoff, but do Adams, Crawford, and Clay receive at least as great a payoff in that coalition as in any other? The problem here is the division of the payoff among the members. Should it be split evenly, or according to weight, or according to some other criterion? In the previous chapter, for example, we noted that the original weight of coalition members—we spoke then of "value" rather than "weight"—was not the only basis for dividing the spoils. In fact, in computing the Shapley value, we assumed that the coalition member who was approached by another member might expect a greater payoff, regardless of relative weight, on the grounds that the member who proposed the coalition must be more anxious for it.

Riker's suggestion for determining how the payoffs should be divided is based on a notion of *initial expectation* which he defines as follows:

An initial expectation for a proto-coalition, X^k, in the $(r-1)$th stage is an imputation for Γ when a minimal winning coalition containing X^k forms, such that the imputation contains a payoff to X^k equal to the maximum of the values of all non-minimal winning coalition that X^k might belong to. (Riker, 1962, p. 129)

The "$(r-1)$th stage" is that point in the bargaining process just before the final bargain. The "imputation for Γ" is the payoff configuration for the particular game which is being played. In simpler terms,

An initial expectation for X^k in his bargaining to enter a minimal winning coalition is an amount equal to the best it can do in the best alternative *nonminimal* winning coalition. (Riker, 1962, p. 129. Italics added)

Riker suggests, then, that there should be two requirements for a minimum winning coalition: (1) that MWC should form which has a *higher value* than any other MWC; and (2) that MWC should form in which every member can obtain his *initial expectation*.

A minimum winning coalition which satisfies these conditions is said to be *uniquely preferred*. Clearly, a *uniquely preferred winning coalition* (*UPWC*) *is a solution concept* as discussed in the previous chapter. Now, the question is whether there is a UPWC in the presidential election example? In order to determine this, we first list all of the nonminimum winning coalitions and their values:

Nonminimum Winning Coalition	Number of Votes	Value of Coalition
Jackson-Adams-Crawford-Clay	24	0
Jackson-Adams-Crawford	21	3
Jackson-Adams-Clay	21	3
Jackson-Crawford-Clay	17	7

As we saw above, the MWC of Adams-Crawford-Clay had the highest value. The question now is whether Adams, Crawford, and Clay obtain at least their initial expectation in this winning coalition. For Adams, the maximum he could obtain in a nonminimum winning coalition is 3, when he joins Jackson and Crawford. This assumes, of course, that Jackson and Crawford receive nothing. But, Crawford and Clay could do better than Adams by splitting the payoff of 7 in a coalition with Jackson. Thus, the maximum total value which Adams, Crawford, and Clay could obtain in nonminimum winning coalitions is 10, while the total value of the Adams-Crawford-Clay minimum winning coalition is 11. Therefore, all three could do better in a MWC. *The MWC of Adams-Crawford-Clay, then, is a uniquely preferable winning coalition,* while Jackson is a *strategically weak proto-coalition* (SWPC). A SWPC "is one that cannot, by reason of a given partition in a putative $(r-1)$th stage, become a part of the most valuable winning coalition" (Riker, 1962, p. 130).

This theoretical reasoning implies that the Jackson supporters should begin to look elsewhere for a better deal; and, in fact, the Jackson coalition of 11 states began to disintegrate as the Illinois and Maryland representatives switched to Adams, while North Carolina switched to Crawford, and Louisiana went to Clay. At that point, the new configuration of votes was as follows:

Candidate	Number of Votes
Adams	9
Jackson	7
Crawford	4
Clay	4

In view of the fact that Clay was not a candidate, the Louisiana move was clearly meant to indicate that it would go to the same candidate as the other Clay votes.

Notice that there are now two minimum winning coalitions with the same weight:

Minimum Winning Coalition	Number of Voters	Weight of Coalition
Adams-Crawford	13	11
Adams-Clay	13	11

Since Clay was not a potential candidate, his demands on Adams, as mentioned above, would be less than those of Crawford, who could justifiably demand much more for his withdrawal and commitment to Adams. This rationale for an Adams-Clay alliance was strengthened irretrievably when Missouri left Clay and joined Adams. At that point the theoretical value of an Adams-Clay alliance (11) was higher than that of an Adams-Crawford alliance (10), and, indeed, Adams was nominated when Clay joined him in return for a position as Secretary of State. The final vote was Adams, 13; Jackson, 7; Crawford, 4.

Riker suggests that this example lends empirical support to the theoretical argument for his size principle. It is, indeed, interesting that despite some very questionable methods of calculating coalition values, the notion of a minimum winning coalition, combined with the uniquely preferable winning-coalition solution concept, does explain the outcome of this historical case. Of course, such evidence does not confirm the theory, but it does suggest that more rigorous studies may be justified.

OVERSIZED COALITIONS

On a more general level, Riker argues that the size principle can be seen at work where overwhelming coalitions—almost grand coalitions—form in American politics, and where these coalitions are then broken up into smaller coalitions nearer minimum winning size. As examples of such developments, he points to the period after the 1816 election when the Republican party emerged as an almost unanimous choice and the Federalists almost disappeared. This situation changed after 1828, when Jackson forged a new minimum winning coalition by alienating segments of the old grand alliance and forming the Democratic party. By the early 1850s, the

Whigs had been decimated and the Democrats verged on being a coalition of the whole. By 1860, however, the Democratic coalition had split up and the smaller Republican coalition under Lincoln was victorious.

A more recent example of an oversized coalition which required pruning was the bloated Democratic coalition of 1964 under Lyndon Johnson, which was narrowly defeated in 1968 by the Republican Nixon. In fact, if we follow presidential elections from the Roosevelt era to the present, we see a succession of emerging grand coalitions which break up just after they reach maximum size. The Roosevelt majority for example, in 1932 was slim, but by 1936 it was overwhelming. The narrow Truman victory in 1948 can be seen as the last gasp of the Roosevelt coalition, for in 1952 Eisenhower led the resurgent Republicans. By 1956, the Republicans became virtually a coalition of the whole, only to be broken up in 1960 by a narrow Kennedy victory. We have already mentioned the Johnson-Democratic grand coalition of 1964 and its demise in 1968. Following the same pattern, the Republicans developed an overwhelming coalition in 1972, only to break up with the Carter Democratic victory in 1976. In other words, the history of the last forty years of American presidential politics seems to provide some evidence for Riker's size principle.

Such evidence, however, is scarcely definitive. These same events, could be interpreted rather differently. For example, we might attribute the cyclical pattern of expansion and contraction during the last twenty-five years to the constitutional amendment limiting a particular presidency to two terms. By this analysis, the great majorities of 1956, 1964, and 1972 could be attributed to the bandwagon effect of incumbency. When the two terms were complete, the competition for the presidency resumed. In addition, these "grand coalitions" represented only slightly more than 60 percent of those who voted, and a much smaller percentage of the eligible voters. Such a proportion does not seem to be significantly higher than a 51 percent minimum winning coalition.

LEGISLATIVE EVIDENCE

Koehler (1972) suggests that the United States Congress is also inclined to form minimum winning coalitions on its role-call votes. Interestingly, however, he does *not* assume that legislative voting is a zero-sum game, which, as we indicated above, creates some conceptual problems. Koehler found that over a period of time, from the 83rd Congress in 1953 to the 90th Congress in 1968, *voting coalitions remained fixed in size and minimum in size*.

While there is not much controversy about the fact that these congressional coalitions remained relatively fixed in size, there has been some dispute about whether these coalitions were minimum winning. What Koehler's data showed was that the *median size of winning coalitions in contested roll-calls—i.e., those which involve at least 15 percent opposition—was about 62 percent* (1972, p. 162). Koehler calls this a minimum winning size in an uncertain world, since "a coalition manager is likely to intentionally build some margin of safety into his coalition" (1972, p. 162). Moreover, the 62 percent actually represents the proportion of those members present and voting. If the entire House membership is taken into account, the proportion is actually closer to 53 percent.

Hardin (1976) makes an interesting comment on Koehler's results. He points out that in a legislature of about 400 members, *random voting would produce coalitions of between 50 percent and 60 percent of the total membership almost 100 percent of the time!* This apparently odd notion can be explained as follows. Suppose we were to consider a legislature of five members, A,B,C,D, and E, in which a majority was needed to pass any resolution. In other words, a coalition of at least 3 members would be needed to win. Let us list all of the possible winning coalitions:

ABC, ABD, ABE, ACD, ACE, ADE BCD, BCE, BDE CDE	Three-member (MWC)
ABCD, ABCE, ACDE, ABDE BCDE	Four-member
ABCDE	Five-member (Grand Coalition)

There are, altogether, 16 different winning coalitions. Of these, 10, or 62.5 percent, are minimum winning. Notice here that a MWC is 60 percent of the total membership. In other words, in a series of random votes, a minimum winning coalition would emerge 62.5 percent of the time. By a "random vote" we mean a situation in which potential coalition members use some kind of random device (e.g., flipping a coin) to determine their vote. Thus, the grand coalition would form only when all five members flipped either heads or tails, clearly an unlikely event.

You can verify for yourself—with the aid of a computer or a great deal of patience—that, *as the size of the legislature increases, the proportion of coalitions which is closest to minimum winning size increases dramatically,* so that in a legislature of 100 members (the size of the U.S. Senate), 99.9 percent of the winning coalitions are smaller than 60 percent of the total membership, while in legislatures of 400 (nearly the size of the U.S. House), 95.4 percent are smaller than 55 percent of the total membership. Given such figures, says Hardin, it is not confirmation of the size principle to observe that the median size of congressional coalitions is 62 percent.

EVIDENCE FROM THE U.S. SUPREME COURT

The U.S. Supreme Court is, of course, a decision-making body whose votes on particular cases can be seen as involving the formation of coalitions. In this case a "winning coalition" involves at least five of the nine justices. In an interesting article, Rohde (1972) presented data which indicated that minimum winning coalitions did tend to form on the Supreme Court bench, even allowing for the fact presented above that MWC's are more likely to occur by chance alone than non-minimum winning coalitions.

Rohde considered two kinds of issues which confront the Court—one in which there is *no external threat* to the Court; the other in which there is an external threat to the Court. By a "threat to the Court," Rohde meant those issues which directly challenged the Court's authority. For example, the cases which arose in the South after the *Brown* v. *Board of Education* decision declaring racially segregated education unconstitutional provided an opportunity for Southern federal judges to resist the Supreme Court's ruling. For that reason, Rohde suggests, the Court would want to present a united front in order to convince the judges that it was determined to maintain its authority. The implication is that when the Court is faced with a threat to its authority, there will be a tendency for the justices to close ranks. In cases where no such threat exists, the more normal tendency toward disagreement will reassert itself. Rohde predicted, therefore, that minimum winning coalitions would occur in those cases where there was no threat to the Court's authority, while much larger coalitions would form when the Court sensed that its authority might be tested.

Rohde recognized that minimum winning coalitions were very likely to occur by chance. In fact, with a nine-member body, the probability of five-member majorities is .492. In other words, almost half of all possible winning coalitions are minimum winning in a group this size. For this reason, he suggested that the size principle would only be confirmed if the proportion of minimum winning coalitions which occurred was "significantly larger than 49.2 percent" (p.176). Conversely, he predicted that where there were external threats to the Court, "the proportion of minimum winning coalitions formed will be significantly smaller than 49.2 percent" (p.176).

Using 76 First Amendment cases decided by the Court between 1953 and 1967, Rohde classified 18 cases as involving issues which threatened the Court's authority, and 58 which did not. Tables 7.5 and 7.6 summarize his results:

TABLE 7.5 DISTRIBUTION OF OPINION COALITION SIZES IN NONTHREAT ISSUE AREAS

	Coalition Size				
Issue Area	5	6	7	8	9
Internal security	16	2	2	0	1
Censorship	9	2	2	0	0
Assembly	5	0	1	1	0
Libel	2	4	0	1	0
Miscellaneous	5	1	1	2	1
Total ($n = 58$)	37	9	6	4	2
	(.64)	(.16)	(.10)	(.07)	(.03)

Source: Rohde, 1972, pp. 176–77. Reprinted by permission of Charles E. Merrill Publishing Co.

TABLE 7.6 DISTRIBUTION OF OPINION COALITION SIZES IN THREAT ISSUE AREAS

	Coalition Size				
Issue Area	5	6	7	8	9
Religion	2	3	1	2	0
Association	3	1	2	0	3
Internal security (1957)	0	1	0	0	0
Total ($n = 18$)	5	5	3	2	3
	(.28)	(.28)	(.17)	(.11)	(.17)

Source: Rohde, 1972, pp. 176–77. Reprinted by permission of Charles E. Merrill Publishing Co.

The figures in table 7.5 do appear to indicate that the minimum winning coalition of five members does occur significantly more than half of the time in nonthreat situations, whereas those in table 7.6 indicate that MWCs occur significantly less than 50 percent of the time where there are threats to the Court's authority. Moreover, statistical significance tests confirm this impression.

GENERAL FINDINGS

There are, then, some interesting though not conclusive studies which show that minimum winning coalitions do tend to occur in rather diverse situations. Nevertheless, there are also studies which show that minimum winning coalitions do not occur in certain situations. For example, in a study of Italian cabinets from 1953 to 1970, Axelrod (1970) showed that the size principle does not predict coalition formation as well as a notion of *ideological similarity,* which we shall discuss shortly. Similarly, DeSwann's (1970) study of coalition-formation in the Netherlands also indicates that the size principle is not so good a predictor as the *minimization of policy distance* among the parties. From these studies, as well as those which support the size principle, Riker suggests a modified version of his theory: "These studies indicate that *where ideology is especially important*—here as a means to maintain coalitions for governing—it may well overwhelm the consideration of size" (Riker and Ordeshook, 1973, p. 194; italics added). The problem with such a formulation, however, is that it leaves open the question of how strong ideological influence must be before the size principle is nullified. It also raises the possibility of circular reasoning: the size principle (i.e. the formation of minimum winning coalitions) holds where ideology is weak; and ideology is weak where larger than minimum winning coalitions form!

SUMMARY: EMPIRICAL TESTS

Our discussion of the application of Riker's size principle has included the following points:

1. The size principle can be tested easily, since it makes a rather unambiguous statement about a particular attribute of coalitions—i.e., their size. Butterworth's maximum positive-gainers principle, on the other hand, is difficult to test, since it is not always possible to ascertain or compare the nature and division of the payoffs.

2. In applying the size principle, certain conditions can be satisfied easily in real political situations. These include the n-person condition, the

rationality condition, and the negatively sloped characteristic function. Other conditions are more difficult to satisfy. These include the zero-sum condition, control over membership in a coalition, and the nature and extent of side-payments. Finally, the condition of perfect information can rarely be satisfied in real situations. Therefore, applications of the size principle must allow for uncertainty. Some authors feel that the uncertainty of the real world will lead to larger than minimum winning coalitions, as coalition builders try to ensure a margin of safety. Others feel that coalition builders will overestimate that strength in an uncertain world and the result will be smaller than minimum winning coalitions.

3. The size principle seems to explain rather well the American presidential election of 1825, in which Adams was elected with Clay's support. The Adams-Clay coalition emerged as a result of the fact that the Jackson coalition was strategically weak (in Riker's technical sense of the term) and the original Adams-Crawford-Clay coalition was a uniquely preferred winning coalition—Riker's solution concept.

4. Riker perceives the cyclical expansion and contraction of political majorities in American presidential elections as further evidence for the validity of the size principle.

5. Evidence on the size principle from studies of the U.S. Congress is ambiguous, while evidence from studies of U.S. Supreme Court decisions appears supportive.

6. In general, the findings on the size principle are indeterminate. Riker suggests that where ideological considerations are strong the size principle is less applicable. This position, however, may involve circular reasoning.

MINIMIZING POLICY DISTANCE

Thus far, we have considered only Riker's size principle and Butterworth's maximum-positive-gainers principle as the basis for coalition formation. In this section, we shall consider another principle—*the policy distance* between proto-coalitions. This principle can also be viewed as the *ideological distance* between proto-coalitions.

In order to see this more clearly, recall our discussion in chapter 5 of spatial models. There, the preferences of voters and the policy positions of candidates or political parties could be represented by points in an n-dimensional space—i.e., one or more issues. Moreover, it was assumed that the policy "distance" between the voters or parties was measurable and could be specified numerically in terms of cardinal utilities. Now, consider a one-dimensional issue space (fig. 7.6) in which policy positions could be ordered, but not assigned cardinal utilities. This would be equivalent to an ordinal ranking of the issue positions. Suppose further that the distance between any two policy positions was called a *space,* and that the policy position itself was called a *hole.* Thus, there is one space on each side of each hole:

	space	hole	space	hole	space	hole	space
		A		B		C	
Policy Position							

Figure 7.6. Policy distance between positions in a one-dimensional issue space.

The points A, B, and C are policy positions on this single dimension. Between A and B there is one space, and between B and C there is also one space. Between A and C, however, there are two spaces and one hole. The policy distance, or ideological distance, then, between positions A and C is greater than that between A and B, or B and C. Moreover, we can specify that distance more precisely by referring to each space and each hole as a unit. Thus, there is one unit (one space) between A and B, one unit (one space) between B and C, and three units (two spaces, one hole) between A and C. Leiserson (1966) refers to these distances as a measure of *ideological diversity.* In symbols, $D(S)$ (read "D of S") is the measure of ideological diversity or policy distance within a coalition S. Suppose, for example, that A, B, and C were political parties of the left, center, and right respectively on our single dimension above. Then the ideological diversity of a coalition involving A and B is 1, while the diversity of a coalition involving A and C is 3. In symbols:

$$D\ (\overline{AB}) = 1$$
$$D\ (\overline{BC}) = 1$$
$$D\ (\overline{AC}) = 3$$

Clearly, the higher number refers to *greater* ideological diversity, the lower number to *less* ideological diversity.

On the basis of such concepts, Axelrod (1970) has argued that *the coalitions which are most likely to form are those with the least ideological diversity*. Moreover, a winning coalition in Axelrod's terms is one which is *minimally connected*. A *minimum-connected winning coalition* (MCWC) is one whose members are ideologically adjacent (connected), and is "minimum winning" in the sense that "the coalition can lose no member without ceasing to be both connected *and* winning." (Taylor, 1971, p. 372). To illustrate this point, consider the following party structure in a parliamentary system (fig. 7.7):

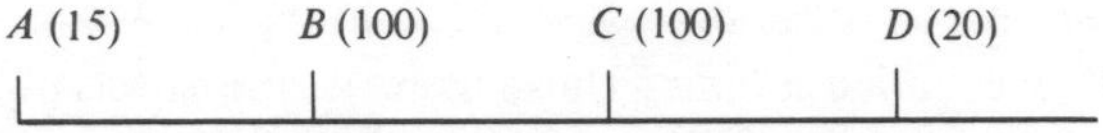

A (15)   B (100)   C (100)   D (20)

Figure 7.7. A 4-party parliament with 235 members.

The numbers in parentheses refer to the number of members in each party. There are, then, 235 members in this four-party parliament. The possible winning coalitions (containing at least 118 members) are: $\overline{BC}$, $\overline{BD}$, and $\overline{CD}$. Of these, $\overline{BC}$ and $\overline{CD}$ are minimally connected, while $\overline{BD}$ is not. Note, however, that all three are minimum winning coalitions in Riker's terms. Presumably, then, coalitions $\overline{BC}$ and $\overline{CD}$ are more likely to form than $\overline{BD}$. In the example, $\overline{BD}$ is a MWC, but not a MCW coalition. On the other hand, *a MCW coalition must be a MWC by the definition given above*. That is, since a minimum connected winning coalition cannot lose a member without ceasing to be winning, it follows that a MCW coalition is also a minimum winning coalition. In other words, the fact that a coalition is simply minimum winning implies nothing about its ideological diversity, while a MCW coalition is *both* minimum winning and ideologically adjacent. The set of MCW coalitions, then, is a subset of all MWCs.

The interesting question, however, is whether these two criteria for coalition formation—i.e., MCW and MWC—are competing criteria. A party which was primarily concerned about being in a minimum winning coalition, and was not concerned about the ideological diversity of the coalition would not be dissatisfied in any MCW coalition. On the other hand, a party which was concerned primarily about the ideological position of its coalition partners might have to join a nonminimum winning coalition rather than a MWC. To see this more clearly, consider the party structure shown in fig. 7.8.

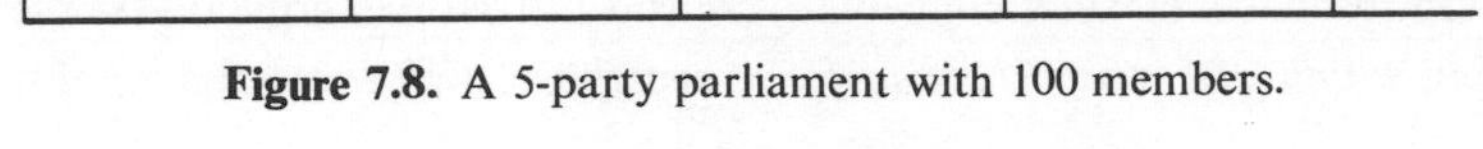

A (25)   B (15)   C (30)   D (10)   E (20)

Figure 7.8. A 5-party parliament with 100 members.

Here there are 100 members in a five-party legislature. A winning coalition requires at least 51 votes. The coalition $\overline{ADE}$ is a minimum winning
coalition with 55 votes and $D = 6$. (*Question:* can you explain how this ideological diversity was computed?) On the other hand, the coalition $\overline{ABC}$ is a
non-minimum winning coalition since party B could be excluded and the coalition $\overline{AC}$ would still be a winning coalition. The ideological diversity of
$\overline{ABC}$, however, is 2. For the party concerned primarily with ideological
diversity, then, the non-minimum winning coalition $\overline{ABC}$ is preferable to the
minimum winning coalition $\overline{ADE}$. This point can also be made by pointing
out that the MWC $\overline{AC}$ (55; $D = 3$) is also less desirable than the non-
minimum winning coalition $\overline{ABC}$ (70; $D = 2$).

For the party primarily concerned about the size of the coalition it enters, then, the criteria MCW and MWC are *not* competing. For the party
primarily concerned with the ideological diversity of its coalition, however,
these criteria can be competing. For that reason, the ideologically oriented
party must always consider the ideological diversity of potential coalitions
before any consideration of size.

There is another problem for the ideologically oriented party. Suppose
two potential winning coalitions of which that party could be a member are
equally diverse ideologically, and both are minimum winning. What criteria
can be used to distinguish them? Consider the following distribution of parties in a five-party parliament (fig. 7.9):

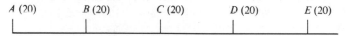

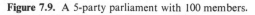

Figure 7.9. A 5-party parliament with 100 members.

Here party C could join coalitions $\overline{ABC}$, $\overline{BCD}$, or $\overline{CDE}$, each with the
same ideological diversity. An argument could be made that the coalition
$\overline{BCD}$ should be the preferred coalition for C on the grounds that C's position
at the ideological center assures the greatest possible satisfaction when policies are implemented by that coalition. In coalition $\overline{ABC}$, for example, party
C faces the possibility that policies implemented by that coalition will be
inclined toward A's position which is farther from C's position than any
possible policy implemented by coalition $\overline{BCD}$. We are assuming, of course,
that policies which winning coalitions implement can be related to a unidimensional ideological position, and that party coalitions in power always
implement policies which at least some member of the coalition approves.

These are very strong assumptions which would undoubtedly have to be modified in a more complex model.

WEIGHING COMPETING CRITERIA

So far, we have considered two main criteria for coalition formation: size and ideological diversity. In the literature on coalition theory, two additional criteria have been suggested. Gamson (1961) suggests another size principle: *minimize the number of members in a coalition*. Obviously, this criterion is sometimes equivalent to Riker's size principle, particularly when all proto-coalitions are of equal weight. Thus, in the five-party parliament in fig. 7.9, all minimum winning coalitions are the same size—i.e., 60 members. Consider fig. 7.8, however, where the MWC $\overline{BCD}$ contains 55 members, while the MWC $\overline{CDE}$ contains 60 members. Here Gamson's size principle tells the parties to join the MWC with the fewest members—i.e., $\overline{BCD}$.

Here again we must consider whether these criteria can ever be competing. Is it possible, that is, to have a MWC which has more members than some nonminimum winning coalition? Consider a five-party parliament composed of 100 members (fig. 7.10).

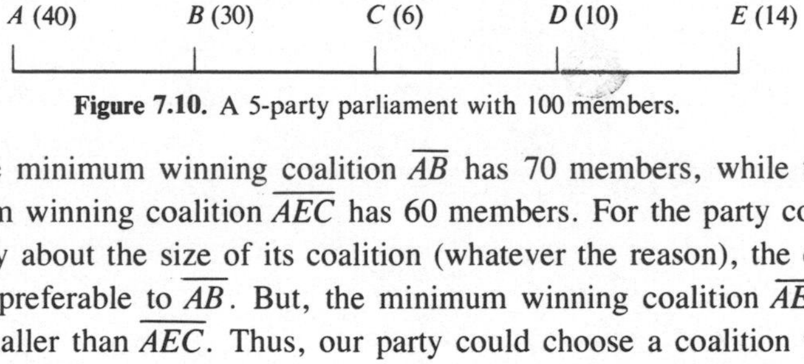

A (40)   B (30)   C (6)   D (10)   E (14)

Figure 7.10. A 5-party parliament with 100 members.

The minimum winning coalition $\overline{AB}$ has 70 members, while the non-minimum winning coalition $\overline{AEC}$ has 60 members. For the party concerned primarily about the size of its coalition (whatever the reason), the coalition $\overline{AEC}$ is preferable to $\overline{AB}$. But, the minimum winning coalition $\overline{AE}$ (54) is even smaller than $\overline{AEC}$. Thus, our party could choose a coalition which is *both* smaller in size *and* minimum winning. It should be fairly evident that the *smallest minimum winning coalition is also the smallest winning coalition, since any winning coalition which is not a MWC can always be reduced in size and still be a winning coalition*. Thus Gamson's size principle is a means of choosing among MWC's of unequal size. It is also evident from our discussion that it does not matter which criterion is used first. If both criteria are used, the coalition chosen will be the smallest minimum winning coalition.

A fourth criterion which could be used is the *number of parties*. Ideally, a single party would like to have a majority of members in a parliament. Short of that, a party might want to minimize the number of other parties with which it joins in order to keep the important cabinet positions under its control. Thus, a two-party coalition divides cabinet positions among two parties, while a three-party coalition must divide the cabinet posts three ways. This becomes a particular problem when a relatively small party is needed to create a winning coalition and, in return for its support, demands control over a cabinet post. In Israel, for example, where no single party has ever controlled a majority of the 120 Knesset seats, the National Religious Party, with only 10 seats in a slim governing majority of 67 seats, has wielded power over important issues far out of proportion to its size, controlling the ministries of Religious Affairs, Social Welfare, and Interior.

The number of parties in a coalition is clearly a criterion which can compete with either of our size principles. In fig. 7.10, for example, the MWC $\overline{AB}$ (70 members) would be preferred to the MWC $\overline{ACD}$ (56 members) by a party which was more concerned about the number of parties in a coalition than in simply the number of members in a MWC. It is not difficult to imagine the rationale for the primacy of either the size principle, or the minimum number of parties principle (MPP). The size principle implies not only a concern with the division of the spoils, but also with the problem of holding together large coalitions. It assumes, in other words, that intraparty discipline is precarious at best. The party principle (MPP), on the other hand, assumes rather rigid party discipline, and so a willingness to join a coalition which is larger in terms of the number of members in order to minimize the number of parties. The party principle joins the size principle, however, in its concern over minimizing the number of those who share in the spoils, whether parties or individuals.

We have, then, introduced four criteria for the formation of coalitions:

1. Minimum winning coalition (MWC)
2. Minimum-size winning coalition
3. Minimum ideological or policy distance (MCWC)
4. Minimum number of parties (MPP)

Obviously these are not the only possible criteria, but they are the ones which have been discussed most frequently in the literature. We should also stress that these are criteria for *coalition formation* only, and do not deal with the question of how payoffs should be distributed once coalitions are formed. In the previous chapter, however, we discussed situations in which the question of which coalition would form was determined by the ultimate division of the payoffs.

If we view the proto-coalitions which are trying to form winning coalitions as voters, and the variety of winning coalitions as alternatives, then the criteria we have just discussed are analogous to the criteria voters use in choosing among alternative policies or candidates for office. More importantly, the theory of coalition-formation is then seen to be structurally equivalent to that of the theory of voting and political parties (see chapter 5). Table 7.7 outlines this structure.

TABLE 7.7 VOTING THEORY AND COALITION THEORY COMPARED

	Voting Theory *(Theory of Political Parties)*	*Coalition Theory*
Choosers	voters, party members	proto-coalitions
Alternatives	policies, candidates	winning coalitions
Criteria	ideological position, issue position, personality of candidate, etc.	minimum winning coalition, minimum-size winning coalition, minimum ideological or policy distance, minimum number of parties
Outcome	implementation of policy, election of candidate	formation of winning coalition

For this reason, it is not surprising when Taylor (1971) shows that

whereas undominated coalitions *necessarily* exist if all actors are assumed to use only the same single criterion, this is not the case when two or more criteria are used, the existence of undominated coalitions being guaranteed only under one very strong assumption about the manner of combining the criteria. Thus, an equilibrium theory of coalition formation will never fail to make a prediction if only one criterion is postulated for all the actors but will be of no explanatory value when several are postulated, unless the theory is based on this assumption (p. 361. Emphasis in original).

The "one very strong assumption" to which Taylor refers is the same one we encountered in chapter 5, that is, a *lexicographic application of the criteria: "every party applies the criteria lexicographically in the same order"* (*Ibid.*, p. 364. Emphasis in original).

In order to see this more clearly, recall that a lexicographic application of criteria in choosing among alternatives means that an individual ranks the criteria in order of importance to him or her, and then compares the alternatives first on the basis of his or her most salient criterion. If this produces a single first choice, then it is not necessary to compare the alternative further. If, however, several alternatives satisfy the most important criterion equally, then the individual must invoke his or her second most important criterion. If that criterion does not distinguish among the alternatives, a third criterion must be invoked. The process continues, moreover, until a single alternative emerges as the most desirable.

In the case of coalition formation, the alternatives, as we said, are the possible winning coalitions, and the criteria are the various minimization goals—size, ideological diversity, and number of parties. Let us consider a simple example of a three-party parliament with 100 seats divided as in fig. 7.11.

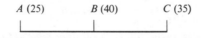

Figure 7.11. A 3-party parliament with 100 members.

Assume that the ideological order is ABC, and that is A is "closer" to B than C. The four possible winning coalitions are: $\overline{AB}$ (65), $\overline{AC}$ (60), $\overline{BC}$ (75), $\overline{ABC}$ (100).

In terms of ideological diversity, $\overline{AB}$ and $\overline{BC}$ are least diverse $(D = 1)$, $\overline{ABC}$ is next $(D = 2)$, and $\overline{AC}$ is the most diverse $(D = 3)$. Note that each party can be a member of any one of three different coalitions. The question, then, is whether there is a coalition which is preferred to every other coalition by at least two of the parties. With no information about the values or goals of the parties, we know that the least preferable outcome for each is the formation of a coalition from which that party is excluded. Thus, for party A, the formation of coalition $\overline{BC}$ is the least desirable outcome; for party B, $\overline{AC}$ is the least desirable; and for C, $\overline{AB}$ is least desirable. The preference ordering for the first three alternatives, however, depends upon the criteria employed. Suppose, for instance, that party A were concerned more with the size of its coalition than with the ideological diversity. Then it would prefer coalition $\overline{AC}$ as its first choice, $\overline{AB}$ as its second choice, and $\overline{ABC}$ as its third choice. Since there were no ties, it was not necessary for party A to use any other criterion than its most salient. *Recall that in apply-*

*ing criteria lexicographically, the second most salient criterion is used only
if a choice cannot be made by using the most salient criterion.*

Suppose, however, that parties B and C consider ideological diversity
more important than size. Then, party B could not choose between $\overline{AB}$ and
$\overline{BC}$ using the ideological criterion, since their diversity was equal. Using
size as a *second* criterion, however, B would prefer the smaller coalition $\overline{AB}$
to $\overline{BC}$. Party C, however, prefers $\overline{BC}$ as its first choice, $\overline{ABC}$ as its second,
and $\overline{AC}$ third. The preference orderings for the coalitions, then, are:

	Party Coalitions		
	$\overline{A}$	$\overline{B}$	$\overline{C}$
Preference order for coalitions	$\overline{AC}$	$\overline{AB}$	$\overline{BC}$
	$\overline{AB}$	$\overline{BC}$	$\overline{ABC}$
	$\overline{ABC}$	$\overline{ABC}$	$\overline{AC}$
	$\overline{BC}$	$\overline{AC}$	$\overline{AB}$
Most salient criterion for coalition formation	Size	Ideology	Ideology

The problem here is that there is no *undominated coalition*. To see this
we shall list the possible winning coalitions and the coalitions which defeat
each of them:

Possible Winning Coalition	Alternative Coalition Preferred by At Least Two Parties
$\overline{AC}$	$\overline{ABC}$ (B, C)
$\overline{AB}$	$\overline{AC}$ (A, C)
$\overline{BC}$	$\overline{AB}$ (A, B)
$\overline{ABC}$	$\overline{BC}$ (B, C)

In other words, no coalition is preferred to every other coalition by a
majority of the parties. This is, of course, the familiar voter's paradox
problem, and the question again is whether it can be avoided in coalition
formation. Taylor's answer, as indicated above, is that there will be no dominated outcomes as long as all of the parties apply the criteria lexicographically and in the same order. In order to illustrate this, let us return
to our example, but this time assume that the three parties apply the criteria
lexicographically and in the same order.

Assume first that ideology is most important. Then, the preference
orders for coalitions are as follows:

	Party		
	A	B	C
Preference order for coalitions	$\overline{AB}$	$\overline{AB}$	$\overline{BC}$
	$\overline{ABC}$	$\overline{BC}$	$\overline{ABC}$
	$\overline{AC}$	$\overline{ABC}$	$\overline{AC}$
	$\overline{BC}$	$\overline{AC}$	$\overline{AB}$

Most salient criterion for coalition formation Ideology Ideology Ideology

Here, the coalition $\overline{AB}$ is preferred to every other coalition by parties A and B, and, therefore, should be the coalition which forms.

In order to generalize his point, Taylor shows that every possible ordering of the four criteria leads to a single undominated outcome. With four criteria there are $4! = 24$ permutations or orderings. But, some of these are redundant or equivalent. For instance, if the minimization of political parties (let us call this criterion E) is applied after the minimum winning coalition criterion (M), this is the same as using E alone. That is because a coalition which is not minimum winning has a surplus of parties in it by definition. On the other hand, the winning coalition with the minimum number of parties must be a minimum winning coalition. In other words, E is a subset of M and, therefore, to choose an E is also to choose an M, but to choose an M is not necessarily to choose an E (see fig. 7.12). That is, all of the coalitions

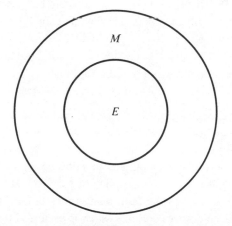

Figure 7.12. All the coalitions within M are minimum winning. All those within E are both minimum winning and minimum in terms of the number of parties.

within the circle M are minimum winning, while all of the coalitions in circle E are *both* minimum winning *and* minimum in terms of the number of parties.

The same is true of M and Gamson's size principle (S) which calls for minimizing the number of members in the coalition as a whole. Here again, S is a subset of M, and if S is applied, M is automatically applied. Taylor also points out that applying E after D (ideological diversity) is the same thing as applying D alone, and that applying S after D is the same thing as applying SE or ES after D. In symbols:

$$MS \equiv S$$
$$DE \equiv D$$
$$DS \equiv DSE \equiv DES$$

(*Question:* Can you explain why the last two equivalencies hold?)

Because of such equivalencies, there are only *six* orderings of the four criteria which are different. These include:

SED	MDSE
SDE	ESD
MDES	EDS

All other orderings are equivalent to one of these. Taylor then shows that all of these orderings will produce a single, undominated outcome if they are applied by all of the parties. To do this he uses a six-party, 100-member parliament with members distributed as in fig. 7.13. The order in which they are presented is also the ideological order. (*Exercise:* Apply each of the six orderings of the criteria above to this six-party legislature and show that each produces a single equilibrium result.)

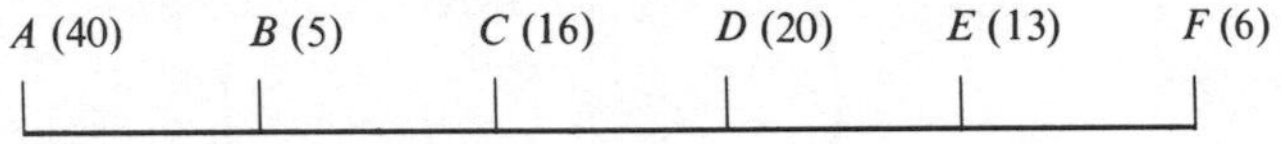

A (40) B (5) C (16) D (20) E (13) F (6)

Figure 7.13. A 6-party parliament with 100 members.

The problem of forming a winning coalition, then, is structurally similar to that of trying to choose among competing policies or candidates. The winning coalition, like the winning policy or party, must be *undominated* in the sense that we have used the term many times before in this book. That is, there cannot be any other coalition which is preferred by a majority to the winning coalition. Stated this way, the problem of coalition formation is subsumed under equilibrium theory. What Taylor is saying is that unless all parties involved apply the four criteria lexicographically *and* in the same order (different orderings of the criteria would undermine this result), undominated outcomes (i.e., undominated winning coalitions) cannot be guaranteed. Note that Taylor is not saying that there will be no undominated winning coalitions but that the *possibility is unavoidable* unless all parties apply the criteria lexicographically and in the same order. In this sense his result is similar to Arrow's.

We must point out, however, that Taylor's concern is different from Riker's, or Leiserson's, or Gamson's. The latter were trying to predict *which* coalition would form by using different theories of coalition formation. Taylor was asking *whether* we could expect the formation of *any* coalition given any of these theories. Taylor's result might be taken as an explanation of unstable parliaments. That is, a parliamentary government might be unstable not simply because it is inept at keeping its winning coalition together, but because there is a rationally better alternative for its coalition partners.

Another important point is that all of the work mentioned above assumes *complete party discipline*. There is no room in these models for party mavericks who vote against their party. Presumably, any weakening of this assumption would make parliamentary coalitions even more unstable. In fact, if the analysis above were correct, it would be extraordinary that government coalitions survive as long as they do. Further theoretical development, then, must account for the stability of so many real coalitions in view of the theoretical arguments thus far which imply instability.

THE CASE OF ISRAEL

In May, 1977, the people of Israel voted for a new government. The outcome was a surprising plurality for Likud, the hawkish party of Menachem Begin: The Labor party, which had governed Israel since its independence in 1948, received fewer voters than Likud. With no majority winner, the problem was to form a new government. Since Likud had a plurality, it was asked to try to form a new government by Israel's president. This meant that, at least in the first round of negotiations, Likud would be a member of the government coalition. Nevertheless, if Likud failed to form a government, it was conceivable that Labor would be given the task and would return weakened but in control of a new government. In this section we shall examine the process of coalition formation in the Israeli parliament (Knesset), trying to relate it to our discussion of coalition theory above.

The incomplete early returns showed the votes divided as follows:

Party	Seats
Likud	43
National Religious Party	12
Democratic Movement for Change	15
Labor	32
Total	102

There are 120 seats in the Knesset. The 18 remaining votes were scattered among smaller parties. For present purposes however, we shall deal only with the four largest parties. A winning majority needs at least 61 seats. In terms of ideology, Likud has been called the party of the Right, strongly opposing the return of captured territory to the Arabs, in favor of strong religious influence on state policy, and inclined toward private enterprise. Labor, on the other hand, is the most "Leftist" of these parties, favoring some territorial concessions to the Arabs, reducing religious influence in state affairs, and developing democratic forms of socialism. On this scale, the National Religious Party is inclined toward Likud, while the DMC leans toward Labor. On an ideological spectrum, then, the parties could be listed as in fig. 7.14.

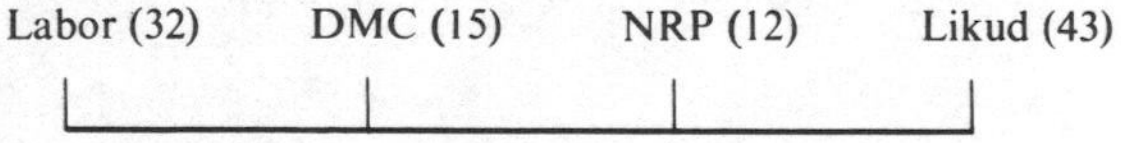

Labor (32)   DMC (15)   NRP (12)   Likud (43)

Figure 7.14. Distribution of seats in the Israeli Knesset, May 1977.

Can we predict which coalition will form? First, let us assume that ideology is the most important criterion for all of the parties. Of the minimum winning coalitions, the ideological diversity would be:

Coalition	Seats	Ideological Diversity
Likud-Labor	75	5
Likud-NRP-DMC	70	2

Notice that these are the only minimum winning coalitions. If ideological diversity were the most important criterion, the Likud-NRP-DMC would form. This would also be true if size were the most important criterion. Only if the number of parties were crucial would the Likud-Labor coalition form. Given the fact that the Likud-Labor coalition was greater in size, as well as more ideologically diverse than the Likud-NRP-DMC coalition which eventually formed, however, it is not possible in this case to determine which factor was more important.

CHAPTER EIGHT

Collective Goods

COLLECTIVE GOODS, or public goods as they are sometimes called, are goods which can provide benefits for many people simultaneously. Clearly, the range of collective goods is enormous—public parks, clean air, safe streets, national security, a just society, and so on. A private good is simply one whose benefits are limited to one or a few individuals. My car and house, my bicycle, my home library, the operation to remove my appendix are all private goods. It is also evident that some goods may be collective for some individuals, and private for others. For all of those who can afford the high-priced tickets, the Metropolitan Opera is a collective good; but for those who cannot afford the tickets, it is someone else's private good.

It should thus be evident that collective goods—as well as private goods—can be supplied either by markets or by government. Ordinarily, however, we tend to make a distinction between the two. Markets provide us with cars, houses, professional football, and television sets; government provides us with hospitals, parks, schools, a criminal justice system, and national defense. Aside from national defense and local police, however, it is evident that many governmental functions are, or could be, supplied by a market, and that many goods now provided by markets are, or could be, supplied by government. Thus, there are private hospitals, schools, and retirement insurance which coexist with similar public activities; and it is evident that the railroads, television stations—in fact, any business—could be nationalized as they are in socialist countries. In addition, many "public" goods are enjoyed by some citizens and not others. In fact, federal, state, and local expenditures are such a hodgepodge that most of us pay for certain goods and services we never use, and use certain goods and services for which we do not pay.

We are all wont to complain about taxes and the inefficiency and corruption of government. This has led some to urge a return to a market system for many goods and services, and a massive reduction of government spending. While this idea may have merit for some goods, it is clearly irrelevant for such important collective goods as clean air and national defense. A market cannot provide clean air or national defense because these are benefits which cannot feasibly be withheld from those who do not pay for them. In a market, goods go only to those who pay for them. In the case of clean air and national security, no one would have an incentive to "purchase" either, since everyone would get them anyway.

The government, then, is assigned the task of reducing air pollution or providing national security through threats of penalties for noncompliance with regulations, and through tax incentives for those who invest in such things as antipollution devices. For these purposes, it uses great sums of tax money, which is collected under threat of penalty for noncompliance. The justification for this great show of government muscle is that clean air and national security are things which people want. This, of course, has an odd ring. If people want clean air and national security, why is it necessary to use coercion? In fact, if Americans are as patriotic as everyone says, Why must taxes be wrenched out of us?

The answer to these questions is the central concern of Mancur Olson's *Logic of Collective Action* (1965). Olson argues that sanctions or private incentives are necessary to overcome the "free-rider" problem. That is, without such sanctions or private incentives, individuals in large groups would have no incentive to help pay for collective goods. Instead, their incentive would be to try to reap the benefits without paying the costs. Such an argument provides a justification for government coercion, just as Hobbes had justified government coercion as necessary to restrain natural human passions for violence. It also provides an explanation for the use of the closed shop in the labor movement as well as the disproportionate burden of funding in such groups as NATO and the United Nations.

In this chapter, we shall analyze Olson's argument in some detail and consider certain criticisms of his position. Then, we shall examine Hardin's (1971) notion that the collective-goods question can be seen as a prisoner's dilemma, though an "agreeable" one; and Taylor's (1976) claims that the prisoner's dilemma analysis does not necessarily support Olson's claims, but that there are other game theoretical situations which do support them. Finally, we shall consider Margolis's (1979) use of the notion of altruism to explain why we might expect collective goods to be provided voluntarily.

THE LOGIC OF COLLECTIVE ACTION

While Olson's analysis is not particularly technical for economists, it might seem very abstruse for most political scientists. In the following sections, therefore, we shall try to explicate his work, using some of his symbols but trying to clarify and simplify the basic logic of his argument.

SUPPLY AND COSTS

Economists are used to discussing such concepts as supply and demand. With some goods, such as cars and refrigerators, the notion of supply is fairly clear and unambiguous. It is simply the number of cars or refrigerators. With other goods, however, the problem is more complex. For example, what is the "supply" of clean air or national defense or safe streets? These notions are difficult to quantify. Nevertheless, it is not impossible. For example, we could measure the "level of supply" of clean air in terms of the amount of pollutants in the air. Then, as the level of pollutants declines, the "supply" of clean air is increased. Thus, we might say that if x is a given amount of pollutants in the air at one time, and if there is a 10 percent reduction in those pollutants, then the supply of clean air has increased by 10 percent. In other areas, of course, even this crude measure may not be possible. Suppose, for instance, that we were concerned with the level or "supply" of national security. Here we seem to have only indirect measures. Thus, we might try to relate national security to levels of defense spending, but clearly there is no necessary relation between the two. Our development of the neutron bomb, for example, may even *reduce* our national security. Similarly, where the collective good is "safe streets," an increase in the number of police does not necessarily reduce crime, as studies have shown; and, the data on crime rates are notoriously unreliable.

Nevertheless, Olson's theory does assume that collective goods can be supplied at various rates. Further, he assumes that such collective goods, like all economic goods, are costly, and that more of the good costs more. Here again, we must note that costs are also difficult to quantify in some situations. Thus, for example, the time we spend organizing a neighborhood patrol to provide the collective good "safe streets" cannot easily be valued. Nonetheless, Olson assumes that any increase in the supply of a collective good costs more, just as two cars cost more than one car. In symbols, let T be the level of supply of a collective good, and C be the cost. Then

$$C = f(T)$$

that is, cost is a function of the level of supply, as shown in fig. 8.1. The exact shape of this curve, of course, depends upon many factors. Note,

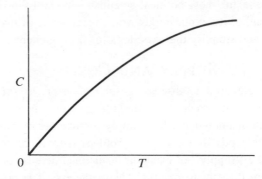

Figure 8.1. Relationship between cost and supply of collective goods.

however, the rather rapid rise of this curve for small initial amounts of the collective good. This is supposed to reflect the fact that the initial costs of providing a good are likely to be relatively high. For instance, if we want to reduce pollution, at least one of our actions must be to build "scrubbers" on factories. This suggests that money must be spent even *before* the first reduction in pollution can be achieved. Yet, once the machinery is in place—scrubbers, catalysts on auto exhausts, and so forth,—the cost remains relatively constant, or rises only slightly, relative to the collective good—clean air—produced. This also means that the cost of the first increment of clean air is relatively high compared to later increments. This is the same in auto production, for example, where the first car produced is relatively expensive, while the one-millionth car is relatively less expensive.

INDIVIDUAL BENEFITS

Just as an individual receives utility or benefits from a private good, so he or she also receives utility from collective goods. The interesting difference between a collective and a private good, however, is that the former can provide benefits simultaneously to more than one individual. This characteristic of collective goods is called *jointness of consumption*. Now, the important point is that every individual associates a particular level of benefits with a particular level of collective good supplied. Thus, individual benefits are also a function of the level of supply, T. In symbols.

$$B = f(T)$$

where *"B"* stands for benefits. But, not every individual associates the same benefit with the same amount of a collective good. In fact, a collective good for some individuals may be a collective "bad" for others. Thus, for example, "safe streets" are a "good" for all law-abiding citizens, but a "bad" for the criminals! Similarly, a tariff on imported Japanese autos may be a collective good for American auto makers, but it is clearly a "bad" for the Japanese. Additionally, some individuals may receive relatively greater benefits than others from a particular level of collective goods. Remember, though, that "benefits" here means subjective utility, and to say that an individual "receives greater benefits" than others, means that he or she *values* that good more.

Since different individuals may place different values on the same amount of a collective good, it is evident that not everyone would want to spend the same amount to purchase a given level of a particular collective good. Moreover, some individuals would want to spend much more of their resources than others on a particular collective good. In standard economic analysis, an individual purchases a good—private or collective—until the point at which his or her *marginal utility* for the good equals its *marginal cost*. Since these notions are so important in economic analysis generally, as well as in Olson's analysis, we shall explain them here in more detail.

MARGINAL UTILITY AND MARGINAL COSTS

"Marginal utility" is the utility we receive from the last increment of any good we purchase. It is distinguished from *total utility*, which we receive from the entire amount of the good we have purchased, and from *average utility*, which is the total utility divided by the number of increments. A standard assumption in economic theory is that marginal utility declines as the supply of a good increases. This means that the first unit of a good brings a certain level of utility, and that each succeeding increment brings less utility. This is not to say that total utility declines—it does not— but rather that the increase in utility from each increment or additional unit of the good is less than the previous increment.

The image behind the diminishing marginal utility concept is that of a satiated appetite. We begin with a need or desire we want to satisfy. When we are most "hungry," we value most whatever will satisfy us. As we are satiated we place less value on additional satisfaction. This applies to such needs as hunger or sex, where the pleasure diminishes as the need is satisfied, until a period of abstention renews our desire.

Figure 8.2 depicts marginal utility in graphic terms. Here the "ath" unit of a particular good has a value a' while the "bth" unit has a value of b'

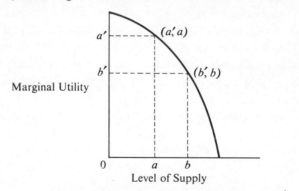

Figure 8.2. Marginal utility and level of supply.

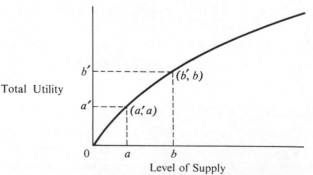

Figure 8.3. Total utility and level of supply.

which is lower than a'. If we were drawing the graph of the relationship between the *total amount* of the good and the level of utility it might appear as in fig. 8.3.

Here the utility of an increasing *amount* of the good *increases,* but at a *decreasing rate*.

Another way of expressing diminishing marginal utility is in algebraic form. For example, suppose G_1 is the first unit of a good, and that G_2 is the second unit, then, according to the notion of diminishing marginal utility:

$$u(G_1) > u(G_2)$$

That is, the utility of the first unit of the good is greater than the utility of the second unit. Also according to diminishing marginal utility:

$$u(G_1) + u(G_2) > u(G_1)$$

Or, the sum of the utilities of G_1 and G_2 is greater than that of G_1 alone.

Now, it is also true that the resources any individual uses to purchase a good have utility. The standard economic activity, then, is an *exchange*. That is, I exchange some goods, services, or other resources which I have for some goods, services, or other resources which I want but do not have. Moreover, the basis for any voluntary exchange is that the utility (for me) of the resources I give up must be greater than the utility (for me) of the goods purchased. In theory, then, economic exchange increases the utility of both parties in an exchange.

In practice, of course, this does not always happen. Sometimes I pay less than I would have been willing to pay for a good. In such cases, we say that I have made a good bargain, or simply, that the good itself is a "bargain." In other cases I am "taken," i.e., I pay "too much" for the good. What this means is that either I do not, in fact, receive the utility from a good which I expect, or I could have purchased it for less elsewhere. Examples of the former abound—my new car which turns out to be a "lemon," the best-selling novel which is uninteresting to me, and so on.

Nevertheless, the goal of a trading individual is to purchase a particular good up to the point at which the value of the good equals the value of the resources spent to purchase that good. In order to see why this is so, consider the following simple example. Suppose that I am deciding how much of a particular private good to purchase, and that the cost of x amount of the good is c. Now, suppose that, in terms of utility, x is greater than c. This means that the utility of the good I have purchased is greater than the utility of the resources I have exchanged for that good. Now, my question is whether I should purchase an additional unit or increment of that good, say x'. Recall that in our discussion of decreasing marginal utility we said that any *increment* of a good brings less utility than a previous increment. Thus, the increment x' should have less utility for our individual than x—assuming, of course, that x and x' are equivalent *amounts* of the good. (*Question:* Can you explain why we must include this restriction?) The additional unit of the good will also cost more, say c'. This will reduce the resources available and, therefore, by the marginal utility assumption, the extra unit of resources spent will have a *greater* utility for the individual. Then, with the declining marginal utility of the good purchased and the increasing marginal utility of the resources spent, at some point the two will be equal. Let us assume, then, that the utility of the last increment of x—i.e., the amount which produces x'—is equal to the utility of the increment of c—the resources—needed to purchase x. At that point, the individual should not purchase any more of x since the next increment will bring less utility than the increment of c needed to purchase it.

It is not necessarily the case, however, that an individual will purchase a particular good until the point at which the marginal cost equals the marginal utility for that particular good. Suppose, for example, that a second good, y, would produce greater utility for our individual. Then, he or she would purchase y rather than x. This point will be especially important in our discussion of altruism below. An individual's overall spending should cease when the value of the resources held exceeds the value of anything that could be purchased.

PRIVILEGED GROUPS

The model which has been presented so far, then, depicts goods—public or private—which are costly to provide, and which require additional resources to purchase additional increments; individuals who receive benefits from these goods, though at a declining rate (declining marginal utility), and not necessarily at the same level as other individuals; and a situation in which goods are purchased by these individuals up to the point where marginal costs equal marginal utility.

For private goods, this picture is relatively straightforward. The same is true of only one situation involving collective goods, and that is the so-called *privileged group*. In the privileged group, there is one, or at most a few, individuals for whom the benefits of a particular collective good outweigh the *total cost* of the collective good. That is, even though all members of the group receive the benefits of the collective good, one or a few members of the group would be willing to pay the entire cost of the good even if the others did not pay their share.

In order to clarify this notion, let us consider some possible examples. Suppose that I am a shipowner whose ship has run aground in a fog on a small island off the coast. Suppose further that this is a continuing condition, that I must send my vessels through that area, and that I cannot convince either the government or other shipowners to build a lighthouse. In such a case, it could be worth it to me to build a lighthouse at my own expense. The light which was provided would be a collective good to all shipowners and sailors who use the waters in that area. Moreover, it would not be feasible for me either to exclude others from its benefits or to charge them for "using" the lighthouse. These are two of the important characteristics of collective goods: *nonexcludability* and *jointness of consumption*.

Consider another example. Suppose several people in a neighborhood felt that an evening patrol was essential to prevent crime. At the same time, they could not convince others to participate in the patrol. Nevertheless, they organized the patrol and shared the costs—time, effort, the use of their cars, and so on. Again, they could not exclude their neighbors from the benefits of the patrol, nor could they force them to contribute to the costs—unless, of course, they tried moral suasion, shaming, or a similar approach. Such a group would also be "privileged" in Olson's terms.

Consider a final example. The political dissidents in the Soviet Union, such as Andrei Sakharov, could be said to be providing all Soviet citizens with a public good—i.e., pressure on the Soviet government to be less autocratic. Of course, the Soviet government is trying to convince the Soviet people that the dissidents are providing a public "bad." Nevertheless, the dissidents themselves are surely bearing the full burden of the costs of this public good, while the rest of the Soviet citizens are receiving benefits without costs.

Olson's point is that such privileged groups *are* likely to provide themselves *voluntarily* with collective goods. Further, he suggests that such groups are likely to be very small. There are at least two reasons why privileged groups are likely to be small. First, it is only in small groups that any one individual's benefits are likely to be large relative to the total benefit of the group as a whole. In large groups, the benefit which any one individual receives will be small relative to the total group benefit. Thus, it is only in small groups that individuals will be likely to bear the entire cost of providing the collective good.

Second, most collective goods, according to Olson, are *crowdable* rather than *pure*. A crowdable collective good is one whose individual benefits are reduced by the consumption of others. This means that as more individuals benefit from the crowdable collective good, the benefit to *each* individual *declines*. The benefits of a public park, for example, are reduced as more people use the park. Conversely, a pure public good is one whose benefits are not affected by the number of people who enjoy it. Thus, clean air is an example of a pure public good, since the benefits any one individual receives from clean air cannot be reduced by the fact that many others are enjoying it. If most collective goods are crowdable, then, relatively large groups should provide relatively small benefits for each individual. At the same time, the total costs of providing collective goods for large numbers of people are relatively high. Consider, for example, the enormous costs of building and maintaining public parks, or keeping the air free of pollutants, or providing national defense. Relative to such enormous costs, the benefits to any one individual, or even a few, are minuscule. We must also consider the fact that such costs would be clearly beyond the means of a few individuals, even if the benefits were great. For these reasons, then, privileged groups are expected to be quite small.

The example of the dissidents, however, does present some problems, since it appears that a relatively few individuals are providing a collective good for a great many individuals, and are bearing the full costs. Several responses are possible. First, this is, indeed, a privileged, large group, and while such groups are rare, they may exist. No one would doubt, however, that martyrdom is an uncommon phenomenon. A second response is that those who feel that the actions of the dissidents are a good are confined to the dissidents themselves, a relatively small group, all of whom share the costs of pressuring the Soviet government. Thus, the majority of the Soviet citizens are not "free riders," benefiting without paying. Finally, we might say that the good produced by the dissidents is a pure public good whose costs are well within the capacity of a few individuals. Again, such situations are probably quite rare, though they should alert us to possible problems in Olson's analysis.

LARGE GROUPS

Olson's main point is that, in *large groups,* collective goods will not be provided voluntarily, and that some form of coercion or special incentive is needed to induce individuals to bear their share of the cost. Now, it is important to stress that Olson is not talking about forcing individuals to do something which they do not want to do. He is positing a large group of individuals all of whom *want* a particular collective good and are able to pay their share for it. Yet they should not do so voluntarily if they are rational. This is because:

A. They will receive the collective good if it is provided, even if they do not pay for it.
B. Any individual share of the cost is so small relative to the total cost that the refusal of any one individual to contribute will not affect the provision of the collective good.
C. There is absolutely no guarantee that others will pay their fair share or anything at all.
D. Since the contribution of any one individual is so small, no one will notice the "free rider" and so the possible costs of community opprobrium can be avoided.

The problem with such reasoning, of course, is that if *everyone* came to the same conclusion, no one would contribute and there would be no collective good. Is it rational, then, for an individual in such a large group to contribute to the collective good so that others will do the same? Again, the answer is no, since no single individual is in a position to assure that others contribute. Thus, while it is true that if everyone reasons the same way no one will contribute, it does not follow, therefore, that any one individual should contribute as a way to induce others to pay, since no individual contribution will have that effect. As a result, Olson expects that large groups will not provide themselves voluntarily with collective goods.

Notice the striking similarity between this discussion and our discussions of the Downsian rational voter in chapter 5, and of the prisoner's dilemma in chapter 6. Recall that the Downsian rational voter asked whether it was rational to vote in a large election. There, as well, the answer seemed to be negative, since the voter could not hope to influence the election by his or her single vote and would reap any benefits or suffer any consequences independently of his or her actions. There the collective good could be the voting itself—i.e., democratic systems (a "good") require the expression of citizens' preferences (also a "good"), which in turn requires something like a voting procedure. It could also be the policies any particular candidate or party implements, in which case, of course, some voters will suffer from collective "bads."

In the prisoner's dilemma, the collective good is the mutually cooperative action, but, in both the two-person and the n-person game, the noncooperative strategy is dominant. This will be discussed in more detail below, but for the present, note that Olson's privileged-group notion can be used as a "solution" to the two-person prisoner's dilemma, not in the more technical "solution concept" sense of the term we discussed in chapter 6 but in the sense of solving the problem. That is, where the strategies are either to contribute to the costs of the collective good or refrain from doing so, a privileged group contains at least one individual for whom the collective good is so valuable that he or she will bear the entire cost. Thus, if the two-person prisoner's dilemma involves a collective good, and if the two players constitute a privileged group, one of them will "cooperate" and pay for the collective good, even if the other is "noncooperative" and refuses to pay. In the n-person case, however, this will not happen for the same reasons which we used to explain the failure of large groups to provide themselves with collective goods.[1]

INTERMEDIATE GROUPS

An intermediate group is a relatively small group in which at best only a few individuals are willing and able to provide a collective good for the group as a whole. In other words, it is not a privileged group. On the other hand, the fact that it is relatively small means that certain informal group pressures will play a role in supporting the provision of a collective good. Thus, in an intermediate group, no individual will pay the full cost of the collective good, but if an individual refuses to contribute anything, it will be highly visible, and it will affect significantly the provision of the collective

1. Of course, as Hardin (1971) points out, the cooperative solution of the n-person prisoner's dilemma is at least a weak Condorcet outcome, and, in that sense, the collective goods situation is an "agreeable" n-person prisoner's dilemma. We shall discuss this further below.

good. Under such circumstances, Olson argues, it can be expected that *some* amount of a collective good will be provided, but that the amount will be extremely *suboptimal*.

In order to understand this notion of suboptimality, recall our discussion above, in which we suggested that individuals would be expected to purchase a good until the point at which marginal cost equals marginal utility. That point is said to be "optimal," in the sense that an individual cannot increase his or her utility by further exchanges, since the utility of the resources needed to purchase the next increment of the good is greater than the utility of the good itself for that individual. Such a point can also be said to be *Pareto optimal* since an individual's utility cannot be increased by any other action. This notion is related to the Pareto principle which we introduced in chapter 2. There, the alternative which is the unanimous choice of all voters is said to be *Pareto optimal*.

Suboptimality, then, means that an alternative has been chosen which is not Pareto optimal. This means that there is another alternative which is preferred to that alternative. Thus, in chapter 1, we spoke of the "dominated-winner paradox" in which a sequential-elimination, simple majority rule procedure resulted in the choice of an alternative which was Pareto dominated by another alternative. In other words, there was an alternative everyone in the group preferred to the alternative which actually emerged as the winner.

In regard to the collective goods case, suboptimality means that, while a certain amount of a collective good has been provided, there are certain individuals in the group who could still increase their utility by exchanging resources for more of the collective good. In other words, "optimality" in regard to the provision of collective goods means that every individual in the group has spent his or her resources up to the point where the marginal utility of the collective good equals its marginal cost. The question, then, is why individuals in an intermediate group do not reach an optimal level of spending.

In order to answer this question, we must first distinguish between groups whose members receive the *same* benefits or utility from the same amount of a collective good, and groups whose members receive *different* benefits or utility from the same amount of a collective good. Ordinary experience and intuition would suggest that groups of the latter kind are probably far more prevalent than those of the former. It seems to make more sense to assume that, for the most part, different individuals will benefit very differently from the same collective good. Thus, for example, freedom of speech means much more to the members of the American Civil Liberties Union than it does to the average citizen, even though the latter may feel that freedom of speech is definitely a "good." Similarly, clean air is probably more valuable to the nonsmoker than to the smoker, and public parks are more useful to the inveterate jogger than to the occasional stroller. The interesting problem, however, is that *collective goods are more likely to be provided at a suboptimal level—if they are provided at all—where benefits are unevenly distributed throughout an intermediate group.* Conversely, an optimal provision of collective goods is more likely where members of an intermediate group receive relatively equal benefits from the same amount of a collective good.

In order to see this more clearly, let us consider first how the costs of a collective good should be shared among the group members. The most obviously fair way is in proportion to the benefits received. Thus, if everyone receives equal benefits, everyone should pay an equal share of the costs, and if some individuals receive more than others they should pay more.[2] Notice that this point is in keeping with our claim above that individuals should spend their resources until marginal utility of the good equals the marginal cost. Thus, if individual A receives u utiles of benefit from x amount of the collective good, and B receives $u + 1$ utiles, then A should pay less than B for x. In Olson's terms, those who benefit more from a collective good are referred to as the "great," while those who benefit less are the "small." (These terms are not particularly significant, and imply only the differences in the rate of benefit. They are not a commentary on the qualities of the individuals themselves!)

Now, the problem is that the "small" members of the group will want to purchase less of the collective good than the "great" members. This is because they receive less utility from a given level of collective goods. But, this means that unless the "great" continue to purchase the collective good after the "small" have stopped contributing, the amount of the good actually purchased will be suboptimal. This is because the "great" have not

2. This is, of course, a very particular notion of fairness, which is not without problems. For example, one individual may benefit more than another and pay less—or nothing—but this could be justified on the grounds that the second individual may have significantly greater resources than the first.

reached the point at which marginal cost equals marginal utility. On the other hand, if the "great" do continue to purchase the collective good after the "small" have stopped, it could be argued, as Olson does, that the "great" are being *exploited* by the "small."

In order to see this more clearly, consider the following simple example. Suppose that there are four individuals, A, B, C, and D, in a particular group, and that they want to purchase collective good *G*. (Perhaps these are members of NATO—the U.S., Britain, Belgium, and Italy—deciding how much "collective security" to purchase in Europe.)

Suppose further that every increment of *G* costs one unit (whatever that may be), and every member of the group has a different marginal utility curve for *G*, as in fig. 8.4. (It may seem strange to suggest that the United States might receive greater benefits from European security than the Europeans themselves, but if the level of past commitment of resources to NATO is any indication, it would certainly seem to be an empirically accurate observation.)

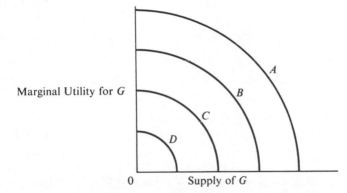

Figure 8.4. Marginal Utility for 4 individuals and collective Good.

Here, A has the greatest marginal utility for any increment of *G*, while D has the least. Suppose also that every member of the group contributes an equal amount when any amount of *G* is purchased. Thus, for the first four increments of *G*, each member will pay one unit. Suppose D feels that the utility received from four units of *G* exactly equals the utility received from the one unit it cost to purchase those four units of *G*. By our assumption above, this would *not* be the case for A, B, and C who would receive *more* utility from the four units of *G* than from the one unit of cost. In tabular form, this could be expressed as follows:

Individual	Units of G	Cost (C)	Utility of G [U(G)]	Utility of C [U(C)]
A	4	1	4	1
B	4	1	3	1
C	4	1	2	1
D	4	1	1	1

Thus, for A, the four units of G, the collective good, produces four units of utility, while the one unit of C represents only one unit of utility. For D, on the other hand, the four units of the collective good provide only one unit of utility, and that is equal to the utility of one unit of C (Cost). At that point, D would have no incentive to purchase more, since the next four units of G would bring *less than* one unit of utility (by the declining marginal utility assumption), while the one unit of C it would cost would be valued at one *or more* units of utility (the resources increase in value as they become scarce).

If the group should stop purchasing the collective good at that point, the supply of G (four units) would be extremely suboptimal, since A, B, and C can all improve their positions by further exchange. Suppose, then, that A, B, and C decide to purchase more of G without D. Then the results might be as follows:

Individual	Units of G	Cost (C)	Utility of G [U(G)]	Utility of C [U(C)]
A	4	1.33	3.75	1.33
B	4	1.33	2.75	1.33
C	4	1.33	1.75	1.33
D	4	.00	.75	.00

Notice that D has not paid anything for the additional 4 units of G, while A, B, and C split the cost of the additional units. Then, D receives an additional .75 units of utility without spending anything. We begin to see here what Olson means by the "exploitation" of the "great" by the "small." The "small" receive utility from G—remember, G is a collective good which cannot be kept from anyone—without paying for it. (In the NATO example, three countries would be paying for the collective security which the fourth shared.)

The total of eight units of G, however, is still suboptimal since A, B, and C would like to purchase more. Thus, we see from this example that there is good reason to expect that the provision of collective goods in inter-

mediate groups with members of different "size" will be severely suboptimal. Or, if the supply is not suboptimal, then the "great" will be exploited.

Of course, in our example, it is not completely clear that it is the
"great" who have been exploited. Notice that after the first unit of payment,
A had received more utility than B, B more than C, and C more than D.
Moreover, it was the willingness of everyone to contribute which enabled
the "great" to prosper. In addition, if we consider the total gain in utility
from G, the "great" do much better than the "small." Thus, A received
7.75 utiles, B 5.75, C 3.75, and D 1.75. Similarly, the net utility
$[U (G) - U (C)]$ was also much higher for the "great"; $A = 5.42$, $B = 3.42$,
$C = 1.42$, and $D = .75$.

There are two more points to be made here. First, this "intermediate"
group begins to look more and more like a "privileged" group as particular
members refuse to pay more of the cost. On the other hand, the fact that everyone pays at least something distinguishes the intermediate group from the
privileged group. Remember, though, we are only discussing relatively
small groups. For large groups, the point remains that no voluntary collective-goods provision is expected.

Our second point is that the small members are in a good strategic position, since they do not care about the collective good as much as the great
members. This means that the small might even be able to induce the great
to spend more on the collective good by threatening not to spend anything at
all. Surely this is the position which the United States has frequently faced
in dealing with smaller countries whose geographical position is of strategic
interest to us.

Similarly, there is an incentive to misrepresent the utility one receives
from a collective good in order to induce others to pay a greater share of the
costs. The difficulty here, however, is that *everyone* has an incentive to pre-
tend that his or her benefits are less than they really are. As a result, suboptimal provision of collective goods is even more likely.

CARROTS AND STICKS

In view of his analysis, Olson concludes that collective goods will be
provided in large or intermediate groups only if there is external coercion or
"side-payments" in the form of private goods given to some members of
the group. Such a conclusion can serve as a justification for state power, just

as state power was justified in the prisoner's dilemma discussion above as a legitimate way of bringing about a situation which everyone wanted, but which was unobtainable without external coordination. We can even see this in the marriage-counselor role, or the mediator role in general, where the third party tries to bring about a settlement of disputes—which is, presumably, a collective good.

Thus, we give the state the power to tax—i.e., to take money from us—and to penalize those who cheat. The power to punish tax evaders, moreover, is justified on the ground that if the payment of taxes was voluntary, no one would pay them.[3] This is particularly interesting, since citizens are supposedly committed by patriotism to doing voluntarily what is good for their country. Moreover, if the state, with all of its propaganda resources, cannot obtain voluntary support for its activities, surely other large collectivities with far fewer resources and far less emotional commitment cannot be expected to have its members voluntarily pay for collective goods. Thus, Olson argues that even trade unions, whose activities in achieving higher wages, better benefits, and shorter hours are surely providing collective benefits to their members, could not survive without the coercion of closed shops.

It is not through coercion alone, however, that individuals are induced to pay for collective goods. Frequently, large groups, such as unions, provide special benefits for particular members, such as college scholarships for union children, social evenings, insurance, discounts on appliance purchases, and so on. In such situations, group membership is simply a way of obtaining access to benefits which were not part of the original group purpose.

INCOME EFFECTS AND CONGESTION EFFECTS

Not everyone has agreed with Olson's conclusions. One interesting criticism is Chamberlin's (1974), which argues that the size of the group is not the

3. It is not clear, of course, that no one would pay taxes, nor is it clear how the payment of taxes by some citizens would affect the payment of taxes by others. It would be an interesting experiment, however, to see how large the federal budget would be under a voluntary system of taxation. It has also been suggested that the probability of being punished in any significant way for evading taxes—e.g. going to jail, as opposed to simply paying more money after an audit— is so low that it pays to cheat, and that, therefore, our tax system is, in many ways, already voluntary!

only factor in determining whether a collective good will be provided. He suggests that two other factors are important—the so-called *income effect* and the *congestion effect*. He concludes that large groups should be expected to provide themselves with collective goods which are *inclusive,* though they would not provide themselves with collective goods which are *exclusive*. We shall define these terms and explain these points below.

Consider first the *income effect*. Suppose an individual is considering whether to spend resources on a particular collective good or a particular private good. Suppose further that another individual provides a certain amount of that collective good before our first individual makes up his or her mind. Presumably, such a situation could arise in a privileged group. At that point, the first individual has received benefits without paying any costs, and can be said to have received additional *income* from the action of another. That is, the resources which might have been spent on that collective good can now be used either to purchase more of the private good than originally intended, or additional increments of the collective good. We are assuming, of course, that the first individual was at least considering whether to spend some income on the collective good.[4]

The decision on how to spend those resources depends upon the individual's *elasticity of demand* for the collective good. The notion of elasticity of demand is very important in economic analysis, and refers to the effect of changes in price or income on our demand for a good. Here "demand" means the so-called "effective demand"—i.e., our willingness and ability to pay for a good.

Consider, for example, the demand for open-heart surgery. If we need such medical attention, we will pay for it even if the surgeon's fee doubles from the time of our first consultation. Such demand is said to be *inelastic*—it does not contract or decrease as the price increases, nor does it increase as the price decreases. On the other hand, when the price of lettuce jumps from 39 cents to 49 cents per head, we may substitute celery and carrots for the lettuce. Our demand for lettuce, then, is *elastic*—it contracts as the price increases, and expands as the price decreases.

A price increase is equivalent to a reduction in income. This has be-

4. If the individual had no intention of purchasing the collective good, it would be difficult to see how the free benefits of the collective good could be seen as additional income—i.e., *resources* to be spent on something else. It is obvious that the collective good can bring unexpected benefits, but unless those benefits released resources which were intended to purchase that collective good, it does not seem that new income was created. And, the notion of income effects implies the creation of new resources which can be spent.

come a very familiar point in the recent discussions of inflation in this country. Thus, our demand is also elastic or inelastic in relation to an increase or decrease in our income, as well as in the price of a good. If our income decreases, our demand for all goods decreases. If our income increases, however, our demand for certain goods may increase, remain the same, or decrease. Specifically, we may decide to spend a greater proportion of our additional income on a good than we did our previous income, we may decide to use the same proportion of our additional income on the good, or we may decide to use a *smaller* proportion of the additional income on the good. In the first case, the good in question is said to be *superior,* in the second *normal,* and in the latter case *inferior.* These terms are not meant to be qualitative judgments about the goods but rather descriptive statements about the behavior of consumers toward these goods as income increases.

To make this distinction clearer, suppose that I am spending 1 percent of my income on gifts to my alma mater, and that when I receive an increase in salary I increase my gift, but the latter still amounts to 1 percent of my income. My alma mater, or what it produces, is then said to be a normal good.[5]

Consider, however, the food budget. Ordinarily, there must be a certain minimum amount of money spent on such necessities. Thus, whether a family of four earns $25,000 or $100,000, the *amount* of money spent on the ordinary food budget should not be dramatically different. (Of course, we are not speaking about eating at restaurants.) Therefore, the proportion of our income spent on the food budget would *decline* as income increases. If our income increased from $25,000 to $30,000, for example, we would not expect any significant change in the gross amount spent on our normal food budget. We would expect, however, that the proportion of our income spent on eating at good restaurants would increase as income increased. Thus, restaurants are a superior good. In general, then, we might say that necessities are inferior goods, while luxuries are *superior* goods.[6] Again, we must not read too much into the connotation of the terms "inferior" and "superior". They are used here descriptively and not normatively. We should also note that there are important exceptions to this generalization. For example, we

5. Of course, the fact that such a gift is tax deductible may mean that the percentage of the increase is really more than 1 percent, but this example is only for purposes of illustrating the notion of a normal good.

6. I am indebted to Russell Hardin for this point.

would certainly expect that an individual receiving a $5000 income for a family of four would spend a greater amount on his food budget as his income increased. At such a low level of income, then, food is also a superior good.

We are not primarily interested here in such goods as food and restaurants, but rather in collective goods which are politically important. Again, we are still considering the possibility of voluntary collective action. Thus, for example, we must ask whether such goods as national security, safe streets, a just society, or clean air might be "superior," "normal," or "inferior" goods. Is it the case, in other words, that we would choose to spend increasing proportions of an increasing income on such goods?

When considering such collective goods, it is evident that we must be dealing with large numbers of people. For this reason, we would not expect privileged groups where these goods are concerned. But, if that is the case, who provides the *initial* increments of the collective good which then provide others with additional "income"? Surely, the strategic problems Olson described for large groups must be overcome before we can postulate such income-producing increments. Moreover, the organizational, or start-up, costs of such goods must also reduce the possibility that some individuals will produce collective goods for others.[7]

In any case, Chamberlin argues that *if* such problems are overcome, and if some individuals provide others with essentially free increments of *superior* collective goods, then the individuals who benefit from those goods, who receive additional income, will spend a *greater* proportion of that increment on the collective good than they had been spending at a *lower* income level. *If that is the case, larger groups should provide greater amounts of such collective goods than smaller groups.* Of course, this is the opposite of Olson's argument. In order to illustrate this point, consider the following case. There are two groups of individuals, A, B, C, and A, B, C, D. The former group purchases a superior collective good, G_1. The cost of G_1 is equivalent to six utiles of benefit. That is, the resources used to purchase G_1 are worth six utiles and each unit of cost has the same value for each individual. At first, individuals A and B share the cost, and C pays nothing, but each receives benefits of five utiles for G_1. This situation can be summarized as follows:

7. This is also a point which Russell Hardin has stressed.

	Cost (in utiles)	Amount of Collective Good	Benefit (Individual Utility)
A	3	G_1	5
Individuals: B	3	G_1	5
C	0	G_1	5

Let us assume also that G_1 is a so-called *pure* public good, or an *inclusive* public good—the terms can be used interchangeably. Now, in this case, C has received five utiles of benefit with no expenditure of resources. Moreover, given our previous assumption that individuals try to equalize marginal utility and marginal cost, we would expect C to spend up to 5 utiles worth of resources on G_1—unless, of course, some other good, collective or private, provided a better return. Further, let us assume that C wants to spend half of his income on the collective good, G_1, the other half on a private good, P_1. This is, of course, a highly simplified view of reality. In any case, C would have been willing to share the cost of G_1 with A and B, and those two utiles of cost (splitting 6 three ways) represent half of his income. Since A and B have purchased G_1 without C, however, C can be said to have received an additional income worth two utiles. Since G_1 has been assumed to be a superior good, C is willing to spend *more than half* of his additional income on the next increment of the collective good which we shall call G_2. The purchase of G_2 produces the following situation:

	Cost (in utiles)	Amount of Collective Good	Benefit (Individual Utility)
A	2	G_2	4
Individuals: B	2	G_2	4
C	2	G_2	4

Notice that the individual benefit of G_2 is less than that of G_1. This is the result of our declining-marginal-utility assumption. Notice also that we have assumed that every increment of the collective good costs the same. Thus G_3, the increment which follows G_2, will cost each individual two utiles worth of resources, and produce three utiles in benefits, while G_4 would cost two utiles of resources and produce two utiles of benefit. At that point, no more of the collective good would be purchased. (*Question:* Why?) This group of three individuals, then, produces four increments of the collective good.

Now, add individual D to the group and use the same analysis. This time assume that individual D receives the additional income:

		Cost *(in utiles)*	Amount of Collective Good	Benefit *(Individual Utility)*
	A	2	G_1	5
Individuals:	B	2	G_1	5
	C	2	G_1	5
	D	0	G_1	5

Notice that since G_1 is an *inclusive* or *pure* collective good, the addition of a new member to the group does not reduce the benefits of G_1 to each individual. Again, assume that D spends half of her income on collective goods, and, since G_1 is a superior collective good, decides to spend all of her additional income on G. In this case, the additional income is only 1.50 utiles rather than 2, since there are four individuals rather than three sharing the costs. The purchase of G_2 then is depicted as follows:

		Cost *(in utiles)*	Amount of Collective Good	Benefit *(Individual Utility)*
	A	1.50	G_2	4
Individuals:	B	1.50	G_2	4
	C	1.50	G_2	4
	D	1.50	G_2	4

Again, G_2 produces less utility than G_1. *Here G_3 will produce three utiles of benefit, and G_4 will produce two utiles of benefit. Recall that in the example above, the group of three individuals stopped purchasing G at G_4. The present group, however, would purchase part of an additional increment, G_5 so long as it produced at least 1.50 utiles for each individual. In other words, *this larger group provided itself with more of a particular collective good than a smaller group, in contrast to Olson's prediction.*

The obvious reason for this result is that we assumed G to be an *inclusive* or *pure* collective good. Suppose we had assumed it to be an *exclusive* or *crowdable* or *congested* collective good.

This would mean that the individual benefits would be affected by the number of people in the group, and that the addition of a new member to the group would *reduce* the benefits for the others. Thus, if the group A, B, C received five utiles of benefit each from G_1, the addition of individual D would *reduce* that benefit by a "crowding" or "congestion" effect. Thus, instead of receiving five utiles of benefit from G_1, they might receive only four when D was added. Since the cost remains the same, however, the group of four actually purchases less of the collective good than the group of three.

Chamberlin's point, then, is that the income effect can result in an *increase* in the level of benefits or amount of collective good provided as group size increases, while the congestion effect results in a *decrease*. These two forces are thus pulling in opposite directions. This means, however, that *larger groups will provide themselves with more collective goods than smaller groups if the collective goods are pure or inclusive and if they are "superior" in terms of demand. Olson's point, then, applies to goods which are crowdable or exclusive as well as to goods which are "inferior" in terms of demand.* Thus, says Chamberlin, size is not the only factor in determining whether collective goods will be provided.

The difficulty with this position, however, is that it does not deal with the strategic question Olson raised: Why should *anyone* in a large group voluntarily contribute to the provision of collective goods? Without a suitable answer to this question, however, it makes little sense to speak of income effects in large groups.

POLITICAL ENTREPRENEURS

So, the Olson problem remains. An interesting analysis by Frohlich, Oppenheimer, and Young (1971), however, suggests that the function of political leaders, or political entrepreneurs as they call them, is to provide a coordinating mechanism for the provision of collective goods in large groups. Thus, the function of political leadership is to overcome the dilemma in which Olson's rational individuals find themselves.

In return for private benefits—income, status, and so on—the political leaders provide collective goods. They do this by collecting resources through both voluntary and coercive means—e.g., taxation—and then purchasing collective goods with those resources. After paying for the resources themselves, as well as the costs of organization and coordination, the political entrepreneurs keep any surplus for themselves. Presumably, if the "business'' of providing collective goods does not pay, the political entrepreneur seeks other employment.

The important question here is how the political leader is kept from "exploiting" the people—i.e., taking their money and not providing collective benefits, or providing collective benefits at a lower level than the public has purchased. Most critiques of American society, of course, suggest that this is precisely what happens. The people do not receive commensurate benefits for their spending. Frohlich, Oppenheimer, and Young, however, argue that there are several important limits on this exploitation. First, competition from other political entrepreneurs means that any political leader must convince the people that he or she has a better "product." Second, if the leader coerces too much from individuals, their voluntary contributions decline. Thus, disillusion with high taxes may produce a less honest society as individuals find ways to avoid exploitation, or opposition to events such as the Vietnam War may produce mass disorder, draft evaders, and the breakdown of military discipline. In the case of taxes, the "voluntary" contribution is the relative honesty of most taxpayers, while in the Vietnam case it is the "voluntary" compliance with government orders. It may seem strange to speak of voluntary compliance where there are real and severe sanctions for noncompliance. Nevertheless, as we pointed out earlier, it is not possible for any government in a large poitical system to apply sanctions for noncompliance on a large scale. All political leaders depend on a certain amount of legitimacy in the implementation of policy. Compliance based on the legitimacy of the leaders, then, can be viewed as voluntary and as a collective good. A leader who loses his or her legitimacy through excessive exploitation, however, cannot count on voluntary compliance. Finally, excessive exploitation will reduce productivity and, consequently, the resources available for the production of collective goods. This, in turn, reduces the leader's ability to compete with other leaders, and to produce a surplus for himself or herself.

In many ways, this analysis is similar to that of Downs. In each case, political leadership is said to be a response to a particular problem. In Downs, the problem was voter uncertainty; in Frohlich, Oppenheimer, and Young the problem is the inability of large groups to provide themselves voluntarily with collective goods. There is also another important similarity. Political leaders in both analyses are constrained in their ability to exploit the people; and they must produce collective goods at some minimum level.

Politics then becomes the struggle over the levels of that exploitation and the production of collective goods.

COLLECTIVE ACTION AS A PRISONER'S DILEMMA GAME

In an important article, Hardin (1971) suggested that the logic of the collective-action problem was essentially the same as the logic of the prisoner's-dilemma problem, which we discussed in chapter 6. To the extent that collective noncooperation is the dominant outcome in the prisoner's dilemma, moreover, Olson's analysis finds support in Hardin's work. On the other hand, Hardin showed that under certain circumstances, the collective-action situation was an *agreeable* n-person prisoner's dilemma in the sense that there was a least a weak Condorcet winner among the possible outcomes. The implication of that analysis was that Olson's conclusions did not apply to those situations. In a more recent work, Taylor (1976) made two important points. First, even if collective action is an n-person prisoner's dilemma, the fact that it is an interative game—i.e., that it is played more than once—makes the cooperative outcome rational. Second, there are important, realistic situations in which mutual noncooperation is the dominant outcome, and in which that outcome is Pareto-optimal. In other words, none of the players has any incentive to change the situation. Taylor's first point, of course, does not support Olson's argument that large groups will not voluntarily provide themselves with collective goods; while his second point does support Olson but not on the grounds of prisoner's-dilemma logic. In the following section, we shall discuss these points.

Recall the structure of the prisoner's-dilemma game. In its most general form it can be represented as in fig. 8.5.

		B	
		Cooperate	Not Cooperate
A	Cooperate	z, z	w, x
	Not Cooperate	x, w	y, y

Figure 8.5. Prisoner's Dilemma game.

Here the letters x, y, z, and w stand for different payoffs or outcomes for each individual, and the preference order for each is $x > z > y > w$. Thus, individual A prefers the outcome (x,w) as his first choice, (z,z) as his second, (y,y) as his third, and (w,x) as his last. Conversely, individual B prefers (w,x) as her first choice. Recall that the second letter in the parentheses is B's payoff, while the first letter is A's payoff. B's second choice is (z,z) and her third choice is (y,y). These preferences are, of course, the same as A's. The outcome B prefers least is (x,w). *The problem, then, in the prisoner's dilemma is that noncooperation is the dominant strategy for both players.* This means, as we discussed in chapter 6, that no matter what the other player does, each player is better off choosing the noncooperative strategy. Moreover, since both players have a dominant strategy, there is an *equilibrium* outcome—that is, an outcome neither player has an incentive to alter. In this case, the equilibrium is (y,y), the mutually noncooperative outcome. What makes the prisoner's dilemma unique, however, is that *while there is an equilibrium outcome which neither individual, ostensibly, has an incentive to alter, that outcome is not Pareto optimal.* That is, there is another outcome, (z,z) the cooperative outcome, which both players prefer to the outcome (y,y).

Now, the question is whether the collective-action problem is a prisoner's dilemma. Consider first the two-person game, and recall our discussion of the Haldeman-Nixon situation. There, the possible outcomes were prison sentences. In collective-goods terminology, the length of the jail sentence can be said to represent the level of the collective good. That is, the avoidance of a long jail sentence is a collective good, while freedom, no jail sentence, represents the highest level of collective good in this case. In terms of collective goods, the higher jail sentence for noncooperation is *less* of a collective good than the lower jail sentence for mutual cooperation—that is, where both remain silent. It is less clear how to interpret the outcome where one individual goes free and the other receives a ten-year sentence. Such an outcome is clearly not a collective good for both, or, more precisely, the prisoners do not receive the same amount of the collective good.

In any case, the lower jail sentence of the cooperative outcome is clearly a greater collective good for both than the higher jail sentence of the noncooperative outcome, and yet, noncooperation is the dominant strategy for both players. Thus, it would appear that the collective goods problem can be seen as a two-person prisoner's dilemma.

The two-person group is clearly not a large (Olson's term is *latent*) or intermediate group. It might, however, be a privileged group. Suppose, for example, that the prisoners happened to be lovers, and that one was willing to be sacrificed for the other. Then, by prearrangement, one would confess, the other would remain silent; the former would go free, the latter would go to jail for ten years. Clearly, the silent prisoner is bearing the full burden of the costs of the collective good, as in Olson's privileged group.

It might also be the case, however, that the fear of retaliation for being a "stool pigeon" could alter the situation and induce mutual cooperation. Suppose, for example, that in the Nixon-Haldeman case, it was known that if either "squealed," he would be executed through extralegal channels. This fact would essentially alter the payoff outcomes. For example, the payoff for the "squealer," where the other prisoner remains silent, is no longer freedom. Rather it is almost certain death, or at least, a lifetime of hiding. Thus, the game is no longer a prisoner's dilemma, the cooperative strategy is dominant, and we can expect a mutually cooperative outcome. The same conclusion may hold even if the possible cost is not retribution in some physical sense but simply the opprobrium of being disloyal. After all, there is obvious value both psychologically and in terms of actual future dealings in having a reputation for being trustworthy. This, however, is essentially Olson's point—in *small groups,* where our actions are more readily apparent, considerations such as social pressure will play a more important role, and will, therefore, contribute toward the provision of collective goods.

There is another interesting point to be made. In the experimental studies of the prisoner's-dilemma game, approximately half of the participants choose a cooperative strategy even when they know for certain that the other player will cooperate. That is, these individuals refuse to exploit a situation in which they would be the certain winner by not cooperating, and the other player would be the certain loser (Rapoport, 1968). Perhaps these players feel that "it is not fair" to exploit their opportunity at the expense of another. In any case, this would provide further evidence for Olson's claim that small groups will be more likely to provide themselves with collective goods. And, this is true even if the situation is a prisoner's dilemma.

The next important question is whether this analysis applies to large groups. In dealing with this, Hardin begins by postulating a group of ten players, and a game in which each player has an option of contributing nothing toward the purchase of a collective good, or one unit. Every one unit contributed can purchase two units of the collective good. In other words, the ratio of benefits to costs is two. In symbols,

$$B(2)/C(1) = r(2)$$

This is an arbitrary assumption whose significance will become clearer below.

Now, let us consider how each individual might reason in this game. First, if everyone pays one unit, everyone will receive one unit net benefit (two units of benefit less one unit of cost). But if no one paid, there would be no gains in benefit at all; and, of course, no loss. If everyone *except* our one individual paid one unit, there would be 9 units paid in. This would produce 18 units of benefit. Now, remember, since this is a collective good, every individual shares in the benefit whether or not he or she contributes to its purchase. Thus, the 18 units of benefit would be split among all ten members of the group. But, since nine members of the group contributed one unit each to the purchase, they would net only 0.8 unit benefit ($1.80 - 1.00 = .80$). On the other hand, the "free rider" gets the full benefit of 1.8 units. Finally, suppose our single individual pays his or her one unit and no one else contributes anything. In that case, the total benefit would be 2 units, and that would be split among the ten players. Each player, then, would receive 0.2 unit benefit. For the nonpayers, this would be their net benefit. The lone payer, however, would have lost 0.8 unit. This discussion is summarized in fig. 8.6.

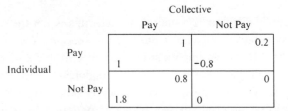

Collective

Figure 8.6. Hardin's Individual Vs. Collective game.

Hardin calls this the Individual versus Collective game. The dominant strategy for the individual is "Not Pay." That is, no matter what everyone else does, it pays for the individual not to pay. Moreover, since *every* individual must reason this way, the outcome is that no one pays.

Here again, it appears that the collective good should *not* be forthcoming. Hardin, however, makes an interesting argument that the cooperative outcome in which everyone pays is, in fact, a Condorcet choice and, therefore, would be chosen in a *voting* situation. To see this more clearly, recall that the usual game situation requires players to choose among strategies rather than outcomes. There is, of course, an implied preference for outcomes in the choice of strategies, but a strategy choice is not always an accurate indicator of preference among outcomes. For instance, where there is a dominant strategy, it is true that the outcomes associated with that strategy are preferred to the outcomes associated with the nondominant strategy. Moreover, it is sometimes true that *every* outcome associated with a dominant strategy is preferred to every outcome not associated with a dominant strategy. This is true in the game shown in fig. 8.7. Here, A prefers either outcome associated with strategy II to either outcome associated with strategy I.

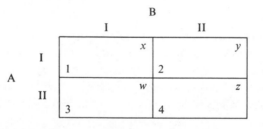

Figure 8.7. Game in which every outcome associated with a
dominant strategy is preferred to every outcome
not associated with a dominant strategy.

In a prisoner's dilemma, on the other hand, this is not the case, since the mutually cooperative outcome is preferred to the mutually noncooperative outcome. This fact is an important element in Hardin's argument.

Hardin distinguishes between a *strong* Condorcet choice and a *weak* Condorcet choice. The strong Condorcet choice is simply the notion we introduced in chapter 1—an alternative which is preferred by a majority to every other alternative in a particular environment. A weak Condorcet choice does not have to be preferred by a majority to *every* other alternative, but it has to be preferred by more people than any other alternative. The notion of a weak Condorcet choice may become clearer if we illustrate it with the two-person prisoner's dilemma game. Recall that the preference orders over outcomes for the two-person prisoner's dilemma is:

$$
\begin{array}{cc}
A & B \\
DC & CD \\
CC & CC \\
DD & DD \\
CD & DC
\end{array}
$$

Where *"C"* is "cooperate" and *"D"* is "defect." Now, if we treat this as an election where these two "voters" present these two preference orders, the pairwise comparisons are as follows:

CC vs. *DD:*	*CC* > *DD* (preference)
CC vs. *DC:*	*CC* = *DC* (indifference)
CC vs. *CD:*	*CC* = *CD* (indifference)
DD vs. *DC:*	*DD* = *DC* (indifference)
DD vs. *CD:*	*DD* = *CD* (indifference)
DC vs. *CD:*	*DC* = *CD* (indifference)

In this case, *CC,* the mutually cooperative outcome, is the *weak* Condorcet choice, since both players prefer *CC* to *DD,* and no other alternative is preferred to *CC* by both players. (*Question:* Why is *CC* not a *strong* Condorcet choice?)

The ten-player case Hardin uses to illustrate his point about n-person games is more complex, but the principle is the same. Thus, in a ten-player game, where each player has a choice of paying one unit of cost or not paying, the individual payoffs can range from a high of 1.8 to a low of -0.8. The payoff of 1.8 arises only when nine individuals pay (remember, $B/C = r$, and in this case $r = 2$; therefore, the nine units of cost produce 18 units of benefit which are then divided among nine individuals) and one individual does not pay. Of course, for the nine who have paid, the *net* benefit is only *one* unit. The loss of 0.8 unit of benefit is the net cost to a *single* paying individual—that is, when one pays and nine do not. We summarize the range of payoffs in table 8.1.

TABLE 8.1 PAYOFFS (NET)

	P_{10}	P_9	P_8	P_7	P_6	P_5	P_4	P_3	P_2	P_1	P_0
Pay	1.0	0.8	0.6	0.4	0.2	0	-0.2	-0.4	-0.6	-0.8	–
Not Pay	–	1.8	1.6	1.4	1.2	1.0	0.8	0.6	0.4	0.2	0
	N_0	N_1	N_2	N_3	N_4	N_5	N_6	N_7	N_8	N_9	N_{10}

Source: Slightly modified from Hardin 1971. Reprinted by permission of *Behavioral Science.*

The letter *"P"* stands for "Pay," the letter *"N"* stands for "Not Pay." The subscript numbers stand for a particular number of people who either pay or do not pay. Thus P_1 means that one person pays, P_3 means that three people pay, et cetera. The symbol *"N_1"* means that one person does not pay, N_5 means that five people do not pay, et cetera. The numbers in the "Pay" and "Not Pay" rows indicate the payoffs for the number of individuals who either pay or do not pay. Thus, under P_{10} (all pay) the net payoff for everyone is 1. Under P_7, the seven people who do pay receive a net benefit of 0.4, while the three who do not pay each receive a net benefit of 1.4. Where only three people pay, they sustain a net *loss* of 0.4 units, while the seven who do not pay receive a net benefit of 0.6 units. At the far right, where no one pays, no one benefits, but neither does anyone lose.

Suppose then, we asked these individuals to rank these outcomes according to the benefits each brings them. Such a ranking would be as in table 8.2.

TABLE 8.2 OUTCOMES RANKED ACCORDING TO BENEFIT

Net Benefit	Configuration(s) Which Produce(s) Net Benefit
1.8	N_1
1.6	N_2
1.4	N_3
1.2	N_4
1.0	P_{10}, N_5
0.8	P_9, N_6
0.6	P_8, N_7
0.4	P_7, N_8
0.2	P_6, N_9
0.0	P_5, N_{10}
−0.2	P_4
−0.4	P_3
−0.6	P_2
−0.8	P_1

Source: Slightly modified from Hardin 1971. Reprinted by permission of *Behavioral Science*.

In other words, everyone would prefer most the situation in which he or she was the one nonpayer while the nine others paid. The next most desirable outcome is the one in which two individuals do not pay while eight others do pay. The configurations in the right-hand column indicate the group which receives the payoff in the left-hand column. Thus, for example, an individual can receive a net benefit of 1.0 *either* by being a part of a group in which all ten pay, *or* by being part of the group of five who do *not* pay when the other five *do* pay. There is one more point to make about this table. Every individual can avoid a net loss simply by not paying. In other words, no one can be forced to accept a lower net benefit than zero by the actions of others. In our game-theory chapter we referred to such a point as a *security level*. In Hardin's terms, none of the outcomes which involve net losses is *realizable*. That is, no one can be forced below the security level.

Consider now whether any of these outcomes would be a Condorcet winner in a vote involving outcomes. While the outcome P_9, N_1 is generally preferred by everyone to any other outcome, the outcome P_{10}, N_0 would be preferred to P_9, N_1 by every group of nine individuals who found themselves paying while a particular individual did not pay. The change from P_9, N_1 to P_{10}, N_0 would raise the benefit of the nine payers from .8 to 1.0, while it would reduce the benefit of the original free rider from 1.8 to 1.0 (*Question:* Is the move from P_9, N_1, to P_{10}, N_0, then, Pareto optimal?) By a similar argument, P_{10}, N_0 would also be preferred to (P_8, N_2), (P_7, N_3) and (P_6, N_4). The majority would decline in each case, of course, (from 8 to 7 to 6), but more people would still prefer P_{10}, N_0 to any of these alternative outcomes. Since the outcomes involving P_4, P_3, P_2, and P_1 are not realizable, the only outcome left to be considered is P_5, N_5. Where the outcome is P_5, N_5, the five individuals who do not pay receive a net benefit of one. But, this is also what they would receive if everyone paid. On the other hand, the five individuals who pay in P_5, N_5 do benefit from a change to P_{10}, N_0, thus they prefer P_{10}, N_0 to P_5, N_5. In other words, P_{10}, N_0 is preferred by a majority to every other realizable outcome except P_5, N_5, in which case, five prefer P_{10}, N_0 to P_5, N_5 and five are indifferent. It is because of this last case involving P_5, N_5, then that P_{10}, N_0 is a *weak* Condorcet winner rather than a *strong* Condorcet winner. But, *the important point is that it is the mutually cooperative outcome which is the weak Condorcet winner, and not the mutually noncooperative P_0, N_{10}*. In this sense, Hardin sees the collective-choice problem as an "agreeable" *n*-person prisoner's dilemma.

This, of course, is the outcome for the ten-person game. Hardin goes on to prove a theorem which says that *the outcome in which everyone pays is the Condorcet choice for any n-person game of collective action so long as n is odd and r > 1. When n is even and r = 2, P_n is the weak Condorcet choice*. Notice that if $r = 1$, the realizable outcomes are P_n and N_n, and the players are indifferent between these two. It is not difficult to demonstrate this in the case above where $n = 10$. Remember, to say that $r = 1$ means that for every single unit of cost, the benefit will also be a single unit. If $r < 1$, no one can gain under any circumstances, and the game will not be played.

Hardin's analysis is important in two respects. First, it shows that the size of a group is not the important factor in determining whether collective goods will be provided, as Olson suggested. He shows that it is the ratio of benefits to cost which is determinative. Second, he implies that a voting mechanism might be appropriate for expressing individual preferences in the collective-goods situations which are also prisoner's-dilemma games, thereby signaling a government to act. That is, in the ordinary collective-goods situations involving large groups and a prisoner's dilemma, the dominant strategy or rational choice for each individual is not to act. In such a case, government may act to provide the collective good on the grounds that it is desired by the people who, for strategic reasons, cannot provide the collective good voluntarily. *Yet, such a rationale is simply an inference from a failure of the populace to act. There is no positive statement from the people. The Hardin analysis shows that such a statement is possible if people are asked to choose among possible outcomes.* (On the other hand, the practical problem of choosing among a large number of alternative outcomes is very difficult in this case.)

There are also problems with the Hardin analysis. For example, how do we arrive at the all-important benefit/cost ratio? Such a notion assumes that we can establish a relatively precise relationship between costs and benefits. But, this may not be possible *even in principle*. For example, "national security" is a presumed collective good, which provides benefits, but it is not clear when our national security increases or decreases and, hence, what is the magnitude of our benefits. Does the national security increase when we develop a new missile system, or does it decrease? That is, have we strengthened our shield against Soviet aggression or have we simply induced a new and more dangerous round in the arms race? A similar problem arises in the prevention of crime. Does the addition of more armed police on the streets reduce crime, or does it simply increase the likelihood of our being caught in a cross fire? Or is it unrelated to the level of crime? As we mentioned above, studies indicate that there is no correlation between safety in the streets and the amount spent on police protection. Under such circumstances, how can we establish a precise ratio of benefits to costs?

NONCOOPERATION WITHOUT PRISONER'S DILEMMA

More recently, Taylor (1976) has argued that the prisoner's dilemma is not the only situation in which noncooperation is a dominant strategy. Consider the two-person game in fig. 8.8. Here, both A and B have dominant strat-

	B	
	Not Pollute (cooperation)	Pollute (noncooperation)
A — Not Pollute (cooperation)	(C, C) 3 2	(C, N) 4 1
Pollute (noncooperation)	(N, C) 1 4	(N, N) 2 3

Figure 8.8. Noncooperation as the dominant strategy in a game which is not a Prisoner's Delemma.

egies, that is, the noncooperative strategy. For purposes of illustration we are using the example of pollution.

Notice, however, that the two individuals here do *not* have a mutual preference for the mutually cooperative strategy, since A is better off with the mutually noncooperative strategy (N,N). This situation, therefore, is *not* a prisoner's dilemma. To see this, consider the preference orders:

A	B
NC	*CN*
NN	*CC*
CC	*NN*
CN	*NC*

The collective relationships are as follows:

NC vs. *CN:*	*NC* I *CN*
NC vs. *CC:*	*NC* I *CC*
NC vs. *NN:*	*NC* I *NN*
CN vs. *CC:*	*CN* I *CC*
NC vs. *NN:*	*NC* I *NN*
CC vs. *NN:*	*CC* I *NN*

Thus, collective indifference prevails. No outcome is preferred to another by both individuals. In such a situation, if there is an equilibrium it is stable, in the sense that there is no incentive to alter the outcome. In the prisoner's dilemma, *both* individuals would be better off, and, therefore, would prefer the mutually cooperative outcome to the mutually noncooperative outcome. An external form of coercion (e.g., government), or an internal form of coercion (e.g., fear of retribution or dishonor), then, is *needed* to bring about the cooperative outcome, *and is mutually desired*. In the example above, however, the cooperative outcome is *not* mutually desired, and therefore there is no dilemma: the noncooperative outcome is the stable equilibrium. Government interference here would not bring about any improvement in the situation. It would simply satisfy one individual and dissatisfy another. But that is the case in this example without government intervention. Of course, politics is frequently the interference by government to aid one group at the expense of another, but here we are considering the ideal possibility of government improving the *collective* utility by improving the position of some *without* worsening the situation of any. The purpose of this example is to show a situation in which a noncooperative outcome *cannot* be collectively improved by being turned into a cooperative outcome. In other words, *cooperation is not always collectively preferred to noncooperation*.

This example is not simply an oddity produced by the arbitrary arrangement of the numbers, but has a meaningful interpretation. It could arise where the cost to A of eliminating B's pollution is *greater* than the cost of putting up with B's pollution. Thus, A would prefer the situation in which both polluted to the situation in which neither polluted. The interesting problem with this example, however, is that if B felt that the cost of eliminating A's pollution was greater than the cost of accepting A's pollution, then polluting (noncooperation) would be Pareto superior to not polluting (cooperating) as well as a strategic equilibrium, and the result would be doubly stable. The matrix payoffs would then be as shown in fig. 8.9.

Here, as in the prisoner's dilemma, there is a noncooperative equilibrium outcome (N,N). The difference, of course, is that here there is no outcome which is Pareto superior to the noncooperative outcome.

We might be tempted to label this outcome a "disaster," and for those individuals not included here it probably would be. But, what these matrices say is that the individuals involved *prefer* the outcome in which pollution prevails to one in which it does not. For individuals with such preferences, then, the pollution outcome is, by definition, *not* a disaster unless the non-

B

	Not Pollute (cooperation)	Pollute (noncooperation)
Not Pollute (cooperation)	2 (C, C) 2	4 (C, N) 1
Pollute (noncooperation)	1 (N, C) 4	3 (N, N) 3

A

Figure 8.9 Game in which mutually noncooperative outcome is a stable equilibrium and is Pareto superior to mutually cooperative outcome.

pollution outcome involves even more calamitous results. Thus, perhaps, a severe shortage of fuel in the future might force us to use vast amounts of coal, whose production spoils the land, and whose consumption ruins the atmosphere. If the alternative is mass death by frostbite, however, pollution appears the lesser disaster.

Where the public-goods situation is a prisoner's dilemma, we say that there are *strategic reasons* for both individuals to choose a noncooperative strategy. This implies that if the only consideration were the relative value of the alternative outcomes, the cooperative alternative would be chosen. It is the concern with the behavior of others, however, or strategic reasons, which causes both to choose noncooperation.

Taylor, however, has argued that the existence of a prisoner's dilemma should not necessarily lead to a noncooperative outcome. One implication of his argument is that government activity is not required simply because a prisoner's dilemma exists. Taylor points out that the important decisions in public life tend to be iterative. For this reason, it is possible to make corrective changes in our behavior if experience indicates that change is necessary. Thus, the more risky cooperative strategy can be chosen in the initial "play" of the public goods game, with the knowledge that the safer noncooperative strategy can always be used if the other player does not cooperate. In the pollution example, one individual might refrain from polluting and see what the other individual does. If the second individual continues to pollute, the first individual can always protect himself or herself by beginning to pollute again as well. Taylor's argument is complex, and will not be presented here. His main point, however, is that *in this series of plays of a prisoner's dilemma game*—or the *supergame* as it is called—the *cooperative* strategy is dominant for both players.

In support of Taylor's claim, consider the following two examples. During the summer of 1977, residents of San Francisco and the Bay Area were called upon by public officials to reduce their consumption of water by 25 percent in order to mitigate the effects of a severe drought. There were no penalties for noncompliance with this request. Water was rationed only to the extent that each household and business was given a maximum allotment of water. If a consumer used more than the allotment, the fees for the extra water would be substantially higher. Nevertheless, the water rates for the allotment, and even the penalty rates, were extremely low relative to other commodities and services in that very expensive area. The two-month allotment water bill for one family of five, for example, was ten dollars. Thus, there were no serious sanctions. It was a truly voluntary system. By August of 1977, consumers had cut back their use of water by 40 percent! Moreover, this reduction had cost the city so much in lost revenue, and had caused such havoc with the sewer system that public officials called on sonsumers to *increase* their consumption or face increased water rates! Clearly, most citizens of San Francisco and the Bay Area were not free riders. They had voluntarily refrained from using water in excess in order to maintain the supply.[8]

Our second example comes from the diamond district in Manhattan, where millions of dollars worth of diamonds are bought and sold daily without contracts or bonds of any kind. Moreover, massive amounts of credit are extended informally and without collateral. The penalty for violating this trust is exclusion from the diamond center. No one will do business with a dealer who has proven untrustworthy. There is, then, a kind of honor system which serves to maintain a thriving market, which is an obvious pure public good. Though this situation is somewhat different from the San Francisco example—since there are, after all, informal sanctions—it has not been necessary to establish an institution to enforce these sanctions, as, for example, the Securities and Exchange Commission does for the stock mar-

8. Not everyone agrees with this description of the San Francisco experience. A New York *Times* article, March 3, 1979, carried the heading "More People Seen Saving Water Under Rations than Voluntarily." There followed a report on a California study which concluded that "people will conserve a scarce resource more willingly and enthusiastically under a rigorous control program than one of bland exhortation." Although the article is relatively vague on the details of the study, it appears that the researchers had classified as "rigorous controls" what this observer saw as essentially voluntary. Such a difference illustrates one of the problems in the application of collective choice theory.

ket. Thus, it does seem to be an example of the voluntary provision of a pure public good.

But why do the citizens of San Francisco or Manhattan's diamond district voluntarily refrain from action which would destroy a public good? We might argue that, unlike polluters of the air or water, they are able to see, or have become convinced, that their actions will have an undesirable effect. This argument, however, misses the point that while any one individual may see the adverse consequences, the important question is whether that individual thinks others will also see the problem and act properly.

We might also suggest that since such decisions are made over time it is always possible to adjust our future behavior if the emerging evidence indicates that we have judged incorrectly. By this reasoning, even though the situation is a prisoner's dilemma, the full penalty for being the "sucker" is not exacted at once as it is in a one-shot prisoner's dilemma. Thus, the opportunity to try the cooperative strategy without danger of suffering the full sucker penalty allows for the possibility of the mutually cooperative outcome.

Unfortunately, such an explanation makes no sense if we assume that individuals are self-interested utility maximizers, since, no matter what anyone else does, it still pays not to contribute to the collective good. If everyone else contributes, the individual can get a free ride; if no one else contributes, the individual certainly should not contribute. In either case, there is no incentive to cooperate.

Altruism

Another way of explaining phenomena such as the San Francisco water conservation or the system of trust in the Manhattan diamond district is to invoke some notion of *duty* or *altruism*. Up to this point, we have assumed that individuals make decisions on the basis of rather narrow self-interest. We have not considered two other possibilities—first, that individuals act out of a sense of *duty,* and second that they are *altruistic*. To act out of a sense of duty simply means to do what an individual thinks he or she *ought* to do, whether or not it satisfies one's self-interest. (We shall not discuss the difficult question of whether a dutiful act is also a self-interested act because of the personal satisfaction which may be realized by doing one's duty.) In such a case, actions are designed to satisfy some moral imperative. An altruistic act is one which considers the effect of that act on the utility of others.

In this section, we shall look more closely at one analysis of the collective-goods problem which assumes the existence of altruistic behavior. The arguments for altruism which we shall discuss here are those of H. Margolis (1979).

ASSUMPTIONS OF THE MODEL

Margolis begins with four simple assumptions:

1. He posits only two goods, one private (x) and one collective or public (y). Obviously, this is a rather simple model, but it is adequate to illustrate his point.

2. There is declining marginal utility for both goods. This is, of course, the assumption which we have adopted for the analysis above, and it is the common one in economics.

3a. It is assumed that the total spending on the collective good by everyone in the society (Y) is much larger than the income of any one individual (I) in that society. That is,

$$Y \gg I$$

where the symbol $\gg$ means "much greater than." For most collective goods on a grand scale, such as national security or clean air, this is quite obviously a realistic assumption.

3b. The marginal utility of the collective good for each individual $[v'(y)]$ is much smaller than the marginal utility of the private good $[u'(x)]$; i.e.,

$$v'(y) \ll u'(x)$$

This point can be understood as follows. If a great many individuals are contributing to a collective good, the contribution of each individual will be relatively small. This means that any one individual is purchasing a relatively small portion of the collective good. It is the marginal utility associated with that small portion of the collective good which is less than the marginal utility of any private good an individual purchases.

To see this more clearly, suppose I switch from less-expensive leaded gasoline to more-expensive unleaded gasoline in order to help the fight against pollution. In terms of altering the environment, such a contribution would be infinitesimal as would be the utility associated with that act. On the other hand, if I had spent the extra few dollars on a private good, such as a tennis racket, the utility would be solely mine, and would be far higher than the virtually negligible utility associated with the minuscule change in the atmosphere produced by my changing to unleaded gasoline. Of course, if everyone used unleaded gasoline, the effect would be enormous, but such an occurrence could not be attributed to the actions of any one individual. The point here is that one simply receives higher utility from spending on private goods than on the type of collective goods Margolis is considering.[9]

4. The goal of each individual, in determining how to allocate his income between the collective and private good, is to reach a point where the weighted (We shall explain below this notion of "weighting.") marginal utility of the private good [$Wu'(x)$] is equal to the marginal utility of the collective good [$v'(y)$]. In other words,

$$Wu'(x) = v'(y)$$

The notion of equating marginal utilities is relatively straightforward. Recall that our earlier discussion assumed that an individual spends income until marginal cost equals marginal utility. If the marginal utility of the good is higher than the marginal cost, then the individual is willing to purchase more of the good. The present assumption simply means that an individual allocates his or her income on collective or private goods until the marginal utility from the former equals the marginal utility of the latter. If the marginal utility of one type of good is higher than the other, then the individual will spend his or her income on that good. Since marginal utility declines, however, the marginal utility of the next increment of that good will be lower. If it is lower than the marginal utility of the other good, then the individual purchases that other good until its marginal utility equals the marginal utility of the first good. This is a dynamic process, then, in which spending alternates between the collective and private good with the goal of equalizing the marginal utilities.

VARIETIES OF ALTRUISM

None of the four assumptions above says anything about whether an individual is self-interested or altruistic, or some combination of the two. In

9. In Olson's privileged group, of course, the utility associated with the purchase of the collective good would be relatively high.

this regard there are several possibilities. First, an individual might be a *pure egoist*.[10] The pure egoist decides how to spend his resources solely on the basis of whether his utility is increased or decreased. There is no concern here with the utility of others, that is, no altruism. In order to illustrate the behavior of the pure egoist consider fig. 8.10.

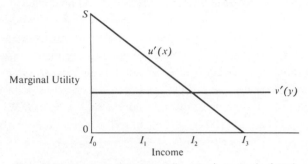

Figure 8.10. Marginal utility for public and private goods plotted against levels of income.

Here, the marginal utility for public and private goods is being plotted against levels of income. The symbols I_1, I_2, and I_3 refer to levels of income, with I_1 being lower than I_2 which is lower than I_3. The line labeled $u'(x)$ represents the pure egoist's marginal utility for the one private good in Margolis's model. The fact that the line slopes downward from the upper left to the lower right simply indicates declining marginal utility. That is, as income rises more of the private good is purchased. At the same time, each additional increment of the private good brings less utility than the previous increment. Notice, however, that the line which represents the marginal utility for the collective good, $v'(y)$, does not decline, and that it is much lower than the marginal utility for the private good at low levels of income. The latter point is essentially assumption 3b. The constancy of the marginal utility for the collective good is explained by the fact that any one individual's contribution to the purchase of a collective good in this model is so small that it scarcely affects the amount of the collective good provided. It is the marginal utility of that tiny increment, then, which remains relatively unchanged.

The pure egoist, then, spends all of his income on the private good and

10. This term and those which follow are not from Margolis. Rather, they represent our interpretation of his categories.

none on the public good so long as his income is below I_2. When that income reaches I_2, however, the next increment of the private good purchased would bring *less* utility than if he had spent the income on the public good. Remember, the pure egoist only considers the utility which his spending will bring to him. For that reason, the pure egoist would begin to spend *all* of his income beyond I_2 on the collective good, and none on the private good.

There are two points to be made about such a scenario. First, given the fact that the marginal utility of the collective good produced by any one individual's spending on it is so small, an individual would have to purchase a great deal of the private good before its marginal utility would be less than that of the collective good. This means that only a very wealthy individual would contribute anything to the purchase of collective goods. That is, I_2 would have to be a very high figure. Second, there would be a point — (I_2 in this example) at which an individual would make an abrupt switch from spending all of his income on the private good, to spending all of his income on the collective good.

Margolis argues, however, that people do not in fact behave this way. That is, at low levels of income, most individuals do spend most of their income on necessities, i.e., private goods, but they also spend at least some portion of that income on collective goods. For example, even relatively poor people contribute to their churches. Similarly, at higher income levels, people spend their resources on *both* private and collective goods. At no point, does it appear that increments of income are spent solely on private or collective goods as the pure egoist model suggests. This model, then, appears to be unrealistic.

Since we cannot explain actual behavior in terms of a pure egoist model, Margolis argues, it is necessary to invoke some form of altruism. That is, *the spending of resources on collective goods cannot be explained solely as an attempt to increase one's own private utility but must be explained as an attempt to increase the utility of others*.

One model of altruism, which Margolis rejects, is what we shall call the *constant altruist* model. The constant altruist is an individual whose degree of altruism (or concern with the utility of others), no matter how high or low, is unchanging. Thus, we have a continuum of constant altruism which has as one end point what we might call the *pure altruist*. The pure altruist cares *only* for the utility of others, and is not concerned with his own utility. This means that the pure altruist purchases only collective goods.

Clearly, the pure altruist is a very rare species! At the other end of the continuum is the pure egoist, that is, an individual whose level of altruism is zero. In between these extremes are various levels of altruism. The difficulty with the constant altruist model is that it implies that the proportion of an individual's income spent on the private or collective good remains constant no matter what the income level. Thus, even if the constant altruist wins a million dollars in the New York State lottery, he will spend the same proportion of his income on collective and private goods as before.

A more realistic model appears to be what we shall call the *variable altruist* model. The main point about the variable altruist is that her level of concern for the utility of others varies as a function of her income and her spending on either private or collective goods. That is, at relatively low levels of income, the variable altruist spends most on necessities, i.e., private goods. Some income can be spent on collective goods, but it is relatively little. As her income level rises, the variable altruist begins to spend relatively less on private goods and relatively more on collective goods. At levels of income considerably above the subsistence level, the proportion of income spent on private and collective goods will vary as a function of the amount already spent on either. That is, as the variable altruist spends more of her income on collective goods, she will begin to feel that she has done her share in contributing to the utility of others, and will begin to spend more of her income on private goods. At some point, she will have satiated her demand for personal satisfaction and will turn once again to increased spending on collective goods.

We are now in a position to explain Margolis' notion of "weighted" marginal utility which is presented above in assumption four. The *"W"* term indicates a level of concern. It varies between zero and one and is inversely proportional to the amount spent on collective goods. That is, as the amount spent on collective goods increases relative to spending on private goods, *W increases,* indicating an increasing concern with the private good. Conversely, as spending on private goods increases relative to that on collective goods, *W decreases,* indicating a decreasing concern with private goods.

The variable altruist model implies that individuals at all levels of income will spend at least something on collective goods. It also suggests that the rich will spend relatively more on collective goods than the poor, but that this spending will vary. For Margolis, this appears to be a relatively re-

alistic description of how people behave, certainly more accurate than implications of the pure egoist or constant altruist models.

One problem with this analysis is that since any individual's spending
on collective goods will be infinitesimally small relative to total spending on
the collective good, one's altruism will also be rather minuscule. That is, an
individual may want to increase the utility of others, but for the most part,
no single individual has sufficient resources to make much of a difference.
Remember, Margolis assumes relatively large groups of people whose individual income is small relative to the total amount spent on the collective
good. This point, of course, is related to that which we made above in the
discussion of assumption 3b, where we said that the marginal utility anyone
receives from the collective good is extremely small. The altruist, therefore,
must identify his altruism with the amount spent on the collective good *relative to* his spending on the private good, and not relative to the actual change
in the welfare of others. In other words, the individual feels that he is altruistic not because he has increased the welfare of others by any substantial
level, but simply because he has spent a portion of his income on that en-
deavor. Of course, such a notion of altruism may not be fully convincing.

Margolis's theory of altruism, then, suggests that we *should* expect voluntary contributions to the supply of collective goods, even in large groups.
This is, of course, different from Olson's theoretical conclusions. Moreover,
Margolis suggests that, in fact, we do observe voluntary spending on collective goods. For example, he sees voting as the voluntary provision of a collective good, as well as contributions to the "community chest" and public
television. Olson, on the other hand, in his work on labor unions, suggested
that there would be no unions without the coercion of the closed shop and
private perquisites to union members. Clearly, we have here an empirical
dispute which can only be settled by detailed empirical studies.

CONCLUSION

In this chapter, we have discussed the notion of collective goods and have
considered whether we should expect collective goods to be provided voluntarily by groups of individuals.

A collective good is defined as a good whose benefits can be enjoyed
simultaneously by more than one individual. This property is called

jointness of consumption. Collective goods include clean air, national security, crime-free streets, parks, roads, and so on. A private good, on the other hand, is one whose benefits cannot be shared.

Collective goods can be further characterized as *pure* or *crowdable.* A pure public good is one whose benefits to any one individual are not reduced when others also enjoy those benefits. Clean air is an example of a pure public good. A crowdable public good is one whose benefits to any one individual *are* reduced when others enjoy it simultaneously. A public park is an example of a crowdable public good. The terms *inclusive* and *exclusive* are also used to mean *pure* and *crowdable* respectively.

In addition to jointness of consumption, collective goods are characterized by *nonexcludability.* This means that collective goods cannot feasibly be withheld from some individuals. If they are available to one, they are available to all.

Mancur Olson argues that, in large groups, collective goods will not be provided voluntarily by rational, self-interested, utility-maximizing individuals, even though they all want them. There are two main reasons for this. First, the contribution of any one individual is so small that it cannot affect the provision of the collective good either positively or negatively. Second, the failure of any one individual in a large group to contribute his share to the provision of the collective good will not be noticeable to the other members of the group. For that reason, there will be no penalty, such as social opprobrium, attached to not doing one's share. Thus, each individual has an incentive to become a "free rider," that is, one who receives benefits from collective goods without paying his share.

If everyone reasons this way, however, no one will contribute toward the purchase of the collective good, and it will not be provided. We are assuming, moreover, that this is a good which everyone wants, and for which everyone is willing to pay. At that point, an institution such as a government is justified in using coercion in order to induce everyone to pay for the collective good. Thus, Olson explains the use of penalties for nonpayment of taxes or avoidance of military conscription, as well as the closed shop in labor unions, as measures necessary to eliminate free riders and to provide collective goods which everyone wants.

This analysis applies primarily to large groups, such as all American citizens, or the membership of a large labor union. In relatively small groups, such as neighborhoods, collective goods are more likely to be provided without external coercion for several reasons. First, in the smaller group, the contribution of any one individual is far more significant than it is in the large group. Thus, my failure to participate in a neighborhood security patrol could undermine that effort. Second, the actions of any individual are more visible in a small group than in a large group. Thus, there will be social pressure on each individual to do his share. For these reasons, Olson expects such smaller groups, which he calls *intermediate groups,* to provide themselves with collective goods without external coercion. Nevertheless, the amount provided will be *suboptimal,* that is, less than the amount which the group members are willing and able to purchase.

Smaller groups may also provide themselves with collective goods because one or several individuals may be willing to bear the full cost of the collective good, even if others do not contribute. This occurs when the benefits of the collective good to that one individual, or those several individuals, is greater than the total cost of the collective good. Olson refers to such groups as *privileged groups.* If I join a few of my neighbors in a security patrol, while most of the neighborhood does not participate, those individuals in that neighborhood constitute a privileged group.

It has been pointed out by Chamberlin and others, however, that the existence of *income effects,* and an elasticity of demand associated with so-called *superior goods* which are also inclusive, could result in the provision of collective goods even for large groups. An income effect is the added income which one individual receives from the purchase of a collective good by another individual. A superior good is one which an individual purchases with such increments, at a greater rate than he had with a lower income.

The difficulty with this analysis is that few goods may be "superior," and, more importantly, it is not clear why any individuals should initiate such a process and provide others with additional income.

Support for Olson's position has come from the analysis of the collective goods situation as a prisoner's dilemma game. In other words, the dominant strategy for every player in an n-person collective goods game, which is also a prisoner's dilemma, is to refrain from purchasing the collective good—i.e., not to cooperate. Hardin, however, suggested that in such a game, the cooperative outcome in which everyone pays his or her share is a weak Condorcet choice, and, therefore, should be the actual outcome. Taylor supports this notion by suggesting that the cooperative strategy is also dominant in repeated plays of the n-person prisoner's dilemma game, and that, therefore, in collective-goods situations in which payments and benefits occur over an extended period of time, it is expected that such collective goods will be provided. Taylor also points out, however, that there are situations in which noncooperation is the dominant strategy, even though the situation is not a prisoner's dilemma. In such cases, it is *not* expected that collective goods will be provided voluntarily nor is there justification for government intervention.

In the final section of this chapter, we considered Margolis's argument that actual behavior in collective goods situations cannot be explained by a model which assumes pure self-interest. He suggests that we can understand such behavior only by assuming that individuals are *altruistic* to some degree. That is, they act in order to increase the utility or welfare of others, and not simply as a way of satisfying themselves. Margolis's analysis implies that we should expect the voluntary provision of collective goods, and that, in fact, there is a great deal of such activity. In both respects he differs from Olson.

Conclusion

IN THE PREVIOUS chapters we have considered a great deal of material. Many concepts were introduced, many symbols were used, and many theoretical results were presented. It is legitimate to ask whether all of these disparate parts are related, and, if so, how? Indeed, it has been suggested that the work presented here constitutes theoretical "islands," with no meaningful relation to each other. In the course of our discussion, however, we have referred to certain attempts to bring these parts together. Thus, for example, we have Hardin's treatment of the free-rider problem in collective goods theory as a prisoner's dilemma. There have also been some systematic attempts to provide a set of bonds between the parts of collective-choice theory. Perhaps the most impressive is Plott's (1976) recent "overview" of "axiomatic social choice theory."[1] In this conclusion, I should like to side with those who see the relationships between the various fields in collective-choice theory, and try to provide a way of organizing the material presented above which stresses those connections.

Table C.1 summarizes the argument. There are eight columns four of which correspond to various parts of the collective-choice field, and seven rows, which indicate the basic terms or concepts, as well as the major results; and the variations of those terms (concepts) in each of the fields. The point we shall argue is that all of the terms in each row represent equivalent concepts. If that is true, two points follow. First, any set of terms in any of

1. See also, Mueller (1976), Aldrich (1977), Miller (1977), and Brock (1978).

TABLE C.1 THE UNITY OF COLLECTIVE CHOICE THEORY

Ordinary Language (1)	Axiomatic Choice Theory (2)	Elections (3)	Legislatures (4)	Spatial Models (5)	Game Theory (6)	Coalition Theory (7)	Collective Goods (8)
Possible collective outcomes	Environment	Candidates	Proposed bills	Candidates	Possible payoffs	Possible coalitions	Possible amounts of collective goods
Actual collective outcomes	Choice set	Winning candidate	Laws	Winning candidates	Actual payoffs	Winning coalition (Actual coalition formed)	Amount of collective good actually provided (level of supply)
Decision rule, or decision procedure	Social welfare function (social choice function)	Proportion of voters (e.g., majority rule)	Proportion of legislators (e.g., ⅔ majority)	Proportion of voters (e.g., simple majority)	Intersection of individual choice sets; characteristic function; solution concept	Solution concept; minimum winning coalition; minimum connected winning coalition	Relationship between number of individuals, and cost and supply of collective good
Individual choosers	Individual choosers	Voters	Legislators	Voters	Players	Parties	Individuals, citizens
Individual preferences among alternatives (possible collective outcomes)	Individual rank orderings of environment	Individual preference among candidates (ranking of candidates)	Policy preferences of individual legislators	Position in policy space	Player preferences among possible payoffs	Individual or party preference among possible coalitions	Indifference curves; utility functions
Individual act (choice)	Vote (reveal preferences)	Vote or abstain	Vote or abstain	Vote or abstain	Make move(s); choose strategy	Join coalition or remain alone	Contribute something or nothing toward provision of collective good
Theoretical results	Arrow Impossibility Theorem; voter's paradox	Voter's paradox	Logrolling and voter's paradox	Absence of equilibrium point; irrationality of voting; function of ideology and political leadership	Minimax theorem; absence of core; prisoner's dilemma	Coalition cycles; MWC in supersymmetric games	No voluntary provision of collective goods in large groups; identity with prisoner's dilemma; possibility of altruism

the seven columns could be considered "basic"; and, second, the disparate fields themselves are also conceptually equivalent. What this means is that the different fields are essentially variations of a common conceptual theme. It is in this sense that we may consider collective-choice theory "unified." This is not to say, however, that these fields are formally equivalent. While we have noted some formal equivalencies—e.g., between logrolling and the voter's paradox—there does not seem to be any evidence of some overarching formal equivalence.[2]

Before setting out this argument, we must comment on some of the terms in table C.1. The label "Ordinary Language" simply indicates that these are the terms we would ordinarily use. They are not necessarily a part of any particular branch of the field. "Axiomatic Choice Theory" refers primarily to the work which develops from Arrow and Black; and, of course, you will recognize the terms from chapter 2. Columns 3 and 4, "Elections" and "Legislatures," are not fields themselves. Rather they are specific applications of collective-choice theory which are included to provide a better intuitive feel for some of the more esoteric terms. The final four columns are the major variants of collective-choice theory which we discussed in separate chapters.

COLLECTIVE OUTCOMES

The first row begins with "possible collective outcomes" in ordinary language. We might also have used the term "alternatives" or "choices" as well as "outcomes" without obscuring our meaning. The stress in this row, however, is on the notion of "collective" as opposed to "individual." We should also note that "possible" means both logically and technologically feasible. That is, we cannot consider George Washington as a candidate for President of the United States in 1980, nor can we consider solar power as a replacement for nuclear energy at this time.

In axiomatic choice theory, this is the "environment." The equivalent notions in the other areas include "candidates" (elections and spatial models), "bills" (legislatures), "Payoffs" (game theory), "coalitions" (coalition theory), and "collective goods" (collective-goods theory). Similarly,

2. For a good example of a formal equivalence between game theory and axiomatic choice theory see Bloomfield (1976).

the actual collective outcomes of ordinary language become the "choice set" (axiomatic choice theory), the "winning candidate" (elections and spatial models), "laws" (legislatures), "actual payoffs" (game theory), "winning coalitions" (coalition theory), and "level of supply" (collective-goods theory).

The individuals who compose the group or collective, those who do the choosing, are the "individuals" of axiomatic choice theory and ordinary language, the "voters" in elections and spatial models, the "legislators" in legislatures and logrolling, the "players" in game theory, the "parties" or "individuals" in coalition theory, and the "citizens," or, simply, individuals, in collective-goods theory.

DECISION RULES

Those previous categories are rather straightforward and provide few problems. The remaining categories are more difficult. The "decision rules" are the *criteria* for making a collective choice. They are the methods by which a particular collective outcome is designated as the group choice from among the possible outcomes. In axiomatic choice theory the decision rule is sometimes called a "social welfare function," whose task is to determine the "choice set" from among the elements in the "environment."

The primary effort in axiomatic choice theory has been to find a reasonable set of conditions or criteria for collective choice, and a decision procedure, or procedures, which will satisfy those conditions. We might ask whether those conditions are also part of the decision rule. For example, majority rule is a criterion for collective decision making, while the Arrow conditions are criteria which majority rule, or any decision rule, should not violate. Now, clearly, majority rule by itself is not a normative criterion. It has been used, presumably, because it implied the satisfaction of other criteria. In particular, as we saw in chapter 1, it represented a compromise between the desire for unanimous consent, and the desire to avoid the stalemate of easy vetoes. Similarly, the Arrow conditions may be seen as a set of desirable criteria for collective decision making, and, in that sense, part of the decision rule.

In elections and in voting for bills in legislatures, the decision rule or criterion is some proportion of the voters or legislators. Thus, while decision rules can vary from 1 to n (the total number of members in the group), the usual rules are simple or special majority, or unanimity.

An interesting problem arises when we consider game theory. What are the decision rules of game theory? For games in extensive form, we saw that the outcome was simply the culmination of a series of moves. For two-person games in normal form, we saw that the collective choice was the outcome in the intersection of the two individual choice sets. For example, in the prisoner's dilemma, the individual choice of either strategy eliminated two possible collective outcomes, and designated the remaining two outcomes as the choice set for that individual. The actual collective outcome— (DD) if both chose their dominant individual strategies—is that outcome which is in the choice set of *both* individuals.

Now, our question is, what is the "decision rule" in such a game? Clearly, it is not simply a numerical proportion as it is in elections involving three or more voters. In this case, the decision rule could be expressed as follows: "The collective choice is that payoff configuration which is in the intersection of the two individual choice sets."

Another way to express the decision rule in such a game is simply to repeat part of the rules of the game. In this case we would say: "If both players choose D, the payoff to each is -5; if both players choose C, the payoff to each is -1, and so on." We say that the decision rule is only part of the rules of the game, since it does not specify such rules as the number of players, whether the moves will be simultaneous or sequential, and so forth.

Still another expression of a decision rule for n-person games is the characteristic function. Recall that the characteristic function specifies the relationship between coalitions of various sizes, or particular coalitions, and their value. The value, of course, is a payoff to the coalition. Where the characteristic function relates coalitions of various sizes to particular payoffs, without regard to the membership in the coalition, as in symmetric games, it seems that a numerical criterion is being used, as it is with majority rule.

Finally, it can be argued that a solution concept is also a decision rule, in the sense that it suggests criteria for a collective choice. The core, for example, says that the collective choice should be that outcome or payoff configuration which satisfies certain rationality conditions.

The decision rules of game theory, then, are functionally similar to those in axiomatic choice theory, elections, and legislatures, but they appear to be more complex. Thus, majority rule simply establishes a numerical proportion of the voters as the criterion for a collective choice, while the core requires that its three rationality conditions be satisfied. If the Arrow conditions are also viewed as a decision rule, however, then the decision rules of axiomatic choice theory are no less complex than those of game theory.

It may sound strange to speak of a solution concept such as the core as a decision rule. It has certainly never been used explicitly and formally as a criterion of collective choice in any voting body. Nevertheless, the core could be used as such a criterion, and, moreover, it has been hypothesized that when a core does exist it will be the collective choice of a group of rational, self-interested, utility-maximizing individuals.[3]

There are, then, differences in the decision rules of axiomatic choice theory, or elections, and game theory. Nevertheless, there is also an important overlap. For example, a majority rule election can be considered a game in which the strategies for each voter (player) involve a vote for one candidate or abstention, while the outcomes are either a victory for one candidate or a tie. In this case it is presumed that the possible outcomes involve payoffs for the voters. Consider a simple two-person, two-candidate election as in Fig. C.1.

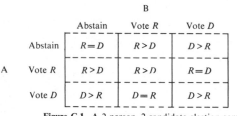

Figure C.1. A 2-person, 2-candidate election game.

The outcomes in the boxes mean that D defeats R, R defeats D, or there is a tie.

Thus, we see that an election can be modeled as a game. The converse is also true. A game can be viewed as an election. Consider again the prisoner's dilemma. There, either player's choice of either strategy can be considered a "vote," and neither player can assure a particular outcome. Nev-

3. See the interesting experimental results on this point in Fiorina and Plott (1978).

ertheless, either player can assure that particular outcomes will not occur. This, of course, is also true in the election game, above, where either player can assure that one candidate will not win. Thus, a vote for R assures that D cannot win, while a vote for D assures that R cannot win.

In coalition theory we saw that various solution concepts are also the criteria for collective choice where coalitions are the possible outcomes. This is understandable, since coalition theory developed from n-person game theory.

We also saw that there were several other criteria for coalition formation, including Riker's minimum winning coalition, and the notion of a minimum connected winning (ideologically adjacent) coalition. The MWC notion is sometimes equivalent to simple majority rule, but sometimes it is not. The MWC notion is applicable to situations where there are blocs of voters. Like majority rule, MWC is a size or numerical criterion. Unlike majority rule, however, MWC is *predictive* rather than *prescriptive*. It does not tell us what ought to be, but rather tries to predict what will be. The MCWC is also predictive in the same way. Nevertheless, both the MWC and the MCWC notions resemble the solution concepts we have discussed in their assumption that rational, self-interested, utility-maximizing individuals ought to join minimum winning coalitions or minimum connected winning coalitions.

In the spatial-model literature, the activity in the original Downsian model was an election of candidates for office, and a competitive political struggle between those candidates. The decision rule for choosing the winner was simple majority, as most of our discussion made clear. In that sense, the spatial model theory is equivalent to any other election theory.

What the spatial model theories added, however, was a theory of reasons why individuals would abstain or vote for a particular candidate. The notion of an *issue space* provided explanations of individual preferences, as well as party strategies. Moreover, the party competition could easily be viewed as a game. Thus, the notion of an issue space connected a game theoretical analysis with a straight electoral analysis.

The actual decision rule, then, in spatial models was not simply majority rule, but rather a more complex multistep rule: first, each individual determines his or her own position in the single or n-dimensional issue space; second, each individual ascertains the positions of the candidates in that same space; third, the individual decides whether to abstain or vote for a particular candidate; and, finally, the candidate who obtains the majority of the votes is the winner.

For the candidates, the decision rule is fairly simple: whichever candidate stands closest to the position of a majority of the voters in the issue space is the winner.

The difference, of course, between this analysis and that of Arrow or the voter's-paradox literature is that the latter does not consider the *reasons* for individual preference orders. Rather, it simply takes individual preference orders and collective preference profiles as given and examines what happens with different decision rules, variations in the number of individuals and issues, and so forth.

Finally, let us consider the decision rules of collective-goods theory. In Olson's analysis, collective goods may not be provided at all, they may be supplied at some suboptimal level, or they may be supplied at an optimal level. Given the definitions of collective goods and optimality, moreover, everyone in a group, for whom the collective good is, in fact, a good, would like to see an optimal amount of that good provided. This fact distinguishes collective-goods theory from any electoral theory in which individual preferences usually differ. Each individual, then, has an option of not contributing at all toward the purchase of the collective good, or providing some contribution. The collective outcome is completely determined by the sum of these decisions. Thus, the decision rule for the collective-goods case seems to be: the amount of the collective good provided is a function of the amount contributed by the individuals in the group. Notice that there is no majority rule here. If some minority of the group contributes to the purchase of the collective good, while the majority does not, then the collective good will simply be provided at relatively low levels. If no one contributes, no collective good will be provided. But, that is a collective outcome. The difficulty is that it is an outcome no one wants, and that there are other outcomes everyone prefers. Compare that situation to the voter's paradox, where there is no outcome everyone prefers to another. There is not even an outcome preferred by a majority to every other outcome.

In the voter's paradox, one of two problems arises. Either the failure to elect a candidate or choose a policy leaves the status quo unchanged; or, if the status quo is one of the possible outcomes, the voter's paradox is a situation where neither the status quo nor any change in the status quo is preferred by a majority to every other outcome. In an actual election for political office, moreover, a voter's paradox would simply leave a very confused and chaotic situation. Imagine, for example, if there were a cyclical majority in the next American presidential election!

The difficulty in the collective-goods case is that the rules allow for jointness of consumption and non-excludability. This is equivalent to a rule which says that if collective goods are available, they will be available to everyone, regardless of whether he or she has paid for them. The Olson analysis shows the results of such a rule.

The decision rules of collective-goods theory differ in another important way from the simple numerical rules of voting theory. In the latter, every vote is equal. Thus, given a particular decision rule, a particular candidate is elected, or a bill is passed, when a particular number of votes is obtained, regardless of who votes for or against.[4] The collective-goods case is more complicated. It is not enough to know simply how many individuals contribute to the collective good in order to know how much of the collective good will be provided or, even, whether the collective good will be provided at all. For example, in a privileged group, a single individual might provide the optimal level of a collective good; while in a large group, no collective good may be provided even if a large number of individuals are willing to pay; or a severely suboptimal level may be provided. In the collective-goods case, then, there is no clear connection between the *number* of people who contribute to the provision of a collective good, and the level of supply. Thus, the specification of the relationship between the cost and supply of the collective good must be included in the decision rule. A decision rule for collective goods, then, would be something like this: "If x number of individuals provide y resources, then z amount of collective good G will be provided." Only in the case where no one contributes will the decision rule be simply numerical.

INDIVIDUAL CHOOSERS

All of these parts of collective-choice theory also include a notion of individual choosers. In fact, it is the stress on this point, as well as the postulate that collective outcomes are a function of individual choice, which marks

---

4. In the axiomatic choice literature this is the *anonymity* condition. See Sen (1970).

this field as "individualistic," and which distinguishes it from certain holistic sociological views, or gestalt views in psychology, which argue that collective outcomes are something other than the product of individual choices. Whether referred to as "individuals," "voters," "legislators," "parties," "players," "citizens," or some other name, they are the individual agents or actors whose choices play a role in determining the collective outcome.

INDIVIDUAL ACTIONS

The actions of these agents represent an attempt to affect the collective outcome. Sometimes the effect is relatively substantial, as in the two-person game, and sometimes the effect is minuscule, as in the American presidential election or in the attempt to reduce air pollution.

In axiomatic choice theory, the individual somehow reveals his preferences over all of the alternative outcomes. This differs, of course, from most actual political situations where individuals simply reveal their first choice. Sometimes, however, the individual abstains from indicating a preference among the alternatives. In actual elections, such abstentions may or may not affect the outcome, but clearly abstention is as much an act as choosing.

In game theory, the individual act is not to reveal one's preferences directly for the possible outcomes, as in an election, but rather to make a move, or choose a strategy, which indirectly reveals one's preferences. As we have seen, however, an election can be modeled as a game. Nevertheless, in game theory an individual cannot express his or her preferences over all of the available outcomes. Of course, since the outcomes are numerical payoffs, and since individuals are assumed to want higher payoffs rather than lower payoffs, it is assumed that we know the preference ranking of the players over the outcomes. Thus, the only question is the strategic one: Will the players try to obtain their highest payoffs, or settle for something less— i.e., a payoff lower in value, but more probably obtainable.

In coalition theory, the individual act is to join a coalition or to remain alone. Here, the notions of bargaining and reaching agreements are central. The individuals or parties communicate with each other, and, in this respect, the process of coalition formation resembles that of logrolling. In ordinary voting and in many game theoretical situations, it is assumed that individuals frequently will not be in communication, that they will not negotiate, and that they will not make agreements. This is not to say that satisfactory agreements will always be made in coalition-formation situations (they will not) or that there will be unsatisfactory outcomes where individuals act independently. Rather, the overt process of coalition formation may be different from the processes by which candidates are elected, policies chosen, or payoffs distributed. Of course, it need not be the case. In game theory, for example, where both players have dominant strategies, the outcome of the game where there is bargaining should not differ from the outcome without bargaining.

In the collective-goods case, the individual choice is to contribute something toward the provision of a collective good, or nothing. Here again, there is no necessary relation between the individual act and the collective outcome. Collective goods may be provided even if some individuals do not contribute, and they may not be provided even if some individuals do contribute.

INDIVIDUAL PREFERENCES AMONG OUTCOMES

Each of the parts of collective-choice theory also presumes that these agents have preferences for certain outcomes, and that they can rank the possible outcomes according to those preferences. In addition to the preference relation, the collective-choice theories also postulate the notion of "indifference."

In axiomatic choice theory, as well as in actual elections and legislatures, the notion of individual preferences seems relatively straightforward. Nevertheless, there is considerable debate about what it means to say that an individual has a preference. Suppose, for instance, that a voter reports, in a public-opinion survey, a preference for Senator Kennedy over President Carter in the Democratic party primary, but that he or she intends to vote for Carter, because of a feeling that Kennedy cannot win, and that a strong Kennedy showing would damage Carter's chances for reelection and open the way for a Republican victory. This kind of reasoning has been described as sophisticated, or strategic, voting. The assumption is that one has "real" preferences, but that one does not necessarily try to implement them.

In some cases, such a dichotomy between our preferences and our acts seems reasonable. Nevertheless, suppose we are told that an individual expresses a preference for integration over segregation, but refuses to live

with blacks and opposes busing and affirmative action. We might be justified in concluding that this person does not really prefer integration at all.
In fact, we call this "giving lip service," and argue that our true values and
preferences are expressed in our actions. By this reasoning, there is no such
thing as sophisticated voting. Our choices are our preferences.

In general, collective-choice theory does not restrict individual preference orders unless it is necessary to avoid a particular problem. In axiomatic
choice theory we saw that such restrictions as single-peakedness were invoked to avoid the voter's paradox. Moreover, we saw that there are sometimes restrictions once a first choice is made. Thus, in our discussion of logrolling, we noted that the additivity condition limited the order of preferences.

A less obvious restriction is involved in the spatial-model literature.
There, an individual's first choice in any policy space fixes the preference
ranking for every other alternative according to the policy "distance."
Thus, no alternative can be higher on the preference scale than an alternative
which is nearer the first choice. The policy-space notion, then, constitutes a
restriction on individual preferences over outcomes.

In collective-goods theory, preference orders are expressed in terms of
indifference curves or utility functions. Indifference curves indicate the set
of alternatives which are equal in terms of utility, and which, therefore,
have the same ranking in the individual's preference order. In the case of a
"frontier," these alternatives are the first choice. Otherwise, there are alternatives which can rank higher or lower. The utility functions relate the alternatives to a utility value; and, the higher that value, the higher the preference ranking of the alternative.

In general, all of the parts of collective choice theory invoke the notion
of utility to explain individual preferences. In game theory, coalition theory,
collective goods theory, and spatial models, cardinal utility seems to have
been accepted without question. Only in axiomatic choice theory have the
ordinalists held sway.

RESULTS

This category is, perhaps, the most important. We have suggested that the
various parts of collective-choice theory are related, but that they differ in
important respects. The theoretical results, then, should reflect our point that
collective-choice theory represents variations on a basic theme.

Before looking at these results, we should make an important distinction. Axiomatic choice theory is basically *normative*. That is, it postulates conditions which any collective-decision procedure *ought* to satisfy, and then inquires whether such conditions are logically consistent. In general, as we pointed out in chapter 2, there have been no extensive justifications of these conditions. They are clearly ethical requirements, but they are simply put forward as being "reasonable" and "weak."[5] Sometimes they are justified on the grounds that they avoid such problems as the voter's paradox.

The term "weak" simply means "not stringent," or "not difficult to achieve." By contrast, "justice" appears to be a "strong" or "difficult" ethical requirement. The implication of claiming that collective-choice conditions are weak is that no one could object to them—i.e., raise ethical objections. As we have seen, however, that position is excessively optimistic.

Nevertheless, our point is that the axiomatic choice theorists are concerned with the question of what is the "best" collective-choice procedure—"best" in the sense of satisfying certain normative conditions. As such, their work is directly related to such political activities as devising constitutions, or trying to implement socialist or centrally planned socioeconomic systems.

In contrast, the work on the probability of the voter's paradox, spatial models, game theory, coalition theory, and the theory of collective goods are all *behavioral* models. That is, they attempt to model real situations, and to produce results which would be empirically testable. This work is not normative or ethical in the same way that axiomatic choice theory is normative.[6]

Given this distinction, it is important to remember that normative or

5. For example, many collective choice theorists seem to think that the Pareto principle is ethically unassailable. Its "strong" version, however, allows severe inequalities (See Sen. 1970) while its "weak" version—the unanimity principle—does not consider the effects of collective action on future generations, fetuses, children, prisoners, or the mentally incompetent.

6. Not everyone would accept this argument. There is, in fact, a long history in game theory traceable to Nash (1953) which is concerned with "arbitration" schemes which are in some sense normatively justifiable. My point here is simply that such justifications do not arise from the game theoretical analysis itself, nor does the analysis produce results which tell us anything about such justifications. Rather, they say that if an arbitration scheme is accepted, then a particular outcome should be chosen. In Braithwaite's (1955) terms: "The recommendations which I shall make for sharing fairly the proceeds of collaboration will therefore be *amoral* in the sense that they will not be based upon any first-order moral principles; but the recommendations themselves will constitute what may be called second-order moral principles giving criteria for *good sense, prudence,* and *fairness*. . . ." (pp. 5-6. Italics in original) See also Raiffa (1953), and Barry (1978).

ethical statements cannot be derived from empirical statements. Or, as the philosophers say, one cannot derive an "ought" from an "is." We cannot say, in other words, that a collective-choice procedure is ethically acceptable simply because people do in fact employ it. Nor can we say that an outcome is ethically acceptable simply because it has been chosen. Thus, the results of the behavioral models cannot be used to solve the problems raised by the normative models.

Despite this rather strict separation, there are important similarities. First, all of the models involve logical inference. The theoretical results are not derived from empirical observation, but rather from a chain of deductions which begin with an arbitrary set of assumptions. For political scientists, the interesting questions which must now be pursued are whether any of the behavioral models adequately explain real political processes, and how the normative models relate to all of the traditional work in political philosophy.

A second similarity is that there are important *negative* results in both the normative and empirical models. The Arrow impossibility theorem, of course, is the major negative result in axiomatic choice theory. Among the behavioral models there are many negative results. The voter's paradox is a situation in which there is no Condorcet winner. In chapter 1, we saw that many voting rules are not compatible in the sense that they produce different results. In the logrolling chapter, we saw that the conditions for logrolling presuppose an underlying cyclical majority, so that logrolling also will not produce a stable outcome. In the spatial-model literature, we discussed Downs's argument that voting in a large election seemed to be an irrational act; as well as the conclusion that equilibria generally do not exist in a multidimensional world. In game theory, the prisoner's dilemma produced an outcome no one wanted, while there were no outcomes in the "core" of *n*- person constant-sum games. In coalition theory, there were situations in which no coalition was dominant. Finally, in collective-goods theory, Olson's central conclusion was that large groups would not provide themselves voluntarily with collective goods, even though the members of the group were willing and able to bear the cost.

A central concern of collective-choice theory has been to avoid or overcome these negative results. Toward that end, restrictions of one kind or another proved necessary. In axiomatic choice theory it was only necessary to alter or abandon one of Arrow's conditions in order to avoid the impossibility theorem. Since these were normative conditions, moreover, this meant abandoning some value judgment.

In the voter's-paradox literature, the probability of the paradox varied according to the assumptions. Thus, if certain preference profiles were forbidden, the paradox would not occur. Nevertheless, it should be pointed out that some restrictions actually increased the probability of the paradox. Thus, while the equiprobable assumptions of the impartial culture produced a relatively low probability, certain arbitrary cultures—which involved restrictions on the preference profiles—produced higher paradox probabilities.

In spatial models there seems to be no way of avoiding Downs's conclusion concerning the irrationality of voting in large elections, except, perhaps by invoking the so-called minimax regret assumption. For spatial equilibria, it appears that they are more likely in a restricted unidimensional, rather than multidimensional, issue space. Here the restriction is on the dimensionality of the issue space.

In game theory, the prisoner's dilemma seems to require an external coordinating or coercive force in order to bring about the mutually desired cooperative outcome. This is also true, as we saw, for the collective-goods case. Thus, it is necessary to restrict freedom of choice in order to avoid these negative results.

There are two restrictions which can avoid the problem of the absent core in game theory. First, the class of games can be restricted to nonconstant-sum games where cores exist. In other words, the problem of the absent core arises only where all n-person games are permissible. If we wanted to avoid this problem in real-life situations, then, we would have to allow, somehow, only nonconstant-sum games.

Another way out of this problem is to weaken the requirements of the core. As we have seen, this amounts to jettisoning one of the rationality conditions. The result, however, is a great increase in the size of the choice set.

Since, as we have argued, these game-theory models are behavioral and not normative, the problems involved in dropping one of the rationality conditions cannot be ethical. Rather, the question must be whether it violates any of the initial assumptions on which the concept of the core is based. In other words, we are arguing that the core conditions must be a *deduction* or an *inference* from certain other assumptions, such as: "All players are rational, self-interested, utility-maximizers." The core conditions, then, would be seen as an implication of such a basic assumption. If we want to eliminate one of those core conditions, then, we must ask whether that move violates any of those basic assumptions. Another approach, however, is to view the core conditions themselves as the basic rationality assumptions of the model, in which case they are arbitrary, and there can be no logical objection to eliminating one of them.

I suspect, however, that the core conditions are viewed by some as *ethical* conditions. This would imply that outcomes in the core are normatively desirable. In that case, the absence of the core indicates that its conditions are incompatible. Such a result is, of course, similar to the Arrow result.

The main objection to this argument that the core conditions are ethical postulates is that, intuitively, they seem so objectionable. They embody a completely self-centered and competitive standard, which may be descriptively accurate—though that is questionable—but normatively repugnant. The Arrow conditions, by contrast, embody important elements of the democratic ideology which are normatively defensible if not completely impregnable.

An even stronger case can be made against the Shapley Value as an ethical standard. There, the ultimate division of the payoffs depends on one's initial endowment or resources. In such an ethic, the rich may not get richer, but the relative positions remain unchanged. The problem here is that there is no assumption about how the resources were originally distributed. Only if that distribution itself was "just" or "fair" can we say that the Shapely Value is "just" or "fair." No such restriction has been related to the Shapley Value, however, so that we must assume that the original distribution of resources may be "just" or "unjust," "fair," or "unfair." Clearly, such an ethical position is seriously flawed.

There is also no discussion about whether it is morally acceptable to maintain an uneven distribution of resources, even if the original distribution were produced in a just manner. Rawls, for example, would argue for an equalization of such resources, regardless of the fairness of the original distribution.

This is not to say that ethical discussions cannot arise out of these game theoretical questions. Indeed, such philosophers as Virginia Held (1977) and Derek Parfit (1979) have done just that. Rather, the point is that the results of game theory cannot be said to have made a contribution to ethical theory as the Arrow result clearly has.[7]

7. Compare this argument with that of Brock (1978).

In coalition theory, Hardin, Frohlich, and others showed that minimum winning coalitions could occur only under very restricted conditions—e.g., supersymmetry, negatively sloped characteristic functions, and so on. In all other cases, the outcome would be indeterminate. Here again restrictions are necessary in order to induce an outcome.

We should make a distinction, in this discussion, between the failure to achieve an equilibrium—or, in other words, the failure to designate a stable outcome from among the possible outcomes—from the achievement of a Pareto-dominated equilibrium—i.e., a stable outcome which no one wants! In the former category are the Arrow result, the voter's paradox, and the absent core. The latter category includes the prisoner's dilemma and Olson's collective-goods result. Clearly, such differences have important practical implications. It is not at all the same to say that we have failed to produce a collective choice as it is to say that no one wants the collective choice which we have produced. The latter situation appears to be remediable, while the former creates insoluble dilemmas.

In this conclusion we have argued that the various parts of collectve choice theory are structurally related. This suggests that the political activities to which these theories may apply are also structurally related. However, we have also described important differences. This is natural, since the various parts of collective-choice theory clearly were developed with particular political phenomena in mind. The task now for political scientists is to take the theoretical results described here, apply them systematically to their empirical fields of study, and determine whether the theory of collective choice has advanced our knowledge of the political process.

References

Abrams, Robert. 1973. *Some Conceptual Problems of Voting Theory*. Beverley Hills: Sage.
—— 1976. "The Voter's Paradox and the Homogeneity of Individual Preference Orders." *Public Choice* 26:19–27.
Aldrich, John. 1977. "The Dilemma of a Paretian Liberal: Some Consequences of Sen's Theorem." *Public Choice* 30:1–21.
Arrow, Kenneth. 1959. "Rational Choice Functions and Orderings." *Economica* 26:121–27.
—— 1963. *Social Choice and Individual Values*. 2d ed. New Haven: Yale University Press.
——1977, "Current Developments in the Theory of Social Choice." *Social Research* 44(4):607–22.
Axelrod, Robert. 1970. *Conflict of Interest*. Chicago: Markham.
Barry, Brian. 1978. "Don't Shoot the Trumpeter—He's Doing His Best! Reflections on a Problem of Fair Division." Paper presented to Public Choice Society, annual meeting, New Orleans, March 1978 (forthcoming in *Theory and Decision*).
Bernholz, Peter. 1975. "Logrolling and the Paradox of Voting." *American Political Science Review* 69(3):961–62.
Black Duncan. 1948. "On the Rationale of Group Decision-making." *Journal of Political Economy* (February), 56:23–34.
——1958. *Theory of Committees and Elections*. Cambridge: Cambridge University Press.
Blau, J. H. 1957. "The Existence of Social Welfare Functions." *Econometrica* (April), 25:302–13.
Bloomfield, Stefan D. 1976. "A Social Choice Interpretation of the Von Neumann-Morgenstern Game." *Econometrica* 44(1):105–14.
Bowen, Bruce. 1972. "Toward an Estimate of the Frequency of Occurrence of the Paradox of Voting in U.S. Senate Roll Call Votes." In R. Niemi and H. Weisberg, eds., *Probability Models of Collective Decision-making*. Columbus, Ohio: Merrill.

Braithwaite, R. B. 1955. *Theory of Games as a Tool for the Moral Philosopher*. Cambridge: Cambridge University Press.

Brams, Steven J. 1975. *Game Theory and Politics*. New York: Free Press.

Brock, Horace W. 1978. "The Shapley Value as a Tool for the Conceptual Unification of Economics, Politics, and Ethics." Paper presented to Public Choice Society, annual meeting, New Orleans, March 1978 (forthcoming in *Theory and Decision*)

Buchanan, James and Gordon Tullock. 1962. *The Calculus of Consent*. Ann Arbor: University of Michigan Press.

Butterworth, Robert L. 1971. "A Research Note on the Size of Winning Coalitions." *American Political Science Review* 65(3):741–48.

Chamberlin, John. 1974. "Provision of Collective Goods as a Function of Group Size." *American Political Science Review* 68(2):707–16.

Dahl, Robert. 1963. *Modern Political Analysis*. Englewood Cliffs, N.J.: Prentice-Hall.

Davis, Otto, Melvin Hinich, and Peter Ordeshook. 1970. "An Expository Development of a Mathematical Model of the Electorial Process." *American Political Science Review* 64(2):426–48.

DeSwaan, Abram. 1970. *Coalition Theories and Cabinet Formations*. San Francisco: Jossey-Bass.

Downs, Anthony. 1957. *An Economic Theory of Democracy*. New York: Harper and Row.

Enelow, James M. 1976. "A Few Remarks on Vote Trading, Logrolling, Coalitions of Minorities and the Voter's Paradox." Unpublished paper, Department of Political Science, University of Rochester (March).

Fein, Jack M. 1978. "Microvascular Surgery for Stroke." *Scientific American* (April), 238(4):58–67.

Ferejohn, John and Morris Fiorina. 1974. "The Paradox of Not Voting: A Decision Theoretic Analysis." *American Political Science Review* 68(2):525–36.

Fiorina, Morris and Charles Plott. 1978. "Committee Decisions Under Majority Rule: An Experimental Study." *American Political Science Review* 72(2):575–95.

Fishburn, Peter. 1970. "The Irrationality of Transitivity in Social Choice." *Behavioral Science* 15(2):119–23.

——1973. *The Theory of Social Choice*. Princeton, N.J.: Princeton University Press.

——1974. "Paradoxes of Voting." *American Political Science Review* 68(2):537–46.

Frohlich, Norman. 1975. "The Instability of Minimum Winning Coalitions." *American Political Science Review* 69(3):943–46.

Frohlich, Norman, Joe Oppenheimer, and Oran Young. 1971. *Political Leadership and Collective Goods*. Princeton, N.J.: Princeton University Press.

Frohlich, Norman and Joe Oppenheimer. 1978. *Modern Political Economy*. Englewood Cliffs, N.J.: Prentice-Hall.

Gamson, William A. 1961. "A Theory of Coalition Formation." *American Sociological Review* 26:373–82.

Gibbard, Alan. 1973. "Manipulation of Voting Schemes: A General Result." *Econometrica* 41:587–601.

——1976. "Social Decision, Strategic Behavior, and Best Outcomes." Mimeographed, Department of Philosophy, University of Pittsburg.

Goldman, Alan. 1976. "Rawls's Original Position and the Difference Principle." *Journal of Philosophy* 73(21):845–49.

Hardin, Russell, 1971. "Collective Action as an Agreeable *n*-Prisoners' Dilemma." *Behavioral Science* 16(5):472–81.

——1976. "Hollow Victory: The Minimum Winning Coalition." *American Political Science Review* 70(4):1202–14.

Harsanyi, John. 1976 *Essays on Ethics, Social Behavior, and Scientific Explanation.* Dordrecht, The Netherlands: Reidel.

——1977. "Morality and the Theory of Rational Behavior." *Social Research* 44(4):623–56.

Held, Virginia. 1977. "Rationality and Reasonable Cooperation," *Social Research.* 44(4):708–44.

Hinich, Melvin, John Ledyard, and Peter Ordeshook. 1973. "A Theory of Electoral Equilibrium: A Spatial Analysis Based on the Theory of Games." *Journal of Politics* 35(1):154–93.

Hinich, Melvin and Peter Ordeshook. 1969. "Abstentions and Equilibrium in the Electoral Process." *Public Choice* 7:81–106.

——1970. "Plurality Maximization vs. Vote Maximization." *American Political Science Review* 64(3):772–91.

Kelly, Jerry S. 1978. *Arrow Impossibility Theorems.* New York: Academic Press.

Koehler, David H. 1972. "The Legislative Process and the Minimal Winning Coalition." In R. Niemi and H. Weisberg, eds., *Probability Models of Collective Decision-making.* Columbus, Ohio: Merrill.

——1975. "Vote Trading and the Voting Paradox: A Proof of Logical Equivalence." *American Political Science Review* 69(3):954–60.

Leiserson, Michael. 1966. "Coalitions in Politics: A Theoretical and Empirical Study." Ph.D. dissertation, Yale.

Margolis, Howard. 1979. "Selfishness, Altruism, and Rationality," Center for International Studies, MIT.

May, Robert. 1971. "Some Mathematical Remarks on the Paradox of Voting." *Behavioral Science* 16(2):143–51.

Miller, Nicholas. 1977. " 'Social Preference' and Game Theory: A Comment on 'The Dilemma of a Paretian Liberal.' " *Public Choice* 30:23–28.

——1977. "Logrolling, Vote Trading, and the Paradox of Voting: A Game Theoretical Overview." *Public Choice* 30:51–73.

Mueller, Dennis C. 1976. "Public Choice: A Survey." *Journal of Economic Literature* 14(2):395–433.

Nash, J. F. 1953. "Two-person Cooperative Games." *Econometrica* 21:128–40.

Niemi, Richard. 1969. "Majority Decision-making with Partial Unidimensionality." *American Political Science Review* 63(2):488–97.

Olson, Mancur. 1965. *The Logic of Collective Action.* Cambridge, Mass.: Harvard University Press.

Oppenheimer, Joe. 1972. "Relating Coalitions of Minorities to the Voter's Paradox, or, Putting the Fly in the Democratic Pie." Paper presented to the meeting of the Southwest Political Science Association, San Antonio, Texas (March).

——1975. "Some Political Implications of 'Vote Trading and the Voting Paradox: A Proof of Logical Equivalence.' " *American Political Science Review* 69(3):963–66.

Page, Benjamin. 1977. "Elections and Social Choice: The State of the Evidence." *American Journal of Political Science* 21(3):639–68.

Parfit, Derek. 1979. "Prudence, Morality, and the Prisoner's Dilemma." *Proceedings of the British Academy* 65.

Plott, Charles. 1967. "A Notion of Equilibrium and Its Possibility Under Majority Rule." *American Economic Review* 57:788–806.

——1976. "Axiomatic Social Choice Theory: An Overview and Interpretation." *American Journal of Political Science* 20(3):511–96.

Rae, Douglas. 1969. "Decision Rules and Individual Values in Constitutional Choice." *American Political Science Review* 63(1):40–56.

——1975. "The Limits of Consensual Decision." *American Political Science Review* 69(4):1270–94.

Raiffa, H. 1953. "Arbitration Schemes for Generalized Two-Person Games." In H. W. Kuhn and A. W. Tucker, eds. *Contributions to the Theory of Games,* vol. 2 Annals of Mathematics Studies, no. 28. Princeton, N.J.: Princeton University Press.

Rapoport, Anatol. 1966. *Two-Person Game Theory.* Ann Arbor: University of Michigan Press.

——1968. Editorial Comments. *Journal of Conflict Resolution* 12:222–23.

——1970. *N-Person Game Theory.* Ann Arbor: University of Michigan Press.

Rawls, John. 1971. *A Theory of Justice.* Cambridge, Mass.: Harvard University Press.

Riker, William H. 1958. "The Paradox of Voting and Congressional Rules for Voting on Amendments." *American Political Science Review* 52(2):349–66.

——1962. *The Theory of Political Coalitions.* New Haven: Yale University Press.

Riker, William and Steven Brams. 1973. "The Paradox of Vote Trading." *American Political Science Review* 67(4):1235–47.

Riker, William and Peter Ordeshook. 1973. *An Introduction to Positive Political Theory.* Englewood Cliffs, N.J.: Prentice-Hall.

Rohde, David W. 1972. "A Theory of the Formation of Opinion Coalitions in the U.S. Supreme Court." In R. Niemi and H. Weisberg, eds., *Probability Models of Collective Decision-making.* Columbus, Ohio: Merrill.

Rosenthal, Howard. 1970. "Size of Coalition and Electoral Outcomes in the Fourth French Republic." In Sven Groennings, E. W. Kelly, and Michael Leiserson, eds., *The Study of Coalition Behavior.* New York: Holt, Rinehart and Winston.

Satterthwaite, Mark. 1975. "Strategy-proofness and Arrow's Conditions: Existence and Correspondence Theorems for Voting Procedures and Social Welfare Functions." *Journal of Economic Theory* 10:187–217.

Schwartz, Thomas. 1970. "On the Possibility of Rational Policy Evaluation." *Theory and Decision* 1:89–106.

——1972. "Rationality and the Myth of the Maximum." *Nous* 6:97–117.

——1977. "Collective Choice, Separation of Issues, and Vote Trading." *American Political Science Review* 71(3):999–1010.

Sen, Amartya. 1966. "A Possibility Theorem on Majority Decisions." *Econometrica* 34(2):491–99.

——1970. *Collective Choice and Social Welfare.* San Francisco: Holden-Day.

Shapley, L. S. 1953. "A Value for in-Person Games." In H. W. Kuhn and A. W. Tucker (eds.) *Contributions to the Theory of Games.* II. (Annals of Mathematics Studies 28). Princeton: Princeton University Press.

Shepsle, Kenneth. 1974. "On the Size of Winning Coalitions." *American Political Science Review* 68(2):505–18.

Stokes, Donald. 1963. "Spatial Models of Party Competition." *American Political Science Review* 57(2):368–77.

Strasnick, Stephen. 1976. "The Problem of Social Choice: Arrow to Rawls." *Philosophy and Public Affairs* 5(3):241–73.

Taylor, Michael. 1970. "The Problem of Salience in the Theory of Collective Decision-making." *Behavioral Science* 15(5):415–30.

——1971. "On the Theory of Government Coalition Formation." *British Journal of Political Science* 2:361–86.

——1976. *Anarchy and Cooperation.* New York: Wiley.

Taylor, Michael and Douglas Rae. 1971. "Decision Rules and Policy Outcomes." *British Journal of Political Science* 1(1):71–90.

Tullock, Gordon. 1967. *Toward a Mathematics of Politics.* Ann Arbor: University of Michigan Press.

——1974. "Communication." *American Political Science Review* 68(4):1687–88.

Von Neumann, John and Oskar Morgenstern. 1944. *The Theory of Games and Economic Behavior.* New York: Wiley.

Wolff, Robert Paul. 1976. "On Strasnick's 'Derivation' of Rawl's 'Difference Principle.' " *Journal of Philosophy* 73(21):849–58.

Index of Names

Abrams, R., 101, 139, 173, 347
Aldrich, J., 329n, 347
Arrow, K., 2, 63, 84, 100, 101, 331, 347
Axelrod, R., 265, 267-68, 347

Barry, B., xi, 341n, 347
Bentham, J., 63
Bernholz, P., 111 ff., 347
Black, D., 2, 66, 100, 331, 347
Bloomfield, S., 331, 347
Borda, J., 2
Bowen, B., 90, 347
Braithwaite, R., 341n, 348
Brams, S., 4, 104, 129-30, 134, 348
Brock, H., 329n, 344n, 348
Buchanan, J., 3, 10, 104, 348
Butterworth, R., 241, 348

Chamberlin, J., 298, 348
Condorcet, M., 2

Davis, O., 166-67, 168n, 169, 171, 178, 348
DeSwaan, A., 265, 348
De Tocqueville, A., 63
Dodgson, C. L., 2
Downs, A., 3, 119, 120, 139, 146 ff., 169, 348

Enelow, J., 124, 348

Ferejohn, J., 182 ff., 348
Fiorina, M., 182 ff., 334n, 348

Fishburn, P., 31, 71, 101, 348
Frohlich, N., 3, 251, 304, 305, 348

Galton, F., 2
Gamson, W., 235, 270, 276, 348
Goldman, A., 88n, 349

Hardin, R., xi, 215n, 245, 249n, 262, 283, 292n, 300n, 301n, 306 ff., 329, 349
Harsanyi, J., 51, 84, 349
Held, V., 344, 349
Hinich, M., 166, 167, 169, 171, 173 ff., 178, 349

Kelly, J., 349
Koehler, D., 113 ff., 121, 254, 262, 349
Kuhn, H. W., 350

Laplace, 2
Ledyard, J., 173 ff., 349
Leiserson, M., 235, 267, 349

Margolis, H., 283, 320 ff., 349
Marx, K., 63
May, R., 93, 349
Mill, J., 63
Miller, N., xi, 73n, 109n, 115n, 118n, 124, 129n, 329n, 349
Mitchell, W., xi
Morgenstern, O., 3, 81, 200, 351
Mueller, D., 329n, 349

Nash, J., 341n, 349
Niemi, R., 97, 99, 349

Olson, M., xi, 3, 282 ff., 349
Oppenheimer, J., 3, 118, 119, 304, 305, 349
Ordeshook, P., 3, 166 ff., 167, 169, 171, 173 ff., 178, 265, 348, 349, 350
Ortega y Gasset, J., 63

Page, B., 177n, 350
Parfit, D., 344, 350
Plato, 62
Plott, C., xi, 329, 334n, 350

Rae, D., 13 ff., 177 ff., 350
Raiffa, H., 341n, 350
Rapoport, A., 3, 308, 350
Rawls, J., 2, 21, 26, 101, 350
Riker, W., 3, 90, 104, 129, 130, 134, 235 ff., 252 ff., 265, 350
Rohde, D., 263, 264, 350

Rosenthal, H., 254, 350
Rousseau, J., 63

Schwartz, T., 77, 121 ff., 135, 350
Sen, A., 69, 70n, 77, 100, 337n, 341n, 350
Shapley, L., 222, 223, 350
Shepsle, K., 249, 350
Stokes, D., 165, 351
Strasnick, S., 2, 77, 85, 351

Taylor, M., 177 ff., 268, 272, 276, 277, 283, 306, 315 ff., 351
Tucker, A., 350
Tullock, G., 3, 10, 100, 104, 134, 351

Von Neumann, J., 3, 81, 200, 351

Wolff, R., 88n, 351

Young, O., 304, 305, 348

Subject Index

Abstention, 150; from alienation, 150; from indifference, 150
Additivity, 115-18, 214; superadditivity, 214
Admissibility, 44
Altruism, 319; pure, 323; constant, 323; variable, 324
Anonymity, 337
Arrow's general possibility theorem, 42-64; proof, 53-62

Bargaining cycles, 244-45
Bargaining set, 226-29; individually rational payoff configuration, 226; objection, 226; counter-objection, 226; justified objection, 226
Borda method (voting), 29
Bribery, competitive, 249

Chairman's gambit, 31
Characteristic function, 237; negative slope, 238; positive slope, 238
Chicken game, 193
Coalition of minorities, 111
Coalitions, decisive, 122; in games, 207; grand coalition, coalition of the whole, 210; rationality of coalition formation, 213-29; minimum winning coalition, 235-41; proto-coalition, 257; uniquely preferred winning coalition, 258; strategically weak proto-coalition, 259; minimization of policy distance, 265; ideological distance, 266; ideological diversity, 267; minimum connected winning coalition, 268
Collective goods, 281 ff.; see also Public Goods
Condorcet method (voting), 29; weak Condorcet winners, 313
Congress, U.S., 261
Consensual decision-making, 13-21
Constitutions, 5-39
Core (of a game), 217-19
Costs, 10; decision costs, 13; external costs, 13
Culture, (preference profile), 93-100; impartial, 93; arbitrary, 94; and paradox probability, 95-100
Cyclical majorities, 30

Decision rules, 332-37
Decisive sets, 55-60; weakly decisive, 55; strongly decisive, 55
Demand, elasticity of, 299; effective, 299
Democracy, 6
Disbursements, payoff, 210
Domination, 108-9; dominant strategy, 192; in coalitions, 220-22

Efficiency, 15; maxima, 18
Egoist, pure, 322
Equilibrium points, 171-73, 201
Extension condition, 71
Externalities, positive and negative, 11-13

Factorial, 45
Forward cycle, 33
Free rider problem, 282

Games; zero sum, 190; prisoner's dilemma, 191; chicken, 193; extensive form, 196; game tree, 196; strategy, 196; move, 196; normal form, 198; two-person zero sum, 200; n-person, 207 ff.; characteristic function form, 210-11; essential and inessential, 213; simple, 238; side payments, 241

Ideology, 163, 265
Imputation, 219-20
Independence, of preferences, 114
Indeterminate outcomes, 249
Indifference, 43; indifference curve, 155
Indifference set, 16, 17
Individualism: economic, 7, 8; political, 21
Intransitivity, 30
Israel, 277-78

Justice, theory of, 2

Leadership, political, 163-64
Legitimacy, 9
Lexicographic models, 177-81
Logrolling, 4; logrolling cycles, 104-8; and the voter's paradox, 111-15; and vote trading, 124-25
Lotteries, 81-84

Majority rule, simple, 21-26
Majority strategy (coalitions), 119
Maximum positive gainers, 241-44
Maximin principle, 21, 26-28, 77
Measurement, problems of, 79-81
Minimax regret, 182-85
Minimax solution, 203
Minimum winning coalitions, 235-41
Minority strategy (coalitions), 119

Ordering (of alternatives), strong and weak, 43
Ordinalist, 51

Paradoxes, voting, 28-36; dominated winner, 31-32; inverted order, 32-33; winner-turns-

loser, 33-34; truncated point-total, 34-35; Borda dominance, 35-36
Pareto optimality, 14; Pareto principle, 53-54
Parties, 147-55; activists, 163
Party differential, 150
Paternalism, 8
Payoff vector, 210
Permutations (of preference profiles), 44
Plurality maximization, 166
Policy space, 142
Political entrepreneurs, 304
Positional preference, 25
Preference, 43, 339-40; profile, 46; intensity of, 51, 78; weighing, 78-79; sincere, 109; sophisticated, 109; preference density function (unimodal, bimodal, multimodal), 158-59
Preference priority, 2, 85-88
Preference set, 15, 16, 17
Prisoner's dilemma, 4, 191, 292; and public goods, 306-25
Probabilistic spatial models, 173-77
Probability (subjective, objective, logical), 88-89; relative frequency, 89; probability vector, 94
Public Choice, 3
Public Choice Society, 3
Public goods, 281-328; jointness of consumption, 285, 289; marginal utility of, 285; marginal cost of, 285; total utility of, 285; average utility of, 285; privileged groups, 288; nonexcludability, 289; crowdable public goods, 290; pure public goods, 290; and large groups, 291-92; and intermediate groups, 292-97; suboptimality and, 293; income effects and, 299; congestion effects and, 299; inclusive public goods, 299; exclusive public goods, 299; goods (normal inferior, superior), 300

Rational voting, 145-46
Rationality, 10; individual, 43; collective, 43; political, 147; of coalition formation, 213-29; conditions in games, 215-16
Rejection set, 15, 16, 17
Response combination, 23
Risk, 84

Saddle point, 203

Scaling, 79-81; interval scale, 80; ratio scale, 80; transformation of scale, 81

Security level, 211

Separability (of preferences), 114

Shapley value, 222-25; as power index, 226

Side payments, 241; competitive bribery, 249

Single-peakedness, 66

Size principle, 237

Social choice conditions, 42-53; connectivity, 42-43; transitivity, 43; free triple, 43-46; positive responsiveness, 46-47; independence of irrelevant alternatives, 47-51, 76; citizen's sovereignty, 52; nondictatorship, 52; unlimited domain, 54-55

Social choice function, 48

Social contract, 8-9

Social welfare function, 8; universal, 43-44

Solution concept, 219; core, 217-19; imputation, 219-20; Shapley value, 222-25; bargaining set, 226-29

Spatial models, 139-88; probabilistic, 173-77; lexicographic, 177-81; minimax regret, 182-85

Stable outcomes, 108-11, 201

Strategic manipulation, 36-37

Strategy-proof (choice procedure), 38

Strategy, contingent and noncontingent, 197; pure, 200; mixed, 201, 204-7

Superadditivity, 214

Support set, 33

Supreme Court, U.S., 263

Symmetry, 245-49; identical symmetry, 245; asymmetry, 245; supersymmetry, 246-49

Transitivity, 10, 30, 43; social, 71

Unanimity rule, 10 ff.; unanimity principle, 74

Uncertainty, 84, 159-63

Utility: cardinal, 10, 15, 50, 76-84; ordinal, 10, 15; interpersonal comparison of, 15, 50; sum of, 50, 51, 76; utile, 50; matrix, 112; utility function, 142, 153, 154; symmetrical utility function, 150; utility loss function, 168; concave utility function, 171; marginal, 285; total, 285; average, 285

Value-restrictedness, 69

Vote maximization, 166-70

Vote trading, 4; paradox of, 104, 129-36; and Condorcet winners, 121-24; and logrolling, 124-25

Voter's paradox, 30-31; probability of, 88-100; and logrolling, 111-15

Voters, rational, 148-55

Voting: unanimity rule, 10-13; simple majority rule, 21-26; Borda method, 29; Condorcet method, 29; sequential elimination, 31; rational, 145-46

Welfare economics, 7, 8